Y0-CYN-238

ECONOMICS

For

Extemp and Debate

Copyright © William H. Bennett, 2003

CDE
P.O. Box Z
Taos, NM 87571

505-751-0514   bennett@laplaza.org   www.cdedebate.com

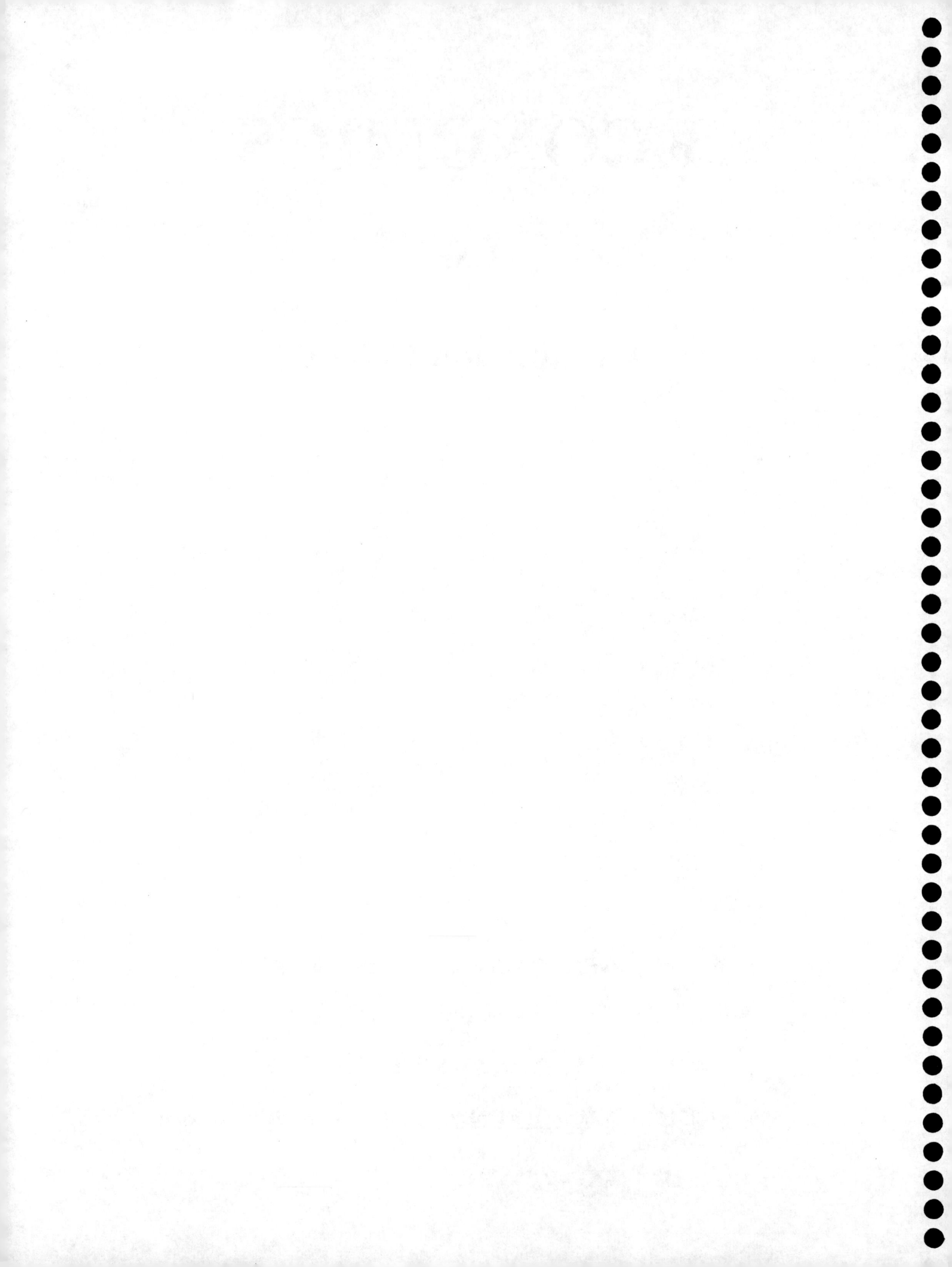

TABLE of CONTENTS

Chapter One
The Basics

What does a good extemper or debater need to know about economics? S/he needs a good working knowledge of the vocabulary of economics. This, in turn, should be used to read, understand, cut and highlight economy and business articles. This book is intended to help you in creating and using both the vocabulary and analysis of economics. Such knowledge increases your education for school and for life, impresses judges, and deepens your analysis.

The book content is relaxed and minimalist. Key vocabulary is highlighted to draw your attention. The more of the vocabulary you can learn and use the more powerful your knowledge and impact.

1. The Concepts

Economics is the study of production, distribution, and wealth. It is sometimes called "the dismal science", a name probably created by a graduate student trying to understand the mathematics formulas that attach to advanced economics study. But for extemp and debate just think of economics as the study of what makes our economy function, the factors that determine the supply and demand of all the goods and services that exist.

Economic issues can be comfortably divided into **macroeconomic** and **microeconomic** categories. The prefixes tell you what each category means. Macroeconomics looks at big issues, large topics and questions. Most extemp topics are macroeconomic concerns. Microeconomics looks at small issues: a single company, one town's economy, and similar limited albeit realistic concerns.

Whether the economics issue is macro or micro they will involve questions of **supply and demand**. These are simple concepts. Supply simply talks about how much of something is available. The quantity that already exists is the supply. **Aggregate supply** is the total amount of a good or service. Supply can be auto parts, flowpads, file folders, or blocks. Supply can be goods or services, the number of pills and the number of doctors are both types of supply. Supply is determined by many factors: raw material availability, the person power required to produce it, investment costs, and most of all by the demand for the good or service. Solutions to some extemp topic questions rest in how to increase or decrease demand. Debaters addressing drug topics, for example, often spend much of their time researching demand control questions.

Demand is the question of how much of something is wanted. In economics it is the desire for something, how much of something consumers want to purchase. **Aggregate demand** is all the demand, the total demand that exists for an item or in an economy. Demand is determined by lust, physical need, price, emotional need, advertising, religion and the full basket of desires that make up every part of human society. It can be impacted by any of these same forces. If price goes up demand usually drops. If something is easier to get (e.g. as the web made research more available) demand often goes up. Extemp topics on inflation, agriculture and global trade policies incorporate demand issues. Cost disadvantages in debate usually include demand analysis.

Supply and demand has very strong effects on each other. **The law of supply and demand** proves that these two factors effect each other. The effect varies according to circumstance but all things being equal, when the price of a particular item goes up, the quantity demanded goes down.

When the price goes down, the demand often goes up. In most situations the quantity supplied of a good or service varies directly with its price.

But there are notable exceptions and variables. A rise in the price of oil or bread does not mean that demand goes down. Some demand is **inelastic.** We all need to eat. Cars need gas. So in the short run demand might not be effected. If prices stay high a long time, however, buyers will look for alternatives and demand will drop. Instead of bread we eat pasta. Instead of gas we go electric or use a bicycle. Thus we see a **substitution effect,** which in the long run, makes almost all demand somewhat elastic.

In extemp and debate our knowledge of these events is also impacted by the statistics that surround them. Debaters argue costs, inflation disadvantages, solvency measurements. Extempers track the **consumer price index, lead indicators,** the stock market averages and other reports that add quantified impact to their speeches.

But not all statistics are equally useful or valid. Some bestsellers (e.g. *How To Lie With Statistics)*, and some scholarly works such as *Evidence* by Robert and Dale Newman testify that statistics can mislead or distort. Reliable economic statistics can usually be found in <u>Business Week</u>, <u>The New York Times</u>, <u>The Economist</u> magazine, reports from the Government Accounting Office, the Congressional Budget Office, and the Organization for Economic Cooperation and Development—the OECD.

2. Web Sites

Government statistics can be usually be found or researched at <u>www.firstgov.org</u>. A general statistical search, domestic or foreign, can often be done by topic on the Google search engine.

3. Sample Extemp Topics

How can the United States increase its energy supply without sparking sectoral inflation?
How can LDCs develop better economic policies?

4. If You Want To Read More...

What Every Debater and Extemper Should Know About Economics

By David Beers

Introduction: Why Economics?

As a policy debater or extemper you are a spinner of tales. Your art is to tell a story that is reasoned, persuasive, fresh—in a word, *compelling*. And you must ply your art better than the speakers who come before or after you in the round. The best, most believable story usually wins.

To be sure, the stories you tell are of a special sort: they have a distinctive structure, sometimes involve specialized lingo, and they tend to quote an awful lot of outside sources to convince the listener that they are true. But beneath the surface every good debate or extemp speech has the hallmarks of a good tale. It introduces characters (politicians, business people, voters, etc.) who face or create some sort of conflict (in debate we sometimes call it a "harm scenario") and it brings about a resolution to the conflict (sometimes good and sometimes bad) through the course of these characters' interactions with each other. Like every good story, a debate or extemp speech describes action and consequence, sometimes stringing together long chains of actions and consequences (often ending in nuclear war if you do cross-examination debate!)

And this is where economics comes in.

You see, economics is the *science of human action and its unintended social consequences*. Economists, too, are storytellers. And the art with which they tell their stories is a highly refined form of reasoning based on simple, mostly self-evident facts about human action. This "economic way of thinking" has been developed over centuries to clarify, systematize and correct all manner of assertions about the way society works. Economics is not a series of settled conclusions about public policy, rather it is, in the words of the economist John Maynard Keynes, "a technique of thinking which helps its possessor to draw correct conclusions." A debater who is proficient in this technique of thinking can analyze circles around his opponents' arguments, identify fallacious links, and quickly sift out promising affirmative and negative positions for further research.

As an extemper, you will find that economics opens up a whole range of fresh approaches to tired old questions and strengthens your personal voice. This will free you from relying exclusively on other peoples' analysis and give you the capacity to evaluate media assertions with authority and clarity. Whichever event is your favorite, an understanding of a few basic economic principles will help you tell compelling, well-reasoned stories that will leave your opponents wondering, "how'd they do that?"

David Beers is a former debate coach at St. John's School, Houston, TX, and Wichita Collegiate School, Wichita, KS. He has a Master's degree in economics from George Mason University. David has coached several debaters to State and National competitions. He currently is a computer programmer and technical writer in Houston, Texas.

So where is a student or coach to turn for a practical introduction to these principles?

A slim volume titled *What Everyone Should Know About Economics and Prosperity* by James Gwartney and Richard Stroup is a superb place to start (a Canadian version is online: www.fraserinstitute.ca/publications/books/ econ_prosp/index.html).

Unlike many otherwise excellent introductory economics books, this one has the virtue of unsurpassed brevity. Clocking in at only a little over 100 pages, it is astonishing how much of the basic core of economics is explained. Each short chapter begins with a simple, one-sentence summary of the point to be made in that chapter. And you would never know the authors were economists by their writing style: the exposition is lucid, punchy and to the point. Mostly what has been left out are the parts of economics that drive college freshmen crazy in Econ 101: the strange terminology, the counterintuitive assumptions, and the inscrutable graphical models. But you will not find watered down or dumbed down economics here. Of the many of books I've used or considered using for high school debaters and extempers over the years, this is the one I have found to be the most practical and helpful. With the tight constraints on our time and curriculum, no book I can think of provides an easier way to learn the economic principles that are most relevant to extemp and debate.

If You Could Only Know 10 Things...

For those of you who need to have the "opportunity cost" of learning economics lowered still further before they will tackle the task, or who need further verification from an experienced debate coach that it's really a task worth tackling, I offer you the following essay. Here is my take on the top ten things every debater and extemper should know from this book. I urge you to accept this essay as an appetizer, rather than the main course. But by the time you are finished digesting it, I think you'll have your own reasons for wanting to learn more about using economics as a tool for debate and extemp. Once you begin to catch on, you will be astonished at the power of the economic way of thinking for making and rebutting arguments about government, the market, and society.

So here is my list of the top things you should know about economics:

1. **TANSTAAFL ("There Ain't No Such Thing As A Free Lunch").**
2. **Incentives matter.**
3. **"Hazlitt's Lesson."**
4. **Private ownership promotes responsibility and cooperation.**
5. **Trade creates wealth.**
6. **Profits direct businesses toward activities that increase wealth.**
7. **Competition increases efficiency and innovation.**

8. **Taxation and regulation discourage production and destroy wealth.**

9. **Political decision-making favors plunder over production.**

10. **Central planning wastes resources and retards economic progress.**

Some of these items may seem simplistic or trite. Simple to state, perhaps, but rich in their application to real-world problems. In economics the skill is usually in the application; the concepts themselves are remarkably simple. I will give plenty of examples to illustrate the applications. Some of the items may seem counter-intuitive or paradoxical. Before I'm through I hope you will see that each is grounded in ordinary common sense—which is good news, since that's often the standard by which your judges will critique your arguments. But before I go on, a clarification of terms is in order.

A Brief Clarification of the Term "Wealth"

Before explaining why these ideas are so useful for debaters and extempers, I'd like to clarify a commonly misunderstood term that plays a central role in much of the discussion that will follow. The word "wealth" is often considered to mean an accumulation of material things or money. Thus, the pursuit of wealth is frequently contrasted with other more elevated pursuits, such as peace, compassion, justice, or spiritual enlightenment. In debate rounds we often hear about a supposed trade-off between economic growth (increasing wealth) and the environment. This is confusion. In fact, wealth is a term that encompasses anything that people place value on—material, moral, environmental, spiritual, or otherwise. Wealth can be defined for the purposes of economic analysis as *the range of opportunities available to people*[1].

When people become wealthier in this sense, it may be (and probably will be) seen as an increase in peoples' money incomes—a higher income, after all, is one of the most obvious ways someone's range of opportunities may be increased. But increases in wealth may also be seen in the enhancement of other difficult to quantify values such as security, a beautiful environment, or good health. For one thing, having a higher income allows one to pursue all manner of "non-material" goals as well as "materialistic" ones. For example, higher money incomes permit more charitable giving, better health care, safer, less polluting automobiles, and better speech and debate programs.

At another level we recognize that the distinction between material and non-material values is artificial and unnecessary. People make daily decisions of how to employ their limited time and resources to enhance their lives, balancing material and non-material goals in a single scale of value to achieve the greatest personal happiness. To arbitrarily separate out the "material" goals for the purpose of defining wealth might help someone put a dollar figure on wealth (a

---

[1] I owe this definition to Paul Heyne, *The Economic Way of Thinking*, 1994, p. 178

questionable endeavor) but it creates an artificial concept of progress that no thoughtful person would be likely to endorse. Economists, by and large are thoughtful people, so they generally reject the idea that there is a conflict between increasing wealth and increasing "other things people value"—wealth to them is *defined* by what people value.

Unfortunately, economists themselves unwittingly promote the myth that wealth is material when they spend so much time looking at statistical measures of economic activity. This has caused non-economists of all stripes to think of economists as "bean counters" who are concerned about "economic performance" rather than quality of life. In fact, statistics and forecasts play almost no role at all in the economic way of thinking—they are just a business that some professional economists have spun off to make a little money on the side!

When statistics *are* used to amplify an economic argument, it is implicitly recognized that the numbers are imperfect shadows or "proxies" for the real, unmeasurable values that underlie them. No serious economist who extols the value of economic growth would exclude progress in health, culture, the environment, etc. from his definition of growth, even though the value of these things is often difficult to measure. All these valued goals are within the increased range of opportunities that economic growth makes possible. Moreover, the extent to which each of them are pursued depends upon the value attached to them by individuals, not on the economic system which generates that wealth or creates the opportunities in the first place.

Now for a closer look at that list.

#1   TANSTAAFL

"There Ain't No Such Thing As A Free Lunch," the saying goes. There is a cost of obtaining any good thing in this world. It may not be a money cost, and the recipient is not always the one who has to pay it, but there is a cost to *someone* all the same—an opportunity that is sacrificed to make that good thing available to the recipient. The reason is that good things are scarce in society—there isn't as much of them as people would like to have. To employ scarce resources to provide a good or service of one sort leaves less for producing others. This is all right if the good produced is more valuable than the goods sacrificed. Otherwise, it's trading good for bad. Tradeoffs are everywhere and arguments are often won or lost depending on who is the best at identifying the relevant tradeoffs for a particular situation.

Politicians and special interest groups are renowned for acting as though scarcity can be repealed by an act of the legislature. Watch for it in your research. Listen to evidence and you will hear the tell-tale signs. The argument will go like this: (1) X is a good thing; (2) There is not enough X; Therefore, (3) a law to increase the amount of X is a good thing. Case in point: The War on Drugs. Here the argument is (1) Drugs are bad; (2) Tougher drug enforcement reduces drugs;

Therefore, (3) getting tough on drugs is good. What elements of scarcity are overlooked here? Well, police, courts, and prisons, to name a few. Leave aside the debatable assumption in (2) that drug enforcement actually reduces drug use. If the time and resources of the justice system are devoted to arresting, convicting, and punishing drug dealers this leaves less time and resources for bringing murderers, rapists, and armed robbers to justice. The 60 percent of federal prison space that is occupied by mostly non-violent drug offenders today is space that is not available for violent criminals[2]. Courts that once had high conviction rates for violent offenders now are clogged with drug cases and plea-bargaining is increasingly common. Meanwhile police spend time chasing dealers while more murder and rape cases go unsolved. Not surprisingly, higher drug enforcement expenditures correspond directly with higher rates of violent crime. Even if we achieve lower drug use, at what cost? There's no free lunch.

The foreign policy debate topic is one where trade-offs abound but are frequently ignored in public discussion. One example is the way public opinion polls are used to promote or defend U.S. "peacekeeping" (i.e. military) operations overseas. People polled about whether they are concerned about "ethnic cleansing" carried out by one Balkan ethnic group on another, or tribal warfare between African tribal clans, overwhelmingly answer that they are. It is not at all clear whether U.S.-backed intervention in the situation will make things better or worse, or that the intervention is in accordance with peoples' values or concerns. Nor is it clear that, given the uncertainty of improving the situation with military intervention, people would still support "doing something" if they knew how many millions of dollars it would cost them as taxpayers. But government will be seen as acting rather than doing nothing. And the unintended consequences of each intervention, after more news reports and polls, can easily become the justification for the next level of intervention.

Basing policy on such polls is similar to finding out that 95 percent of people surveyed would like a better car and then instituting a program of heavy taxation to finance new cars for everyone. Wanting a better car is one thing. Having to pay the cost is another altogether!

#2   *Incentives Matter*

A common assumption underlying many policy proposals is that human behavior is somehow fixed, regardless of the new circumstances the policy would put in place. Economists, on the other hand, emphasize that human behavior by and large is the result of choices among alternatives. Any change in the alternatives available or the relative attractiveness of those alternatives will have an effect on peoples' choices. Incentives do matter.

---

[2] David Kopel, "Prison Blues: How America's Foolish Sentencing Policies Endanger Public Safety," *Cato Policy Report*, May 17, 1994

Experience bears out the importance of incentives for altering behavior. When Congress raised the tax on luxury goods like yachts, private jets, and fur coats they were shocked to learn that the higher tax reduced the revenue generated rather than increasing it. Faced with a higher effective price on these goods, consumers of luxury goods sought out substitutes (leasing their jet instead of buying, refurbishing the old yacht, wearing more cashmere and less fur). In the end the demand for these goods was so much lower that the taxes collected didn't even cover the cost of the additional paperwork. This is an illustration of the "Law of Demand" in operation: the price of a good and the quantity demanded are inversely related.

When Congress strictly designated strong encryption technology as "munitions" that could not be freely exported out of the country, their intent was to prevent American technology from falling into the hands of terrorists or other criminals that might use it to hide communications about their activities from law enforcement officials. They gave little thought to the ways this changed incentives for producers of domestic computer software. Encryption technology today is included in almost any software that involves Internet transactions or communication. While some companies could afford to make two versions of their software—one with strong encryption for the American market and another with weaker encryption for the export market—others could not do so profitably. By raising the cost of marketing new Internet applications, Congress imposed disincentives against entering this market and gave the economic advantage to foreign software makers. Today, it is widely recognized that foreign software manufacturers have closed the gap in the market for encryption software and ended any superiority that American products once enjoyed.[3] Harder to see are the American software products that were never produced because of reduced market incentives.

#3   "Hazlitt's Lesson"

Henry Hazlitt, probably this century's greatest journalistic expositor of the economic way of thinking wrote that:

> The art of economics consists in looking not merely at the immediate but at the longer effects of any act or policy; it consists in tracing the consequences of that policy not merely for one group but for all groups.[4]

He went on to say that nine-tenths of the economic fallacies that work harm in the world today are the result of ignoring this lesson. While Hazlitt's Lesson is not exactly a separate economic principle, it is a form of mental discipline that must be exercised when constructing or analyzing policy. The Gwartney and Stroup book provides excellent examples of how rent control laws destroy urban housing, protective tariffs and quotas harm American consumers *and* workers, and jobs programs fail to create a single job overall. In each case the counter-intuitive result

---

[3] See www.cato.org/pubs/briefs/bp-042es.html for an analysis.
[4] Henry Hazlitt, *Economics in One Lesson*, 1979, p.17

is found by consistent application of Hazlitt's Lesson: look not just to the immediate effects on one group, but the long run effects on all groups.

Hazlitt's book, *Economics in One Lesson*, is still one of the best examples of the economic way of thinking put into practice. Each chapter of only a few pages traces the surprising, but inescapably logical effects of a different government policy and explains why "the law of unintended consequences" has so plagued interventionist attempts to control the economy or engineer society. More often than not, the harm of these policies falls not only on people who were never considered at the time, but on the supposed beneficiaries of the programs.

Debaters and extempers are advised to spend time with each of these books to get a feel for the way Hazlitt's Lesson is put into practice. Examples are the best teacher. A few words of practical advice: use three ideas to help you think of unintended consequences that your opponents may not have: *opportunity cost, substitutes, and competition. Opportunity cost* reminds you that when government creates a beneficiary somewhere there is a cost being paid. Who pays it and how does it affect their choices? The idea of *substitutes* reminds you that people are born circumventers—close off one avenue or make it more costly, and they will leave that activity and switch to another. How will this adjustment affect other people? *Competition* reminds you that helping one group harms others that compete with that group. (This, by the way is a useful consideration not only for analyzing the impact of policy, but for evaluating the credibility of evidence sources!)

While Hazlitt's law is the basis of the economic way of thinking, it provides a useful framework for evaluating foreign policy decisions as well. No where has the "law of unintended consequences" been more distressingly apparent than in American foreign policy since World War II. As we consider expanding the membership in the North Atlantic Treaty Organization (NATO) to put ever more of Europe under the protective umbrella of American and European military forces, we would do well to consider the way such alliances have worked out in the past. The history of post-war U.S. foreign policy in the Middle East illustrates what happens when we fail to look to the long term and to the consequences for all groups.

In 1953 America allied itself with the Shah of Iran to help him overthrow the government of Mohammed Mossadegh and preserve (we thought) security in the region—security for access to its oil and against Soviet influence. Failing to consider the hostility this act might foster against America, the U.S. watched with dismay as a revolutionary torrent built up in Iran converting its strategic alliance into a violent cauldron of anti-Americanism. By 1979 the Islamic fundamentalist revolution of Ayatollah Ruhollah Khomeini had swept the Shah out of power and taken Americans hostage in the U.S. Embassy in Tehran.

Within a year, Iran went to war with neighboring Iraq, a centuries-old rival. In the early 80s America formed a new de facto alliance to "correct" the errors of the last—this time providing critical aid and legitimacy to Iraqi leader Sadaam Hussein. With the help of the U.S. and American allies who armed Hussein with fighter planes and missiles, Iraq was to become the world's new guardian against Muslim fanaticism. Yet, two years after Iran accepted a cease-fire from Iraq, the huge military establishment that Sadaam had built during the conflict was used to invade Kuwait. To protect the secure flow of Arab oil, America went to war with Iraq, which had been a de facto ally only a few years before.

Since the Persian Gulf War, the U.S. military presence on the soil of Arab allies such as Saudi Arabia has ignited still more hostilities from forces opposed to the American-friendly governments there. The recent devastating bombing of the U.S. Embassies in Tanzania and Kenya were apparently organized and funded by Saudi Osama bin Laden in retaliation against U.S. military presence in his country. While nothing can excuse such acts of terrorism, the failure to understand their origin in America's penchant for "entangling alliances" can only ensure repetitions of this sad history.

In considering the question of enlarging NATO are we taking into account the long-range effects this might have on conflicts in which our new allies could easily become involved? With Bosnia-style ethnic conflicts already brewing between Hungary and Serbia, the loose cannon of Russian-backed Belarus on Poland's flank, and Russia touchy about the proposed encirclement of its Kaliningrad enclave by an expanded NATO, security commitments in this region have all the dangers of our Middle East alliances of the past. But where the stakes in the Middle East were mainly about oil, there is an even greater concern in the Russia/NATO interface: the vast, poorly controlled nuclear arsenal of a highly unstable ex-superpower.

#4   *Private ownership promotes responsibility and cooperation.*

Private ownership is one of the least understood institutions of the free society—a fact that can be of enormous value to debaters and extempers looking for a fresh, unexpected angle on an issue. Many people assume that because ownership entails the right to use property as one sees fit and to exclude others from using it, private property is anti-social and dangerous. A resource owned by a private individual (rather than commonly owned, or government-owned) is subject to whatever capricious idea that person might have about its use. The public has no recourse to prevent irresponsible or even dangerous uses of resources, the argument goes, when property rights are consistently defended. From there the argument claims government control is the answer, either through outright public ownership or through regulations that take away some of the property owners' rights. Economic reasoning shows that this argument gives too little credit to private owners and too much to government's wisdom and beneficence.

Private property does give owners a degree of freedom but it also makes them accountable for their actions. The owner of a dog is legally responsible for the damage his dog does to his neighbor's rose garden. The owner of a building is responsible for making repairs if the roof leaks on his tenants. This accountability ensures that property is not used in a way that harms other peoples' rights.

Consider furthermore that one of a private owner's rights is the right to sell his resource to someone who values it more and has the resources to pay for it. This opportunity forces people (both owners and potential buyers) to take into account the value that others place on the property. When natural gas was discovered under the Rainey Wildlife Preserve in Southern Louisiana, the environmentalist group that owned the land considered the commercial value of the gas and sold the right to extract it under tightly controlled conditions.

The environmentalists didn't care so much about heating homes as they did about the additional wilderness areas that the gas revenue would permit them to buy. Likewise, the gas company that won the bid for the right to drill didn't develop special extraction technologies with low environmental impact because they loved the wildlife but because they knew that this would increase their chances of winning the drilling rights. Each party had the incentive to cooperate with the other and to take their values into account.

When property rights are not clearly established or property is held in common, the incentives are reversed. This typically results in irresponsible resource use. The water crisis is a good example[5]. Farmers who share the water in underground aquifers throughout the Western United States know that the aquifers are being exhausted faster than they can be replenished. Without plentiful ground water, millions of acres of valuable cropland will some day be useless, yet no farmer has much incentive to conserve this dwindling resource. Each knows that his own conservation efforts will be to no avail unless others do the same. Each pays little or no cost for wasteful uses of water. He may as well use the water while it lasts and hope that his children don't go into farming.

By contrast, if each farmer had a share of the water that was his own, his conservation efforts would be rewarded since he could sell the rights to any unused water to other water users. If water became more scarce the price would increase and the reward for conservation would become even greater. Responsible water use would prevail.

The reckless waste and abuse of commonly owned (or unowned) resources has been dubbed the "Tragedy of the Commons" by economists and is a problem that is evident in some form in almost every area of public policy. Here are just a few examples. Learn to watch for the signs of the "Tragedy" and to trace its cause:

- **Housing**: Publicly owned housing projects quickly fall into disarray and disrepair since no one has any stake in maintaining them. Apartments that the

---

[5] See Terry Anderson, *Water Crisis: Ending the Policy Drought*, Cato Institute, 1983 for a more detailed exposition.

government deeds back to the tenants are better maintained and the owners take more responsibility for getting involved in issues that affect their building.

- **Endangered Species**: Unowned blue whales are hunted to extinction while privately owned African elephants flourish in Zimbabwe, despite (or because of?) large profits to be had from the sale of their tusks[6].

- **Law Enforcement**: Much of the time and resources of "commonly-owned" government police is wasted with false alarms, low-priority calls, and functions inessential to providing security. Meanwhile hired private police focus on the crime problems most important to the customers who hire them and charge customers who have excessive false alarms[7].

- **Wilderness Land Use**: Timber companies operating on private land have the highest rate of replanting and sometimes generate extra income by maintaining scenic areas for hunters, hikers, and other sportsmen. Meanwhile companies on public land have the highest rates of clear-cutting and are not allowed to collect revenue from sportsmen.

- **Health Care**: People who pay for their health care out of a common insurance pool spend 25 percent more on health care and are more likely to receive unnecessary treatment than people who spend their own money from a medical savings account. Today only 19 cents out of each dollar of physician's fees is paid by patients using their own funds. Meanwhile the demand for health care has exploded, and health care costs with it. Countries where all health care is financed out of tax revenues are scrambling to privatize their systems[8].

Many of these examples also illustrate the conflict that results when political forces are inevitably brought to bear to control common-pool resources. Political control of resources does not eliminate competition; it only changes it from market competition to competition among political interest groups. Whereas competitors for privately owned resources have strong incentives to accommodate each other (as in the Rainey Wildlife Preserve example), political competition is usually a winner-take-all affair. Political struggles over health care, the environment, and now the legal protection of private, personal information have been heated and sometimes even violent because competing groups have nothing to gain from accommodating each other and everything to lose.

#5   *Trade creates wealth.*

For centuries people believed that for exchange to occur the goods exchanged must be of equivalent value. Old habits die hard. This is still one of the most common economic fallacies. But the intense interest that people take in trading, whether they trade dollars for a new stereo, or their labor for a paycheck

---

[6] See Randy Simmons and Urs Kreuter, "Herd Mentality," *Policy Review*, Fall 1989, pp. 46-49
[7] See Bruce Benson, *The Enterprise of Law*, 1990
[8] John Goodman and Gerald Musgrave, *Patient Power*, 1992, p. 20

gives the lie to this misconception. With only a little reflection it is easy to see that in every exchange we make we give up something we value *less* than what we receive…and so does the person with whom we are trading. Voluntary exchanges benefit both parties to the exchange and this benefit is rightly seen as an increase in wealth for both. Remember, more wealth doesn't mean "more stuff"; it often means getting stuff into the hands of the people who value it most. Air conditioners in Arizona and space heaters in Saskatchewan.

Exchange creates wealth in indirect ways, as well, by creating the possibility of specialization and division of labor. Most of us would be desperately poor, even to the point of starvation, if we had to produce everything we needed for ourselves. But by specializing in one type of production that we do very well and exchanging that product or service for the other things we need, we can be much better off. Along with the division of labor comes division of knowledge—people gaining specialized knowledge and skills that benefit millions of other people who can be blissfully unaware of how it all comes together. The increased division of labor and division of knowledge are the chief sources of the economic growth that has occurred in human history. And they are only possible because of the freedom to exchange.

The significance for debaters and extempers is this: be alert to proposals to limit, regulate, or restrict free exchanges between people. Many a nation has choked off economic progress and trapped its people in poverty by imposing a morass of regulations, licenses, permits, taxes, and fees on every type of transaction. Gwartney and Stroup use the extraordinary example of Peru as a nation whose economy has stagnated under the weight of bureaucracy and regulation, yet the U.S. may be almost as good an example. Economist Thomas Hopkins has estimated that the current cost to the U.S. economy of government regulations is over $500 billion per year [9]. Tariffs and quotas on imports alone cost consumers $80 billion a year—over $1,200 per family[10]. These trade restrictions destroy American jobs by reducing the dollars available for foreigners to purchase American exports and by leaving consumers with less money to spend on other things.

Licensing restrictions and regulations on small business have especially hurt minority and low-income entrepreneurs by blocking entry to markets where they can sell their goods and services. Rationalized in the halls of government as a protection to consumers, these restrictions are mainly backed by businesses who fear the competition of new entrants that might provide better service or a lower price. Minimum wage laws, too, reduce the demand for low-skilled labor and close off economic opportunities for young people just entering the job market. Trade restrictions that impact people with low skills and low income are doubly costly in that they drive disappointed job-seekers into the welfare system and add to the burden of taxes in the economy.

---

[9] Michael Tanner, *Cato Handbook for Congress*, 1995, p. 181.
[10] James Bovard, *The Fair Trade Fraud*, 1991, p. 5.

In short, every policy that restricts free trade, free contract, or free entry into the market diminishes wealth for individuals and the nation as a whole.

Trade issues are central to the foreign policy topic. Trading relations between countries bring benefits to people in both countries and these trading networks reduce nationalistic tensions. Americans may shout in anger at French national bicycling team beating the American team at some international competition. But their anger diminishes when consuming a bottle of fine French wine. Many Americans were terribly upset when a Chinese fighter plane collided with an American spy plane in international air space. But thousands that same day purchased inexpensive electronics equipment made in China.

Though governments regularly stir up resentment between the people of different nations, people on their own gradually specialize in producing some goods and services and trading for others goods and services produced in other countries.

It is worth noting that not everyone benefits from open trade. Those companies in the U.S. that are struggling to compete with inexpensive goods made in China naturally harbor resentment and are often the first to call for boycotts of Chinese-made goods when foreign-policy tensions erupt. Lobbyists for U.S. manufactured goods are often the first to back dramatic trade restrictions under the guise of national defense measures.

#6   *Profits direct businesses toward activities that increase wealth.*

"Profit" is often considered to be a derogatory term today, especially when it's referred to as a motivation for human activity. It is fashionable today to talk about the need for business to temper its pursuit of profits by being more socially or environmentally conscious. The concern that business people behave responsibly and with all due awareness of the ways their decisions affect other people is certainly noble and good. But the implication that pursuing profit is socially irresponsible is based on economic misunderstanding.

Profits are not snatched from the mouths of hungry children by greedy businessmen. They are earned by people who provide a product or service that other people are willing to pay for. More accurately, they are earned by the people who most creatively and judiciously employ their resources to satisfy the needs of others. The pursuit of profit demands the imagination and alertness to anticipate those needs and the wisdom to meet them without wasting scarce resources. Even if the entrepreneur's immediate goal is making money, the economic criterion for doing so is to help others accomplish their own goals.

There is nothing automatic about this process. Many business people suffer losses because the cost of the resources (labor, capital, materials, etc.) was higher than anticipated or they were inefficient in employing them. Others lose money because the demand for the product was insufficient. In all these cases, losses signal to the entrepreneur that the resources would be more valuably employed in a different manner. Those entrepreneurs who persist in losing ventures eventually lose their businesses and the resources are freed up for other more socially beneficial lines of production. While sad for the owner who must sell the business, this process is beneficial for the public as a whole since scarce resources are conserved for only the uses that consumers value most highly.

"Corporate downsizing," the practice of trimming excess workers and managers from company payrolls to lower costs and increase profitability, is often described as a symbol of weakness or corruption in our economy. This is because people judge only by the obvious visible consequences without tracing the invisible ones—they ignore Hazlitt's Lesson. What is seen are people losing their jobs. What is not seen are the new goods and services which the economy can now produce because this valuable labor and know-how is available for starting new businesses. This is one reason why this period of corporate downsizing has corresponded with very low rates of unemployment, rapid innovation, and low prices for consumer goods.

Internet businesses have been vilified of late for trampling consumer privacy by tracking consumer behavior and sometimes sharing the information with other businesses. The fact that some of this is actually beneficial, on balance, to consumers has already been discussed. The more interesting story, perhaps, is the extent to which the profit incentive has forced businesses to regulate their own use of consumer information and offer convincing assurances that they are respecting the privacy of consumers who are sensitive to this issue. It is the interest in profit that has drawn software companies into the market for technologies that afford greater privacy protection, not just a sense of moral obligation to the public. Profits encourage people to cooperate in providing what other people want and are willing to pay for.

#7   *Competition increases efficiency and innovation.*

Competition is a source of discipline in the market, or in any social organization for that matter. Producers who are earning profits for the time being can rarely afford to rest on their laurels. A single new entrant producing a better, cheaper product can turn those profits to losses very quickly. As long as entry into the market is open, competition (actual or potential) ensures that entrepreneurs stay on their toes by constantly increasing efficiency and finding new, better ways to produce. It is the producer's perpetual "reality check."

When competition is reduced by legal restrictions, regulations, tariffs, or quotas market discipline is partially suspended. Efficiency, innovation, and quality of service are reduced since they are no longer as necessary for the protected industry to stay profitable. When the author moved from Wichita, Kansas to Houston, Texas he learned this lesson first hand. In Wichita, trash collection is a competitive industry. Dozens of local companies offer subscriptions to pick up residential waste. The fact that a dissatisfied subscriber can make two phone calls and change her trash company has resulted in low prices, and excellent service. Companies provide and maintain free 90-gallon trash barrels with sturdy wheels and hinged tops. On trash day (twice a week) they come up to the house to get the barrel and take it out to the street. Most services pick up almost any kind of trash that is left for them—even large appliances!

In Houston, by contrast, the city maintains a legal monopoly in residential waste pick-up. Competition is forbidden. No barrels are provided. In fact, Houston trash collectors won't touch trash barrels of any kind—all trash must be placed by the resident in plastic bags at the curb. What about heavy items that won't go into bags? Houston residents must remember to put those at the curb on a particular day that comes once each month. *Sometimes* the city will pick them up then. If not, haul the stuff back in the garage and try again next month!

Competition is one of the most important reasons why the market is superior to government as a system for producing goods and services. Those who fear that economic freedom will allow producers to take unfair advantage of people often neglect this fact and call for industries to be tightly regulated or taken over by government. As a rule, these government-run industries are inefficient, costly to taxpayers, and far less innovative than private firms operating in a competitive environment.

Privacy regulations may be a serious threat to competition if they limit the capacity for new entrants to the market to gain critical information about consumers and prevent them from playing profitably on a field where established firms are already quite dominant.

#8   *Taxation and regulation discourage production and destroy wealth.*

How hard we are willing to work depends on how much we are offered in pay. Incentives matter. Taxes lower our incentive to work just like a reduction in pay, since that is exactly what they are. If allowed to keep only half of every dollar we earn, alternatives to working for money begin to look more attractive. Some people will work less overtime and enjoy more leisure, some will find non-taxable work in the home (and stop paying daycare and cleaning people), some will retire earlier, etc. Businesses whose income is heavily taxed may withhold undertaking new ventures since the share of the profits they are allowed to keep doesn't justify the risks. Investors, too, find alternatives to putting their money to work in a high-tax environment: they invest in countries where the tax rates are lower or they simply consume more of their surplus income. All these choices illustrate that high taxation discourages productive activity, and thereby reduces the wealth that is created in society.

Equally important for the general welfare is the fact that taxation diverts enormous amounts of time and resources into non-productive activities. Businesses and individuals spend billions of worker-hours each year (in America,

5.5 billion, to be exact[11]) just completing taxation paperwork. This includes the wasted talent and labor when lawyers and accountants are hired to find legal and not-so-legal ways of sheltering income from the tax collector. These jobs in the tax industry create no wealth for society as a whole, rather they deprive us all of the valuable services these individuals could be producing for the market. The higher the tax rate, though, the more people hire such experts to help them.

Tax cuts reduce the *percentage* of income government collects, but because of the stronger incentives to produce they also increase the tax *base* (the total amount of taxable income generated in the economy). This means that cutting tax rates doesn't necessarily reduce the revenue government takes in. When taxes are very high, tax cuts have even *increased* total tax revenue, thanks to the economic growth produced. This is not "voodoo economics"—it is just common sense. Consider that if we were taxed at a rate of 100%, government revenue would be almost zero since few people would bother working for money knowing they would receive no take-home pay. Tax cuts from that level and from levels substantially lower would obviously increase income-producing activity, and tax revenue along with it. Significant tax cuts during the Kennedy and Reagan administrations were attended by increased tax revenues in the years that followed, just as this theory would predict.

For debaters this means that raising taxes is a questionable option for funding plan mandates! For everyone, the economic reasoning provides a framework to assess conflicting claims about taxes within the media.

#9   *Political decision-making favors plunder over production.*

The great French political economist, Frederic Bastiat, wrote in 1850:

> Man can live and satisfy his wants only by ceaseless labor; by the ceaseless application of his faculties to natural resources. This process is the origin of property.

> But it is also true that a man may live and satisfy his wants by seizing and consuming the products of the labor of others. This process is the origin of plunder.[12]

Bastiat went on to say that the purpose of law is to protect property by preventing people from using plunder against each other. This is a pretty important function. For one thing, the entire market economy is based on this foundation of secure property rights, which creates strong incentives to produce and to cooperate through peaceful, voluntary exchange. Preserving this fabric of civil society by protecting individual rights is usually the primary reason people give for having a government with the legitimate right to use force.

But governments often do much more than protect people from plunder and coercion. Government's power to tax can indeed be used to pay for police,

---

[11] James Gwartney and Richard Stroup, *What Everyone Should Know About Economics and Prosperity*, 1993, p. 76
[12] Frederic Bastiat, *The Law*, 1990, p. 10.

courts, and military defense but the same power may be used to dispense other benefits. To someone who can influence the government, its power can be a tool for gaining access to other peoples' property. Bastiat called this "legal plunder" and argued that it was no more just and no less destructive than the criminal plunder of a thief. If people can compete for legal access to their neighbors' wallets and purses through the political process, it will not be long before a government designed to protect peoples' rights becomes one of the greatest threats to those rights.

Understanding the dangerous incentives inherent in concentrating power in a central government, the founding fathers sought to constrain the government with a binding Constitution. Under the Constitution, Congress was to have only those powers delegated to it as enumerated in the document. "The powers not delegated to the United States by the Constitution, nor prohibited by it to the States, are reserved to the States respectively, or to the people." Specifically Congress was permitted to raise taxes to "provide for the common Defense and the General Welfare" of the people, but not for the special defense or welfare of particular groups. Madison and Jefferson insisted that this clause be included as a shield guarding against the misuse of federal powers.

The majority of the modern federal budget is devoted to the transfer of resources from the taxpayers to various particular groups in society: farmers, industry, small business owners, homeowners, scientists, artists, the poor, the elderly, nature lovers, classical music lovers, even peanut lovers. In fact, government has grown so large with programs for each special interest group that today more than 35 percent of what we produce (GDP) is consumed or redistributed by federal, state, and local governments[13].

A great deal more legal plunder is perpetrated by regulations that protect one group's economic interests at the expense of others. Labor unions lobby for a higher minimum wage to protect union jobs from competition by cheap labor. Taxi drivers and hairdressers ask for mandatory state licensing to reduce competition from upstart new entrants. And hundreds of domestic industries pressure the International Trade Commission and Commerce Department to impose heavier tariffs on consumers when they try to buy foreign-made goods. Those who benefit most directly by subsidies, tariffs or protective legislation have strong incentives to be politically organized, while the much larger group who share the costs tend to be less vocal. Government officials pay most attention to those who are paying attention to them.

As more of what people receive comes to them through government and less through their individual labors, this has predictable effects on their productivity. More resources are devoted to plunder and less to production. Living standards grow more slowly, or even decline. Poverty becomes entrenched. International comparisons cited in the Gwartney and Stroup book show that a

---

[13] William Niskanen and Stephen Moore, *Cato Handbook for Congress*, 1995, p. 73.

nation's economic progress is generally inversely related to the size and scope of its government[14].

For debaters and extempers the lesson here is clear. Be wary of proposals to expand the aspects of our economic lives over which politics has control. Political decision-making delivers the spoils to the groups that are most politically organized (most likely to determine election outcomes). In the free market, by contrast, resources tend to flow to where they are most valuably employed in satisfying consumers. Whereas market competition tends to increase wealth by expanding the range of opportunities available, political competition tends to consume wealth by diverting resources into organized legal plunder. Lobbyists, lawyers, and government relations departments are the private sector counterparts to the government bureaucracies and agencies that spend billions of tax dollars each year directing benefits to various special interest groups.

#10   *Central planning wastes resources and retards economic progress.*

Human reason has given us enormous control over our environment. The technology that reason has produced helps to feed, clothe, and shelter us from the cold blasts of nature which kept our prehistoric ancestors huddled and half-starved. With the Enlightenment came the faith that nothing was beyond man's ultimate capacity to control if reason was his guide. If science could help us design a better bridge, then why not a better society—one that is organized and planned to suit our needs, instead of one where everyone pursues their own disconnected plans in that bewildering, competitive, uncontrolled game called capitalism? As well as we have done muddling along with nothing but profit and loss to guide us, one might imagine that the messy process of market competition would be better replaced by a consciously designed economic system that is rationally planned.

This basic line of reasoning is at the foundation of a great many debate cases, as well as countless real-world proposals for reforming our economy. But as reasonable as it sounds, it is fallacious. In fact it is possibly "The" great economic fallacy of the 20th century; the one that brought us Soviet socialism and German fascism, to say nothing of the untold economic misery of dozens of Third World countries who patterned their policies after socialist governments in Europe. It is also the essential vision behind proposals for comprehensive national health insurance, national industrial policy, social engineering, government-funded scientific research, and all manner of government-business partnerships.

The fallacy of central planning, which Nobel Laureate Friedrich Hayek[15] called the "fatal conceit," lies in a misunderstanding of the kind of knowledge

---

[14] James Gwartney and Richard Stroup, *What Everyone Should Know About Economics and Prosperity*, 1993, pp. 110-112
[15] See Friedrich A. Hayek, The Fatal Conceit, 1988

required to organize the plans of a large number of people into a successful economy (or health care industry, etc.). The knowledge to construct even the simplest item we use—say, a pencil—is known to no individual on earth. It is dispersed among millions of individuals who neither know each other nor are aware of each others' activities. Graphite miners, tool manufacturers, forestry experts, mill designers, paint chemists, rubber growers, truck drivers and machine operators each contribute their specialized knowledge to the production process. No central planner could hope to understand even a fraction of the detailed knowledge needed to guide the construction of a single pencil, much less an industry or an economy.

And even if a planner could master this knowledge, how would he go about evaluating which resources should be devoted to which projects in the economy? What would tell him which things are most important or valuable? In a free, competitive market, fluctuating prices signal the value of resources and guide production decisions. If a large chromium mine collapses in Zaire, the American pencil maker is signaled that he needs to substitute paints with non-chromium dyes. How? By the higher price of chromium paint. People with less urgent needs for chromium reduce their consumption without having to know the details—or even that chromium is in the paint they use. Thus, supply and demand generate prices which spontaneously direct resources to the most important uses. Without competitive markets and prices to guide him, the central planner has no way to accurately judge what are efficient uses of resources.

The problem of central planning is deeper still when incentives are taken into account. People who gain resources by virtue of their position in "the plan" rather than by better satisfying consumers tend to have a stronger interest in catering to the planner than to the supposed beneficiaries of their work. The collapse of communism is now widely understood to have occurred because of perverse incentives that rewarded corruption and waste, while neglecting even the most pressing needs of the people.

Centrally planned government programs in America show the same pathologies. Medicaid clinics, paid by the government according to the number of clients they serve, often churn patients through as quickly as possible. Bureaucratically set prices for many Medicaid services are too low to compensate doctors for the liability risks involved, so these services—including prenatal care—are becoming less and less available[16]. A pregnant Medicaid patient who is willing to supplement the doctor's reimbursement with her own money to receive prenatal care or a higher quality of service cannot legally do so since this would defeat the purpose of the plan. Similar irrational results can be found in other "rationally planned" government programs.

For debaters and extempers the principle to keep in mind is that individuals are generally better able to produce, purchase and provide for

---

[16] John Goodman and Gerald Musgrave, *Patient Power*, 1992, p. 59

themselves what they need than even the best-intentioned bureaucrat in a remote office. With economic freedom, society tends to spontaneously order itself to maximize peoples' chances of carrying out their plans successfully. This coordination may seem mysterious—we are trained to believe that where there is order there must be a designing hand that created it. But most of the order and cooperation in a complex society such as our own must be generated in this spontaneous manner, for no designer could ever accomplish the task.

Conclusion

The economic way of thinking begins with just a few common-sense ideas: goods are scarce, incentives affect peoples' behavior, and the consequences of individual actions and government policies usually extend far beyond the obvious short-term effects on their immediate beneficiaries. But as you begin to apply these common-sense ideas you will often come to conclusions strikingly different from what you are accustomed to hearing. This is because few people make the effort to be consistent and persistent in tracing the logic of human affairs. Learning to do this will put you at a tremendous advantage in analyzing policy issues before and during your tournaments. And it will give you the rare capacity to make reasoned, independent judgments on complex issues, without always having to uncritically accept the opinion of self-proclaimed "experts" in the media or the political arena. That's a powerful edge to have in competition and in life.

An online version of this essay, along with other articles and links for speech and debate students, is available at the Foundation for Economic Education's speech and debate website: www.freespeaker.org

Chapter Two
Making The Economy Run

1. The Concepts

    The formation of society usually overlaps with the creation of an economy. Individuals, families, and small clans do not create an economy. They hunt or grow simply to survive. Only when production creates a surplus does the opportunity for economy creation open. Until approximately 700 A.D. the Anasazi were neither a society nor did they have an economy, they were hunter-gatherers. Only when summer rain cycles improved did they even have the chance to plant enough to develop a surplus, and thus the chance at trade and an economy. Surplus also creates leisure time in which artisans can develop and expand, where goods production can diversify. We owe the beauty of Navajo rugs and Chinese porcelain to the conditions that promoted economic evolution.

    Moving from survival to surplus creates the question "what should be produced?". Trade, barter, and buying all measure **demand**. The time and effort used for each determines its **opportunity costs**; the time you use to produce one item is time you cannot use to produce another item. The interaction of demand and opportunity cost begin to formulate what the price of a simple product will be. Greed, lust, love, and all the human emotions create demand. Maslow's hierarchy attempts to identify and place our needs in a hierarchy. But whatever needs and desires exist they form the basis for demand, the stimulus for economic production and product diversity.

    Answering the "what should be produced?" question also introduces us to the **substitution effect.** If prices go high the potential buyer will use substitutes instead. OPEC could charge even higher prices when group cohesion is high; they do not because (among many reasons) they don't want to increase incentives to develop petroleum substitutes. Debate counterplans often use the substitution effect to get their net benefit or competitiveness.

    As economies develop they become more complex. New factors enter the "what should be produced" equation. The early Anasazi of America's southwest, or the Cossack communities of the Ukraine, made only a few products. Each could be made by a single person or a small family. But successful small economies often see population growth and with that an evolution and exploration of new product opportunities. Enter the **factors of production: labor, raw materials, capital goods, and capital formation.**

    Early Athens, Babylon, Memphis (in Egypt) and Chaco Canyon all faced evolutionary economic questions. Nobody necessarily said it out-loud. The idea might not even have been conceived of in the way we would think about it today. But in each of these evolving societies some citizens realized they had a choice. They could do what their parents had done (pottery, farm, hunt...) or they could find something new that would give them enough to live on. Teachers, medical products, new clothing options, weapon design advances, and perhaps even some governmental and or religious posts stem from these economic realizations.

    To take advantage of or create new choices one or more **factor of production** had to be used. If more people needed to work together **labor** became a production factor. If a jeweler wanted to add turquoise to jewelry or home designs improved **raw material** access became important. If a machine or tool was needed to make the end product then **capital goods** had been discovered. And if it took money for an item to be produced the economy and business had entered the era of **capital formation.** The more of these factors involved in an economy the more complex and advanced it became.

These same four factors can be thought of as variables. Adding or reducing the amount of each in an economy greatly affects its success. Therein lays the gleam of an answer to many an extemp topic or debate case solvency.

But extemp and debate analysis can answer the question of "what should be produced?" by approaching the question from a new or second direction. The speaker can ask **what, how, and for whom.** This approach often works best when combined with the concept of **economic scarcity.** Whether an economy is just leaving its beginning phases, or is a complex machine like the twenty-first United States, the economic system has to find answers to what should be produced, how it will be produced, and who will get the final products. Since most things, such as time, labor or raw materials, are finite economic scarcity always limits the choices any economy can make.

Economies are thus always making choices. How efficiently the economy makes the choice impacts its success, its citizens quality of life. Growth disadvantages and extemp topics that ask how we can solve country x's economic woes address parts of these issues.

The form of government impacts the success of every economy, and every economy effects the success of a government. Anarchy, no or minimal government, leaves production decisions to individual participants. It is akin to **laissez-faire** (no government interference) economic systems. Democratic systems run the full gamut from minimal marketplace interference to Sweden's **democratic socialism** with extensive governmental ownership of natural resources, and production input. Dictatorships often promote **oligarchies** or **state owned businesses** as extensions of the ruler's tyranny.

2. Web Site

http://economics.about.com/ labels itself the "Complete Guide to Economic Resources on the Web". Good access to statistics and a nice list of economic subject groupings for the user to pick from.

3. Sample Extemp Topics

How can the emerging economies of Eastern Europe successfully move from central planning to consumer-controlled economies?

Does United States policy maximize our factors of production?

4. If you want to read more...

econDash

Econ 101

Would you like to learn more about economic data and how it impacts you?

You've come to the right place! EconDash™'s Econ101 will provide an easy-to-read tutorial on basic economic concepts, focusing on those that impact the entire United States region (these concepts are called macroeconomics).

There are three basic concepts that tie economics together:

1. Demand - Demand represents the order or requirement for a given item. Demand varies based on Price - in general, as price goes down, demand goes up. As prices rise, demand goes down.

example: Digital TVs initially were priced over $3,000. Very few could afford this pricing, so demand was low. If digital TVs drop to $300, demand will skyrocket.

2. Supply - Supply is the availability of a particular item. Supply usually also varies with Price changes - in general, as price goes down, supply goes down. When prices rise, supply typically increases as well.

example: When oil prices are at $10 per barrel, drillers cannot make money, so they do not explore for new sources of oil. However when oil is over $30 per barrel, significant profits can be achieved so oil exploration significantly expands.

3. Price - In a perfectly competitive world (Adam Smith called this the "invisible hand"), price is established where supply of an item equals demand of an item at that price point.

example: In the stock market, the price of Microsoft shares is the price at which sellers are willing to sell and buyers willing to buy at that point in time. If sellers wanted to sell more of their shares, they would have to lower the price to get more buyers interested in buying. If buyers wanted to buy more shares, they would have to offer a higher price to get more sellers interested in selling.

The familiar integration of Demand, Supply and Price looks similar to the following chart.

24

Supply and Demand Curve Example

DEMAND CURVE   SUPPLY CURVE

Price per unit $ (y-axis: $0, $10, $20, $30, $40, $50, $60, $70, $80, $90, $100)

Market price

Volume in millions (x-axis: 1, 3, 5, 7, 9, 11, 13, 15, 17)

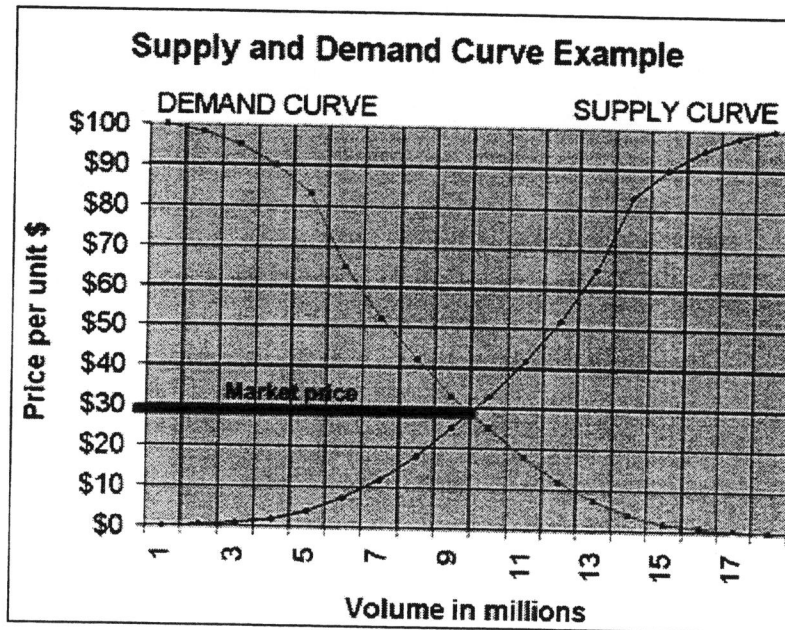

What is "the economy"?

First: a look at the dictionary: Economy is defined as "the structure of economic life in a country, area or period". Economic is defined as: of, relating to, or based on the production, distribution and consumption of goods and services

From MSN Encarta Dictionary: the production and consumption of goods and services of a community regarded as a whole

Our major concern is the links to production, distribution, consumption, and pricing of goods and services. All indicators in the Dashboards are linked to these in one way or another. What we will see is how they relate to the production, distribution, consumption, and pricing of goods and services, and more importantly, how these are related one to another.

Production, distribution, consumption, and pricing are not natural phenomena. People are doing them. They invest, and start firms, which produce and distribute goods and services. People consume goods and services. What we observe and measure with the indicators is the result of the interaction of a huge number of individuals and firms. All these "agents" make decisions along a large number of dimensions. Understanding how the economy works, and trying to predict it, involves studying an extremely complex object, which is not an easy task.

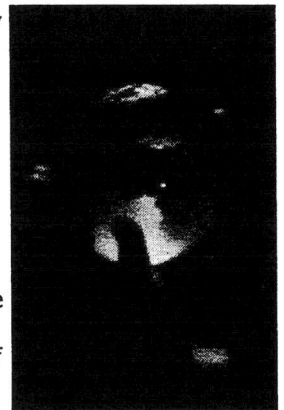

In what follows, we will try to be as simple as possible, and we will try to stay as practical as we can: the point is to teach you how to use some economic reasoning in order to better understand news and better grasp economic data and its implications.

If you want to take a few minutes to try and understand how economists do their job, you can make a detour through our what do economists do section.

What do economists do?

We have seen that the economy is extremely complex; the result of the interaction of a lot of agents, either individuals, or people grouped into firms making decisions along a large number of dimensions.

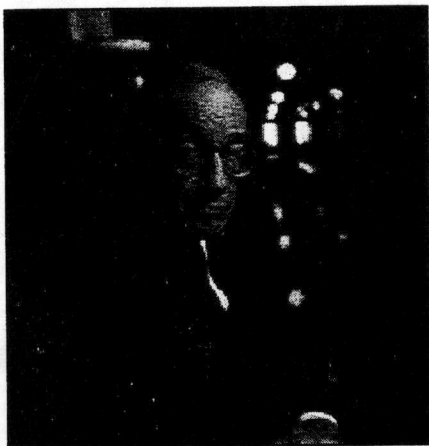

How can we try to understand what is going on? First we need to evaluate what is happening, by gathering data. It is the data that we want to understand. Economists do this by constructing models, or mathematical equations, that they hope will be able to demonstrate patterns in the data. The purpose of the exercise is to understand what has happened and predict what is going to happen to the economy in the future. This is important in several respects. For instance, when governmental policies are changed, what happens to the economy? Knowing this for sure would allow us to evaluate policies. Unfortunately, there are not enough certainties. The more we understand the economy, the better we can predict what will happen. Also, when a firm is looking whether to invest, knowing how the economy will fare is crucial. Of course, experiments would make it a lot easier to understand how things work. This, of course, is not a possibility when studying the economy: we can't ask a state to tax at 90% income, and observe if what happens corresponds to the prediction in our model. So, we are left with models that we constantly compare against actual data.

Models are logical constructs, built on numerous assumptions. But the economy is very complex, so what economists do is simplify as much as possible. Using stringent assumptions, they try to understand as much as possible with simple models, and then increase the complexity of the models.

The US government has assembled some of the best economists to help guide US monetary policy. By evaluating economic data and models, they try to predict proper monetary policy to optimize the economy. These independant individuals lead the Federal Reserve, which controls the interest rates charged to banks by the US Federal Reserve System and the cash reserve requirements of US banks. These two factors are a large part of the US monetary policy. The Federal Reserve Open Market Committee (FOMC) evaluates monetary policy in meetings throughout the year.

Nobel Prize Winners:

JAMES J. HECKMAN for his development of theory and methods for analyzing selective samples
and
DANIEL L. MCFADDEN for his development of theory and methods for analyzing discrete choice.

Later on, you should be able to use very simple constructs, or models, to grasp some of the implications in changes in the indicators. We will not claim that the models replicate the economy, just that they allow us to understand some part of the mechanism that makes up the economy. You may want to check out what a **model** is in a little more detail, with simple illustrative **examples**.

On the use of models, an example

Let's model the market for wine. We want to simplify things, so assume there is only one quality of wine (a stringent assumption, of course). Assume also that all trade takes place at one site.

If you are a producer of wine, and you expect prices to go up, then you will want to increase your production level. However, if prices go down, you'd rather lower your production level and produce something else that is more profitable. If you are a wine buyer, well you will buy more if the price is low, less if the price is high. Despite the producers desires, short term price is determined in large part by the buyers willingness to pay.

If there are many wine makers and many buyers, no one will be able to set prices: if you increase over the market price, all customers go to the next merchant who sells at the market price and nobody will buy from you. So how is the market price determined? Well, it is the price at which the total quantity of wine produced is equal to the total quantity of wine demanded.

In a simple example, let's say there are 10 wine buyers. They like wine, but if it's too expensive, they will buy beer instead. The buyers have the following secret profile.

At this price	# of bottles we will buy
$2.50	400
$3.00	300
$4.00	200
$5.00	100

Now let's take our 3 sellers of wine. In our market let's assume the sale of wine happens one day in the town center. The sellers come with 300 bottles, feeling good and start by asking for $4.00 per bottle. What happens? Then 10 Buyers offer to buy only 200 of the bottles. The sellers are stuck with 100 bottles left. Instead, they offer $3.00 per bottle, which sells all the bottles available, for $100 more in total proceeds.

Suppose there is frost in the late spring, so wine makers cannot make as much wine as they used to. They now only have 100 bottles. What is the effect on the market price and the quantity sold? If demand fundamentals do not change, then at the "no frost" price, there is more demanded than supplied, so the price has to be greater. And at a higher price, demand will be lower. So the result is an increase in price when there is a decrease in production. In our example, the sellers will get $5.00 per bottle to sell their 100 bottles, versus $3.00 the year before, when 300 bottles were available.

Cycles, Leading variables, lagging variables

> GDP is value of the goods and services generated by companies of a certain country.

The main measure of aggregate economic activity is GDP, or output. Most people think the economy is going well if GDP growth is high They become depressed if growth becomes negative (Negative growth has inspired thoughts of suicide).

GDP in the USA

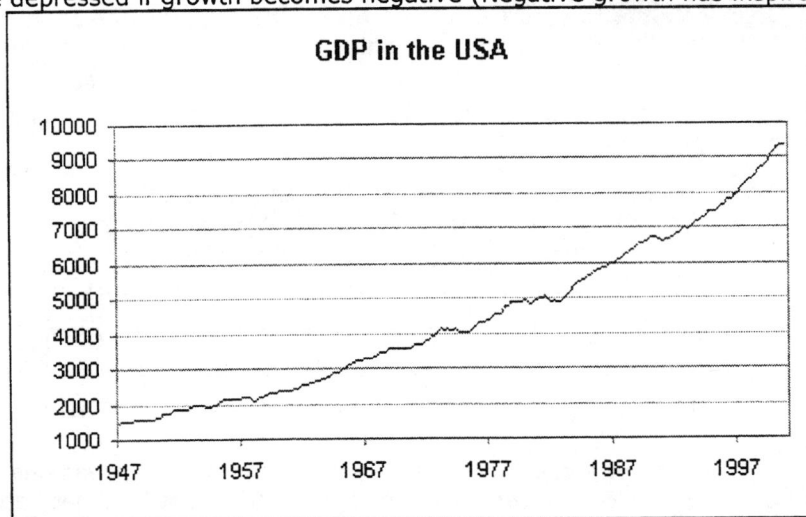

In the long term series of GDP output, two main things are noticeable: one is that output has been increasing steadily over the last 50 years. However, it wiggles up and down from one year to the other. We can break down this series into a trend (long term growth), taking away the wiggles, and in cycles, taking away the trend.

GDP in the USA
Long term Growth Component

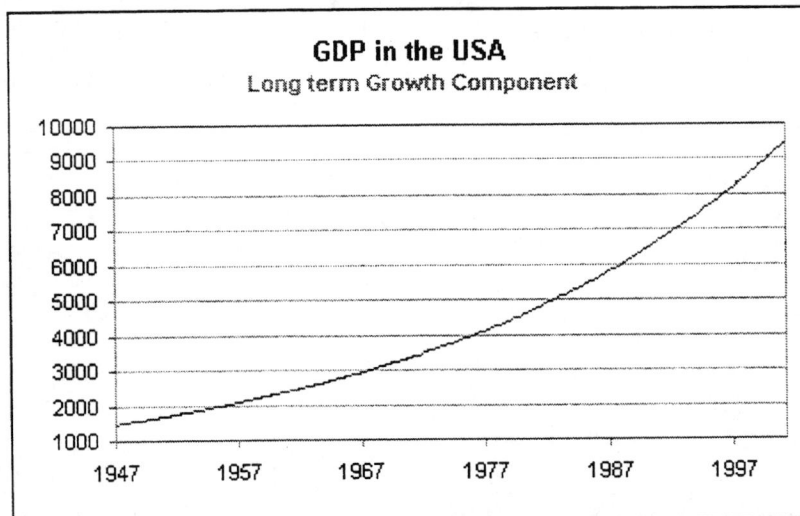

http://www.econdash.net/econ101_all.html

GDP in the USA
Cycle Component of GDP

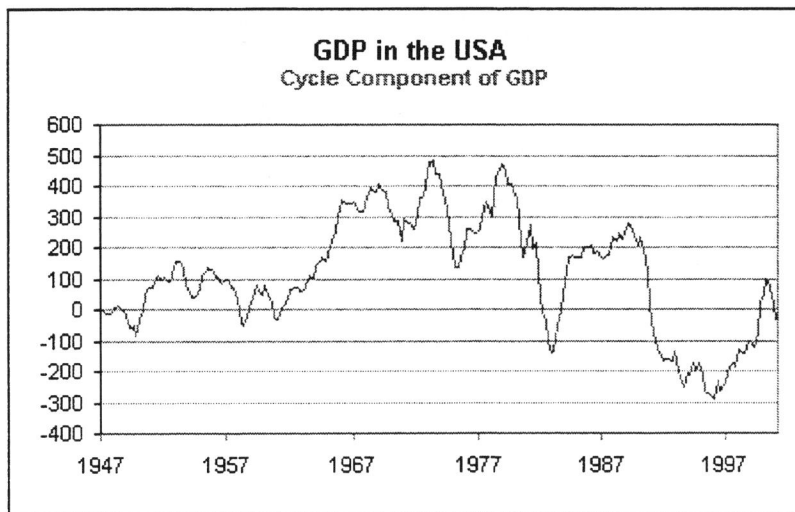

Information most often reported in the news relates to cycles. The question we are concerned with is how the economy, represented by output, will evolve in the next few months. More rarely do we wonder what is going to happen in fifty years. Of course, one question is not independent of the other. For instance, today's decisions in government spending could affect the economy in the long term (in the case of Belgium: huge government debt of the 70s influences the economic process now). Although there are important interdependencies, we will focus on the cycles, at least for now.

Cycles, Leading variables, lagging variables

Procyclical, Acyclical and Countercyclical Variables

When we look at the GDP growth rate, we notice that it reaches maximum and minimum points (peaks and troughs) with a certain regularity. Generally, after a boom, there is a slowdown. One cycle of the economy is defined as 'the period between two peaks'. A question we want to ask is, "Where are we in the current cycle?" Some element of an answer can be given by looking at other indicator series.

> A data series is made by taking an indicator and saving it at regular intervals of time

The economy is described by a series of documenting movements in variables that are related in some way to output (GDP, GNP, growth, employment, unemployment, prices, job creation, interest rates, housing, consumption, etc.) Some variables follow a cycle similar to GDP; when GDP is growing faster, they are also growing faster, and vice versa. These variables are said to be *procyclical*. Other variables go in the opposite direction, and are said to be *countercyclical*. Finally some variables are *acyclical*, meaning they are not moving in a way that is linked somewhat systematically to GDP.

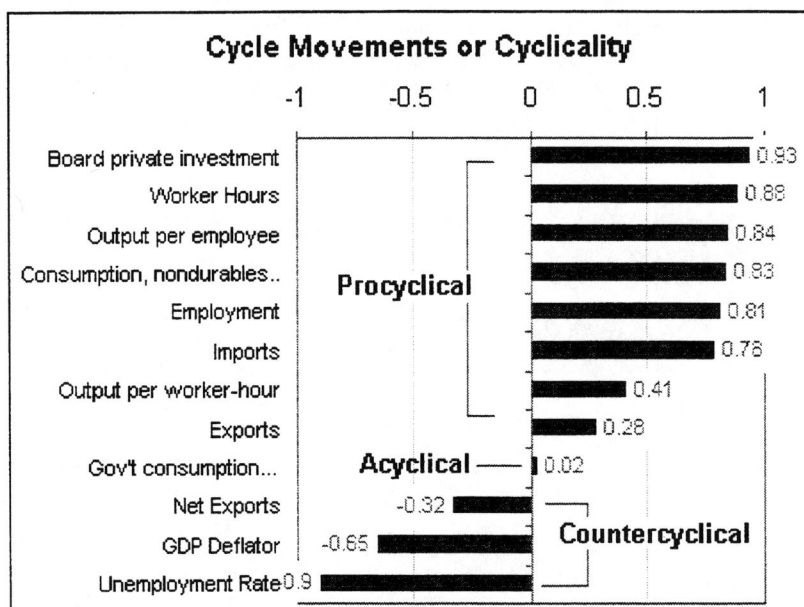

Cycle Movements or Cyclicality

Variable	Value
Board private investment	0.93
Worker Hours	0.88
Output per employee	0.84
Consumption, nondurables..	0.83
Employment	0.81
Imports	0.76
Output per worker-hour	0.41
Exports	0.28
Gov't consumption...	0.02
Net Exports	-0.32
GDP Deflator	-0.65
Unemployment Rate	0.9

Procyclical / Acyclical / Countercyclical

Volatility

Another important concept is that of *volatility*. By volatility, we mean how big is the deviation from the mean. This is usually measured by the standard deviation. A variable is more volatile if the swings from a peak to a trough are big. GDP is relatively volatile: it does swing around. Later on, we will want to explain why it does so. By looking at the variables that compose GDP, and comparing the share of GDP they are accountable for, as well as their relative volatility, we can form an idea of which of them influences the changes in GDP the most. Consumption of non durables and services accounts for roughly 60% of our measure of GDP, with broad investment and government consumption accounting for 20% each.

Consumption it's self is not very volatile: the average swing is less than half that of GDP. Government consumption is as volatile as GDP, but, as we see in the chart above, acyclical. Investment, on the other hand, is much more volatile than GDP so, although it doesn't account for much of the measure, it seems to be an important factor in explaining the swings in output.

The bottom line: understanding the link between investment and output will be crucial to understanding business cycles.

Leading and Lagging variables

If we want to answer the question in hand ("Where are we in the current cycle?") it is interesting to look at procyclical variables and ask whether these variables reach a peak at the same time, or before or after, the GDP. Variables that reach a peak before GDP are called leading indicators. Variables that are behind in the schedule are called lagging indicators. Those that reach a peak at the same time are called coincident indicators.

Microeconomics and macroeconomics

Microeconomics is the study of the behavior of individual agents, either households or firms. Understanding the response of a household to changes in prices and wages, or similarly, trying to understand how firms make their production and pricing decisions, all are microeconomic subjects.

Macroeconomics studies the aggregate economy. It tries to understand why economies grow, and why they go through cycles, and how various economies interact. It is the sum total of microeconomic behaviour in a given geographic area. In other words, macroeconomists try to explain the patterns that can be found in time-series data, data that is the basis for the indicators used in EconDash. Hence our main concern in this site is macroeconomic.

Historically, micro and macro were studied independently, using different tools. *Macroeconomists* would model "an economy", just as a black box, without taking into account the agents that interact and de facto are the economy. In the 1970s, this approach was criticized, and *macroeconomists* have used individual agents as the starting point of their models ever since. This is the approach taken here.

Chapter Three
Improving A National Economy

1. The Concepts

Are there actions that government or groups can take to make the economy stronger? To increase personal and national wealth? To fight back **recession** and **depression**? In 1776 Scotsman **Adam Smith** addressed those questions in his classic **The Wealth of Nations.** A major argument in the book was that market prices and quantities should be permitted to adjust to their equilibrium levels without any interference from the government. Smith argued that a nation's wealth would be maximized by allowing each person and company to make decisions based on marketplace forces mainly **supply and demand**), unhindered by government regulations.

He was a strong advocate of **laissez-faire economics.** He argued that by pursuing their own self-interests people would be guided by an *invisible hand* to maximize their personal contribution to the economy, and balance supply with demand while helping both the rich and the poor. But Smith also recognized that special interests backed by the government could profit at the expense of the general public. That was a strong reason why Smith wanted the government kept out of economic actions.

In Smith's days an economy could suffer a full range of economic woes: **inflation** (when prices rise faster than income), **deflation** (when prices and profits drop thus threatening unemployment plus owners' income), depression, **recession**, shortages, and unemployment. As the decades passed the growing complexity of businesses, production methods and production cycles, added to growth but also to big swings in the **business cycle** (alternating periods of growth and recession).

Inflation often challenged **market equilibrium.** As economies grew more complex so have the types of inflation. There is **cost-push inflation** which results from reduced supplies increasing prices (e.g. an oil shortage pushes energy prices up and these higher costs are passed through to other product price increases.) There is **demand-pull** inflation, a rise in the general price level that occurs because **aggregate demand** (total demand) exceeds **output capacity** (examples: gold prices in the 1890s, high digital resolution televisions at the start of the 21st century). In the twentieth century **hyperinflation** (double digit monthly inflation rates, such as Germany suffered in the late 1920s) reared its head. The late 1970s in the United States saw **stagflation,** a horrible combination of concurrent inflation and recession or **stagnant** economic growth, added to our economic vocabulary.

Monopolies and **oligopolies** (when a small number of companies control an entire business sector) became a growing threat starting in the nineteenth century. The twentieth century saw a new problem, **cartels** such as OPEC artificially increased prices in important commodities, distorting the natural laws of supply and demand – a bruising assault on Smith's *invisible hand.*

The biggest, most common and important harm resulting from most of these problems was unemployment. Unemployment reduces family income, lowers demand and thus risks national recession or depression, and has a negative effect on the **labor force participation rate.** Prolonged unemployment increases suicide rates, crime, and poverty.

- ❑ **Structural** unemployment (unemployment that results from a business sector contracting or collapsing. Example: the reduced number of blacksmiths the resulted from people moving from horses to cars for transportation.)

- **Frictional** unemployment (unemployment that results when people quit one job to move to another.)
- **Cyclical** unemployment (unemployment that comes from the time of year or point in the consumer purchase cycle. Examples: an unemployed construction worker in a snowy winter, or Santa Claus after Christmas.)
- **Underemployment** (people who can find only part-time work even though they want full time jobs.)
- **Hard core unemployment** (those who have been unemployed 12 or more consecutive weeks).

Solutions followed slowly on the heals of problem realization. By 1820 **David Ricardo** introduced a major theoretical advance, his **law of comparative advantage**. Ricardo argued correctly that two steps would increase growth and stability in any economy: producing what you have the biggest advantages in and maintaining free trade. If Brazil can produce coffee, ethanol, and computer circuits at a profit but ethanol gives the biggest peso-per-work-hour return its comparative advantage lies in ethanol production, and trading with less efficient economies for the other two commodities. Trade barriers promote inefficiencies, they reward by protecting those who focus on producing products without a comparative advantage, and thus they hurt growth and prosperity.

Underpinning the writings of several early economists are two realizations that form the basis for rational decisions on economic policy. The first is **the law of demand**, and the second is **the principle of diminishing marginal utility**. Extempers use the first often, debaters nuclear disadvantages often rely on the second. The law of demand says simply that as the price of a thing rises (assuming other factors do not change) the quantity demanded by buyers will fall. So if an item is rare demand is controlled by pricing it high. This discourages consumption and encourages the search for substitutes. If the United States, for example, wants to aggressively promote renewable energy development it could put a big tax on oil and coal and use those monies to fund expanded alternative energy research and development.

The principle of diminishing marginal utility tells us that as we obtain more and more of the same item we will get less and less use or satisfaction from each additional unit. Debate disadvantages sometimes remind us that we don't need enough nuclear weapons to destroy the world ten times over, once is enough. Population growth attacks center around the same idea, do families and mother earth really benefit from a third child in each family? Concurrently businesses often diversify a product line rather than just produce more of the same item at a cheaper price; Henry Ford was overtaken in car production by General Motors because he ignored the principle while GM thrived on it.

As the decades passed many economists in different countries recognized and contributed to the next solution, **human capital** improvements. The better quality work a person can do the greater the **productivity**, the greater the product output per hour. Concurrently the better worker knowledge, education, training, health, capital goods quality, and psychological support for his firm the more output will increase. **Full employment** (defined as the absence of all but frictional unemployment) is more likely when the workforce, our human capital, is developed. That is why Singapore has a higher **per capita** income than Mexico or Zimbabwe; Singapore puts huge efforts into training and protecting the quality of its workforce.

By the 1940s most economists had recognized that good quality economic data and statistics were essential to predicting the future trend of regional and national economies. And they quickly learned that not all statistics were equally important. **Lag indicators**, such as unemployment rates, are not very valuable because they reflect economic conditions two to six months ago. Since businesses are slow to react to expansion or contraction by hiring and firing unemployment rates do not tell us where the economy is headed, they tell us where we've been. But there are **lead indicators**, statistics that very often accurately predict the near-term economic future. Stock market index trends and the

wholesale price index are examples of good lead indicators for growth and inflation rates. The amount of money in circulation, the **money supply**, can also be both a growth and inflation rate indicator. But some statistics are neutral. **Inventory rates** and the **consumer price index,** for example, are good statistics for extemp speeches and disadvantage internal links but they are most often status quo measurements, tools without a good predictive future.

Governments in developed countries started to use these statistical and money supply measurements. Inflation, for example, was battled in by built-in **economic stabilizers**. Income tax brackets assured that if you earned more money you would pay more in taxes. This helps to control money supply and keep the multiplier effect moderate. **COLAs** (cost-of-living-adjustments) were integrated into some entitlement programs (in the United States these included Social Security and military pensions) to mitigate inflationary-related loss of purchasing power.

Statistics and intelligent observation gave governments new tools by the mid-twentieth century. Recent years have seen increased successful use of the tools that came into being then. An appreciation of human capital development, an economic concept first popularized in the early 1960s, offers good ground for in-speech analysis on many current issues and topics.. Investing in human capital is one example of **economic efficiency**, producing the maximum amount from what you have available. Japan is a classic example of economic efficiency. It is the second richest country on the globe. It has few natural resources but has developed the **infrastructure** (the underlying foundation, the basic facilities and installations) and **joint ventures** (business to business, or business to government cooperative enterprises) plus human capital to import and produce effectively. Conversely Russia has more natural resources per capita than any other nation on Earth but has not acted to become economically efficient. As a result its **GDP** (gross domestic product, a measure of all goods and services that helps define the comparative wealth of a nation) is no bigger than the Netherlands, and its per capita income is low.

Developing a nation's human capital and other parts of its infrastructure takes money. Part of this can come from taxes and moderate deficit spending. **Capital formation** (accumulating needed money) is always a key focus for both business and government. The better your capital formation the better your **liquidity** (your ability to pay for what you need when you need it, the less need to borrow or get credit or postpone payment). Increasing national comparative advantage and developing new joint ventures are classic examples of tools to improve capital formation. A vibrant **stock** and **bond market** also are very successful tools that enable sound companies to raise capital.

Some types of investment are more likely to stimulate non-inflationary growth than are other alternatives. New small businesses are the most successful growth engines. Their new products and or new services combine with the intensity of new management and workers to have a great **multiplier effect** (i.e. the money invested turns over quickly). Many larger businesses and product markets eventually confront **the law of diminishing returns**, the fact that each new dollar invested will give you less per dollar profit. A company like Dell Computer, for example, usually gets a great productivity bounce if it upgrades its assembly line and robotics machinery. But if it does such upgrades often, or does it in parts of the production process not amenable to these tools, the return per dollar invested will be increasingly low.

For the last two decades technology and healthcare products have been strong bastions of **noninflationary growth investment**. New genetics and DNA research, software, biotechnology, and robotics research and development have received large government subsidies and private investment because of their high investment to profit potential. Governments also see such industries as major sources for future job growth. **The ripple effect** from successful product development in these arenas can be tremendous.

2. Web Site

EconDebate Online is a very useful tool with diverse controversial topics covered in-depth. Its "Hot Debates" section gives you a nice long list of topics phrased much like ext6emp or debate topics. Click on the one you like and up comes issues, background, quotes, primary resources and data. Its self-description: EconDebate Online keeps you informed on today's most crucial economics policy debates. Each EconDebate, created by John Kane (SUNY-Oswego), provides a primer on the issues and links to background information and current, in-depth commentaries from experts around the world." www.swcollege.com/bef/econ_debate_main.html

3. Sample Extemp Topics

Is the president using all the macroeconomic policies he should to strengthen the American economy?

What economic problems confront Japan and what tools should they use to solve them?

4. If you want to Read More...

Learn From the Shipwreck!

We will understand how the economy works, through a story of a shipwreck on an island. Although we want to understand aggregates (or the total impact on an economy), we will always start by looking at individuals, in order to understand how these individuals, or agents, make decisions. This allows us to derive implications for the economy as a whole. To be able to understand what happens, we need to make significant assumptions that simplify the situation to better understand basic economic concepts. As you will see, a lot can be learned by using models and stories that have unrealistic or extreme assumptions.

We will start by taking a look at the simplest possible scenario: a person, on an island, who only has the resources to make goods by himself. This situation will allow us to introduce some relatively simple concepts that will then be used in most of the subsequent analyses.

Once this island economy is established, we will allow our "poor lost friend" to be joined by more people, and progressively the features of the island will change making it resemble (though not too closely) a real economy: money, bonds, a labor market, capital equipment, a government...and another island ("the rest of the world").

At all stages, we will compare the conclusions that we get from working with our simple island world to data we have on the U.S. and other world economies.

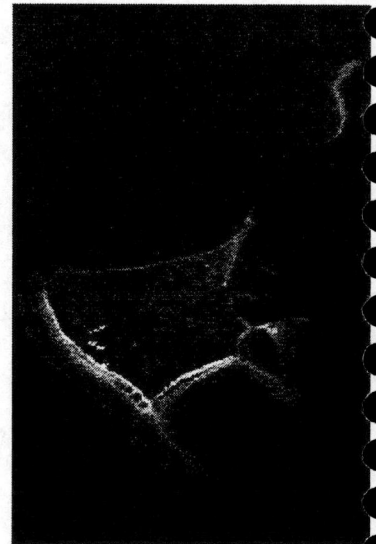

After the shipwreck...

Imagine Robinson, the lone survivor of a shipwreck. He is stranded on an island, where he has very few alternatives. He can stay on the beach ("leisure"), or he can use his time to produce some goods. For instance, he could try catching fish in the sea or climbing a coconut tree to grab fresh coconuts. He could also construct a shelter. (We assume for now that there is a lot of driftwood, so we do not to count driftwood as capital in the production process.)

To sum up: Robinson enjoys two things: leisure, and consumption. He does not like work per se, and so would be very happy to spend all his days doing nothing but leisurely activities, like learning to surf. However, to get the goods that he enjoys, he needs to work. How is he going to choose how much time to work and how much time to spend on the beach?

Before proceding, we need to make assumptions about Robinson's preferences and his ability to produce. How much extra consumption or additional goods does he need to motivate him to work an extra hour? If he has close to no consumption, then he is more than willing to give up leisure time to work and produce more goods. Hence, he does not need to be compensated by many units of goods to work one hour more. When he has a lot of goods at disposition, such as when he had been fed and had shelter, then he doesn't feel the same need for extra goods: he'd rather keep some of his time for leisure. Hence, to remain as happy, working one extra hour, he will require a big increase in consumption.

What about his ability to produce? If he is working very few hours, then working one hour allows him to produce a lot more goods than before. If he has already been working for a long time, then one extra hour won't allow him to produce much more. Hence there is diminishing productivity in labor!

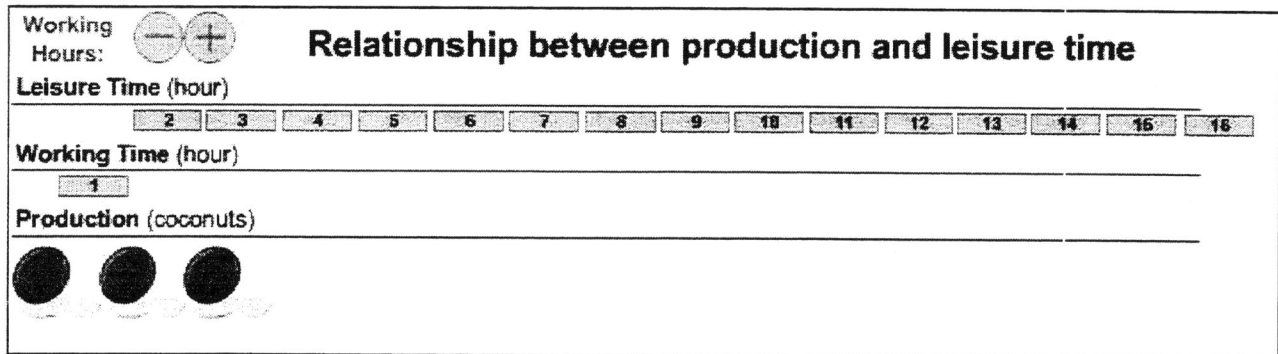

So, how much will Robinson work? Assume he is working 5 hours a day. Does he want to work one more hour? Taking into account diminishing productivity of labor, he can know how many goods he can produce by working the sixth hour, and compare this to the amount of goods he would like to be compensated for that hour of work. If he produces more goods in the last hour (the 6th) than he needs to be compensated from that extra labor, he will work more. If he gets less, then he won't. Since he can do this for every starting work effort, it seems clear that, as long as working a bit more yield more than enough product, he will increase his work load, and vice versa. So the point where he doesn't want to increase or decrease his work effort is where the last hour worked yields just enough extra goods to compensate him for his work: no more, no less. From that point, working one hour more produces less than what he needs to be compensated, hence he would be less happy by working more. And working one hour less does increase his leisure time, but the number of goods that he produces decreases, and that decrease is more important in terms of loss of well being than the gain due to the extra time off!

Production Shocks on the Island

Now that we have a simple guide to Robinson's decision making, we are ready to shock his production process and look at the changes that occur after these shocks. Notice that, since our economy only has one inhabitant, the GDP of the island is the total number of goods that Robinson produces.

In the real world, most changes in the production process combine a change in level (for any hours worked, the total production changes by a constant amount) and a change in marginal productivity (adding an hour's work adds more or less goods than it would have before the shock). It is convenient to decompose any shock into these two effects, called wealth effect and substitution effects. Notice that there are cases where only the wealth effect appears: for instance, for an individual, winning at the lottery, and for an economy, if there is a big tempest that greatly increases the quantities of fish that can be harvested. For Robinson: imagine that a crate full of goods washes onto the shore. For any effort choice he possibly has, the total production in that moment has increased by the number of goods in the crate.

A pure substitution effect is more difficult to see in the real world, as there are always wealth effects . But it is very useful to see what happens in the hypothetical case in which there is a pure substitution effect: In the wealth effect, changes in GDP are accompanied with changes in consumption and labor in a certain direction (increase in wealth), lead to more consumption and less labor. If there are changes in productivity, then there are different changes due to the substitution effect.

So, what is the pure wealth effect? Robinson has all those extra goods. At his current labor choice, he can therefore consume more. However, leisure is relatively more attractive to him, so he decides to work a little less. There is then an increase in consumption and a decrease in labor. What is the pure substitution effect? Now, working a bit more increases his production by more than before... So Robinson has extra incentives to work. The pure substitution effect is thus an increase in labor, and an increase in consumption (Robinson can use all the extra goods he produces, like a sturdier shelter, in addition to the ones he had!).

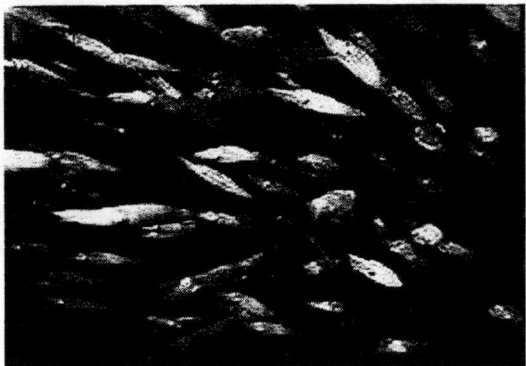

Now, let's imagine a shock that combines both effects: for some reasons, there are a lot more fish in the sea, more coconuts on the trees, but Robinson also has refined his technique to prepare his shelter. Hence GDP on the island will go up. Since both effects allow Robinson to consume more, consumption goes up (it is procyclical). But the total effect on labor is unclear: since food is easy to get, Robinson can decrease the number of hours he puts in getting it. But since he is more productive at preparing a nice shelter, he also wants to work more on the shelter. In total, we don't know which effect dominates. In economics, we can go to the later data and see, based on the end result, which factor is more important by noting whether it increased or decreased. A labor increase would dictate that the substitution effect is stronger, for example.

Cyclicality

38

A Second Survivor...

After some time living alone on the island, Robinson awakens one day to find another human being on the island. Nick survived a few weeks barely holding on to a piece of wood...to finally reach Robinson's island. Once Nick is back in shape, the two men discover that Nick has a similar production capacity as Robinson, but for a different set of goods: he is very good at catching rabbits. Hence the two men can now engage in trade. There is one problem to this: there aren't always fishes to exchange for rabbits or at least not the right amount. And the men don't know each other well so they are not confident enough to exchange goods now for goods in the future...(They don't have paper, and have no confidence in their ability to remember who owes what when). Exchanges are hard to come by on this island until a few boxes of golf balls are found (it seems that the boat that was carrying Nick was carrying a huge number of golf balls). The two men have no use for the golf balls until they have the idea of using these balls as medium of exchange. So now when Robinson does not catch fish, he pays nick a golf ball to eat some rabbit, and vice versa. Nick and Robinson are happy. Nick and Ribinson fine tune their system over time. For example, if Robinson catches a lot of fish, he may sell two fish to Nicks for a golf ball. Robinson my hunger for a rabbit other days and offer two golf balls for a rabbit dinner.

How does the island's economy respond to change in production shocks? The main difference now is when there is a shock to one sector, say, fishes are relatively tough to catch due to a storm. Then the price of fish will increase relative to that of rabbits.

But effects of a general change in production opportunities on labor and consumption will be the same as before. We thus need another shipwreck to make the analysis more interesting! It is important to notice at this stage that what matters are relative prices (the price of one good relative to another). If all prices go up by the same proportion, then this should not motivate any change in consumption.

...And More

To make the situation more interesting, we now need 2 women to survive a wreck and to let some time pass. Imagine now that a second generation has reached adulthood. There are 10 individuals, each specializing in some activities (fishing, rabbit hunting, shelter repairing, etc.). Golf balls are still used as currency, but now there is a possibility to save: a crate with paper has reached the island, and all of the inhabitants have decided to keep the paper for the purpose of writing bonds. Some people have more golf balls in some periods while others have less, and bonds are going to allow them to lend and borrow. Bonds have a one period (say, a month) maturity. Selling a bond for 1golf ball amounts to borrowing 1 golf ball today, and requires a repayment of (1+R) golf balls in the following period, where R is the nominal interest rate.

We thus have on this island two markets: one for commodities and one for bonds. Looking at the market for bonds is not very instructive, however, since for every golf ball that is lent, a golf ball has to be borrowed. If Robinson sells a bond with a 1 golf ball face value to Nick, Robinson holds -1 worth of bonds and Nick holds 1 worth of bond. Hence at the aggregate, the sum is zero. We assume that there is a possibility to hold interest-bearing bonds. So why would anyone want to hold money (golf balls, in this economy), which doesn't pay any interest? For this to happen, we must assume first that no one will exchange goods for bonds. The only mean of buying commodities is using golf balls. But we also need to assume that there is a cost of transforming bonds in liquidity. If we do not assume this, then people would just transform some bonds for the exact amount of money they need to buy their desired goods. There are two opposing effects on the demand for money: first, if the interest rate R increases, it is relatively better to hold bonds, even though you incur the cost of transforming back into money, so an increase in R will decrease the demand for money. But to consume more goods, one needs relatively more money; hence an increase in consumption entails an increase in the demand for money. (Notice that the money supply on our island is fixed: there is a fixed number of golf balls) An increase in the demand for money will tend to make the general worth (or buying power) of money higher, decreasing the price level. A decrease in the demand for money will tend to bring up the prices. If there is little demand for money, people want to get rid of their extra golf balls (the value of money has decreased), and the only way to do this is to buy more goods, which is going to make the price level go up - this is inflation.

How does one individual decide how much to consume today, and how much to save in bonds (and to consume tomorrow)? Well, if the interest rate is high, then the agent has incentives to save more today (thus consuming less and working more today), because he will get relatively more tomorrow. Hence, an increase in the interest rate R will increase production (by increasing work effort) and decrease consumption demand.

We now need to examine what will happen when there are shocks to the production function. An important distinction will be whether the shocks are permanent (they last forever, as a change in technology) or temporary (lasting only one period, as a natural cataclysm). Once again, we will try to decompose the effects into wealth and substitution effects.

After doing this, we will see what changes if we let people on the island organize a labor market.

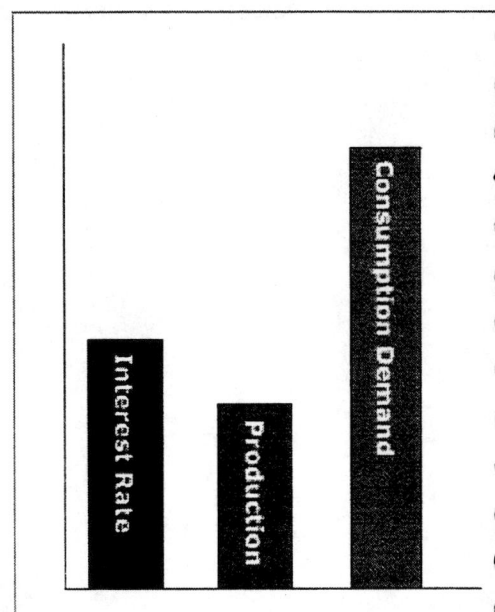

Shifts in Production

Temporary shift in the production function

Imagine that, due to a weather front, goods are a lot easier to produce in general on the island. Fish, for example, become more plentiful for a time. What happens if we only consider this wealth effect? With supply increases price will decrease and quantity purchased and consumed will increase. Also, since the shock is temporary, people will tend to not change their behavior too much. They will tend to spread the benefits of the positive shock over future periods. (Imagine if you won at the lottery. You know this happens only once. Of course you do change your consumption pattern, but you will also spread the benefits over many years) Thus, people will tend to save more, driving down the interest rate. This reduction of the interest rate induces consumption to be higher since additional income is not needed as much, and people will tend to work less.

Now there is also a change in marginal productivity: not only has the weather made the level of production increase, but for every level of effort, increasing effort a bit has now a bigger incidence on production (the same net catches more fish). We saw above that this would trigger a substitution effect: people will find it more attractive to work a bit more, because each hour gets you more production. The wealth effect above, however, makes work less attractive because you already have more to consume and would prefer more leisure time. Hence, as before, we have the prediction that an increase in GDP has a positive effect on consumption and a negative effect on the interest rate, but we can't be sure about the impact on labor in the economy. However, since the wealth effect is rather small (people prefer to spread the shock), we can suspect that the substitution effect dominates, so we should have a slight increase in the total number of hours worked.

Notice that the extra consumption will tend to make the demand for money increase, and since the supply of money is fixed, the general level of prices will move slightly upwards. But apart from that, changes on the commodity market do not affect the price level. This is one side of a phenomenon usually called "Neutrality of Money," and follows the view of Monetarists like Milton Friedman.

Permanent Shift

Now, imagine that the change in the production possibilities is permanent: people have improved at what they are doing, and there are lots of plants and animals, and it is only getting better. Again, there is a wealth and a substitution effect. The first one implies an increase in consumption demand and a decrease in labor supply, while the second one implies an increase in labor supplied. So aggregate demand and aggregate supply increase. So, what is different from a temporary change? The fact it is permanent makes it neutral to savings. Think of the lottery example once more: if you know that you will win at the lottery every month from now on, you will just increase your spending. Why save, since the extra income is coming every month? It is the same for the case of the production shock on the island: the fact the shock is permanent implies no change in the interest rate. Consumption and GDP increase, since total spending increases, and so money demand will increase. These factors will again lead to an inflationary economy.

Impacts

Increase in Money supply

There is no Central Bank on our island. The only way for more money to show up is the unlikely arrival of another few boxes of golf balls. Let's assume that this happens (a ship carrying the balls to the US Open was lost at sea) Let's assume further that the inhabitants of the island decide to share the balls equally. What happens? The supply of Money increases, but demand for money doesn't.

Initially, this may look like a temporary wealth effect - but it is not, since everyone has same impact and it does not change real products or production, only money (golf balls). Imagine the market for fish the day after these US Open golf balls wash up on shore. Consumers are smiling, having more golf balls than ever before. When two consumers approach the fish seller, prices may start where they were yesterday, but the fish buyers soon will find they are willing to pay more because they have more golf balls. These same buyers may also be sellers of thatch for housing, and they find that they get more for thatch in the same way.

So all prices will rise so as to increase the need for golf balls, and thus equate supply and demand for money. So a change in the monetary base of an economy, under our assumptions, will increase the prices, but not affect any quantities (goods, hours, etc.). This is, once again, the neutrality of money in action.

Labor market

After a while, people have decided to specialize a lot in their production. And some have good ideas for making more complex goods. Instead of working individually, they find they can create more value by working together - one cutting and another assembling and yet another selling, for example. Owners start these organizations and pay an hourly wage to the workers. This is also great for some people who did not like how their income fluctuated before, when they were selling each day. We assume that the wages are very flexible, and that an hour worked is worth the same for everyone, so there is only one wage level in the economy. The wage will act as a market clearing device: if there is too much labor supplied, compared to the demand, wages will go down, making some people opt for more leisure, and vice versa. It is very important to realize that what matters is the real wage (wage divided by general price level). What the workers look at is how many goods they can buy if they work one more hour, not how many golf balls they get. Hence, the neutrality of money will hold on the labor market as well as on the commodity market: only changes on the money market (money demand and money supply) will change the general level of prices. Furthermore, given that there are no changes in labor supplied or labor demanded, nominal wages will change in proportion to the change in the level in prices. Changes in labor supplied or labor demanded will have an effect on the real wage, since the change on the labor market will not affect the price level but will affect the wage level.

What would happen if there were a temporary increase in productivity? For example, four people used to fish, clean, and sell fish, averaging 100 fish a day. Then they join forces, with two fishing exclusively, one cleaning, and one selling, and they find they can average 150 fish a day.

With the wealth effect, consumption demand increases and labor hours (supply) decreases (can work less and still have more consumption). This remains exactly the same here. The change is the substitution part. Workers only respond to changes in wealth (including changes in real wages), but an increase in productivity makes it more attractive for the entrepreneurs to hire laborers, increasing labor demand. The overall effect is that the real wage increases, but once more the total effect on hours worked on the island is unclear. When the shock is temporary, we can safely assume that the demand effect will be stronger, thus increasing total hours worked in the economy. In the case of a permanent shift, it is less clear.

Capital

Until now, on this island, most goods were perishable goods: if you did not eat them or use them right away, then they would spoil. We even assumed that shelters were very basic, and counted them as consumption goods. Imagine that, after a while, inhabitants found ways to build goods that are useful in the production processes of their consumption goods. For instance, they managed to build a rowboat which they could use to fish, ladders which help pick fruit, and "machines" which turn the soil, flatten it and to build better shelters. All these goods are used as physical capital in the production process. Hence now, when deciding how much to produce, and individual must not only decide how much to work, but also how much capital to buy for the next period. People will now have to make an investment decision.

If you remember, we assumed that the marginal productivity of labor (the increase in production from working an extra hour) typically decreases. It seems natural to have a similar assumption regarding the marginal productivity of capital. We also assume that capital goods depreciate at a fixed rate: each period, because of usage, part of the capital breaks down. Hence, part of the investment serves just the purpose of replacing capital that no longer works, such as when a rowboat sinks. This is called depreciated capital. We usually call gross investment the total quantity of capital purchased. If we take away from gross investment the quantity that just replaces capital that no longer works (depreciated capital), then we have net investment.

How much will a person living on the island invest in capital? Well we now that the inhabitants of the island can always buy bonds, on which they have a return of R, the interest rate. It seems clear that when people decide where to place their money, they will compare the return on bonds to the return on capital investment. So what is the return on capital? Buying an extra unit of capital increases production by the marginal productivity of capital (which is diminishing, remember).

Buying a ladder allows the orange grower to generate 10 more golf balls a month. This is the return on the golf balls she paid for the ladder. If she paid 500 golf balls for the ladder, she gets 2% back each month (10), or a 24% annual return on capital. Pretty good. Diminishing returns means the second ladder may only generate a 10% return, for example.

If the orange grower is confidant she can get a 10 golf ball return, she would be willing to borrow money at a rate close to the 24% rate, leaving some difference to make it worthwhile. If she thinks it could be a broader range, say 6-14 golf balls of benefit, she will also want to ensure there is enough profit to take the risk if the return is only 6 golf balls.

So producers will continue to invest in new capital projects until the returns approach the bond returns. If bond returns are high, fewer capital projects will be invested in, and vice versa. If capital project risks decrease, more projects will be invested in as well.

What affects the demand for capital? It is clear that an increase in the interest rate will decrease the demand for capital goods, as more people buy bonds. But there are other factors that affect capital demand. Of course, if productivity of capital increases, then demand for capital will increase (this is similar to the effect of a change in labor productivity on labor demand). If depreciation increases, then the return on capital decreases (less money is made selling the capital after its use) and so this lowers the demand for capital. Finally, if a disaster (such as a typhoon) destroys a lot of the old stock of capital, then at the return on capital suddenly increases and the demand for capital increases as well.

Business Cycles

We are now ready to take a look at what happens to the island during both permanent and temporary shifts in production (which is the GDP for the island) and look at the behavior of variables like investment, labor, consumption, and interest rates. We will be able to compare the prediction of the model with the data: more precisely, we will compare the cyclicality of various variables in the model to that in the data. (Cyclicality)

Let's first take a look at what happens when there is a temporary change in the production possibilities. Because the weather was nice (ie. new, lower branches grew for the oranges), it is a lot easier to initially produce goods, but marginal productivity of both labor and capital is unaffected. Hence there is no substitution effect. What happens? Because of increases in production, the quantity of goods sold increases and prices drop. The increased wealth in this economy incites people to consume more and work less, hence demand for goods increases and labor hours (supply) decreases. On the labor market, since there is no change in productivity, labor demand is unchanged, thus real wages will increase to reconcile demand and supply of labor.

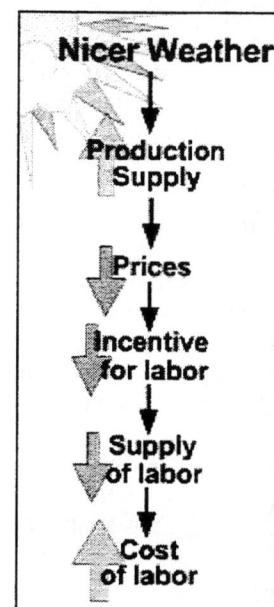

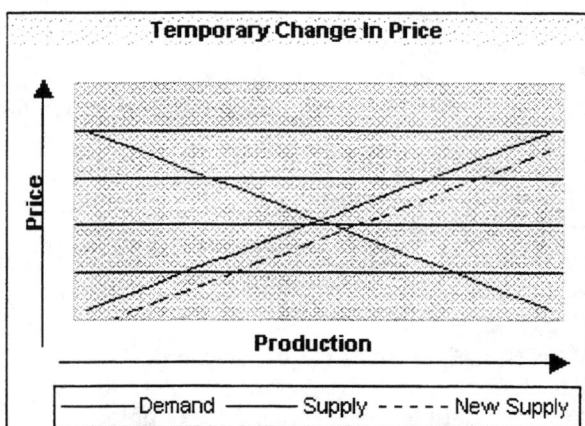

Temporary Change In Price

Price / Production

— Demand —— Supply - - - - New Supply

Temporary Change in Labor

Price of labor / Total Labor

— Demand —— Supply - - - - New Supply

Nicer Weather → Production Supply → Prices → Incentive for labor → Supply of labor → Cost of labor

On the goods market, since the change is temporary, the change in demand is relatively small compared to the change in supply. People want to save part of the wealth for future periods. Hence the interest rate decreases, thus increasing a bit the incentives to consume.

Let's assume the shock is now permanent: technology on the island has improved, and will stay at a higher level. There is both a change in levels of production and in the marginal productivity of labor. However (and unrealistically), let's keep the marginal productivity of capital constant for a while. Since the shock is permanent, there is no incentives to increase saving in this economy, so in this case the interest rate is going to remain the same. Output and consumption will increase by similar amounts. As in the temporary case, labor supply decreases but labor demand increases, increasing the real wage and increasing labor slightly.

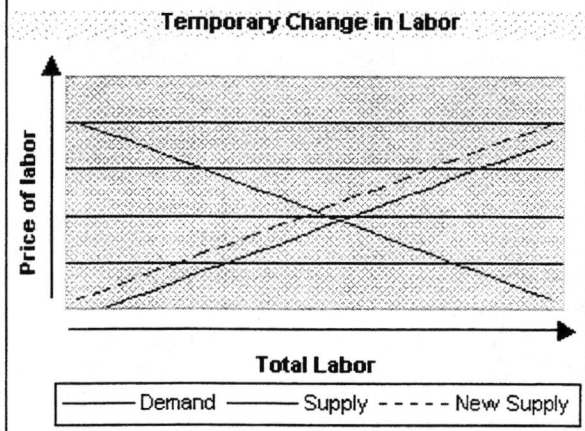

By introducing a change in the marginal productivity of capital, which is more realistic, we can reintroduce an increase in investment. This of course increases demand on capital, increasing interest rates slightly (interest rates are slightly procyclical as well). Since machines are more productive, they yield higher returns, thus giving incentives to invest more. This, of course increases demand on capital, increasing interest rates slightly (interest rates are slightly procyclical as well). In the discussion about volatility, we saw that investment is a lot more volatile than consumption. Changes in output are absorbed by changes in capital investment, due to a mix of temporary and permanent shocks. Many the temporary shocks have some persistence: they affect not only the current period, but also future ones, although by a different magnitudes. These persistent shocks support the fact that changes in output are absorbed by capital investment changes.

Government

After some time, residents on the island decide to organize their society in a more formal way, and elect a government. The government decides to spend some resources to provide public services. Government spending mixes two roles: first, it affects people's happiness directly, as any other form of consumption. Perhaps the government organizes a big gathering with free food, gives kids nutritious lunches, or organizes a nice plaza with plants and fountains. Second, government spending also improves production. We assume that a unit of government spending increases the supply of goods in the economy by a small positive amount. For example, the government may help build a nursery for plants and a factory for fountains needed for the plaza.

How does the government get the money it spends? By taxing residents, of course. At first, we assume that the tax is of the same amount for every inhabitant, no matter the income. This type of taxes is called a lump-sum tax, and it does not create distortions in economic incentives: individual behavior cannot affect it, so leisure/labor choices are unaffected. Obviously, this is not the most realistic tax we can introduce. Later, we will introduce an income tax. But by concentrating on this lump-sum tax, we can isolate the effects of changes in government spending on individual spending.

What happens when government spending increases temporarily? Individuals see their level of happiness go up, due to this increase. They will decide that some of their private consumption is superfluous, and substitute public services for private consumption (For instance, if the government provides a free lunch, people won't spend for that lunch. Also, remember that consumption's extra benefits decrease as the level of consumption increases.) An increase in government spending thus reduces private consumption. Based on US macroeconomic data, an increase in government spending by 10 units decreases private consumption by 2 to 4 units. Overall consumption demand increases, but not by the full amount of government consumption.

What happens then with interest rates? The increase in total consumption reduces savings. With fewer savings, the supply of money drops and interest rates rise. This is especially true when governments spend more than they tax, or deficit spending. In this deficit spending the government borrows money, increasing money demand and also increasing interest rates. These effects are often referred to as the crowding out of private spending.

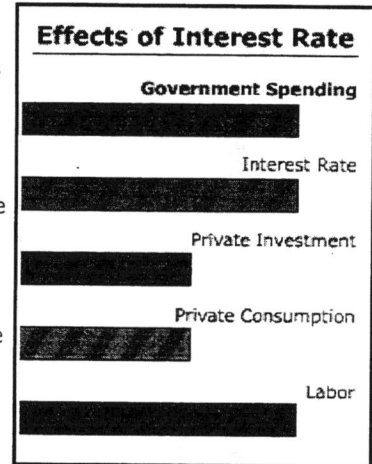

Effects of Interest Rate

Government Spending

Interest Rate

Private Investment

Private Consumption

Labor

Now, it is time to get more realistic in the type of tax imposed. Let us assume an income tax with a flat rate. The government takes a certain percentage of the income of all individuals on the island, including savings. When choosing how much to work and how much to invest, individuals now look at the after tax wage and the after tax return on investment. Changes in the tax rate will then affect the labor-leisure choice of individuals, as well as the savings behavior. Let's assume that there is an increase in the tax rate, but not the government spending or the transfer, to isolate the effects of the increase in taxation. A higher tax rate lowers the incentives to work, lowering the after-tax return on investment, and so reducing investment. Consumption and investment decrease, and labor decreases. Thus both supply and demand of goods decrease (demand decreasing by more). We conclude that the permanent increase in the tax rate decreases output and decreases consumption, work effort and investment. Since investment translates into capital in the future, there are long run effects of the change in the tax rate: less investment means less capital in the future (or a lesser increase in the capital stock), so it decreases long term growth.

Of course, there are no reasons for the government to tax if it is not spending. Let's assume now an increase in government spending financed by an increase in the tax rate. The permanent increase in government spending, we saw earlier, translates in lower wealth. Hence private consumption decreases and work effort increases. However, the change in the tax rate distorts the incentives to work, and decreases work effort. It also decreases private consumption and investment (recall that investment is not affected by the permanent change in government spending). We are thus unclear whether labor effort increases or decreases. Also, the overall demand for goods increases (since the government increases its demands). The long-run capital stock is reduced, however, since investment is reduced.

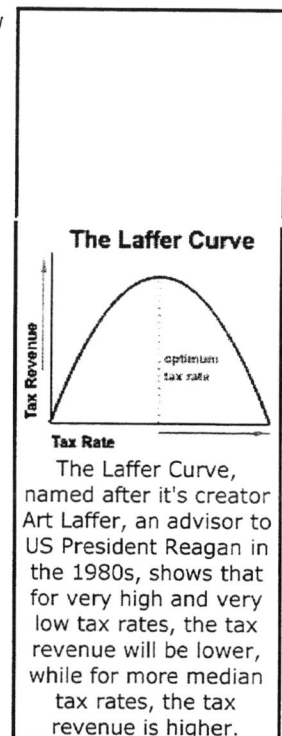

The Laffer Curve

Tax Revenue

optimum tax rate

Tax Rate

The Laffer Curve, named after it's creator Art Laffer, an advisor to US President Reagan in the 1980s, shows that for very high and very low tax rates, the tax revenue will be lower, while for more median tax rates, the tax revenue is higher.

Another Island

Now imagine the people on the island discover that there is another island not so far away. The other island is also populated, and produces the same set of goods. On this island, goods are exchanged against tennis balls. Let's assume for a moment that people on both islands decide to consider tennis balls and golf balls as worth the same. If we assume, in addition, that there are no transportation costs for goods, it is the case that prices of goods are the same on both islands. If the price of a certain good differs from one island to the other, then all who desire the good will buy from the cheapest location, bringing that price up and the other down. Under these assumptions, then, we get a very simplified version of the law of one price.

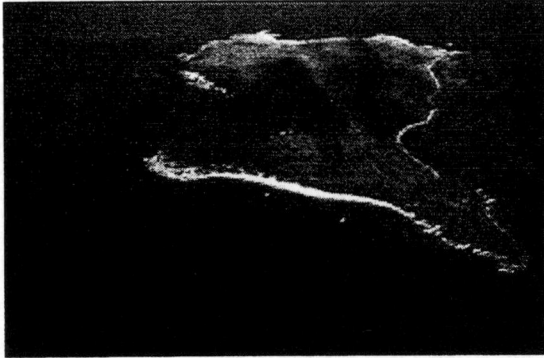

In our bi-island world, there is now possibility to have excess savings or borrowing: it is possible to lend to foreigners, or to borrow from foreigners. The difference between income and spending in a country is called the current-account balance. It has to be equal to net-foreign investment. If the current-account is in deficit, then the country is spending more than its income, and is a net borrower from abroad. (This is the case with the United States)

So what happens when there are changes in the production function? Well, the existence of an international credit market allows savings and borrowing in the economy to be different. Hence, if we assume that the economy we are looking at is small relative to the rest of the world (which clearly is not the case in our world), then wherever we had changes in the interest rates for the closed (single) economy analysis, now the interest rate doesn't change, but the current-account balance changes. For instance, in the case of a temporary negative shock in our first island, say a harvest failure, at the given interest rate, people want to borrow more, to spread the negative effects of the shock. In our previous analysis, this would push the interest rate upwards, thus making it more costly to borrow, and more attractive to lend, and reconciling borrowing and lending. Now, however, borrowing is going to increase, and the interest rate is going to stay at its level. But the island is going to borrow from the other island, hence pushing its current account balance towards higher deficits. Basically, the island is using foreign funds to finance part of its consumption.

Similarly, if instead of a supply shock we consider a demand shock, say because capital got a lot more productive, inducing an increase in investment demand, in our previous analysis, this would have resulted in an increase of the interest rate. But now, the other island will finance part of the increase in home investment, and the current-account is going to be pushed towards higher deficits.

The analysis above assumes that the country is relatively small, and doesn't weight enough in world borrowing markets. This is the case for countries like Belgium, Austria, Portugal, and Ireland. But it is not the case for each of our islands in our two island world (since each island accounts roughly for half of the influence), and it is not the case for the U.S. If we consider the case in which each island weights a lot in the world borrowing market, then we get a situation that is a mix between the case of a closed economy and the case of a small open economy. The interest rate is going to increase, but by less as in the closed economy case, and current accounts are pushed towards deficits. This is how one significant country can have an impact on the world economy.

Until now, we have assumed that golf balls and tennis balls are exchanged on a one to one basis. Let's relax that assumption in order to introduce exchange rates.

The exchange rate expresses the number of foreign currency units needed to buy one unit of home currency. For instance, it is possible that 2 tennis balls are required to get a golf ball. The exchange rate is then 2. Each island has now a central bank of some sorts, and the central bank's only role is to hold some of the other island's currency in reserve. These reserves will be used to defend the currency is some cases: for instance, if demand for golf balls is going down, so that the value of golf balls relative to tennis balls dips, Robinson's central bank might want to buy golf balls in exchange for tennis balls to keep the exchange rate at a reasonable level. Before we take a look at fixed and flexible exchange rates, let's take a look at the two main propositions in international economics.

First, there is the purchasing-power parity, or PPP. This is a generalization of the law of one price: if there are no transportation costs, the prices, corrected for the level of the exchange rate, should be the same across countries. Second, a similar proposition holds for interest rates: if people can freely borrow and save on both islands, then the interest rates corrected for the level of the exchange rate, should be the same on both islands. This is called the interest-rate parity.

An often used example of Purchasing-Power Parity is the Big Mac Index. You can read more on the Big Mac Index at The Economist's website

Let's take a look at fixed exchange rate systems. Basically, our two islands decide that the exchange rate is going to remain fixed at 2 tennis balls for a golf ball. The respective central banks commit to exchanging tennis balls for golf balls at that rate and vice-versa, whenever someone requests it. Why would such a system break down? Imagine that because of government policies, people feel that golf balls are worth relatively less than 2 tennis balls...then they will all go and request from Robinson's central bank tennis balls in exchange for their excess golf balls. Although the central bank holds a lot of tennis balls, eventually, it is going to run out of them. Hence if this keeps on for long enough, the system will break, and the exchange rate will have to fluctuate freely. Will it break when the central bank holds zero tennis ball or before? The answer is before: at some point, people will realize that the central bank can't keep giving out tennis balls. If suddenly it runs out of them, then people holding golf balls will have lost, since golf balls will be worth a lot less than 2 tennis balls. Hence many people will go exchange their golf balls, accelerating the process. When the exchange rate is allowed to float, then the exchange rate level is determined by the demand for the currency in the world economy. In this case, the exchange rate just varies whenever people want more or less of the currency relative to other currencies. This allows the 2 tennis balls to a golf ball to change to 2.2, 2.5, 1.8, or whatever, depending on the demand on tennis and golf ball exchanges.

Chapter Four
Different Governments,
Different Economic Systems

1. The Concepts

The type of government in a nation directly affects what types of economic problems exist, and which solutions are used. The most common governments are **representative democracies, oligarchies, dictatorships,** and **theocracies**. A democracy is where the people vote or elect representatives for a congress or parliament to represent their views. The United States, Great Britain, and Sweden are examples of modern democracies. An oligarchy is rule by the elite. The right to vote is very restricted or nonexistent. China, Saudi Arabia, and Egypt are oligarchies. Dictatorships are totalitarian regimes with power held by one or a very small number of people. North Korea, Cuba, and Iraq are dictatorships. Theocracies are states ruled by religious oligarchies or dictatorships. Iran and Vatican City are theocracies.

Economic systems are often also divided into types or categories. Common ones are **market economies, democratic socialism, Marxist socialism, mixed economies, command economies**, and **oligopoly oligarchies (semi-fascistic states)**. Market economies minimize government intervention and come closest to laissez faire economics and full appreciation of the law of supply and demand. Businesses are privately owned and operated. They are also susceptible to business excesses (e.g. monopolization tendencies). Tax rates usually are lower than other governmental economic systems. Market economies come closes to pure capitalism and are most often found in democracies. Examples: Canada, United States, and Australia.

Democratic socialism operates under elected governments. The government owns most natural resources and large industries, but middle and small businesses are privately held. The government usually provides more welfare programs than in market economies. Unemployment rates tend to be higher than in market economies, poverty harms are lower but so is worker productivity. Tax rates tend to be higher than democratic market economies but lower than Marxist socialist states. Examples include France, Denmark, and Sweden.

Marxist socialism is tyranny with an economic rationale. These are command economies. The government controls the means of production, owns all natural resources, and decides what goods and services will be produced. Sometimes called communist countries no Marxist socialist state has ever come close to achieving the goals of that theory: a classless society with no government where each contributes according to his or her ability and takes only according to his or her need. Tax rates are huge but are hidden since it is the state that pays salaries. Cuba and North Korea are Marxist socialist tyrannies.

Karl Marx and Frederick Engels added important vocabulary and viewpoints to economic and social discussions. They described capitalism as a struggle between the **proletariat** (the workers) and **bourgeois** (the capitalist middle class, the owners of land, factories, and or capital goods). Marx argued that private ownership of the means of production was the heart of the conflict, and he urged the workers to rise up and overthrow capitalism. From 1917 to 1989 large parts of Eastern Europe and all of Russia were under communist rule. Over the years many communist countries had to repress bloody revolts as oppression, corruption, poverty and inefficiencies were rampant. Human rights abuses were very common and very widespread. The political system was discredited throughout most of the world.

Command economies create many state-owned businesses and industries.

Mixed economies have important parts of two or more economic and or governmental systems. China is Marxist socialist in stated ideology, but oligarchial in political structure and has both capitalist and socialist elements in its ownership of business and property. Their business protection laws (e.g. copyright and patent protection, **intellectual property rights**) are weak. Mexico seems to be moving from oligarchial socialism towards a democratic mixed economy, but as a **burgeoning democracy** its path is not certain. Since the late 1980s changes in India's elected governments has supported moving from an almost economically **xenophobic** socialist society with heavy **import substitution** industries, to a more open, capitalistic, and free trade supportive corporate outlook. Joint ventures have increased.

Oligarchial states tend to encourage oligopolies and monopolies, because this feeds oligarchial power and because they see oligopolies as powerful tools to compete effectively in the international trade market. Tax rates are not as high as socialist states. While perfect oligarchial oligopoly states are rare many East Asian nations have many of their characteristics. China, Singapore, South Korea, and Taiwan all have strong oligopoly and trade-oriented economic patterns within their governments. Japan with its **keiretsu** (firms that cooperate with each other to create a national competitive advantage in the world export market) is a classic example. In such countries government-business relations tend to be strong and well coordinated. The East Asian examples are also among the world's leading examples of **export driven** economies.

2. Web Sites

The Fraser Institute has many research areas you can select from on their home page. This includes good support for economic freedom, editorials, environment, fiscal policy, and more. Visit it at www.fraserinstitute.ca/.

3. Sample Extemp Topics

What economic and governmental systems would best help the underdeveloped world achieve their political and economic needs?

Should Cuba abandon socialism?

Chapter Five
Business Profit Issues

1. The Concepts

For an economy to grow or even to remain stable businesses have to be sound. Many extemp topics, affirmative cases and disadvantages center around the question of how to solve business problems. If business declines unemployment skyrockets, profits decline, crime escalates, poverty increases political stability erodes, the rich-poor gap widens. To know how to answer these topics or case issues you should know most of what it takes to make a business successful.

To start, and then to expand, businesses need **capital formation**. You can start a business using personal money, you can borrow it, you can sell stock in the business, if you have the technical know-how you can sell **bonds** (promissory notes that pay interest until redeemed). When government makes it easier to raise capital it makes it easier for businesses to expand or start new ventures. So tax cuts (especially reduced business related taxes), incorporation laws, increased money supply, and reduced interest rates are all good for business because they make it easier to gather in investment capital.

The higher the **startup costs** the fewer new entrees and the less perfect the competition in any business area. Agriculture and food have many participants, many producers because startup costs are low. The result is intense competition and low consumer costs. Aircraft manufacturing has high capital goods, infrastructure and licensing/patent use costs and a limited market size. The result is that there are only two large aircraft firms in the entire world: Boeing and a European conglomerate.

But there are barriers to entry other than money. Business licenses, knowledge of how to design and construct a product, a reliable trained workforce (even if its just one good employee), **marketing** skill, distribution **infrastructure**, raw material access, appropriate **capital goods**, and product protection (e.g. through copyright and patent laws) are all important too.

Once a business is in operation *many* factors will determine if it is successful. **Infrastructure** and **product development** play very important parts. In this context infrastructure means the basic facilities, services, and installations needed for a business to operate well. All businesses have finite resources, so the decision where to spend is critical. Money put into a new store is money not spent on advertising. Capital put into a new machine is capital not used to research an improved product design. To the beleaguered manager every part of infrastructure factor is important to survival so these are important issues.

But no business will prosper for long unless there is also significant research and development. For a publishing firm it may be a new book or an improved Internet site. For a car firm it might represent a new hydrogen fuel cell design. But competition is a fierce taskmaster. The firm that does not upgrade its old products and offer good new ones is leaving the door open for its competitors to seize large **market share** and thus destroy our heroes.

As businesses mature they work to benefit from **economies of scale** without being hurt by **the law of diminishing returns**. Specialization and division of labor result in increased efficiency in the production process. Economies of scale occur when a large volume of output is produced at a lower cost per unit than can a small volume of output. If a tool die in a Mercedes auto plant produces ten fenders a day the economies are much lower than if sales justify it producing two hundred bumpers a day; the cost of the **capital good** (the tool die machine) remains the same no matter how many units it produces so the economies are much greater for the business, and thus for profits, if the unit produces more each day.

Three basic factors restrict production: land, labor, and capital. Expanding just one or two will always reach its limits because it will be constrained by the third factor. The law of diminishing returns states that increasing the quantity of one factor of production while quantities of other factors remain fixed will result in smaller and smaller gains. And eventually there will be no gains at all. If a farmer, for example, adds more seed to an acre it will increase the corn crop. But add too many seeds and growth actually goes down because the seedlings crowd each other out in their fight for water and nutrients. Next the farmer could add technology in the form of seeds that need less water and nutrients but even those will show diminishing returns if too many are planted. Only by expanding *all three* components (land, labor, and capital) can unlimited growth continue. The same law applies with a successful computer chip firm. It can upgrade capital goods and robotics to increase output in a plant, it can train its workers more and invest in thinner lighter materials, but eventually it will still run out of room unless it enlarges the plant or builds a new one. And in the meantime the cost to increase production in the single plant will likely exceed the per chip production gain.

For the most successful of firms expansion will eventually take it beyond the borders of its original country. The United States like almost every country on earth is host to and sponsor of **transnational** and **multinational corporations**. In some poorer countries the power of these firms is impressive. They can be and are both forces for development and a better quality of life, and a threat to the environment and democratic will. Size and market domination can also invoke the risk of monopolization. Monopolies distort **the law of supply and demand** by artificially controlling the supply. Within the United States a variety of laws, beginning with the **Sherman Antitrust Act** are available to control monopolies and, to a lesser extent, oligopolies.

Business prosperity is not important just to the company itself; it is a large part of governmental concerns. When businesses do well there are jobs available, more tax money for good projects, and a higher level of **consumer confidence** that reflects itself in not only robust economic health but in reduced social ills. At the national level that is why **export promotion** is a main part of almost every government. After all, one billion dollars in exports generates 16,000 new jobs. In the United States it is also the reason local governments will offer lower or waived taxes, free land or generous leases, and even subsidies to firms to move into their area.

2. Sample Extemp Topics

How can federal and state government better promote job creation in the private sector?

How can the world community assure that multinational corporations better respect the environmental and cultural rights of underdeveloped nations?

3. Web Site

The Almanac of Policy Issues has an "Economic Issues" section that is great for both extemp and debate research. The home page overviews its well-categorized entrees (which includes its own search engine) "Economic policy often drives other forms of policy. A nation's economic strength often dictates how much it can afford to spend on public needs like health care, transportation, science or education. It can also affect a nation's ability to afford new regulatory policies targeting things like the environment or safety in the workplace.

More fundamentally, economic policy often drives elections, and elections affect issues across the political spectrum. As a wag once noted when prioritizing the most important issues in a presidential campaign, 'it's the economy, stupid.'

Economic policy has many components, including **fiscal policy** (government spending and taxes), **monetary policy** (determining the size of the money supply), and **regulatory policy** in all its forms, including regulation of business, labor relations, consumer protection, and rules of international trade. In fact, most matters of public policy, even those that are not primarily economic in nature, have some impact on the economy." www.policyalmanac.org/economic/index.shtml

Chapter Six
The Government's Role

1. The Concepts

What role should government have in an economy? Is it more important to protect the environment or increase **per capita disposable income** (the amount each person has to spend after mandatory deductions and unavoidable expenses)? Should government help business and promote exports, or should it actively prosecute oligopolies and monopolies? Should the government be more anxious to guard against inflation, or give its priority to keeping unemployment low? There are no known absolute answers to any of these questions, but they do make good extemp topics and debate attacks.

Certainly most governments accept that they ought to increase personal disposable income so long as disadvantages (e.g. inflation or undesirable deficits) do not occur. How to do this is the question. Governments can chose a variety of both **fiscal policies** and **monetary policy**. Fiscal policy is the use of taxes and government to affect aggregate demand. In both the United States and most other countries the central government is a big taxer and a big spender, so any changes in taxes or government spending is bound to impact the whole economy. In the 1920s John Maynard **Keynes** of Great Britain did much of the groundbreaking work to discover and explain the large role of governmental fiscal policies on the economy. Many economists credit Lord Keynes with the basic concept that in recessions and depressions the government should use **deficit spending** to stimulate demand and renew growth; in prosperous times to increase tax rates to reduce **inflationary pressures.** Regrettably the United States government got addicted to deficit spending, keeping it even in prosperous times. The result was to run up interest payments that by the 1970s were a major drain on the budget. Bond money for private business expansion, corporate funds and major capital goods grew more expensive because the federal government soaked up so much investment capital with its huge bond sales, bond sales being the key way to finance and structure the deficit. Not until the budget surpluses of the late 1990s was there a serious attempt to reduce or pay off the deficit and that ended when the Bush tax cut of 2001 combined with the September 11 terrorists attacks to gut the American economy.

The tools Keynes developed take advantage of the **ripple effect** or **multiplier effect** found in major governmental financial actions.

Monetary policy is the attempt to control the business cycle by influencing the supply of money and interest rates. The creation and use of the **Federal Reserve Board** is a United States example of monetary policy. Monetary policy holds that increasing the money supply increases disposable income and makes it cheaper for businesses to borrow and finance expansion. In recessionary periods increasing the money supply seems a logical (and sometimes successful) policy. In times of high growth increased interest charges help to discourage inflationary growth and, combined with changes in the discount rate, reduce the money supply – a classic answer to too many dollars chasing too few goods.

The Federal Reserve Board (the Fed, or the FRB) is a semiautonomous government agency that in several ways is like a central bank for the United States. Ruled by a **Board of Governors** the FRB Chairman is one of the most powerful economic figures in the world. Most banks in the United States are **depository institutions** meaning that they are members of the Fed. The Federal Reserve Board (1) sets **reserve requirements**—the minimum amount of reserves that a bank or depository institution must have on deposit, stated as a percentage of its deposits. Lowering the reserve level increases the money in circulation, increasing it is anti-inflationary but slows growth. The Fed also (2) sets the **discount rate**, the interest rate charged by the Fed on loans in makes to banks or other depository institutions. And the FRB (3) runs **open market operations** which is when it buys or sells government bonds to implement its monetary policy.

Prof. Milton **Friedman** of the University of Chicago, the second American to win the Nobel Prize for Economics, is the main force in the monetarist school of thought. While accepting and encouraging the appreciation of the importance of money supply policy his revisionist approach argues that **the Fed** (the Federal Reserve Board) should not tinker with the money supply in response to current economic conditions. Friedman argues that it seldom works because there is too much of a time lag between FRB policy change and its effect on the economy. Rather he argues that in most times the Fed should increase the money supply at a regular rate, at the same rate as the GDP. Some monetarists argue that Fed fine-tuning efforts can even hurt the economy if the statistics is based on are too old or incomplete.

Since Ronald Reagan Republican presidents have advocated **supply-side** strategies to achieve income growth. Supply-siders want to increase supply by increasing the level of production. Their biggest tool has been the tax cut. **Supply-side theory** maintains that lower taxes provide incentives to producers and investors to increase capital investment and output. It holds that lowering taxes also makes available the investment funds for new plants and equipment. People who are employed will have an incentive to work longer and harder because they get to keep more of their income. The unemployed and **labor force dropouts** (those who have stopped looking for a job) will be drawn back into the labor force as a result of higher production creating more job openings. Supply-siders argue that, in the mid and long term the growth of investment and output resulting from lower taxes actually increases total tax returns.

But the **business cycle** (alternating or periodic periods of growth and stagnation or recession) is an undeniable force. Just as government must use policies to increase personal income in upswings it must have policies to shorten and minimize the damage of downswings. One tool is to create a set of **built-in economic stabilizers**. In the United States unemployment compensation, welfare payments, income tax (because as your income drops your taxes decrease too), and international currency exchange rates are all semiautomatic stabilizers. The goal is to stop recession (two or more quarters of negative growth) from becoming depression (intense, severe and prolonged economic decline).

Many governments (though not all) also think it is their task to protect or promote competition. Holding that competition controls inflation, improves product quality and diversity, and creates jobs most economists agree with this interpretation of governmental responsibility. In the United States many regulatory agencies have been created (e.g. **the Security and Exchange Commission, the Federal Communication Commission**) to promote this goal.

Antitrust legislation exists to promote increased competition. Citable examples for your speeches include the **Sherman Antitrust Act of 1890**, and the **Clayton Antitrust Act of 1914** that established the **Federal Trade Commission** as an enforcement agency. Such legislation exists because burgeoning and existent monopolies are prone to skimp on product quality and development. They are also more likely to use **predatory businesses practices** such as pricing below cost to bankrupt potential competition, **kickbacks and bribery**, charge horrendously high prices to consumers who have no purchase option, and use their deep pockets to buy up start-up firms that might offer them competition.

Monopolies are **horizontally integrated** firms, companies that control the market in one or more products. Companies can be **vertically integrated** and not be monopolies, because vertical integration means that divisions of one company produce the different stages of a product and sell their output to one another. In its early days Ford had divisions that produced raw materials, parts, the finished car, dealerships, and handled marketing. Sometimes this is efficient but, as the Ford example demonstrates, it does not mean that a monopoly exists. Other manufacturers exist and compete.

A third governmental decision is how to prioritize limited spending. A classic example is the battle between defense and **infrastructure** investment. On the defense side is the ultimate responsibility of the government to protect the cultural integrity and political freedoms (if any) of the homeland. On the other side is that without a good economic infrastructure (education, transportation, communication networks and all the other tools necessary for an economy to function well) the national quality of life will deteriorate or stagnate. The challenge is especially challenging for the United States. As the world's only superpower it maintains a need to defend itself and has a huge investment in defense (armaments, bases, weapons, person power).

The risks of over-investing in defense are real. A wonderful book by Paul Kennedy, *The Rise and Fall of the Great Powers*, documents how excessive military spending has been the downfall of every great power in history. Money spent on defense is money diverted from research and development, from schools, from lowered taxes. But, critics properly respond, too little money on defense endangers us all. Too little on defense caused wars throughout history, most recently it caused millions to die in World War II. Madmen, dictators and enemies are enticed to war when rich nations are poorly defended.

Governments also have to decide how much to tax the population. Levels and the types of taxes to use create debate disadvantages. In the real world they impact everyone's lives. Good government balances government finance needs with excessive tax levels. Too heavy a tax load is recessionary and ends up actually raising less for government programs. Taxing less than you could under-funds schools, defense, welfare, and the good social structure a government can promote.

2. Sample Extemp Topics

How can the United States improve its tax policies and tax rates?
Are LDCs guilty of sacrificing development to military spending?
What are the strengths and weaknesses of current FRB policy?
Does EU welfare and budgetary policies moderate the business cycle?

3. Web Site

The Fraser Institute promotes economic freedom, which they define as "the extent to which one can pursue economic activity without interference from government". One of the best entrees on the site is their annual *Economic Freedom of the World Report*. The left side of the home page has a lot of domestic research areas you can use. www.fraserinstitute.ca/economicfreedom/

4. If you want to read more...

You and the Fed

Introduction

We're all very much affected by what the Federal Reserve Bank (known as the Fed) does—whether as employees or employers, savers or borrowers, producers or consumers. But what, exactly, does the Fed do, and how does that affect us?

Monetary Policy

The Fed is best known for its role in making and carrying out the country's monetary policy—that is, for influencing money and credit conditions in the economy in order to promote the goals of high employment, sustainable growth, and stable prices.

Goals of Monetary Policy
Sustainable growth
High employment
Stable prices

PROMOTING BALANCED ECONOMIC GROWTH

The long-term goal of the Fed's monetary policy is to ensure that money and credit grow sufficiently to encourage non-inflationary economic expansion.

The Fed cannot guarantee that our economy will grow at a healthy pace, or that everyone will have a job. The attainment of these goals depends on the decisions of millions of people around the country. Decisions regarding how much to spend and how much to save, how much to invest in acquiring skills and education, how much to spend on new plant and equipment, or how many hours a week to work may be some of them.

What the Fed can do, is create an environment that is conducive to healthy economic growth. It does so by pursuing a goal of price stability—that is, by trying to prevent inflation from becoming a problem.

Inflation is defined as a sustained increase in prices over a period of time.

A stable level of prices is most conducive to maximum sustained output and employment. Also, stable prices encourage saving and, indirectly, capital formation because it prevents the erosion of asset values by unanticipated inflation.

Inflation causes many distortions in the market. Inflation:

- hurts people with fixed income—when prices rise consumers cannot buy as much as they could previously
- discourages savings
- reduces economic growth because the economy needs a certain level of savings to finance investments which boosts economic growth
- makes it harder for businesses to plan—it is difficult to decide how much to produce, because businesses can't predict the demand for their product at the higher prices they will have to charge in order to cover their costs.

COMBATING INFLATION

Inflation is sustained by excess money and credit in the economy. Money refers to cash in circulation, plus the amounts that people and businesses have in bank accounts. Credit refers to amounts that banks and other lenders can lend.

Inflation will result if money and credit rise too rapidly compared with the ability of the economy to produce goods and services. And it will enable sellers to raise prices. However, the growth of money and credit should not be too slow, or people and businesses will not be able to get loans they need for major purchases that stimulate the economy.

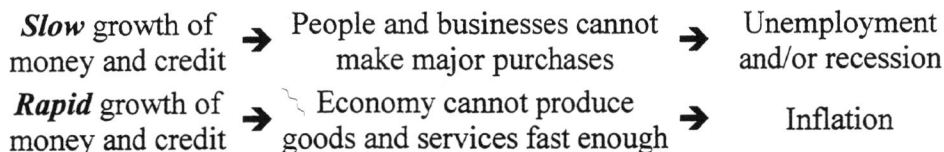

| **Slow** growth of money and credit | → | People and businesses cannot make major purchases | → | Unemployment and/or recession |
| **Rapid** growth of money and credit | → | Economy cannot produce goods and services fast enough | → | Inflation |

The Fed has to maintain an appropriate pace for the growth of money and credit—one that will produce sustainable economic growth and price stability. The Fed has a number of tools to do this job.

Tools of Monetary Policy

The Fed has three monetary policy tools—open market operations, reserve requirements, and discount window lending.

Open market operations are the most important and active tool of monetary policy that the Fed uses. These operations consist of the Fed buying and selling previously issued U.S. Government securities, or IOUs of the Federal Government.

The Fed adds extra credit to the banking system when it buys Treasury securities from the dealers, and drains credit when it sells to the dealers. As the laws of supply and demand take over in the reserves market, the cost of funds for the remaining reserves finds its level at the federal funds rate.

The Fed's open market operations are conducted in the following manner:

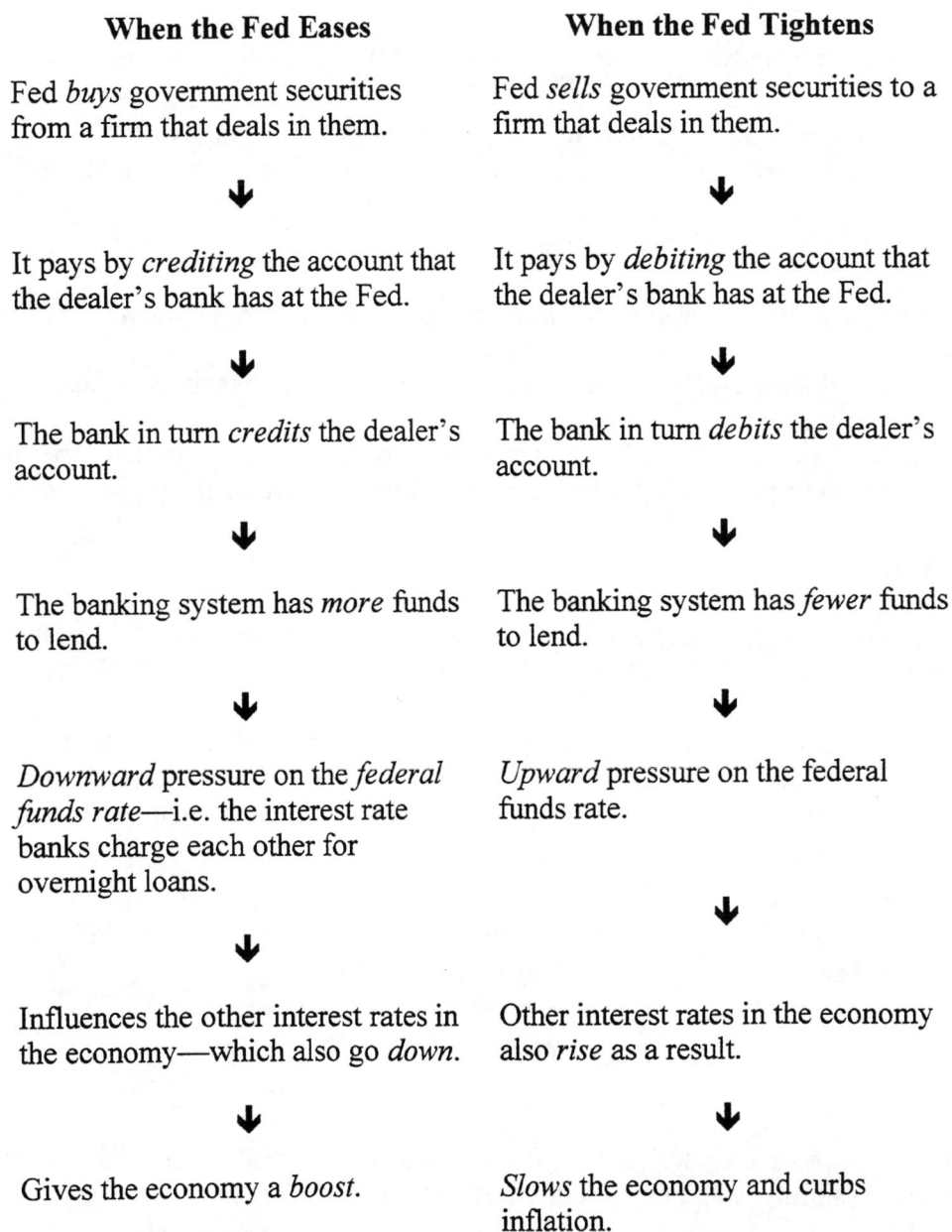

When the Fed Eases	**When the Fed Tightens**
Fed *buys* government securities from a firm that deals in them.	Fed *sells* government securities to a firm that deals in them.
↓	↓
It pays by *crediting* the account that the dealer's bank has at the Fed.	It pays by *debiting* the account that the dealer's bank has at the Fed.
↓	↓
The bank in turn *credits* the dealer's account.	The bank in turn *debits* the dealer's account.
↓	↓
The banking system has *more* funds to lend.	The banking system has *fewer* funds to lend.
↓	↓
Downward pressure on the *federal funds rate*—i.e. the interest rate banks charge each other for overnight loans.	*Upward* pressure on the federal funds rate.
↓	↓
Influences the other interest rates in the economy—which also go *down*.	Other interest rates in the economy also *rise* as a result.
↓	↓
Gives the economy a *boost*.	*Slows* the economy and curbs inflation.

Interest rates affect the level of activity in the economy. When rates are low, people find it easier to buy cars and homes, and businesses are more inclined to invest in new machinery and buildings. And when the rates are high the

58

opposite occurs as the Fed tries to curtail inflation and maintain economic growth.

Open market operations typically are conducted several times a week. A majority of the open market operations are not intended to carry out changes in monetary policy. Rather, they are conducted to prevent some technical, temporary forces from pushing money and credit conditions in some undesired direction.

The public's demand for cash varies, depending on the season, the day of the month, and even the day of the week. When people hold more cash, the reserves of the bank go down. And that could push short-term interest rates up, if the Fed did not use open market operations to offset the increase.

The Fed has to be watchful, not only for any signs of impending inflation or recession, but also for how technical factors may be affecting the supply money and credit in the economy.

> Federal Funds rate is the interest rate banks charge each other for overnight loans.

RESERVE REQUIREMENTS AND DISCOUNT WINDOW LENDING:

- *Reserve requirements* are the percentages of certain types of deposits that banks must keep on hand in their own vaults or on deposit at a Federal Reserve Bank. The Fed has the authority to set reserve requirements on checking accounts and certain types of savings accounts.

Reserve requirement	Impact on bank lending
Raised	Reduce lending
Lowered	Increase lending

The Fed rarely changes the reserve requirements. The last change made to the reserve requirement was in April 1992, when they lowered the rate from 12% to10% of transaction deposits.

Changes in reserve requirement make planning difficult for lenders, and any increase imposes a cost on them. The Fed generally does not change the reserve requirement when there is an alternative way of achieving the same policy result.

- *Discount rate*, another tool of monetary policy, is the interest rate that the Fed charges banks for short-term loans. Changes in the discount rate typically occur in conjunction with changes in the federal funds rate.

Through the discount window, Federal Reserve Banks lend funds to depository institutions. All depository institutions that maintain transaction accounts or non-personal time deposits subject to reserve requirements are entitled to borrow at the discount window.

Discount Rate	Impact on Economic Activity	Policy
Raised	Slows economic activity	Check inflation
Lowered	Stimulates economic activity	Economic growth

Increases in the discount rate generally reflect the Federal Reserve's concern over inflationary pressures, while decreases often reflect a concern over economic weakness.

For the latest figures for federal funds rate, reserve requirement and discount rate.

Fed's International Roles

The foreign-exchange value of the dollar has an effect not only on the prices we pay but also on prices in the entire U.S. economy. That's why it is of concern to the Fed.

Depending on the strength or weakness of the dollar with respect to other currencies, the impact on individuals and businesses will vary. When the dollar is strong, the cost of buying goods and services from abroad is lower than when the dollar is weak.

Value of dollar	Impact on imports/exports	
Falls	Cost of imports rise	➜ Increases U.S. inflation
	Cost of exports fall	➜ Boosts U.S. output
Rises	Cost of imports fall	➜ Decreases U.S. inflation
	Cost of exports rises	➜ Reduces U.S. output

The Fed closely monitors developments in the foreign exchange (FX) market. This is largely due to its impact on the U.S. economy that results from the increased economic interdependence among countries of the world.

FOREIGN EXCHANGE INTERVENTION

The Fed does more than observe the changing value of the dollar; it also influences it—both through its monetary policy and by direct intervention in the FX market.

> Fed raises interest rates ➜ Foreigners want to invest funds in U.S. ➜ They convert their currencies into dollars ➜ Demand for dollars rise ➜ Value of the dollar rises

At times, the Fed enters the FX market, either buying or selling dollars in exchange for a foreign currency. The U.S. Treasury Department officially has the primary responsibility for international financial policy. But its decisions are always made in consultation with the Fed. Moreover, when there is a decision to intervene in the FX market, the Federal Reserve Bank of New York conducts the intervention.

Fed *buys* dollars for yen	➜ *Raises* the value of dollar, lowers the value of yen
Fed *sells* dollars for yen	➜ *Lowers* the value of dollar, raises the value of yen

The intervention is conducted with funds belonging to both the Fed and the Treasury. Since the size of the Fed's intervention is small compared to the total amount of FX trading, it does not influence the demand and supply conditions in the FX market. However, it influences the market sentiment relating to the value of the dollar. The frequency of the Fed's FX intervention varies.

OTHER INTERNATIONAL ACTIVITIES

The Federal Reserve conducts other activities in the international arena, providing a wide range of services to over 200 foreign customers, including:

- central banks
- foreign governments

- official international institutions, such as the International Monetary Fund.

The services the Fed provides to its international customers include:

- maintaining checking accounts
- investing funds
- executing foreign exchange operations
- holding assets for safekeeping

The foreign-owned gold stored in the gold vault at the Federal Reserve Bank of New York constitutes the world's largest known concentration of monetary gold.

Bank for Banks

The Fed provides many services for U.S. banks. These activities are vital to the financial health of the economy.

CASH PROCESING

The cash in the banks is generated from deposits made by customers and acquired from the Fed. Both coins and paper money are produced by the U.S. Treasury, but put into circulation by the Federal Reserve.

When the banks need cash they order it from the Fed. Banks maintain accounts at the Fed for several reasons, one of which is to meet their reserve requirements. The Fed collects payment for the cash it ships to a bank by debiting the bank's account with the amount. When a bank has more cash than it needs, it ships the excess to the Fed for a credit to its account.

The Fed uses state-of-the-art, high-speed machines to verify the deposit amounts and to identify possible counterfeits, which it sends to the U.S. Secret Service for investigation.

The Fed shreds bills that are no longer fit for circulation. Most of the shredded money is disposed off in landfills, while some is sold to businesses, under Treasury Department rules, and some turned into stationery products under contract with the company that makes paper on which currency is printed.

PROCESSING CHECKS

Check processing is another important service provided to banks by the Fed. The Fed processes 35 to 40 percent of the inter-bank checks (that is, the checks that are deposited in a bank other than the one on which they are drawn) written in the United States each year. The rest are processed through private clearing arrangements.

To promote competition in the check-processing field, Federal law requires the Fed to charge fees that reflect the Fed's full costs of providing the service.

Here is how a check is processed:

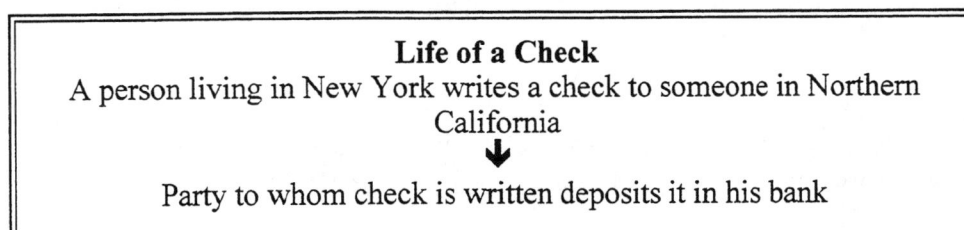

| **Life of a Check** |
| A person living in New York writes a check to someone in Northern California |
| ↓ |
| Party to whom check is written deposits it in his bank |

```
                              ↓
        Bank credits depositor's account and sends check to Federal Reserve
                          Bank of San Francisco
                              ↓
        San Francisco Fed credits the amount of the check to the account that the
                          bank has with them
                              ↓
        San Francisco Fed sends the check to Federal Reserve Bank of New York
                              ↓
            New York Fed debits the check issuer's bank's account
                              ↓
            New York Fed sends the check to issuer's bank, which then debits
                          issuer's account
```

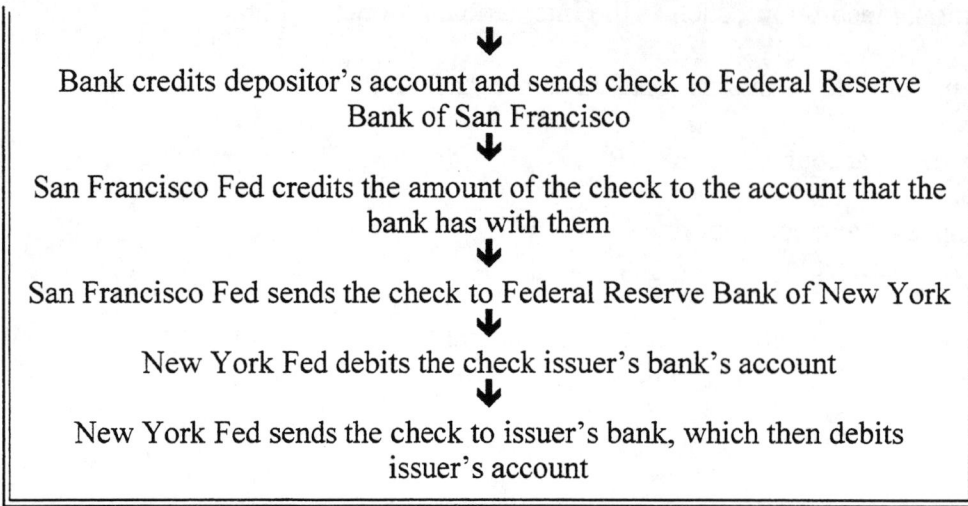

ELECTRONIC PAYMENTS

The Fed provides two electronic payment services:

I. *Fedwire*: Allows banks to make large electronic transfers of funds or U.S. Government securities in a matter of seconds. During 2000, an average of $1.5 trillion per day was transferred over Fedwire. Not many individuals use this service; the average Fedwire transfer was for $3.5 million in 2000.

II. *Automated Clearing House (ACH)*: Individuals are more likely to use this service as it provides a more efficient alternative to checks, especially when recurring payments are involved. This service is typically used for payments such as:

- salaries,
- Social Security benefits,
- corporate dividends, and
- consumer payments such as rent, phone bills etc.

While cash or checks are used for most transactions in the United States, the dollar volume of electronic payments is much larger than that of cash and check payments combined. In 2000, the Federal Reserve System processed over 4.8 billion payments through ACH with a total value of more than $12 trillion.

LENDING TO BANKS

The Fed has three major lending programs for banks:

- *Adjustment credit* consists of loans that the Fed makes overnight or for a few days to a bank that has run into a short-term liquidity problem due to situations such as unusually large withdrawals of deposits.

- *Seasonal credit* program involves the Fed extending loans for up to nine months to banks that experience recurring annual funding needs because of seasonal swings in their deposits and loans. Main users of this facility are banks in farm and tourist areas.

- *Extended credit* program provides loans for periods longer than permitted under the adjustment credit program to banks that are experiencing financial difficulty. To receive extended credit a bank must submit a financial plan showing how it will solve the difficulty it faces.

The Fed serves as a *lender of last resort* to depository institutions. In the pre-Fed era—i.e., prior to 1914—financial panics gripped the country from time to time, when demand for money and credit outran the supply. The creation of the Fed was intended to prevent such panics.

Because the Fed is a *lender of last resort*, banks are not supposed to borrow from it too often and that they are to exhaust alternative credit sources before approaching the Fed.

Thus, while the discount rate which the Fed charges on adjustment credit usually is lower than the federal funds rate, at which banks make short-term loans to each other, the Fed does not allow banks to borrow in order to turn around and lend the funds at a higher rate.

Bank for the Government

The Fed serves as a bank, not only for other banks, but also for the Federal Government. The Government maintains accounts at the Fed, and makes its payments by writing checks against these accounts or by transferring funds from the account electronically.

When a Social Security payment or a Federal income tax refund is sent, it consists of a check or electronic payment from a Government account at the Fed.

HELPING THE GOVERNMENT BORROW

The Fed helps the Government borrow funds that it needs. It processes the vast majority of bids that individuals and institutions make to buy securities at the Treasury's weekly, monthly, and quarterly auctions.

More About Treasury Securities
- Securities that mature in three months and six months are sold each week.
- Securities with longer maturities are sold less frequently.
- The term bills, notes, and bonds are used to refer to Treasury securities of different maturities.
- Bills mature in a year or less, notes in 2 to 10 years, and bonds in 30 years

The Fed also issues and redeems U.S. Savings Bonds for the Federal Government. Whether a Savings Bond is bought through payroll deduction or by placing an order at a bank, the application is processed by the Fed, which then sends the bond to the buyer.

Difference between Savings Bonds and Treasury Securities

Although both are obligations of the U.S. Government, there are differences:

- Savings bonds are sold in paper form while other Government IOUs are issued only as book entries—that is, as electronic accounting entries on Fed and bank computers. This allows the securities to be transferred more easily and reduces their vulnerability to theft and loss.
- Unlike savings bonds, Treasury bills, notes, and bonds are transferable, and can be bought or sold in the securities market.
- Treasury bills, notes, and bonds can be bought for a minimum of

$1,000, while savings bonds can be bought for as little as $25.

FISCAL AGENT FOR THE GOVERNMENT

The Reserve Banks, as the operating units of the nation's central bank, provide several important services to the Federal government. As the banker for the Federal Government, the Fed clears checks drawn on the Treasury's account. Acting as fiscal agents for the Government, the Reserve Banks sell, service and redeem Treasury securities.

Further, currency and coins are placed into or are withdrawn from circulation in response to seasonal and cyclical shifts in the public's need for cash. Almost all U.S. currency now consists of Federal Reserve notes, which were first issued in 1914.

Supervision and Regulation

The Fed is one of the several Government agencies that share responsibility for ensuring the safety and soundness of our banking system. The Fed has primary responsibility for supervising bank holding companies, financial holding companies, state-chartered banks that are members of the Federal Reserve System, and the Edge Act and agreement corporations, through which U.S. banking organizations operate abroad.

The Fed and other agencies share the responsibility of overseeing the operation of foreign banking organizations in the United States. To insure that the banking system remains competitive and operates in the public interest, the Fed considers applications by banks for mergers or to open new branches.

Fed's Role under GLB Act

The passage of the Gramm-Leach-Bliley (GLB) Act in November 1999, was the culmination of a multi-decade effort to eliminate many of the restrictions on the activities of banking organizations.

Some of the main provisions of the GLB are:

- Repeals the existing limitations on the ability of banks to affiliate with securities and insurance firms.

- Creates a new organizational form that allows banking organizations to carry new powers. This new entity called a "financial holding company," (FHC) and its non-banking subsidiaries are allowed to engage in financial activities such as insurance and securities underwriting.

The Fed's enlarged role as an umbrella supervisor of FHCs is similar to its role in supervising bank holding companies. The Federal Reserve Banks will supervise and regulate the FHCs while each affiliate is still overseen by its traditional functional regulator.

The Fed has to delineate the financial relationship between a bank and other FHC affiliates. Its primary goal is to establish barriers protecting depository institutions from the problems of a failing affiliate. To do this efficiently the Fed has to ensure increased communication, cooperation, and coordination with the many supervisors of the more diversified FHCs.

The Fed has access to data on risks across the entire organization, as well as information on the firm's management of those risks. Regulators will be in a position to evaluate and presumably act on risks that threaten the safety and soundness of the insured banks.

For more information on the GLB Act.

BANK EXAMINATIONS

In supervising banks for safety and soundness, the Fed relies on both on-site examinations and off-site inspection of financial and other information. The examinations focus on:

- the quality of the loans that the bank has extended (that is, how likely are they to be repaid);
- the liquidity of the bank's assets (that is, how quickly can the bank turn them into cash without losing any of their value);
- the amount of capital and other assets that the bank has in relation to the level of risk in the bank's portfolio;
- sensitivity of the bank's financial structure to risks;
- the quality of the bank's management.

When the Fed detects a problem at a bank, it brings it to the attention of the bank's management, which usually remedies the matter. In more serious matters the Fed can instruct the bank or someone associated with it to take actions to correct the problem.

The Fed also has the power to assess fines against banks and individuals, and even to bar someone from working in the banking industry.

APPLICATIONS FOR MERGERS AND ACQUISITIONS AND FOR NEW BRANCHES

The Fed is assigned primary responsibility for supervising and regulating the activities of bank holding companies. An existing bank holding company must obtain the approval of the Fed before acquiring more than 5 percent of the shares of an additional bank and must file certain reports with them.

The Federal Reserve is mandated to act on proposed bank mergers when the resulting institution is a state member bank. During the 1950s, bank mergers, especially those in the same metropolitan area, rose sharply. Fearing that a continuation of this trend could seriously impair competition in the banking industry and lead to an excessive concentration of financial power, Congress passed the Bank Merger Act.

The Bank Merger Act sets forth the factors to be considered in evaluating merger applications including:

- financial and managerial resources;
- prospects of the existing and proposed institutions; and
- convenience and needs of the community to be served.

The Fed may not approve a merger that could substantially lessen competition or tend to create a monopoly. However, if it finds that the anti-competitive effects of the transaction are outweighed by the probable beneficial effects on the convenience and needs of the community to be served, it may allow the merger.

When a member bank wants to open a new branch or close an existing one, it has to get approval from the local Reserve Bank. The Fed reviews the application and supporting materials in light of factors such as location, level of competition in the area and so on. After a complete examination it may grant approval.

CONSUMER AND COMMUNITY PROTECTION

The Fed enforces a variety of consumer protection laws. Among these are:

- *Community Reinvestment Act*: which encourages the banks to meet the credit needs of the community, particularly in low- and moderate-income neighborhoods.

- *Truth in Lending Act*: which requires lenders to provide detailed information about mortgages, auto loans, and credit card loans, so that when you borrow you can compare annual percentage rates and know the true cost of borrowing.
- *Equal Credit Opportunity Act*: which says that you cannot be discriminated against in credit transactions on the basis of race, sex, marital status, and some other factors.
- *Fair Credit Reporting Act*: which says that credit-reporting agencies must allow individuals to correct any erroneous information on their files that these agencies maintain.

Structure of the Federal Reserve System

The major components of the Federal Reserve System are the Board of Governors in Washington D.C. and 12 Federal Reserve Banks spread across the country.

BOARD OF GOVERNORS

The Board of Governors consists of seven members, who are appointed by the President of the United States and confirmed by the U.S. Senate. The Governors are appointed for 14-year terms, and the terms are staggered (one expires every two years). The length of the term and the staggered nature are designed to insulate the Fed from day-to-day political pressures.

The Fed is financially self-sufficient which ensures its political independence. It does not depend on appropriations from the Congress. The Fed owns a large portfolio of U.S. Government securities, and the interest from that portfolio provides the Fed enough income to carry out its activities. The Fed returns to the U.S. Treasury the excess of what it takes in over what it spends.

The Board of Governors also has the following responsibilities:

- set the reserve requirements and approve the discount rate that the Reserve Banks recommend;
- exercise authority over the activities of the Reserve Banks;
- approve the annual budgets of the Banks;
- appoint three of the nine members of the board of directors of each Bank; and
- approve the directors' choice of a Bank president.

The Board of Governors also issues a variety of regulations, some in the area of consumer protection, that apply not only to banks, but also to other lenders, such as retailers and finance companies.

The Board also publishes statistics and information about the Federal Reserve System's activities and the U.S. economy. For more information on the Board of Governors.

RESERVE BANKS

There are 12 Reserve Banks spread across the country, although they are concentrated in the eastern part of the United States. The reason is that when the Federal Reserve System was created in 1914, U.S. population and business activity was concentrated more in the East than is the case today.

All Reserve Banks, except those in Boston and Philadelphia, have Branches that help them carry out their work. There are 25 branches in all.

The Board of Governors mainly carries out policy and supervisory functions, and the Reserve Banks and their Branches carry out the operations of the Federal Reserve. While all of the Reserve Banks perform the bank supervisory and payment services, some activities are unique to particular Reserve Banks, especially the Federal Reserve Bank of New York.

FEDERAL OPEN MARKET COMMITTEE

The group that formulates the monetary policy for the Fed is the Federal Open Market Committee (FOMC). The FOMC meets in Washington D.C. eight times a year. The meetings are attended by the seven members of the Board of Governors and by all 12 Federal Reserve Bank presidents. However, there are only 12 voting members on the committee. They include the seven members of the Board and the presidents of five Federal Reserve Banks.

The president of the New York Fed is a permanent voting member of the FOMC, and the presidents of the other Reserve Banks serve one-year terms as voting members on a rotation that is set by law.

Before each FOMC meeting, staff members at each Reserve Bank prepare a report on economic developments in their Bank's district, and Board staff members prepare reports on the performance of the national economy. However, the monetary policy decisions are based on national, rather than local economic conditions. At the meeting, economic developments, as well as the economic forecasts and condition in the banking system, FX markets, and financial markets are discussed.

For more information on the FOMC.

MEMBER BANKS

At the end of 1999, about 3,400 banks were members of the Federal Reserve System. Banks chartered by the Federal Government (national banks) must belong to the System, while those chartered by state governments may choose to belong if they meet standards set by the Fed. While these member banks are less than half those in the country, they control three-fourths of the country's bank deposits.

By law, all banks, whether members of the Federal Reserve System or not, must meet the Fed's reserve requirements and may use the Fed's services such as the discount window.

Member banks must buy stock in a prescribed amount in their local Reserve Bank, and they receive a 6 percent annual dividend on their stock. However, this stock cannot be traded and can be owned only by member banks.

Special Role of the Federal Reserve Bank of New York

The Federal Reserve Bank of New York has supervisory jurisdiction over the Second Federal Reserve District, which encompasses:

- New York State;
- 12 northern counties of New Jersey;
- Fairfield County in Connecticut;
- Puerto Rico; and
- the Virgin Islands.

Though it serves a geographically small area compared with those of other Federal Reserve Banks, the New York Fed is the largest Reserve Bank in terms of assets and volume of activity.

The New York Fed has three unique missions. Foremost is the implementation of monetary policy. The other two missions involve international operations, and supervision and regulation.

In addition to the responsibilities the New York Fed shares in common with the other Reserve Banks, it has several unique responsibilities, including conducting open market operations, intervening in foreign exchange markets, and storing monetary gold for foreign central banks, governments and international agencies.

Through open market operations, the New York Fed buys or sells U.S. Treasury securities in the secondary market in order to produce a desired level of bank reserves. These securities are held in the System's portfolio. The "primary dealers," authorized to do business with the New York Fed, serve as its counter parties in open market operations and other securities transactions.

Only the Federal Reserve Bank of New York conducts the open market operations for the System under the direction of the twelve-member FOMC. The president of the New York Fed is a permanent voting member of the FOMC and uniquely, the Bank's first vice president may vote at the meetings in the president's absence.

The New York Fed, representing the Federal Reserve System and the U.S. Treasury, is responsible for intervening in FX markets to achieve dollar exchange rate policy objectives and to counter disorderly conditions in these markets. Such transactions are made in close coordination with the U.S. Treasury and Board of Governors, and most often are coordinated with the foreign exchange operations of other central banks.

The New York Fed serves as fiscal agent in the United States for foreign central banks and official international financial organizations. It acts as the primary contact with other foreign central banks. Among the services provided for these institutions are:

- receipt and payment of funds in U.S. dollars;
- purchase and sale of foreign exchange and Treasury securities;
- custody of almost $800 billion in currency, securities and gold bullion held for over 200 foreign account holders; and
- storage of monetary gold for foreign central banks, governments and official international agencies.

For more information on the activities of the New York Fed, visit their website.

Chapter Seven
International Trade Issues

1. The Concepts

Chapter Three introduced us to **the law of comparative** advantage. Ricardo was right when he wrote that unrestricted trade, **free trade**, was best for all economies. But that has not stopped countries from trying to gain an edge by restricting some types of trade while vainly hoping no one will retaliate against them. **Protectionism** has taken many forms: **tariffs** (taxes on imported goods to raise their prices as compared to domestic goods), **quotas** (a numerical limit on the number of each item imported, e.g. a quota of 10,000 foreign cars allowed into a country each year), **license requirements** (not allowing an item or service to be imported into the country until it has obtained a sometimes unavailable license or licenses), **government subsidies** (direct payments to a business or sector used both to fight imports by lowering prices to domestic consumers and by making our goods cheaper to sell abroad, the most common example in many nations is agricultural subsidies), and more.

Some governments promote or cooperate with **oligopolies** in order to promote exports. South Korea and Japan have often been charged with these tactics. Oligopolies and monopolies give producers great **economies of scale**, more money for research and development, better marketing coordination, and other cost saving advantages that result from reduced competition. Governments promote exports because of job creation and profit potential, one billion dollars in exports creates 14,000 to 16,000 new jobs*. Monopolies and oligopolies can cross borders to interfere with free trade. In international affairs **cartels**, monopolistic combinations of independent business organizations have sometimes restricted trade in diamonds, copper, coffee, and notably (with **OPEC**) oil.

A few nations, most notably the United States, sometimes use trade as a club or threat. **Embargoes** (against Cuba and North Korea for example) deny trade in hopes of getting enemy governments to change their policies in exchange for restored trade. Almost always conspicuously unsuccessful embargoes are anti-trade; as Ricardo predicted the result on both sides have been lost jobs and lost profits, higher costs and other **economic inefficiencies**. Embargo proponents do have two arguments in their favor however. Embargoes are a way to express moral outrage short of war, and very occasionally they do create great change (e.g. the international embargo against South Africa got it to drop its apartheid; policies and give the vote to black and Indian citizens).

Intelligent leadership knows that free trade brings greater prosperity than trade restrictions. With free trade markets open, the most efficient and inventive firms survive, and (absent government monetary policy stupidity) the competition keeps inflationary risks at bay. The increased competition increases both the quality and diversity of goods, and stimulates new product creation. To promote freer trade good leadership creates bilateral and multilateral free trade agreements. The United States has incorporated this policy under the umbrella **most favored nation** trade policy.

But "opening up" or increasing trade can cause short-term harm. The owners and workers in a sector may be hurt because of the opening trade. Farmers in France and Japan, textile workers and sugar farmers in the United States, and soft drink manufacturers in India were all hurt as freer trade entered their nations. Those companies that cannot compete must find a new approach or fall by the side, which is the harsh wonderful truth of laissez faire competition. But governments have an obligation to their citizens' quality of life. So one solution has been to give free retraining, subsidized relocation, and other forms of **trade adjustment assistance** to workers displaced by new trade agreements.

Common markets or free trade zone are also tools that respect Ricardo's edicts. Free trade zones are not automatically beneficial, occasionally one will increase trade barriers to non-members, but most often they do more to decrease rather than increase the net number of trade barriers. Good examples include the **European Union** (also known as the Common Market or the EU) and the **North American Free Trade Association** (NAFTA). In Asia **APEC** and **ASEAN** both show aspects of modest trade organizations. Africa and Latin America have shown similar signs of developing free trade groups.

While both individual countries and groups of nations show free trade activity the largest is the **World Trade Organization**, the **WTO**. In 1948 most of the world's first and second world nations signed GATT, the General Agreement on Trade and Tariffs. Designed to reduce trade barriers the treaty lead to several successful but long and laborious rounds of trade cut negotiations. But there were flaws in the treaty and the agreements, the most obvious being that there were no courts to interpret and enforce the agreements. This lead to sometimes valid charges of cheating

The Uruguay Round of GATT negotiations thus resulted not only in new barrier and tariff reductions, but also in a new organizational format—the World Trade Organization. The WTO has better structure because it created a permanent enforcement and court bureaucracy.

But successful international trade requires more than free trade. It also requires an agreed-upon method of payment, agreed upon international currency exchange rates, governments that honor their financial obligations, and governments with **viable economies**. Bad leadership, uncontrollable or unforeseen events, and or bad economic systems have often challenged the needed viability. The result has sometimes been **debt default**, big swings in exchange rates, bank collapse, inflation, recession, and other disasters. These instabilities are the stories of debaters' disadvantages. But since 1947 and the **Bretton Woods Agreement** the developed nations have developed controversial tools to try to more effectively deal with these problems. The most important are the **IMF** (the **International Monetary Fund**) and the **World Bank**.

The IMF is an emergency loan organization. Funded by most of the world's developed nations the IMF gives short-term loans to nations whose economies are collapsing. In return for the loan the Fund often requires significant changes in their national economic policy. Sometimes budget deficits must be cut or ended, other times tax reforms and banking policies must be changed. Controversies arise because the changes sometimes create hardships, and succeed in restoring **national economic integrity** only about fifty percent of the time.

The World Bank is a long-term international loan organization. It is designed as a foreign aid tool to promote infrastructure development. Loans fund dams, energy development and distribution networks, underwrite **joint ventures**, and support other expensive economic development projects. Loan rates are below what commercial banks charge. But sometimes the Bank has bankrolled projects that are environmentally damaging or ignore the need to protect some indigenous cultures.

Developed nations can also suffer short-term harms from trade imbalances. To measure trade ratios writers use the phrases **balance of trade** (amount compared mathematically to the amount exported) and the **balance of payments** (the balance of trade plus banking costs, fees, and service transactions). Governments sometimes get very worried in their balances are negative or "in the red". Whether or not they should worry is very unclear, it makes an excellent debate. There are strong advantages as well as harms to a trade deficit. But so long as the government does not artificially interfere in the market and in trade the problem is self-correcting. Inefficient businesses fail, exchange rates adjust, and life goes on. But governments, especially fragile or democratic ones, are often overly sensitive to short-term problems. Thus trade imbalances create pressures for trade barriers, a disadvantage both in debate and in the real world. Trade barriers create **trade wars**, and trade wars cause unemployment and inflation. And sometimes they create real wars.

One impact of not focusing on producing the products in which your nation has a **comparative advantage** is that fewer nations want your goods, so not only does your trade balance look bad but also the exchange rate of your national currency declines. **Currency appreciation and depreciation** affects how well a nation's goods sell. If your currency is cheap (i.e. it only takes a little foreign currency to get a lot of purchasing power in your currency) its easier to sell your goods so exports increase. If your exchange rates are high, if for example it takes a lot of dollars to get a decent amount of German Marks, then you will sell less; in this case it means Americans would buy fewer German goods. The value of a nation's currency is determined by how much demand there is for it. In the short term a nation's banks sometimes intervene to buy up national currency to keep its exchange rate staple, butt in the long run demand determines currency value. A few countries **peg** the value of their currency to another currency. Argentina for a while pegged its currency to the American dollar guaranteeing that a certain number of Argentinean pesos could be exchanged for United States dollars. Under a few conditions countries will actually **devalue** their currency in order to increase their exports and make it easier top pay off foreign debts with their inflated currency.

There is no single currency that everyone uses for international transactions. **International liquidity**, assuring there is enough valued currency in circulation to do international trades, is assured by the United States dollar. In Cuba, Russia and a few other countries the dollar even serves as a defacto currency more valued than the native money. The strength of the United States economy since 1944 has served to make our money the most commonly accepted worldwide. Gold and the EU "**Euro**" are also sometimes used for major international transactions.

*United States Department of Commerce, March 1, ANNUAL TRADE REPORT

2. The Web Site

The Institute For International Economics is a **think tank**. From its home page you can access a search engine, policy briefs, speeches, testimony, "Hot Topics", and publications. Visit it at www.iie.com/homepage.htm.

3. Sample Extemp Topics

How can the United States improve its trade policies?
Does either the IMF or the World Bank need to revise its policies?
What can we do to improve our relations with the EU?
Is globalization a gain or a tragedy?

4. If you want to read more…

The Basics of Foreign Trade and Exchange

Growing Trade, Shrinking World

Americans drive cars made in Germany, use VCR's made in Japan and wear clothing made in China. Japanese watch American movies, Egyptians drink American cola and Swedes jog in American running shoes. The world economy is more integrated than ever before.

What is international trade?

International trade shapes our everyday lives and the world we live in. Nearly every time we make a purchase we are participating in the global economy. Products and their components come to our store shelves from all over the world.

International trade is the system by which countries exchange goods and services. Countries trade with each other to obtain things that are better quality, less expensive or simply different from what is produced at home.

Goods and services that a country buys from another country are called **imports**, and goods and services that are sold to other countries are called **exports**. Trade mostly takes place between companies. However, governments and individuals frequently buy and sell goods internationally.

World Trade is Diverse

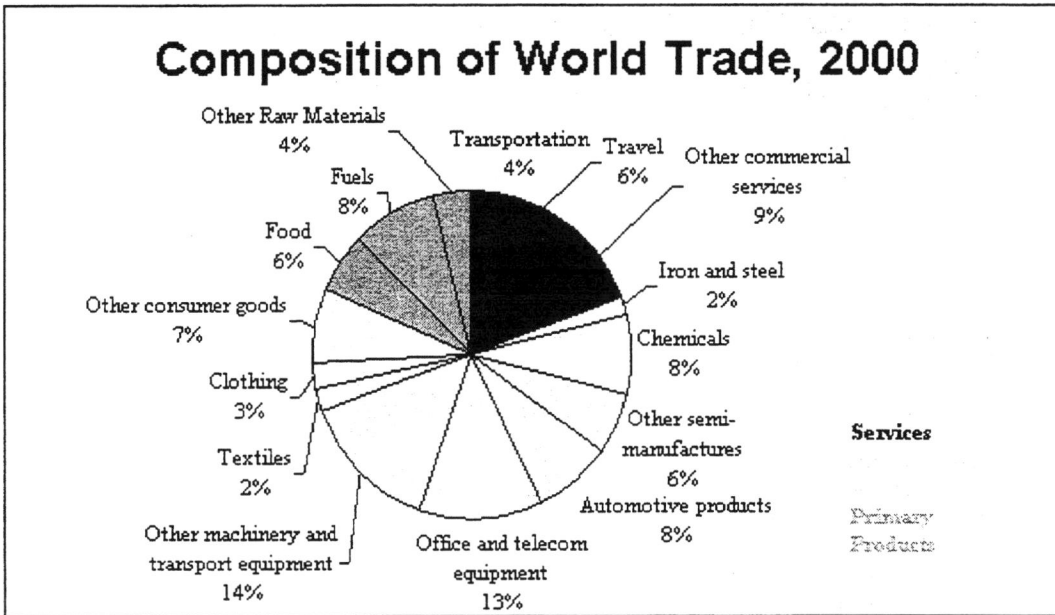

Composition of World Trade, 2000

Other Raw Materials 4%
Transportation 4%
Travel 6%
Other commercial services 9%
Fuels 8%
Food 6%
Iron and steel 2%
Chemicals 8%
Other consumer goods 7%
Clothing 3%
Other semi-manufactures 6%
Textiles 2%
Automotive products 8%
Other machinery and transport equipment 14%
Office and telecom equipment 13%

Services

Primary Products

Most international trade consists of the purchase and sale of industrial equipment, consumer goods, oil and agricultural products. Services such as banking, insurance, transportation, telecommunications, engineering and tourism accounted for one-fifth of world exports in 2000.

WORLD EXPORTS ARE UP SHARPLY

Since the end of World War II, there has been a rapid increase in international trade.

- In 1950, total world merchandise exports amounted to $58 billion
- In 2000, exports were $6.3 trillion, over a 100-fold increase

More information on world trade statistics.

Trade: Important for economic well being

With the increase in volume, trade has become very important to the economic well-being of many countries. In early 1960s, the United States bought less than $1 billion of foreign cars and parts. By 2001, this figure had increased to *more* than $189 billion.

Financial ties between United States and the rest of the world have grown significantly over time:

- Number of foreign banking offices operating in the United States rose from fewer than 40 to over 600 at present.
- Amount of **foreign direct investment** (FDI) was $158 billion in 2001.
- Gross transactions of long-term U.S. government securities by foreigners rose from $144 billion in 1978 to over $9.1 trillion in 2000.

72

Foreign direct investment is the amount of money individuals invest in companies, assets and real estate of another country.

The cost of international transportation and communication has fallen drastically, resulting in greater integration among the economies of the world. Because of this **interdependence**, economic trends and conditions in one country can strongly affect prices, wages, employment and production in other countries. Events in Tokyo, London and Mexico City have a direct effect on the everyday life of people in the U.S., just as the impact of events in New York, Washington and Chicago is felt around the globe.

If stocks on the New York Stock Exchange plummet in value, the news is transmitted instantly worldwide, and stock prices all over the world might change. This means that countries have to work together more closely and rely on each other for prosperity.

For data on FDI in the U.S.

Trade: Why do it?

International trade occurs because individuals, businesses and governments in one country want to buy goods and services produced in another country.

- Trade provides people with a greater selection of goods and services to choose from.
- Often these goods are available at prices lower than those in the domestic economy.

Benefits of Trade

Specialization and Its Benefits

To become wealthier, countries want to use their resources—land, labor, capital and entrepreneurship—in the most efficient manner. However, there are differences among countries in the quantity, quality and cost of these resources. The advantages that a country may have, vary:

- abundant minerals
- climate suited to agriculture
- well trained labor force
- new innovative ideas
- highly developed infrastructure like good roads, telecommunications system, etc.

Instead of trying to produce everything by themselves, countries often concentrate on producing things that they can produce most efficiently. They then trade those for other goods and services. In doing so, both the country and the world become wealthier. Learn more about the theory of specialization and trade.

Specialization and Trade

Two economies, Cottonland and Woodland, have the same resources and produce both cloth and furniture.

Cottonland

- Without trade, produces
  - 8 bales of cloth

Woodland

- Without trade, produces
  - 4 bales of cloth

73

- 4 pieces of furniture
- Total production 12 units
- Time taken to produce
  - 1 bale of cloth – 1 hour
  - 1 piece of furniture – 2 hours
- With trade
  - 16 bales of cloth
  - 0 pieces of furniture
  - Total production 16

- 8 pieces of furniture
- Total production 12 units
- Time taken to produce
  - 1 bale of cloth – 2 hours
  - 1 piece of furniture – 1 hour
- With trade
  - 0 bales of cloth
  - 16 pieces of furniture
  - Total production

Since Cottonland is more efficient in cloth production, it can double its cloth output to 16 bales a day by transferring all its resources to that industry. By doing so Cottonland will eliminate the furniture industry. However, it can trade the surplus cloth for furniture.

Similarly, Woodland can direct all its resources to the production of furniture and produce 16 pieces of furniture. Although its cloth industry will suffer it can trade the surplus pieces of furniture for cloth bales.

Through specialization and trade, the supply of goods in both economies increases, which brings the prices down, making them more affordable.

Trade also provides a wider variety of goods to consumers: cars from Japan, salmon from Scandinavia, bananas from South America, are just a few.

Most industrialized countries can produce just about anything they want. For instance, the U.S.:

- could conceivably devote all its resources to the production of tropical fruits.

➔ such reallocation of resources makes no economic sense.

- could compensate for the unsuitable weather by building hothouses, developing irrigation techniques and retraining workers.

➔ the resources that are directed towards the tropical fruit industry could be used more efficiently elsewhere.

- would never have to import tropical fruit again.

➔ countries achieve greater total wealth by devoting resources to their most productive industries.

Law of Comparative Advantage

Even if a country can produce everything more efficiently than another country, there is still scope for trade. A country can maximize its wealth by putting its resources into its most competitive industries, regardless of whether other countries are more competitive in those industries. This is called the **law of comparative advantage**.

Law of Comparative Advantage

Suppose Cottonland produces both cloth and furniture better than Woodland:

	Cottonland	*Woodland*
Bales of cloth per day	10	2
Pieces of furniture per day	05	3

Cottonland has an *absolute advantage*—is more efficient—in the production of both cloth and furniture. However to achieve greater wealth, each country should specialize in the item in which it enjoys greatest advantage among all the products it produces—*comparative advantage*.

In terms of *opportunity cost*, or the cost of not transferring resources, Cottonland is twice as efficient in producing cloth as furniture.

Opportunity Cost

Cottonland	1 piece of furniture = 2 bales of cloth
Woodland	1 piece of furniture = 2/3 bales of cloth

Since Woodland's opportunity cost for producing furniture is less than Cottonland's, it makes economic sense for Woodland to focus on furniture. Cottonland should continue producing cloth and trade for Woodland's furniture. Whereas, Woodland should concentrate on furniture and trade it for cloth with Cottonland. Channeling resources into the most productive enterprise in each country will result in more products to trade.

Benefits of Diversification

Even though it makes economic sense to allocate resources to the most productive industries, no country wants to rely on only a few products. This makes the country vulnerable to changes in the world economy, such as recession, new trade laws and treaties, and new technologies.

A country that relies too heavily on one product is especially susceptible to market forces. If demand suddenly drops or if a cheaper alternative becomes available, the economy of that country could be damaged.

Many Middle East countries that are largely dependent on their oil exports see their economic fortunes rise and fall in tandem with the oil market.

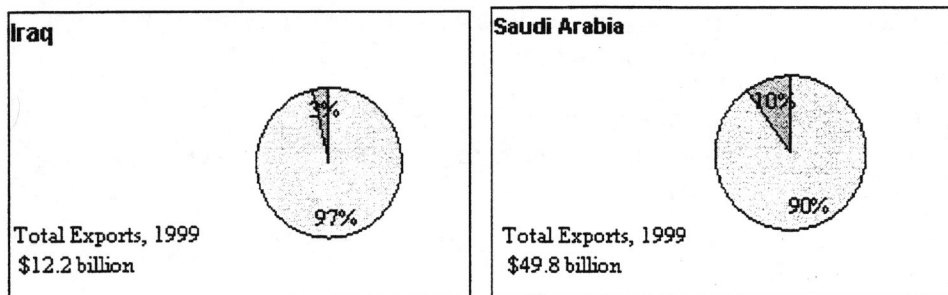

Iraq
3%
97%
Total Exports, 1999
$12.2 billion

Saudi Arabia
10%
90%
Total Exports, 1999
$49.8 billion

The degree to which countries specialize is influenced by that country's *terms of trade*—i.e. the relative prices of a country's imports and exports. It is most advantageous to have declining import prices compared with the prices of exports. Exchange rates and productivity differences affect the terms of trade more than any other factors.

By developing a diversified economy, a country can make sure that even if some industries are suffering, other, more competitive industries will keep the economy relatively healthy. The United States is competitive in finance, entertainment, aerospace, industrial equipment, pharmaceuticals and communications, among others.

Competitiveness

Competitiveness is used to describe the relative productivity of companies and industries. If one company can produce better products at lower prices than another, it is said to be more competitive. This is a matter of concern for governments, since it is difficult for uncompetitive industries to survive.

In the long run, competitiveness depends on:

- a country's natural resources,
- its stock of machinery and equipment, and
- the skills of its workers in creating goods and services that people want to buy.

Natural resources are predetermined and must be used efficiently, but a country's infrastructure and its workers' skills have to be developed over time. The ability of a society to do this effectively determines whether it can remain competitive in the global economy.

Economies of Scale

The law of comparative advantage says that a country can become more competitive by directing its resources to its most efficient industries. This enables a country to achieve **economies of scale**—increasing its output in a particular industry so that its costs per unit decrease. Such lower-cost goods are more in demand in international markets.

Certain industries that require heavy research and development or capital expenditures cannot be competitive unless they can spread the costs over many units. If a sophisticated weapons industry knows that it has access to foreign markets and could export, it may increase the scale of its manufacturing operations and become more efficient and competitive in the international markets.

Other factors affecting a country's trade competitiveness can be complex.

- Sometimes it is difficult to move resources from one industry to another—it would cost a great deal of money to turn a shoe factory into a car factory.
- Governments often attempt to restrict or encourage international trade to achieve domestic economic goals— increasing employment in certain industries, or maintaining economic independence.

Knowledge-Intensive Products Contributed to a U.S. Export Boom

From 1986 to 2001 there was an enormous boom in U.S. exports, especially in manufactured goods. Exports went up from $227 billion to $731 billion. One of the driving forces behind the increase in exports was the success of U.S. companies in selling "knowledge-intensive" manufactured goods to other industrialized countries.

The value of knowledge-intensive products depends on the skills that went into producing them, rather than the actual cost of the components. For example, while producing a new compact disc, the expenses of paying the artist, advertising, marketing and legal and other fees far outweigh the actual cost of the physical disc.

Production of such knowledge-intensive goods relies more on a well-educated and skilled workforce than on natural resources. A number of products fit this description, from computer software to custom-built aircraft engine parts. Such products are produced for specific market niches and substitutes are not easy to come by.

These knowledge-intensive products are becoming a major force in international trade and a source of wealth for economies well positioned to compete in those markets.

Merchandise Exports Since 1982

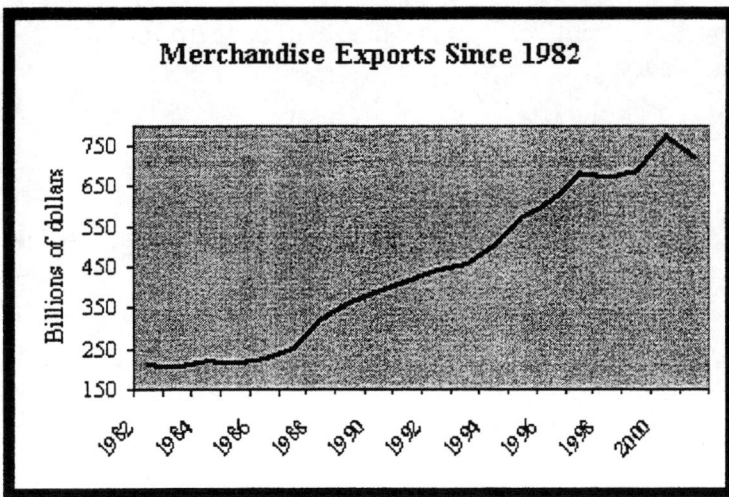

More data on <u>U.S. exports</u>.

Free Trade vs. Protectionism

All governments regulate foreign trade. The extent to which they do so is a matter of great controversy and debate. The news is full of reports of various groups protesting about:

- new trade agreements,
- adverse effects of trade on domestic industry, and
- dilution of the environmental and labor standards, especially in the developing economies.

Free trade proponents stand for an open trading system with few limitations and little government involvement. Advocates of **protectionism** believe that governments must take action to regulate trade and subsidize industries to protect their domestic economy.

Although the amount of government involvement in trade varies from country to country and product to product, overall barriers to trade have been lowered since World War II. All governments practice protectionism to some extent. The debate is over how many, or how few, such measures should be used to reach the country's long-term macroeconomic goals.

Completely free trade would:

- deliver the most goods and services at the lowest possible cost;
- provide consumers the freedom to buy from whomever produces the goods and sevices most efficiently; and
- result in competition for domestic industries which may lead to unemployment and slower growth at the least efficient companies.

If cars can be produced more efficiently in another country and consumers are free to buy them from anywhere, the domestic auto industry will lose business and may ask for government protection by limiting imports of lower-cost cars.

Arguments for protection

There are many arguments forwarded by advocates of protectionism:

- *Cheap labor:* Less developed countries have a natural cost advantage as labor costs in those economies are low. They can produce goods less expensively than developed economies and their goods are more competitive in international markets.

- *Infant industries:* Protectionists agrue that infant, or new, industries must be protected to give them time to grow and become strong enough to compete internationally, especially industries that may provide a firm foundation for future growth, e.g. computers and telecommunications. However, critics point out that some of these infant industries never "grow up."

- *National security concerns:* Any industry crucial to national security, such as producers of military hardware, should be protected. That way the nation will not have to depend on outside suppliers during political or military crises.

- *Diversification of the economy:* If a country channels all its resources into a few industries, no matter how internationally competitive those industries are, it runs the risk of becoming too dependent on them. Keeping weaker industries competitive through protection may help in diversifying the nation's economy.

- *Lowering environmental standards:* In the rush to meet the world demand for their exports, some countries may compromise on critical environmental standards. This is particularly true for less developed countries that do not have well defined environmental protection laws in place.

Methods of Protection

Governments use a variety of tools to manage their countries' international trade positions.

- *Tariffs*: Tariffs are taxes on imports. Tariffs make the item more expensive for consumers, thereby reducing the demand.

Learn more about tariffs.

Tariffs

Suppose there is a U.S company and a foreign company producing widgets:

	Cost to produce
U.S.- made widget	$1.00
Foreign-made widget	$0.75

The American widget factory will find it difficult to stay competitive under this scenario. Now, if the U.S. were to impose a tariff of 60 percent:

	New cost to U.S consumers
U.S.-made widget	$1.00
Foreign-made widget	$1.20 = [(0.75x.60)+0.75]

If consumers base their purchases only on price, the demand for the foreign widget would fall and the U.S. widget industry would prosper.

If no tariff were imposed, as under free trade, Americans would have saved money by buying the cheaper foreign widget. The U.S. widget industry would either have to become more efficient in order to compete with the less expensive imported products or face extinction.

Tariffs need not push the price of an import above the price of its domestic counterpart. They should be just high enough to reduce the price differential between the import and the domestic good. Tariffs are usually levied as a percentage of the value of the import, although sometimes a flat rate may be charged.

- **Import Quotas:** Governments sometimes restrict the sale of foreign goods by imposing import quotas. These limit the quantity of foreign goods that can be imported and help domestic producers by limiting the share of the market that can be taken by foreigners.

- **Voluntary restraints:** Sometimes governments negotiate agreements whereby a country agrees to voluntarily limit its export of a certain product. Japan voluntarily limited its export of cars to the United States in 1992 to 1.65 million cars per year.

With tariffs, it is the importing country that stands to gain through increases in the tax revenue. However, in case of quantitative restraints, the exporting country gains as the price of the imported good rises.

Both import quotas and voluntary restraints thwart the functioning of the free market. The quantity of goods remains constant while the price changes, instead of demand and supply determining both quantity and price.

- **Subsidies:** Another way to achieve the goals of protectionism is to make the domestic industry more competitive. Subsidies, which are grants by the government to an industry, can accomplish this. Subsidies can be:
  - Direct—outright payments
  - Indirect—special tax breaks or incentives, buying of surplus goods, providing low-interest loans or guaranteeing private loans.

For example, the United States subsidizes the sugar and dairy industries, among others.

- **Trade ban:** Sometimes governments ban trade with certain countries for political reasons—during times of war or political crises. Governments also ban import of certain products to protect domestic industries. For instance, Japan bans importation of rice to protect its domestic rice industry.

- **Imposing standards:** Health, environmental and safety standards often vary from country to country. These may act as a barrier to free trade and a tool of protectionism. For example, the European Union has very stringent health and safety standards that goods have to meet in order to be imported.

- **Others:** Apart from the legal restrictions there may be other less formal obstacles that impede trade. Cultural factors are one such obstacle.

Arguments for Free Trade

The debate about how free a trading system should be is an old one, with positions and arguments evolving over time. U.S. free-trade advocates typically argue that consumers benefit from freer trade and forward many reasons in support of their theory:

- Free trade and the resulting foreign competition forces U.S. companies to keep prices low.
- Consumers have a larger variety of goods and services to choose from in open markets.
- Domestic companies have to modernize plants, production techniques and technologies to keep themselves competitive.
- Any kind of protectionist measures, like tariffs, often bring about retaliatory actions from foreign governments,

which may restrict the sale of U.S. goods in their markets. This may result in inflation and unemployment in the U.S. as the export industries suffer and prices of imports rise.

- An open trading system creates a better climate for investment and entrepreneurship than one in which there is fear of governments cutting off access to certain markets.
- The cost of protection often outweighs the benefits. Learn more.

Protectionist Measures: The Costs Involved

Suppose the United States placed a tariff on imported wrenches that were less expensive than domestic wrenches. There would be four basic costs to the economy:

- wrench-buyers will have to pay more for their protected U.S.-made wrenches than they would have for the imported wrenches;
- jobs will be lost at retail and shipping companies that import foreign-made wrenches;
- jobs will be lost in any domestic industries that suffer from retaliatory tariffs; and
- the extra cost of the wrenches gets passed on to whatever products and services use these wrenches.

These costs will have to be weighed against the number of jobs the tariff would save to get a true picture of the impact of the tariff.

Measures of Trade

Balance of trade and balance of payments are two of the statistics most widely used to measure a country's international trade position.

Balance of trade is the difference between a nation's exports and imports of both goods and services.

Balance of payments gives a complete summary of all economic transactions that involve money flowing into or from a country.

Exports are the value of goods and services sold abroad over any specific period of time.

Imports are the value of goods and services purchased from foreign countries over a specific period of time.

A "favorable" balance of trade, or **trade surplus,** occurs when exports exceed imports. A "negative" balance, or **trade deficit**, occurs when the imports surpass exports.

From the mid-1970s through 2001, the United States ran persistent trade deficits. Economists disagree as to what effect these deficits had on the economy, but they allowed:

- foreigners to accumulate U.S. dollars from U.S. import payments; and
- facilitated the purchase of U.S. goods, services and assets, such as real estate and companies, by foreigners.

U.S. Merchandise Trade Deficit Since 1970

The balance of trade alone does not give the whole picture. The detailed record of all economic transactions between a country and the rest of the world is called the **balance of payments**. This includes trade in:

- goods and services; and
- financial and non-financial assets

The balance of payments is separated into two main accounts:

- *Current account*—records transactions that involve the export or import of goods and services and interest payments. The entire merchandise trade balance is contained in this account.
- *Capital account*—records transactions that involve the purchase or sale of assets or investments, like companies, stocks, bonds, bank accounts, real estate and factories.

If you buy an automobile made by a factory in Germany, the transaction will be recorded in the current account. However, if you buy the automobile factory or stock in the automobile factory, the transaction will be a part of the capital account.

Table 1: U.S. International Transactions, 2001
(Billions of dollars)

	Credits	Debits
Current account		
1. Exports	1,298.3	
Of which:		
Merchandise	720.8	
Investment income received	293.8	
Other services	283.7	
2. Imports		1,665.3
Of which:		
Merchandise		1,147.4
Investment income paid		312.9
Other services		204.9
3. Net unilateral transfers		50.5
Balance on current account		

[(1)+(2)+(3)]		417.5

Capital Account

4. U.S. assets held abroad
   Of which:

Official reserve assets	4.9	439.6
Other assets		
5. Foreign assets held in U.S.	895.5	434.7
Of which:		
Official reserve assets	6.1	
Other assets	889.4	
Balance on capital account	455.9	
[(4)+(5)]		
Statistical discrepancy		
[sum of (1) through (5)]		38.4

Source: U.S. Department of Commerce, Bureau of Economic Analysis, U.S. International Transactions Accounts Data. Totals may differ due to rounding.

Every international transaction automatically enters the balance of payments twice, once as a credit and once as a debit, resulting in two equal and opposite entries. A transaction that involves money flowing into the country is recorded as a *balance of payment credit* and anything that draws money out of the country is a *balance of payment debit*.

For example, if you buy a camera from a Japanese company, XYZ Inc., and pay by check, your purchase results in the following two entries in the balance of payments statements:

	Credit	Debit
Current account		
Camera purchase (U.S. import)		$1,000
Capital account		
Sale of bank deposit (U.S. asset export)	$1,000	

Your payment to buy a good (the camera) from a foreign company is recorded as a *debit* in the U.S. *current account*. Let's say XYZ Inc. deposits the check in their account at ABC Bank in New York. This means, XYZ Inc. has purchased, and ABC Bank has sold, a U.S. asset (a bank deposit) worth $1,000—and the transaction will appear as a *credit* in the U.S. *capital account*.

This system of double-entry bookkeeping tries to ensure that the current and capital accounts are balanced. However, due to accounting conventions and differences in the recorded values of transactions, this does not always happen. Accounting for these differences, called *statistical discrepancies*, makes possible the following fundamental identity of the balance of payment accounts:

Current account + Capital account + Statistical discrepancy = 0

CURRENT ACCOUNT

The current account consists of four sub accounts:

- *Merchandise* trade consists of all raw materials and manufactured goods bought, sold, or given away. Since early 1990s, the merchandise trade account has been combined with services to determine the "*balance of trade.*"

- *Services* include tourism, transportation, engineering, and business services, such as law, management consulting, and accounting. Fees from patents and copyrights on new technology, software, books, and movies also are recorded in the service category.

- *Income receipts* record investment incomes made up of interest and dividend payments and earnings of domestic owned firms operating abroad.

- *Unilateral transfers* are payments that do not correspond to the purchase of any good, service or asset. These usually take the form of international aid, gifts, or worker remittances from abroad.

Table 2: Calculating the balance on the current account
(Refer to Table 1 above)

Current Account:		Billions of dollars
Exports		1,298.3
+ Imports	(-)	1,665.3
+ Net unilateral transfers (inflows minus outflows)	(-)	00050.5
Balance on current account	(-)	**$417.5 (1)**

CAPITAL ACCOUNT

The capital account measures the difference between sales of assets to foreigners and purchases of assets located abroad.

- *U.S.-owned assets abroad* are divided into official reserve assets, government assets, and private assets. These assets include gold, foreign currencies, foreign securities, reserve position in the International Monetary Fund, U.S. credits and other long-term assets, direct foreign investment, and U.S. claims reported by U.S. banks.

- *Foreign-owned assets in the United States* are divided into foreign official assets and other foreign assets in the United States. These assets include U.S. government, agency, and corporate securities; direct investment; U.S. currency, and U.S. liabilities reported by U.S. banks.

Table 3: Calculating the balance on the capital account
(Refer to Table 1 above)

Capital Account:		Billions of dollars
Purchase of assets abroad (U.S. owned assets abroad)	(-)	439.6
+ Sales of assets to foreigners (foreign-owned assets in U.S.)		895.5
Balance on the capital account	(2)	**$455.9**

BALANCE OF PAYMENT DEFICIT AND SURPLUS

In theory, the current account should balance with the capital account. The sum of the balance of payments statements should be zero. Therefore, when a country buys more goods and services than it sells (a current account deficit), it must finance the difference by borrowing, or by selling more capital assets than it buys (a capital account surplus). A persistent current account deficit amounts to exchanging capital assets for goods and services. Large trade deficits mean that a country is borrowing from abroad and it appears as an inflow of foreign capital in the balance of payments.

The accounts do not exactly offset each other, due to statistical discrepancies, accounting conventions, and exchange rate movements that change the recorded value of transactions.

Calculating Statistical Discrepancy on the Balance of Payment Accounts
(Refer to Table 2 and Table 3 above)

If (1) and (2) are not equal, the difference (with the sign changed) is attributed to statistical discrepancies.

- (-)417.5 + 455.9 = 38.4

Thus *statistical discrepancies* were **(-) \$38.4** billion for 2001.

2001 U.S. BALANCE OF PAYMENTS

In 2001, the U.S imported goods and services worth \$1,352 billion, while its exports were only \$1,004 billion. And with net unilateral transfers of \$50.5 billion, the deficit on the current account amounted to \$417 billion. To cover this deficit, the United States required a capital inflow of the same amount. That means net borrowings or net sales of assets to foreigners of the same magnitude.

In the same period, the capital account registered an increase of \$439 billion in U.S assets located abroad and a \$895 billion increase in foreign assets held in the U.S. giving us a surplus balance of \$456 billion.

The difference, of approximately \$39 billion, was attributed to statistical discrepancy, leaving a zero balance in the balance of payment statement.

More information on the U.S foreign trade statistics may be accessed on the Department of Commerce, Bureau of Economic Analysis web site.

BALANCE OF PAYMENTS AND INTEREST RATES

The balance of payments is influenced by many factors, including the financial and economic climate of other countries. If the U.S banks are offering higher interest rates for deposits than banks abroad, foreign funds will flow into the United States. Conversely, if interest rates are higher abroad, U.S. investors will choose to invest their money abroad.

Interest rate in U.S.	*Interest rate abroad*	*Fund flows*	*U.S.Capital Account*
High	Low	Into the	Improves
Low	High	U.S.	Weakens
		Abroad	

Statistics Can Have Different Interpretations

Interpretations of trade statistics sometimes can differ sharply, depending on the questions being asked. The U.S. trade deficit has been viewed as good, bad, irrelevant, overstated, understated and illusory.

For example, a company that exports goods to the United States will view the deficit as a sign of a healthy U.S market. On the other hand, a U.S. based trade union may consider the deficit a sign that domestic industries are unable to compete in the world markets.

In a global economy that is measured in trillions of dollars, not every transaction is going to be reported accurately. Statistics for many types of transactions rely heavily on estimates made by statisticians, and even the best estimates are sometimes incorrect. This can produce a skewed measurement of what is actually happening in the economy.

Measuring imports and exports

Imports: U.S. importers file tax documents with the U.S. Customs Service describing the type and value of imported goods. These reports are processed and tabulated to arrive at the overall level of U.S. imports. Inaccurate reports, delays in processing data, and smuggling can affect their value.

Exports: There is no tax on exports, so to collect information, the U.S. Department of Commerce developed a form called the Shippers' Export Declaration (SED) form, which is filled out when goods are sent overseas. These are tallied to arrive at export totals.

Access more data on U.S. trade.

The Bretton Woods Agreements Act of 1945 requires the publication of balance of payments information. The statistics are generally reliable although the collection process is often difficult, especially in case of data on travel, services, direct foreign investment and financial transactions.

Sometimes it is difficult to classify a good as an import or an export. Trade is usually tabulated on the basis of national origin rather than national ownership. If a product is shipped from the U.S. to Germany, it is considered a U.S. export and a German import. It makes no difference whether a foreign company owns the U.S. factory or if it is a U.S. firm in Germany that imports the product.

If a U.S. company owns a plant in Brazil and sells a product to a Japanese company in Canada, the transaction is recorded as a Canadian import and a Brazilian export.

It is also difficult to assign a value to goods. To compare the exports of two countries in a given year, it is necessary to convert the figures into the same currency. However, there can be distortions due to:

- *Exchange rate fluctuations*: The exchange rate may distort the value of trade statistics. It may appear that one country is exporting more than another when, in fact, the distortions could be attributed to variations in exchange rates and not the quality or quantity of exports.

- *Real estate values:* Real estate values have to be adjusted to current market prices.
- *Depreciation:* Allowances for equipment, plant and machinery and other real assets that depreciate over time have to be made.
- *Inflation:* Rising prices of commodities must be taken into account before assigning a value to exports.

Changes in trade statistics do not necessarily signify changes in a nation's trading patterns; the change may merely result from a change in the way the data is presented.

Foreign Currency Exchange

Foreign Exchange Market: What is it?

To buy foreign goods or services, or to invest in other countries, companies and individuals may need to first buy the currency of the country with which they are doing business. Generally, exporters prefer to be paid in their country's currency or in U.S. dollars, which are accepted all over the world.

When Canadians buy oil from Saudi Arabia they may pay in U.S. dollars and not in Canadian dollars or Saudi dinars, even though the United States is not involved in the transaction.

The **foreign exchange market,** or the "**FX**" market, is where the buying and selling of different currencies takes place. The price of one currency in terms of another is called an **exchange rate**.

The market itself is actually a worldwide network of traders, connected by telephone lines and computer screens—there is no central headquarters. There are three main centers of trading, which handle the majority of all FX transactions—United Kingdom, United States, and Japan.

Transactions in Singapore, Switzerland, Hong Kong, Germany, France and Australia account for most of the remaining transactions in the market. Trading goes on 24 hours a day: at 8 a.m. the exchange market is first opening in London, while the trading day is ending in Singapore and Hong Kong. At 1 p.m. in London, the New York market opens for business and later in the afternoon the traders in San Francisco can also conduct business. As the market closes in San Francisco, the Singapore and Hong Kong markets are starting their day.

The FX market is fast paced, volatile and enormous—it is the largest market in the world. In 2001 on average, an estimated $1,210 billion was traded each day—roughly equivalent to every person in the world trading $195 each day.

More statistics on the foreign exchange market.

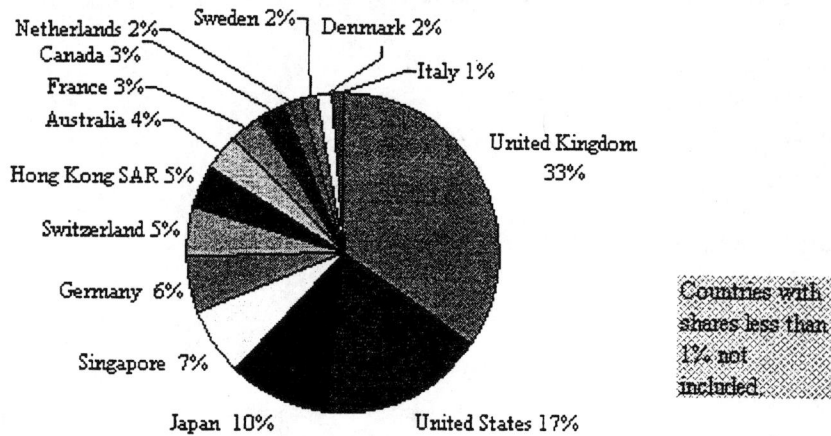

**Three Countries Dominate the Foreign Exchange Market
2001**

- Netherlands 2%
- Sweden 2%
- Denmark 2%
- Canada 3%
- Italy 1%
- France 3%
- Australia 4%
- Hong Kong SAR 5%
- Switzerland 5%
- Germany 6%
- Singapore 7%
- Japan 10%
- United States 17%
- United Kingdom 33%

Countries with shares less than 1% not included

Foreign Exchange Market Participants

There are four types of market participants—banks, brokers, customers, and central banks.

- *Banks* and other financial institutions are the biggest participants. They earn profits by buying and selling currencies from and to each other. Roughly two-thirds of all FX transactions involve banks dealing directly with each other.
- *Brokers* act as intermediaries between banks. Dealers call them to find out where they can get the best price for currencies. Such arrangements are beneficial since they afford anonymity to the buyer/seller. Brokers earn profit by charging a commission on the transactions they arrange.
- *Customers,* mainly large companies, require foreign currency in the course of doing business or making investments. Some even have their own trading desks if their requirements are large. Other types of customers are individuals who buy foreign exchange to travel abroad or make purchases in foreign countries.
- *Central banks*, which act on behalf of their governments, sometimes participate in the FX market to influence the value of their currencies.

With more than $1.2 trillion changing hands every day, the activity of these participants affects the value of every dollar, pound, yen or euro.

The participants in the FX market trade for a variety of reasons:

- to earn short-term profits from fluctuations in exchange rates,
- to protect themselves from loss due to changes in exchange rates, and
- to acquire the foreign currency necessary to buy goods and services from other countries.

Foreign Exchange Rates

Most common contact with foreign exchange occurs when we travel or buy things in other countries.

Suppose a U.S. tourist travelling in London wants to buy a sweater. Price tag is 100 pounds.

Current exchange rate   **Price of sweater in dollars**
$$100 \times 1.45 = \$145.00$$

$1.45 to £1	Pound falls	100 x 1.30 = $130.00
$1.30 to £1	Pound rises	100 x 1.60 = $160.00
$1.60 to £1		

Thus, small changes in exchange rates may not seem significant. But when billions of dollars are traded, even a hundredth of a percentage point change in exchange rates becomes important.

Stronger US dollar implies	1. U.S. can buy foreign goods more cheaply	➜	Cost of purchasing foreign goods falls
	2. Foreigners find U.S. goods more expensive and demand falls	➜	Does not help firms that produce for exports
Weaker U.S. dollar implies	1. Foreigners buy more U.S. goods	➜	Helps firms that rely on exports
	2. Foreign goods become more expensive	➜	Demand for imports falls

It would seem logical that if the dollar **weakens**, the trade balance will improve, as exports would rise. However, this does not always happen. U.S. trade balance usually worsens for a few months.

The **J–curve** explains why the trade position does not improve soon after the weakening of a currency. Most import/export orders are taken months in advance. Immediately after a currency's value drops, the volume of imports remains about the same, but the prices in terms of the home currency rise. On the other hand, the value of the domestic exports remains the same, and the difference in values worsens the trade balance until the imports and exports adjust to the new exchange rates.

Exchange rates are an important consideration when making international investment decisions. The money invested overseas incurs an exchange rate risk.

When an investor decides to "cash out," or bring his money home, any gains could be magnified or wiped out depending on the change in the exchange rates in the interim. Thus, changes in exchange rates can have many repercussions on an economy:

- affects the prices of imported goods
- affects the overall level of price and wage inflation
- influences tourism patterns
- may influence consumers' buying decisions and investors' long-term commitments.

Determination of Foreign Exchange Rates

Exchange rates respond directly to all sorts of events, both tangible and psychological—

- business cycles;
- balance of payment statistics;

- political developments;
- new tax laws;
- stock market news;
- inflationary expectations;
- international investment patterns;
- and government and central bank policies among others.

At the heart of this complex market are the same forces of demand and supply that determine the prices of goods and services in any free market. If at any given rate, the demand for a currency is greater than its supply, its price will rise. If supply exceeds demand, the price will fall.

The supply of a nation's currency is influenced by that nation's monetary authority, (usually its central bank), consistent with the amount of spending taking place in the economy. Government and central banks closely monitor economic activity to keep money supply at a level appropriate to achieve their economic goals.

Too much money → inflation → value of money declines → prices rise

Too little money → sluggish economic growth → rising unemployment

Monetary authorities must decide whether economic conditions call for a larger or smaller increase in the money supply.

Sources for currency demand on the FX market:

- The currency of a growing economy with relative price stability and a wide variety of competitive goods and services will be more in demand than that of a country in political turmoil, with high inflation and few marketable exports.
- Money will flow to wherever it can get the highest return with the least risk. If a nation's financial instruments, such as stocks and bonds, offer relatively high rates of return at relatively low risk, foreigners will demand its currency to invest in them.
- FX traders speculate within the market about how different events will move the exchange rates. For example:
    - News of political instability in other countries drives up demand for U.S. dollars as investors are looking for a "safe haven" for their money.
    - A country's interest rates rise and its currency appreciates as foreign investors seek higher returns than they can get in their own countries.
    - Developing nations undertaking successful economic reforms may experience currency appreciation as foreign investors seek new opportunities.

Foreign Currency Trading

"Yoshi, it's Maria in New York. May I have a price on twenty cable."	*Yoshi it's Maria in New York. I am interested in either buying or selling 20 million British pounds."*
"Sure. One seventy-five, twenty-thirty."	*"Sure I will buy them from you at 1.7520 dollars to each pound or sell them to you at 1.7530 dollars to each pound."*

"Mine twenty."	*"I'd like to buy them from you at 1.7530 dollars to each pound."*
"All right. At 1.7530, I sell you twenty million pounds."	*"All right. I sell you 20 million pounds at 1.7530 dollars per pound."*
"Done."	*"The deal is confirmed at 1.7530."*
"What do you think about the Japanese yen? It's up 100 pips."	*"Is there any information you can share with me about the fact that the Japanese yen has risen one-one hundredth of a yen against the U.S. dollar in the past hour?"*
"I saw that. A few German banks have been buying steadily all day...."	*"Yes, German banks have been buying the Japanese yen all day, causing the price to rise a little...."*

Traders in the foreign exchange market make thousands of trades daily, buying and selling currencies while exchanging market information. The $1.2 trillion that is traded everyday may be used for varied purposes:

- for the import and export needs of companies and individuals
- for direct foreign investment
- to profit from the short-term fluctuations in exchange rates
- to manage existing positions or
- to purchase foreign financial instruments

In the volatile FX market, traders constantly try to predict the behavior of other market participants. If they correctly anticipate their opponents' strategies, they can act first and beat the competition.

Traders make money by purchasing currency and selling it later at a higher price, or, anticipating the market is heading down, selling at a high price and buying back at a lower price later.

Trader *purchases* a lot of currency	→	*long* on the currency (e.g. long dollar, long yen)
Trader *sells* a lot of a currency	→	*short* on the currency (e.g. short sterling)

To predict the movements of currencies, traders often try to determine whether the currency's price reflects its fundamental value in terms of current economic conditions. Examining inflation, interest rates, and the relative strength of the country's economy helps them make a determination.

Currency underpriced	→	price will go *up*
Currency overpriced	→	price will go *down*

CURRENCY TRADING BETWEEN BANKS

Banks are a major force in the FX market and employ a large number of traders. Trading between banks is done in two ways—through a broker or directly with each other.

Brokers: If a U.S. bank trades with another bank, a FX broker may be used as an intermediary. The broker arranges the transaction, matching the buyer and seller without ever taking a position and charges a commission to both the buyer and seller. About a third of transactions are arranged in this way.

Direct: Mostly banks deal with each other directly. A trader "makes a market" for another by quoting a **two-way** price i.e. he is willing to buy or sell the currency. The difference between the two price quotes (the **spread**) is usually no more than 10 **pips**, or hundredths, of a currency unit.

Most currencies are quoted in terms of how many units of that currency would equal $1. However, the British pound, New Zealand dollar, Australian dollar, Irish punt and the Euro are quoted in terms of how many U.S. dollars would equal one unit of those currencies.

The currencies of the world's large, industrialized economies, or *hard currencies*, are always in demand and are actively traded. In terms of trading volumes, the FX market is dominated by four currencies: the U.S. dollar, the euro, the Japanese yen and the British pound. Together these account for over 80 percent of the market.

It is not always easy to find a market for all currencies. The demand for currencies of less developed countries, *soft currencies*, is a lot less than for the hard currencies. Weak demand internationally along with exchange controls may make these currencies difficult to convert.

Types of Transactions

There are different types of FX transactions:

I. **Spot transactions**: This type of transaction accounts for almost a third of all FX market transactions. Two parties agree on an exchange rate and trade currencies at that rate.

Spot Transaction: How it works

- A trader calls another trader and asks for a price of a currency, say British pounds.

  This expresses only a potential interest in a deal, without the caller saying whether he wants to buy or sell.

- The second trader provides the first trader with prices for both buying and selling (two-way price).
- When the traders agree to do business, one will send pounds and the other will send dollars.

  By convention the payment is actually made two days later, but next day settlements are used as well.

Although spot transactions are popular, they leave the currency buyer exposed to some potentially dangerous financial risks. Exchange rate fluctuations can effectively raise or lower prices and can be a financial planning ordeal for companies and individuals.

Exchange Risks in Spot Transactions

Suppose a U.S. company orders machine tools from a company in Japan.

- Tools will be ready in six months and will cost 120 million yen.
- At the time of the order, the yen is trading at 120 to a dollar.
- U.S. company budgets $1 million in Japanese yen to be paid when it receives the tools (120,000,00 yen ÷ 120 yen per dollar = $1,000,000)

There is no guarantee that the rate will remain the same six months later.
Suppose the **rate drops** to 100 yen per dollar:

- Cost in U.S. dollars would increase (120,000,000 ÷ 100 = $1,200,000) by $200,000.

Conversely, if the **rate goes up** to 140 yen to a dollar:

- Cost in U.S. dollars would decrease (120,000,000 ÷ 140 = $857,142.86) by over $142,000

One alternative for a company is to pay for the foreign good right away to avoid the exchange rate risk. But no one wants to part with money any sooner than necessary—if the company does pay the money in advance, it loses six months' interest and risks losing out on a favorable change in exchange rates.

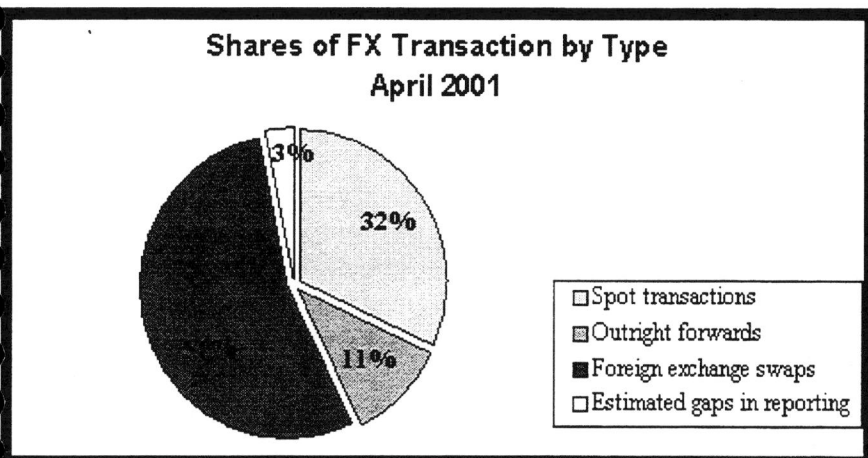

Shares of FX Transaction by Type
April 2001

- □ Spot transactions
- ▨ Outright forwards
- ■ Foreign exchange swaps
- □ Estimated gaps in reporting

3%
32%
11%

II. **Forward transaction:** One way to deal with the FX risk is to engage in a forward transaction. In this transaction, money does not actually change hands until some agreed upon future date. A buyer and seller agree on an exchange rate for any date in the future and the transaction occurs on that date, regardless of what the market rates are then. The date can be a few days, months or years in the future.

- *Futures*: Foreign currency futures are forward transactions with standard contract sizes and maturity dates — for example, 500,000 British pounds for next November at an agreed rate. These contracts are traded on a separate exchange set up for that purpose.

- *Swap*: The most common type of forward transaction is the currency swap. In a swap, two parties exchange currencies for a certain length of time and agree to reverse the transaction at a later date.

In all of these transactions, market rates might change. However, the buyer and seller are locked into a contract at a fixed price that cannot be affected by any changes in the market rates. These tools allow the market participants to plan more safely, since they know in advance what their FX will cost. It also allows them to avoid an immediate outlay of cash.

Swap Transaction: How it works

Suppose a U.S. company needs 15 million Japanese yen for a three-month investment in Japan.

- It may agree to a rate of 150 yen to a dollar and swap $100,000 with a company willing to swap 15 million yen for three months.

- After three months, the U.S. company returns the 15 million yen to the other company and gets back $100,000, with adjustments made for interest rate differentials

III. **Options**: To address the lack of flexibility in forward transactions, the foreign currency option was developed. An option is similar to a forward transaction. It gives its owner the right to buy or sell a specified amount of foreign currency at a specified price at any time up to a specified expiration date.

For a price, a market participant can buy the right, but not the obligation, to buy or sell a currency at a fixed price on or before an agreed upon future date. The agreed upon price is called the *strike price*.

Depending on which—the option rate or the current market rate—is more favorable, the owner may exercise the option or let the option lapse, choosing instead to buy/sell currency in the market. This type of transaction allows the owner more flexibility than a swap or futures contract.

Option to **buy** currency   ➔   **Call option**

Option to **sell** currency   ➔   **Put option**

Get more information of different types of FX transactions.

Option: How it works

Suppose a trader purchases a six-month call on one million euros at 0.88 U.S. dollars to a euro.

- During the six months the trader can either purchase the euros at the 0.88 rate, or purchase them at the market rate.
- Option can be sold and resold many times before the expiration date.
- Options serve as an insurance policy against the market moving in an unfavorable direction.

Floating and Fixed Exchange Rates

The FX market was not always quick to respond to changing events. For most of the 20th century, the exchange rates were **fixed**, or kept constant, according to the amount of gold for which they could be exchanged. This was called the **gold-exchange standard**.

Gold-Exchange Standard

Under this system, the value of all currencies was fixed in terms of how much gold for which they could be exchanged.

For example, if one ounce of gold was worth 12 British pounds or 35 U.S. dollars, the exchange rate between dollars and pounds would remain constant at just under three to one.

There were many advantages of the gold-exchange system:

- It served as a common measure of value.
- It helped keep inflation in check by keeping money supply in the gold-exchange standard economies fairly stable.
- Long-term planning was easier as rate changes were infrequent.

This system was put in place in 1944, when the leaders of allied nations met at **Bretton Woods**, New Hampshire, to set up a stable economic structure out of the chaos of World War II. The U.S. dollar was fixed at $35 per ounce of gold and all other currencies were expressed in terms of dollars.

The Bretton Woods system began to weaken in the 1960s, when foreigners accumulated large amounts of U.S. dollars from post World War II aid and sales of their exports in the United States. There were concerns as to whether the U.S. had enough gold to redeem all the dollars.

With reserves of gold falling steadily, the situation could not be sustained and the U.S. decided to abandon this system. In 1971, President Nixon announced that U.S. dollars would no longer be convertible into gold. By 1973, this action led to the system of floating exchange rates that exist today. Currently, currencies rise and fall in value according to the forces of demand and supply.

After the abandonment of the gold-exchange standard, the foreign exchange market went from a relatively unimportant financial specialty to the forefront of international economics.

Under another system, the **gold standard**, U.S. households and businesses could exchange their dollars for gold. This practice was abandoned in 1933 during the Great Depression to allow freer expansion of money supply. However, foreign governments were still able to exchange their dollars for gold until 1971, when the United States terminated the gold-exchange standard entirely.

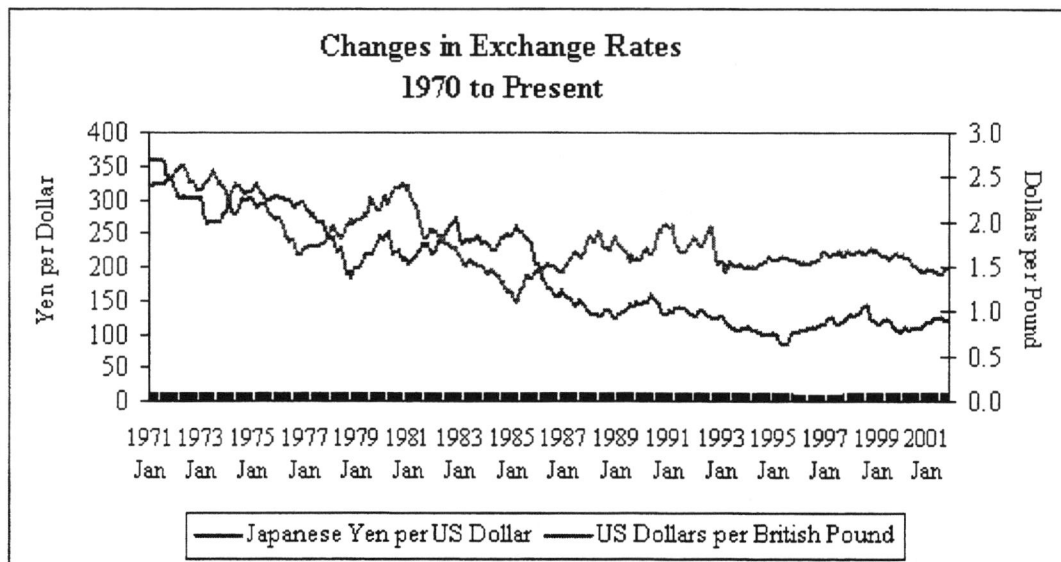

Changes in Exchange Rates 1970 to Present

Japanese Yen per US Dollar ──── US Dollars per British Pound

Role of Central Banks

Despite the size and importance of the foreign exchange market, it remains largely unregulated. There is no international organization that supervises it, nor any institution that sets rules. However, since the advent of the flexible exchange rate system in 1973, governments and central banks, such as the Federal Reserve System in the United States, occasionally intervene to maintain stability in the FX market.

There is no standard definition of instability or a disorderly market—circumstance must be evaluated on a case-by-case basis. Sharp rapid fluctuations of exchange rates and traders' reluctance to be ready to either buy or sell currencies (maintaining a "two-way" market) may be signs of disorderly market.

To restore stability, the central banks often work together. However, a country taking a conservative view on intervention would act only in response to unusual circumstances that require immediate action, like political unrest or natural disasters. Most monetary authorities would be less likely to intervene to counteract the fundamental forces that drive FX markets, such as trade patterns, interest rate differentials and capital flows.

Intervention

The U.S. Treasury has the overall responsibility for managing the U.S. government's foreign currency holdings. It works closely with the Federal Reserve to regulate the dollar's position in the FX markets. If the Treasury feels that there is a need to weaken or strengthen the dollar, it instructs the Federal Reserve Bank of New York to intervene in the FX market as Treasury's agent.

The Federal Reserve Bank of New York buys dollars and sells foreign currency to support the value of the dollar. The Fed also sells dollars and buys foreign currency to try and exert downward pressure on the price of the dollar.

The transactions in the intervention are small compared to the total volume of trading in the FX market and these actions do not shift the balance of supply and demand immediately. Instead, intervention is used as a device to signal a desired exchange rate movement and affect the behavior of investors in the FX market.

The frequency of intervention in the FX markets by the U.S. monetary authorities has reduced tremendously over the last decade. The Federal Reserve Bank of New York intervened only once since 1995.

Central banks in other countries have similar concerns about their currencies and sometimes intervene in the FX markets as well. Usually, intervention operations are undertaken in coordination with other central banks.

Most of the Federal Reserve Bank of New York's activities in the foreign exchange market are for far less dramatic purposes than to influence exchange rates. The New York Fed often intervenes in the FX market as an agent for other central banks and international organizations to execute transactions related to flows of international capital.

Learn more about the Federal Reserve Bank's role in the FX market.

Some countries have special arrangements with other countries to help them keep their currencies stable. Many less developed countries have their soft currencies pegged to hard currencies, so their value rises and falls simultaneously with the stronger currency. Some peg, or target, their currency to a basket of hard currencies, the average of a group of selected currencies.

Countries that are part of the European Union (EU) had pegged their currencies to the euro. There were formulas set for converting from the euro to the currency of each member nation. However, since January 2002, all currencies that were part of the Economic and Monetary System of the EU ceased to exist.

Intervention in the FX market is not the only way monetary authorities can affect the value of their countries' currencies. Central banks can also affect foreign exchange rates indirectly by influencing interest rates.

Higher interest rates ➔ Value of currency goes up ➔ Investors want to buy currency to invest at high rates

| German interest rate | U.S. interest rate | ➔ | Demand for German mark goes up |
| 8% | 3% | | |

Concerns about Eurocurrency

An important side effect of the increase of international economic activity over the past few decades has been the creation and growth of the **Eurocurrency market**. This is the name given to any bank deposits in any country held in a different country's currency, like U.S. dollars in a British bank. A great deal of foreign exchange market activity involves the transfer of Eurocurrency deposits.

Eurocurrency, especially eurodollars (approximately two-thirds of Eurocurrency are U.S. dollars) are a source of concern to central banks and regulators because they are "stateless money"—subject to very little regulation. Rules governing currency and bank deposits— such as taxes, restrictions on capital movements and exchange controls—do not apply to the currency in the Eurocurrency markets.

Banks around the world use the Eurocurrency market to move and store funds more profitably than they could in many countries. This poses a problem for countries attempting to regulate capital flows.

International trade and foreign exchange cannot be viewed as two separate economic processes. The two are intimately connected on many levels. Increased trade and investment has brought the FX markets to their present level. Together, trade and foreign exchange affect peoples' living standards and livelihoods all over the world.

Working across Borders

Many large companies are "multinational" in that they have branches and subsidiaries all over the world. By some estimates, intra-firm trade, or trade between branches of the same company in different countries, accounts for 40 percent of U.S. exports.

Many companies buy and sell goods overseas and others form partnerships with foreign companies so that cooperation replaces competition. This has a profound effect on how companies operate in the global marketplace. Businesses around the world work side-by-side to produce and market products, thereby reducing the economic risks of global production and marketing.

For instance, there may be a running shoe company:

- headquartered in the United States,
- financed by a Japanese bank,
- buying rubber from Indonesia and leather from Spain,
- manufacturing in Mexico,
- employing a U.S. company for the legal and accounting work,
- and a British firm to handle all its advertising and marketing.

Multinational companies shift resources from one country to another to maximize profits and productivity.

The running shoes may be sold all over the world. If a shoe is shipped from

San Francisco to Indonesia, it is simply a U.S. export. However, if Indonesia imposes a tariff on the shoe, it harms more than just the U.S. exporter; all businesses around the world that were involved in the process are affected, including Indonesia's own rubber exports. With globalization, it is increasingly difficult for governments to target trade policies effectively.

To remain competitive, individuals, companies, and governments all must adapt to the changing global marketplace.

Business practices vary from country to country and may require new approaches to making profits. In the United States, a signed contract is considered all but sacrosanct; in the Far East, southern Europe and the Middle East, the spirit of the agreement can sometimes matter more than the letter.

The "get down to business" approach that the U.S. and German businesses usually favor may be considered brusque or harsh in Japan or Korea. Even small details of business behavior—whether or not to look someone in the eye, tone of voice, exchange of gifts—vary significantly from country to country.

International Organizations and Trade Issues

As trade becomes more and more important to economic well being, international organizations have been formed to facilitate cooperation on trade issues.

The **World Trade Organization** (WTO), established on January 1, 1995, is the only global international organization dealing with the rules of trade between nations. It was created by the Uruguay Round of negotiations over a 14-year period and has 144 member countries (as of January 2002).

At the heart of the WTO are the various agreements, negotiated and signed by the bulk of the world's trading nations and ratified in their parliaments. These agreements cover a range of topics:

- reductions in tariffs;
- fairer competition in agricultural trade;
- textiles trade;
- trade in services;
- protection and enforcement of intellectual property;
- issues related to anti-dumping, export subsidies, and safeguards; and
- other non-tariff barriers.

The goal of the WTO is to help producers of goods and services, exporters, and importers conduct their business. The agreements have three main objectives:

- to help trade flow as freely as possible,
- to achieve further liberalization gradually through negotiation, and
- to set up an impartial means of settling disputes.

To learn more about the activities of the WTO.

Another organization, the **International Monetary Fund** (IMF), was founded at the United Nations Monetary and Financial Conference at Bretton Woods in 1944. The IMF is an international organization of 183 member countries, established to:

- promote international monetary cooperation, exchange stability, and orderly exchange arrangements;
- facilitate the expansion and balanced growth of international trade,;
- foster economic growth and high levels of employment; and
- provide temporary financial assistance to countries to help ease balance of payments adjustment.

The purpose of the IMF has remained unchanged but its operations — which involve surveillance, financial assistance, and technical assistance — have developed to meet the changing needs of its member countries in an evolving world economy. Lean more about the IMF.

A related organization, the **World Bank**, was founded in 1944 with the primary focus of helping the poorest people and the poorest countries. Its mission is to fight poverty for lasting results and to help people help themselves and their environment by providing resources, sharing knowledge, building capacity, and forging partnerships in the public and private sectors. Learn more about the World Bank.

The **Bank for International Settlements** (BIS) in Basel, Switzerland, is an international organization that fosters cooperation among central banks and other agencies in pursuit of monetary and financial stability.

The BIS functions as:

- a forum for international monetary and financial cooperation;

- a bank for central banks, providing a broad range of financial services;

- a center for monetary and economic research, contributing to a better understanding of international financial markets and the interaction of national monetary and financial policies; and

- an agent or trustee, facilitating the implementation of various international financial agreements.

The Basel Committee on International Banking Supervision, a committee of the BIS that consists of representatives of some of the world's largest countries, meets to establish uniform financial and performance guidelines for commercial banks around the world. Learn more about the working of the BIS.

The **Group of Seven**, or G7, was created in 1975 with the objective of setting up a forum, at the highest decisional level and having formalities reduced to a minimum, in which to discuss important macroeconomic and monetary issues. The group was established with the intent of filling the gap created in the management of the monetary system following the breakdown of the Bretten Woods agreement in 1971.

The G-7 consists of the leaders of the United States, Germany, Japan, France, Great Britain, Canada, and Italy. The Birmingham Summit in 1998 marked Russia's official entry in the Group and the creation of the **G8**. Among other things the Group discusses

- economic issues
- trade relations
- foreign exchange markets

While economic issues still dominate the G8 meetings, discussions on environmental issues and arms control have been included in recent years. Learn more about G7.

A major change in the economic structures in recent years has been the creation of the **European Union** (EU). It is the result of a process of cooperation and integration that began in 1951 between six countries (Belgium, Germany, France,

Italy, Luxembourg and the Netherlands).

After nearly fifty years, and four waves of accessions, the EU today has fifteen Member States.

One of the main objectives of the EU is to promote economic and social progress. Towards this end, Member States established the single market in 1993 and the single currency was launched in 1999. The completion of the EU's internal "single market" boosted intra-EU trade, which represents two-thirds of the total EU Member States' trade.

Suppliers of goods, services and investment from outside the EU have benefited from the single market program, just as much as people and companies within the EU. The EU has been busy consolidating its single market. Traders at home and overseas can market their goods in the EU based on one set of rules. The single market experience may include valuable elements for the multilateral system of the future. Learn more about the European common market.

Other nations have moved to build free-trade zones and common markets as well. Under the **North American Free Trade Agreement** (NAFTA), the United States, Canada and Mexico have agreed to eliminate barriers to trade and to facilitate the cross-border movement of goods and services. The agreement also aims to promote conditions of fair competition in the free trade area and to substantially increase investment opportunities. Learn more about NAFTA.

Many smaller "**trade blocs**" are developing all over the world, in North Africa, South East Asia, different parts of Latin America, Eastern Europe and the Middle East. Over the last 50 years more than 100 regional economic agreements have been created.

A **trade bloc** refers to a regional arrangement among countries that have established formal mechanisms for cooperation on trade issues. The term does not necessarily imply a protectionist stance with respect to nonmember countries, although it is sometimes used in this way.

Trade blocs commonly include six types of arrangements: *economic union, common market, customs union, free trade area, preferential arrangement,* and *regional cooperation organization.*

A possible problem is that competing trade blocs will adopt protectionist policies and slow worldwide economic growth by restricting trade among groups of nations. However, rapid proliferation of trade blocs and free-trade zones has occurred because countries want the benefits of increased trade that accompany lower trade barriers.

The WTO has created a committee to study regional groups and to assess whether they are consistent with WTO rules. The committee is also examining how regional arrangements might affect the multilateral trading system, and what kind of relationship they might have.

Useful Web Links

U.S. related:
U.S. Department of Treasury: Capital Movements Bulletin:
   http://www.fms.treas.gov/bulletin/b21cm.pdf
U.S. Department of Commerce: Export Portal:
   http://www.export.gov/docTSFrameset.html
White House: Economic Statistics Briefing Room:
   http://www.whitehouse.gov/fsbr/international.html
Census Bureau: Foreign Trade Statistics:

http://www.census.gov/
http://www.census.gov/foreign-trade/www/
Bureau of Economic Analysis:
http://www.bea.doc.gov/bea/di1.htm
Federal Reserve Board: Research and Data:
http://www.federalreserve.gov/rnd.htm
Federal Reserve Board: Flow of Funds Data:
http://www.federalreserve.gov/releases/Z1/Current/Coded/coded.pdf

International Sites:
World Bank:
http://www.worldbank.org/
http://www1.worldbank.org/wbiep/trade/services_data.htm#Flows
Bank of International Settlements:
http://www.bis.org/
European Union:
http://europa.eu.int/index_en.htm
G-7 Home page:
http://www.g7-2001.org/en/frames_c.htm
OECD National Accounts:
http://www.oecd.org/std/nahome.htm
World Trade Organization:
http://www.wto.org/
http://www.wto.org/english/res_e/statis_e/technotes_e.htm
General Agreement on Trade and Tariff (GATT):
http://gatt.org/
North American Free Trade Agreement (NAFTA):
http://www.nafta-sec-alena.org/
International Monetary Fund:
http://www.imf.org/
International Finance Corporation:
http://www.ifc.org/

Chapter Eight
L. D. C. Economies

1. The Concepts

L.D.C.s, less developed countries, are common extemp topic arenas. Their economic problems almost always overlap with intriguing political situations. An occasional nuclear disadvantage link will also stem from this area. But how do less developed countries differ from developing countries? How can you differentiate developing countries from developed countries?

It will help your analysis if you compare national economies *two* ways: how developed the economy is now, and what its potential is. The United States, for example, is number one in the world in terms of where our economy is now, but Russia is number one in potential. The United States has done a great job of maximizing the resources it has, but our resources are no match for Russia. Russia has more rare minerals, natural gas and gold deposits than any other nation in the world. It is number two in oil reserves. Some key parts of its infrastructure are excellent. Russia's current per-capita income is very low, but its potential is immense. So how do we categorize such disparate economies?

There are various labels that can help your speech and analysis. Countries can be described as **north-south**, **resource rich** verses barren, **first-second-third** and **fourth world**, or with an adjective proceeding or surrounding developed (e.g. **un**developed, **under**developed, develop**ing**, or as in the chapter title **less** developed). Each option gives you a slight but sometimes important different meaning.

The "north" in north-south means the developed economically dominant nations in the world. Most are in the northern hemisphere. Underdeveloped and poor countries are often in the south of continents or in the southern hemisphere. Resource rich countries are not always developed, but they always have the potential. The Union of South Africa, Russia and the United States are good examples of resource rich countries.

First, second, third and fourth world are labels that combine potential and actual development. The **first world** is economically developed countries (United States, Japan, Germany, Switzerland, etc.); **second world nations** are developing but not yet rich enough to be called fully developed (Mexico, Brazil, India, China, and so forth). **The third world** is undeveloped but has the resources to become developed if it can combine the right economic and governmental policies (e.g. Congo, Burma or Myanmar, Cuba, etc.). **The fourth world** is composed of those countries that lack the resources to ever become rich and prosperous even if they are lucky enough to get good governments. Bangladesh, Mali, Mauritania, and East Timor probably fit in this last category.

Most LDCs share many or all of the following lamentable characteristics: high poverty rate, excessive agricultural dependence, unequal income distribution (**the rich-poor gap**), and excessive population growth. The harms of rapidly rising population have been explored since Thomas Robert Malthus (1766-1834) wrote his *Essay on Population*. Malthus postulated that the population of the world was rising so rapidly that we would soon outrun our food supply and have massive starvation. He was wrong because he forgot to factor in agricultural technology and scientific advancements. Developed countries also avoided famine because prosperity brings very sharp drops in the birth rate. Modern Malthus disciples, such as Prof. Paul Ehrlich of Stanford University, still proclaim that doom is coming. They write of water shortages, regional famines, pollution and death. In the third and fourth worlds these warnings sometimes come true.

Assuming that the undeveloped or underdeveloped nation is third world, and thus has the resources to become developed, governmental error is probably delaying the right moves. The most common mistakes and problems are (1) diverting too much budget to the military, (2) bribery, (3) corruption, (4) excessive debt, (5) nationalizing industries, (6) inattention to AIDs, (7) under funding infrastructure improvements, and (8) adopting those banking and taxation policies that are responsible for creating an **underground economy**.

Solutions are obvious (e.g. stop taking bribes) but other than waving the extemper's magic wand how are they to be accomplished? Putting solutions together and then keeping in place the right amount of time is challenging. Most importantly it takes or is greatly aided by prolonged quality leadership with non-dictatorial but nevertheless extensive powers (similar to DeGaulle's powers in 1960 France). Regrettably most LDC leaders are "in it" for power and ego, or are corrupted by easy money and the lure of profitable bribery.

If an LDC is lucky enough to get good leadership many steps need to be taken. Some of the steps are unique to the individual country. But many apply to almost every underdeveloped nation. An incomplete but useful list includes (1) promoting **joint ventures** so that the host government gets new industry, new jobs, and modest access to or increased on-the-job training guarantees, (2) cutting defense spending and redirecting the money into education and other infrastructure investments, promoting political stability, **human capital** development via training programs and schools is especially important, (3) increasing political stability by respecting term limits and enforcing all parts of the constitution, (4) dramatically increasing **police and judicial salaries** so that they value their jobs too much to take bribes or tolerate internal corruption, (5) promote constitutional revision to assure that the judiciary is independent of the executive and the legislature, (6) focus government sponsored new business development on **labor intensive industry**, (7) stop **import substitution policies**, (8) take advantage of the **green revolution** (the use of fertilizers, new seed varieties, rotation, and other tools to dramatically increase crop production), (9) massive diverse promotion of **population control** (birth control pills, free condoms, subsidies to vasectomies, abstinence advertising), and to fund it all (1) lobby to obtain the maximum amount of aid from the World Bank, donor countries (the E.U., United States, Japan), regional development banks, the United Nations, the Peace Corps, charities and foundations.

Underdeveloped nations cannot or should not focus on a random mixture of business investments and opportunities. Some businesses will help an LDC much more than others. An exploitative hardwood tree-stripping multinational is not as good a joint venture as is a textile manufacturing plant. The criteria for businesses should include job creation and human capital development. Arguments against a firm should give a high priority to **environmental degradation**. Countries that have made the successful LDC to developed transformation usually (but not invariably) start by taking advantage of its raw resources, evolving to the promotion of labor intensive industry, then to an expansion of heavy manufacturing, and finally high technology development and production. Starting as a net capital importer when underdeveloped most developed countries become capital exporters.

2. Sample Extemp Topics

How can LDCs improve their economic status without sacrificing their environment?
How can Sudan (or Mali or Mauritania or Bolivia or…) better promote economic growth?
Do north-south tensions signal a growing worldwide economic division?

3.   Sample Web Sites

- The World Bank (http://www.worldbank.org/) maintains economic data (http://www.worldbank.org/html/extdr/country.htm) on the regions and countries of the world. The World Factbook (http://www.odci.gov/cia/publications/nsolo/wfb-all.htm) maintains region—and country—specific economic, political, and cultural profiles.
- Visit the Agency for International Development (http://www.info.usaid.gov/), part of the Department of State (http://www.state.org/)
- PRAXIS: Resources for Social and Economic (http://caster.ssw.upenn.edu/~restes/praxis.html) PRAXIS provides a library of links to resources on international and comparative social development.
- World Bank (http://www.worldbank.org/) The World Bank Provides news, publications, and country and regional economic reports.
- Economic Development Institute of the World Bank (http://www.worldbank.org/html/edi/home.html) The Economic Development Institute promotes awareness of development strategies through publications and educational incentives.
- Visit NetDay (http://www.netday.org/) to review data for Internet access in Africa (http://demiurge.wn.apc.org/africa/). Africa Online provides Internet information for Africa (http://www.africaonline.com/).
- The Bureau of African Affairs (http://www.state.gov/www/regions/africa/index.html), part of the State Department, provides data and information about Africa. Africa.com (http://www.africa.com/) and Africa Online (http://www.africaonline.com/) also offer news, information, and resources about Africa.

4.   If you want to read more…

DEVELOPING NATIONS

4

STUDENT OBJECTIVES

Students will be able to demonstrate an understanding of the economic challenges facing developing nations

Students will be able to compare and contrast the views of developing and industrialized nations on significant global economic issues

Students will be able to demonstrate an understanding of the significance of global economic interdependence

TAKING ADVANTAGE OF GLOBALIZATION

As the new millennium begins, developing countries face the challenge of how to reap the benefits of globalization. Countries that succeed will derive significant benefits—improved living standards, lower unemployment, faster growth, and expanded trade. Nations that struggle to keep up will fall further behind.

Most developing nations face daunting obstacles as they attempt to compete in the global marketplace. An obvious problem in many developing countries is the low level of income. While the per capita output of the United States economy is about $30,000, in some countries the figure is only about 1% of that.

Many other problems, such as poor health and illiteracy, often go hand in hand with low per capita income. The World Bank reports, for example, that while life expectancy at birth was seventy-nine years for a female born in the United States in 1997 (and even longer for those born in a number of other countries, including Canada, Japan, and Norway), it was only about one-half as long in countries such as Sierra Leone and Uganda. (An excellent source for data on these socioeconomic indicators is *Entering the 21st Century: World Development Report 1999-2000*, published by the World Bank.) More than half the children under age five in countries such as Bangladesh and India suffer from malnutrition, compared with 1% in the United States. Moreover, in many countries the adult illiteracy rate is more than 50%.

In addition, labor productivity is low, not only because of low education levels, but also because of a low level of capital investment. For example, according to the World Bank, the United States has more than 1,400 tractors per 1,000 agricultural workers; in many countries around the world, the figure is zero or one per 1,000 farm workers. Because of low productivity levels, many countries employ the majority of their labor forces in agriculture—that is, it takes more than half the labor force just to produce the country's food. In contrast, less than 3% of the U.S. labor force works in agriculture—the remaining 97% can produce non-food goods and services.

Clearly, two major priorities for developing countries are to improve people's education and skills and to increase the level of capital investment. In these efforts, however, the countries run into a host of "the poor get poorer" hurdles. For example, there is the problem of the *brain drain*—what happens if some of the country's brightest young people, sent abroad to a college or university, find the higher standard of living abroad too attractive to resist and decide not to return home? Also, where will the savings needed to finance investment come from if the people need to consume their entire income merely to subsist?

CHANGING A CULTURE

Samuelson and Nordhaus (on page 544 of the 16th edition of *Economics*) identify another major need of the developing countries, one less tangible than those described above: "One of the key tasks of economic development is the fostering of an entrepreneurial spirit. A country cannot thrive without a group of owners or managers willing to undertake risks, open new plants, adopt new technologies, confront strife, and import new ways of doing business."

WEB RESOURCES

Information on matters related to developing nations may be found at the following sites:

www.worldbank.org

This is the official site of the World Bank, whose goal is to fight world poverty by helping people help themselves and their environment by providing resources, sharing knowledge, building capacity, and forging partnerships in the public and private sectors. It contains four sections: *The Bank at Work,* which gives information about the Bank and the status of current projects; *Resources,* which provides current data, reports, a list of publications, and suggested teaching ideas; *Partners,* which highlights some of the work of the World Bank's partner organizations; and *Development News Features,* which covers topics of special interest.

www.oneworld.org

By combining the resources of hundreds of development organizations, One World offers diverse perspectives on various development topics. Its focus is on covering current news headlines, by offering editorials, dispatches, and regional outlook pieces. It also emphasizes interactivity, through chat rooms and radio, to give voice to people who ordinarily would not have the opportunity to express themselves.

www.ita.doc.gov/bems/index.html

The U.S. Department of Commerce operates this site, dedicated to emerging market nations. Among the nations featured are Brazil, China, India, and South Africa. The site provides an economic overview of each nation, information about the nation's trade policies, data about the nation's economy, and links to other sites covering big emerging market nations.

Obviously, the government must play a major role in helping an economy develop. Because of the existence of what economists call *externalities*—when someone gets educated or inoculated against a disease, it's not just the person receiving the service who benefits—the government must take the lead in creating programs to improve the country's human resources. The government must take the lead, too, in building the country's infrastructure, such as an efficient road system.

One advantage that poor nations today have, and that countries that developed earlier did not, is that modern technology is now available, albeit in other countries. Moreover, as Samuelson and Nordhaus show (page 546), there have been some major development success stories in recent years: "A generation ago, countries like Taiwan, South Korea, and Singapore had per capita incomes one-quarter to one-third of those in the wealthiest Latin American countries. Yet, by saving large fractions of their national incomes and channeling these to high-return export industries, (these Asian countries) overtook every Latin American country by the late 1980s."

ACTIVITY OVERVIEW

Students will become familiar with key economic issues confronting developing nations in their relation-ships with the industrialized world. They will be able to support or argue against differing points of view on the issues.

TEACHING STRATEGY

In this activity, students will role-play delegates from highly industrialized and developing nations attend-ing a Global Economic Summit conference.

Handout Exercises

. Assign one student to be the chairperson, and two or three students to each of the following nations: Angola, Bolivia, Canada, Ethiopia, France, Germany, Italy, Japan, Myanmar, Nicaragua, the United Kingdom, the United States, Vietnam, and Yemen. In order to become familiar with their country, have students complete the activity for Handout 4B, *Summit Nation Profile*, page 45, based on the following web site:

www.odci.gov/cia/publications/factbook/indexgeo.html.

Discuss with students their responsibilities, the summit resolutions, and agenda. In order to become familiar with the issues in the summit, have students refer to the following web sites:

The Free Trade Debate
www.rich.frb.org/equilibria/issue3/otoh.html
www.globalissues.org/TradeRelated/FreeTrade/ProtectOrRegulate.asp

Forgiving World Debt
news.bbc.co.uk/hi/english/special_report/1999/06/99/debt/newsid_353000/353608.stm
www.globalissues.org/TradeRelated/Debt.asp?Print=True

Development and the Environment
www.harvardchina.org/magazine/article/environment.html
www.oneworld.org/ips2/mar98/economy.html

4 A GLOBAL ECONOMIC SUMMIT

In this activity, you will participate in a GLOBAL ECONOMIC SUMMIT conference, playing the roles of delegates, from one of the following highly industrialized or developing nations: Angola, Bolivia, Canada, Ethiopia, France, Germany, Italy, Japan, Myanmar, Nicaragua, the United Kingdom, the United States, Vietnam, and Yemen.

The summit has been called to debate and vote on these resolutions:

1. ALL BARRIERS TO FREE TRADE BETWEEN NATIONS (E.G., TARIFFS)
SHOULD BE ELIMINATED.

2. THE WORLD'S WEALTHIEST NATIONS SHOULD FORGIVE
ALL THE DEBT OWED THEM BY THE WORLD'S POOREST COUNTRIES.

3. A NATION SHOULD BE ALLOWED TO TAKE ALL NECESSARY STEPS TO
DEVELOP ITS INDUSTRIES, EVEN IF THEY HARM THE ENVIRONMENT.

AGENDA

The chairperson will conduct the summit according to the following agenda:

☐ Call to order.

☐ One member of each delegation will present an overview of his or her nation's economy, briefly discussing the nation's greatest economic strengths and challenges.

☐ *Discussion of Resolution 1.*
A spokesperson from each delegation should present his or her nation's position on the resolution.

☐ *Vote on Resolution 1.* Each delegation shall have one vote.

☐ *Discussion of Resolution 2.*
A spokesperson from each delegation should present his or her nation's position on the resolution.

☐ *Vote on Resolution 2.* Each delegation shall have one vote.

☐ *Discussion of Resolution 3.*
A spokesperson from each delegation should present his or her nation's position on the resolution.

☐ *Vote on Resolution 3.* Each delegation shall have one vote.

ACTIVITY OVERVIEW

Students will draw conclusions about how developing and industrialized nations view key global economic issues.

TEACHING STRATEGY

In this activity, the teacher will debrief the Global Economic Summit and lead a discussion on key global economic issues facing developing nations.

Debriefing the Global Economic Summit – *after completing the Global Economic Summit*

Debrief the Global Economic Summit by asking students to explain their answers to the following questions:

- What did you learn about the importance of the three issues (free trade, debt forgiveness, and the effects of economic development on the environment) discussed at our summit to the developing nations?
- Which of the three issues did you find most interesting to discuss?
- To what extent did the world's developing nations agree with the world's highly industrialized nations on the three issues? To what extent did the two groups disagree on these issues?
- What were the most important arguments presented for ending all barriers to free trade? What were the most important arguments presented against a free-trade policy? Which side presented the stronger case?
- What were the most important arguments presented for forgiving the debt owed by the world's poorest nations? What were the most important arguments presented against forgiving the debt owed by the world's poorest nations? Which side presented the stronger case?
- What were the most important arguments presented for allowing a developing nation to take all necessary steps to develop its industry, even if the steps harm the environment? What were the most important arguments presented against allowing a developing nation to take all necessary steps to develop its industry, even if the steps harm the environment? Which side presented the stronger case?
- To what extent do you believe that developing nations should be responsible for solving their own problems? To what extent do you believe that the highly industrialized nations should be responsible for solving the problems of the world's poorest nations?
- In what ways can the highly industrialized nations best support developing economies' efforts to improve standards of living?

4B SUMMIT NATION PROFILE

Go to www.odci.gov/cia/publications/factbook/indexgeo.html. Click on your
country. Then click on Economy. Based on what you find on the web site, complete
the exercise below.

**[1] Summarize the information in the section labeled Economy–overview, highlighting the
country's economic strengths, weaknesses, and recent economic history.**

_____

_____

_____

_____

_____

**[2] Complete the chart below, first providing the data for your country with the information
found on the web site. Then, for purposes of comparison, find the same data for the United
States.**

Category	Your Country	United States

**3. Based on what you have learned so far about the country you were assigned, state two
conclusions about its greatest economic challenges.**

(i)_____

_____

_____

(ii)_____

_____

_____

Chapter Nine
The Stock Market

1. The Concepts

Debaters run bond disadvantages and business confidence disadvantages on many topics. Extempers often draw business related topics, questions on the effects of tax policy changes, corporate honesty, or even choices that directly ask about the stock market. So it is important to know about this issue.

The most challenging things about "the market" are not the concepts behind it, but the vocabulary that surrounds it. Stocks and bond themselves are quite simple. A **stock** is one share, one small part in the ownership of a business. If you buy or sell stocks you are buying or selling partial ownership of a corporation. A **bond** is a loan. If you buy a bond you are lending the cost you pay for the bond to the company that issued it. In return they promise to pay you back in a pre-announced period of time, and pay you a set interest rate on the bond principle until the bond is **redeemed** or "**reaches maturity**".

The stock market is really a variety of places where stocks can be bought and sold. In the United States the biggest are the New York Stock Exchange and the NASDAQ. Every major European country has one and Japan has the NISEI. Many stocks are listed on more than one market.

The fun and pain both come from decisions on which stocks to buy, and when to sell. As these decisions are repeated tens of thousands of time daily they affect business stability, ability to buy capital goods, the ease or difficulty of promoting company growth, and the health of the *national* economy. Business growth almost always determines unemployment rates and GDP figures. Growth, or the lack of it, is tied directly to the health of the stock market. If a company can sell bonds at low interest it has more money to expand with. If corporate stock is selling at a high price the **board of directors**, the **CEO** (the Chief Executive Officer), and the **CFO** (the Chief Financial Officer) can take advantage of it by selling stock still held by the corporation and using it to expand.

The **SEC**, the Securities and Exchange Commission, is in charge of keeping accounting honest, business records honest, and making sure the public is informed. A semiautonomous government agency sometimes accused of being captured by the vary entities its charged with controlling the SEC has useful but limited powers. Until 2002 most corporate ethical lapses resulted only in fines (albeit some of the fines are huge). Corporate executive responsibility improved some that year when some laws were modified to allow prison time for executives who cheated. These ethical violations are the stuff of legend, and certainly the thing that eats at **consumer confidence**. The fraudulent railroad stock offerings of the late nineteenth century ruined many investors. The Teapot Dome scandal of the 1920s helped bring down the Harding Administration. Charges of insider stock trading at Martha Stewart, Enron and Arthur Anderson combining to claim transactions through dummy corporations, and blatant bookkeeping fraud at WorldCom contributed to a stock market collapse in 2002 and put the economy at great risk. In corporate America what business and the stock market does effects the entire economy.

A **bull market** is charging, it has rising prices and an aggressive confident attitude. During a bull market investors are more likely to **buy on margin** (pay only part of the cost of the stock, using the value of the stock to take a short term-loan from their broker to cover the difference). A sudden downturn in the market risks a **market call,** which means that the rest of the purchase price must now be paid. A **bear market** sees falling prices and nervous investors. Since the stock market is a **lead**

indicator investors have proven they know what they're doing, the direction of the market usually tells us the direction the economy will he heading three to six months from now.

What determines if a stock is a "good buy"? Many, many factors. And most people agree what the factors are. They just do not agree which are the most important, which the least. Factors considered include **return on equity** (equity is the residual value of a business after deducting mortgage and debts), **cash flow** (how much money comes in each month), **debt level**, **market share** (what percentage of the product sold is sold by this company, e.g. if Coke has a 27% market share then out of every 100 cans of pop sold 27 will be Coke products), **growth potential**, **management quality**, **brand identification** (how well known your product[s] is by name, e.g. Kellogg's Corn Flakes has good name recognition while Buster's Flakes does not), **patent protection**, and **entry cost** (the more it costs for new companies to start production the less likely new companies will enter, e.g. Boeing Aircraft has great protection while Kellogg's Cereals does not).

2. ___ An Introduction To Investing

STOCKS

Stocks are essentially shares of a particular company. If you are a stockholder of a company, you have ownership of that corporation. When stock is initially issued by a company, that company makes the money from that initial offering. Afterwards, stocks are traded and the stockholders make (or lose!) the money based on the price of the stock at the time of purchase and sale; the company itself receives no additional income. Stock is much like other goods sold in that its price or value is based on how much investors like yourself are willing to pay for it.

Common stock represents the bulk of the stock in the U.S. Common stock is because there are no guarantees that the stock will increase in value, and in many cases, it decreases. **Preferred stock**, on the other hand, offers a little less risk because **dividends** (the portion of the company's profit that is paid back to the stockholders) are paid out before dividends are paid out for the common stock. But because that dividends do not increase even if the company profits and the preferred stock's prices does not increase as rapidly as that of common stock, preferred stock has less potential growth that goes along with less risk.

A company may choose to issue different **classes of stocks** for several reasons. A different class of stock may be issued for a particular division of a company, or it may have different dividend rules, trade at different prices, or have different selling restrictions. **Stock splitting** occurs when corporations exercise the option to "split" their stock because the value of the stock may have reached its peak. If the company has 1000 shares of stock each reading at $50 and it decided to split the stock, there will be 2000 shares out there, each worth $25. As a stockholder, you just doubled the amount of shares you have (but each share is worth half as much!). In many cases, splitting will increase interest in the company's stock, which would drive the price of those shares up. The opposite can also occur. A company may **reverse-split** their stock, where the amount of shares is cut in half and the value of each share doubles.

In order to make money with the stocks you own, you can sell the stock for more than you paid for it or earn dividends on the stock while you own it. Of course, you have to figure in taxes and brokerage fees in order to determine the probability of your investment. However, if you keep the stock for at least a year, it is considered a **long-term gain** and you will pay fewer taxes on it.

Selling short is an interesting (and confusing!) way to trade stocks. When you sell short, you borrow stocks from your broker without purchasing them for a certain price, believing that the price of the stock will actually go down. When it does go down, you buy the shares at the low price (because you have essentially sold the shares at the high price before you even owned them) and then receive the difference in price (minus taxes and fees, of course).

Buying on Margin is a stock investor's term for borrowing money. If you think a particular stock is going to increase in value and you would like to buy more stocks than you can afford, you can buy on margin. Your broker, in turn becomes the lender of your loan. The potential rewards of buying on margin are obviously high . . . if the stock you borrowed money to purchase goes up in value. However, as you can guess, if the value of the stock decreases in value, you stand to lose all your money PLUS the money you borrowed. Most brokers allow you to borrow up to half the amount of the total stock purchase (so you if you wanted to buy 500 shares of a particular stock that is worth $10 a share, you need to have at least $2,500 in order to buy the $5,000 worth of stocks.)_ In addition, all brokerage firms require that you maintain a certain percentage of the margin purchase (minimum 25%) in the form of cash in an account, so that you can only go into so much debt. In the previous example, if your $5,000 margin purchase loses value and is now worth only $1,000 then its value below the minimum 25% and you would be required to either sell the stock (and lose $1,500 you initially invested as well as the $2,500 you borrowed from your broker) or ass $250 to your account to meet the 25% requirement.

BONDS:

Essentially **bonds** are loans. You as an investor can loan money (in the form of a bond) to corporations and governments. Bonds work in much the same way as a loan from a bank does. There is a specific time in which the bond matures, or must be repaid to the lender (you). The percentage rate at which interest is repaid to you, the lender, is also typically fixed. This is the reason bonds are usually much less risky than stocks (depending on your definition of risk . . . if you get 4% interest on a bond that is guaranteed but you might get 15% interest on a stock, it may actually be considered riskier to tie up your money in a bond). Bonds may also be riskier because the value of the interest a bond pays may actually be less towards the end of the loan period. This is because of inflation. If your 20-year bond pays $100 a month in interest, that $100 is worth much less in the twentieth year of the bond than in the first.

Also, bonds can be traded much like stocks. Since the interest rate of a long-term bond is fixed and usually correlates with the current interest rates of mortgages (since a 30 year mortgage is much like a 30 year bond), then as interest rates begin to fall, the value of your bond may actually increase. Investors may want to purchase your $10,000 bond at 10% for $12,000 if the current interest rates are only 5%. If they expect the interest rates to stay low, they will begin to make more money for their extra $2,000 in the third year since your bond will have much higher interest rates than those that are currently being offered. Bond trading is also risky since the interest rates constantly fluctuate.

To determine whether a particular bond is a good investment, you have to look at how much the bond yields and how much it will yield in the future. Since the interest rates on bonds never change, than you really must determine the rates and economic conditions surrounding the bond to determine its true value. Inflation is probably the single biggest factor in determining a bond's future value. If the inflation rate is expected to increase above the interest rate of your bond, then your bond's real value (what you can purchase with the money generated from your bond, also known as **purchasing power**) will decrease.

Bonds are rated based on the financial and economic condition of the institution that has issued the bond. In other words, a corporation that issues a bond would be rated based on how secure the company is financially and how likely that company will actually repay the loan (bond) plus the advertised interest rate. If a bond issuer receives a low rating, then they will have to issue the bonds at high interest rates to attract buyers. SO as with stocks, the greater the risk, the greater the potential yield . . . and potential loss. **Junk bonds** are the lowest rated bonds available. The interest rates for junk bonds may be substantially higher than those of bonds issued by companies that are ranked better and are therefore safer. However, there is a good chance that the company offering the junk bonds will not be able to repay the loan and/or interest to you.

Municipal bonds are those that are federally tax-free of less taxed than regular bonds. Government agencies may offer municipal bonds as a way to attract investors to pay for schools or highways. In addition, if you purchase a municipal bond from your own state government, you will not have to pay state taxes of the interest earned from those bonds either. **Treasury bonds**, notes, and bills are offered by the federal government as a way of paying for current debt. Bonds have a 30-year term and are offered only in February, August, and November. **Treasury Notes** have a five-year term or a ten-year term and are offered in February, May, August, and November. Two-year notes are offered once a month. **Treasury Bills** that have one year terms are also offered every four weeks and shorter term bills are offered every week. Treasury certificates, which are also traded on the secondary market (after the initial purchase and often for different amounts than face value much like regular bonds), are considered by many investors to be the safest investment on the market since they are backed by the United States Government.

MUTUAL FUNDS:

Mutual Funds take the idea of the investment club one step further. Many mutual funds pool money from hundreds or thousands of individual or corporate investors and invest that many in hundreds or thousands of stocks, bonds, bills, notes, other mutual funds, and several other investments. Each mutual fund will have one or more professional financial managers whose job it is to maintain the value of the fund.

Stock funds are mutual funds that invest primarily in stocks. Some stocks funds invest only in established companies, while others may invest in newer or start-up companies. Other stock funds invest in foreign countries. Some stock funds concentrate on stability (or steady income) while others are riskier and concentrate on high potential on higher potential yields.

Another mutual fund is one that invests primarily in bonds, and are therefore named **bond funds**. Since the funds invest in different bond of varying terms and interest rates, there is no maturity date or fixed interest rate for bond funds. If you want an investment with a fixed interest rate and maturity date, you would buy a bond. If you like the idea of investing in bonds but would like to take a slightly higher risk to beat inflation, you would invest in bond funds, where you are essentially paying a company to invest your money in several different bonds with the hope that their expertise will help you gain a higher yield.

Money market funds are considered a safe investment because the managers of the fund work to maintain a value of $1.00 per share. Therefore, the money you are making on your investment is the interest rate that the money market fund yields. Money markets are similar to a bank CD or **Certificate of Deposit** in that the value of the fund is maintained and the money you make is from the interest. Savings and checking accounts from banks work much the same way. When you purchase a CD from a bank, the bank is guaranteeing a certain rate of return for the money you are lending them (so that they may invest that money and make more money for themselves). Money market funds work in a similar ways, except the interest rates can fluctuate based on how good of an investment the institution that you purchased the fund from makes. One thing to consider when investing in bond funds or money market funds is that you have the option to purchase tax-free funds that usually pay lower interest rates. If you predict that the interest rate of a taxable fund will be higher than the percentage you will get taxed on, then taxable funds would be a wise decision. However, if you think the taxes that you would pay on a taxable fund will be higher than the extra interest you would receive for taxable funds, then you would be better off purchasing a tax-free fund.

INITIAL PUBLIC OFFERINGS

Initial Public Offerings, or IPOs, are a company's first (initial) sale of stock to the public. Securities offered in an IPO are often, but not always, those of young, small companies that are looking for startup funds and stock exposure. Generally, there is tremendous risk that accompanies the potentially tremendous gains that go along with investing in IPOs.

Some of the truly remarkable yields and gains ever made in the stock market are the result of initial public offerings. An IPO is launched when and existing company decides to sell shares to the public.

Notable IPOs, such as Netscape and eBay took a company from relative obscurity to stellar status, virtually overnight. Those who got in early got rich. Those who got in late may have bought overvalued stocks and, consequently, lost or stand to lose a great deal, depending on when or if they sold.

Assessing IPOs is tough. After all, these are fledgling stocks with no trading record to go by, no market perception to use as your own gauge. These days, many IPOs don't even have earnings, or the hope for profit anytime soon. Yet for those who prefer to pick stocks, IPOs are alluring rafts of profit in an insecure investment environment.

3.   Sample Extemp Topics

Should we criminalize corporate misconduct?
How can democratic governments do a better job of working with multinationals to promote economic growth?
What explains the recent machinations in the stock market?

4.   Sample Web Sites

Two sites recommend themselves. First is *edustock*, an educational web page designed to teach what the market is and how it works. The menu includes company profiles, an educational tutorial, and links to other good sites. At http://library.thinkquest.org/3088/welcome/welcome.html. Sample pages are included at the end of this chapter. The National Center For Policy Analysis also deserves a look at www.ncpa.org/pd/economy/econ11.html . These pages have a long good list of useful articles and essays on financial markets.

EDU STOCK

edustock

Edustock is an educational web page designed to teach young and old alike, what the stock market is, and how it can work for them. It includes tutorials on the stock market and how to pick good stocks. It also provides information on a select group of companies to help you start your research into what stock is going to make your fortune. Last of all, it provides a **FREE 20 minute delayed Stock market simulation** on the World Wide Web.

the menu

welcome

This is the page you are looking at right now. This page is here to welcome users, and explain what EDUstock is all about, and how to use it. This page also tells what is new at EDUSTOCK.

company profiles

Are you confused when it comes to what stocks to buy? If so, look here for some ideas and pointers. We have chosen a group of companies for you to look at.

simulation

This section is the only FREE realtime stock simulation on the World Wide Web. Get a real idea of what the stock market is like, and how much money you can make with stock investments. The stock simulation data is 20 minutes delayed, and updated everytime you use it.

the stock market

This page is an educational tutorial on the stock market. You can learn about how the stock market works, and what a stock really is. You can also learn more about picking a stock, and managing your portfolio.

feedback

Any suggestions? How about comments? Well, if you want to communicate with us, use this feedback page.

Our page is only one of the financial pages on the World Wide Web. We have found many others that we thought you might find

http://library.thinkquest.org/3088/welcome/welcome.html

THE STOCK MARKET

I NTRODUCTION

The center of our Nation's economy does not rest at Fort Knox with its millions of dollars worth of gold, or even the Treasury that prints the money that you use. At the center of the United States economy is Wall Street. Almost every larg e company in the US and around the world is traded on a Stock Exchange; from McDonalds to Lockheed Martin.

To learn more about how the stock market can earn money, and even keep the economy healthy, we have to look at how it works. With this tutorial, you will learn how the stock market was created and about the inner workings of the Stock Exchang e, brokerage firms, buying and selling, mutual funds, and much more.

Some of you might be wondering why should you care about the stock market. Maybe you are too young to be investing, or can't see how the market relates to your every day life. The fact is, even if you have no money in the stock market, or ar e in school, the stock market does affect you. It affects everything you do, from going to the mall, to buying that new outfit you have always wanted. After all, Calvin Klein has to get money to make those outfits!

This tutorial is designed to let you decide what you want to learn about. It is recommended that you read the topics sequentially, but it is not required. If you already know about a topic you may want to skip over it. After all, learning s hould be fun. So jump right in and select a topic.

◄ PREVIOUS   ► NEXT

Any questions or comments should be addressed to 3088@advanced.org .

(taken from www.deil.uiuc.edu/)

WRITTEN TASK: Definition of "Stock"

Directions: Read all 4 definitions of "stock" below, then turn the page over and write 1 new definition in your own words. You may turn back to reread the original passages, but it is encouraged to read <u>carefully</u> the first time so that this is unnecessary. Plagiarism is, of course, not permitted. (Time: 15 min.)

Some helpful vocabulary:
Capital: Money invested in a business.
Certificate: Piece of paper recognizing legally as proof of ownership.
Corporation: Large company.
Dividends: Profit from a company divided among the owners.
Proprietorship:Ownership.
Shares: Ownership divided into equal units.

---

1. "a. The capital that a corporation raises though the sale of shares entitling the holder to dividends and other rights of ownership. b. A certificate that shows such ownership."
   The American Heritage Dictionary.
   Dell Publishing Co., Inc. 1980.

2. "1) the proprietorship element in a corporation usually divided into shares and represented by transferable certificates. 3) stock certificate."
   Webster's Ninth New Collegiate Dictionary
   Merriam-Webster, Inc. 1988

3. "Capital stock is a right of ownership in a corporation. The stock is divided into a certain number of *shares*, and the corporation issues stockholders one or more *stock certificates* to show how many shares they hold. The stockholders own the company and elect a board of directors to manage it for them."
   World Book encyclopedia. Vol. 18.
   World Book, Inc. 1990

4. "Capital stock represents ownership of an incorporated business. Total ownership is divided into a number of shares of stock, each share representing an equal fractional equity in the venture. Thus 100 shares of stock in a corporation with 50,000,000 shares outstanding represents 1/500,000 of that business"
   Encyclopedia Americana, vol. 25.
   Grolier, Inc. 1988.

Chapter Ten
Energy

1. The Concepts

Energy drives a developing economy. Manufacturing and transportation are **energy intensive**. Access to and the cost of energy often determine whether an economy is in recession or enjoying a healthy growth spurt. Energy cost increases are highly inflationary. When the price of energy rises the price of almost everything rises because manufacturing, transportation, and farming have high energy costs. In agriculture, for example, planting, harvesting, transport and fertilizer production all require high energy expenditures.

Most of the world's developed countries (Japan, the United States, and the European Union) are highly dependent on imported oil. United States dependence has and will increase because our own **reserves** are being **depleted**. Oil is the most common type of energy because it is the most versatile, and convenient for transportation. And both the national and international **energy infrastructure** have been built around oil.

Oil is a classic **fossil fuel**. Fossil fuels are derived from hydrocarbon deposits, what was living matter in the dinosaurs' time and has gradually compacted and decayed and transformed into coal, oil, and natural gas. There are huge deposits of fossil fuels around the world. Russia's Caspian Sea basin has the world's largest natural gas reserves, Saudi Arabia leads the world in oil production (with Iraq, Kuwait, and Russia also important sources), and both the United States and China have large coal deposits. More than 25% of the world's known coal reserves are in the United States.

Fossil fuel use releases high amounts of carbon dioxide. Coal is the worse pollutant, natural gas the least. But all contribute to the **greenhouse effect** and other forms of air pollution. The greenhouse effect is the buildup of pollutants, mostly carbon gas and methane, in the upper atmosphere. This **gaseous buildup** traps heat in the atmosphere. As it increases **global warming** occurs.

Increasing costs of energy and its environmental effects, plus the risks to national security (e.g. the potential for a devastating embargo), have increased **energy conservation** efforts. Speed limits have been lowered in some locations at some times. Home insulation has increased significantly. Light bulbs have been improved. In the United States the Department of Transportation mandates improved fuel efficiency levels in cars sold in the United States. California has a rigorous law requiring even higher per-mile gasoline averages. Recycling centers are widespread; aluminum cans, newspaper and glass recycling reduce energy waste. These and similar steps have reduced the growth in energy demand significantly, but it has not eliminated it.

The combination of finite reserves, pollution, **security vulnerability** and global warming has combined to create modest support for research and development of **alternative energies**, especially **renewable** energy sources. Alternative energies are non-fossil fuels. The most common is nuclear energy that generates ten percent of America's electrical power. Very clean and efficient energy, support for nuclear power has been destroyed by great troubles in storing its long-lasting radioactive wastes, and by the meltdown and deadly contamination of the Chernobyl nuclear plant in Ukraine. **Synthetic fuels** such as gasohol and ethanol mix gasoline with agriculturally derived fuels (corn oil is a common alternative) but there is little or no net energy gain because of the energy used in converting the agricultural material.

Renewable energies have been popular in the press and scored high in public opinion polls since the late 1960s. But their costs are high and public vocal support has never been matched by a willingness to pay *substantially* higher prices for energy from renewable energy. Government research and development support has been modest and erratic. Privately owned energy firms have made modest steps but profit potential is severely limited unless fossil fuel prices go up dramatically, so heavy corporate investment is not yet justified. But debate topics and extemp speakers love to look at the options. They include

- **Fuel cells**. Very efficient tools to chemically alter substances into energy. Chrysler and Mercedes Benz, for example, are developing a hydrogen fuel cell to power cars.
- **Wind farms**. A variety of windmills, turbines, are already in place around the world to generate electricity. Most are already cost competitive. But so far locations with sufficient wind throughout most or all of the year are limited.
- **Solar cells** have been used on everything from satellites to roofs. The wonderful idea of turning sunlight into electricity remains elusively expensive. Solar farms still encounter high chip costs. Astropower is the only solar power firm showing a profit.
- **Hydroelectric** power from dams has already been fully developed in most industrialized nations. Many LDCs could still expand its use. But there are harms to species (e.g. salmon **species destruction** in the American northwest) and the **ecosystem**.
- **Hot Rock Geothermal** is power from geysers and fissures in the earth where heat is released. Useful in limited locations, such as northern California and Iceland, there is only modest room left to expand this source.
- **Dry Rock geothermal** uses drilling to tap hot subsurface areas, insert liquid and recycle it in steam to power electric turbines on the surface. A loop or cycle can be established so that as the steam cools it is reinserted below ground to become steam again. Not yet cost efficient this approach no longer receives any development funding.
- **Tidal power** uses large changes in sea level to power ocean turbines near the shore. But very few places have enough daily tidal rise and drop to make the turbines cost-effective. Only the Bay of Fundy in Nova Scotia and a very few other spots around the globe could use this technology.
- Other exotic options include **ocean thermal gradients**, which would use temperature variations in the ocean to generate electricity, **hydrogen** as a transportation fuel, and commercially produced **biomass** (the use of wood and other living material as fuel).

2. Sample Extemp Topics

Are we overly concerned with global warming?

How can the international community better support development on nonpolluting alternative energy sources?

What are the national security risks to our dependence on imported oil, and how should we reduce them?

3. Sample Web Sites

The Alliance To Save Energy "promotes energy efficiency worldwide to achieve a healthier economy, a cleaner environment, and energy security". Good internal search engine, check options listed at left of home page for what interests you. www.ase.org/ Recent visit found good summaries of recent studies on reducing carbon emissions.

For those who like the leftist view try Sustainable Energy & Economy Network. The home page has a very good NEWS section at the lower left. www.seen.org/ Moderates can see a business view of energy issues at the American Petroleum Institute. It has good internal searches and policy issue publications. http://api-ec.api.org/policy/

Foreign extempers and debaters working on disadvantages should also look at the International Energy Agency which deals a lot with global warming and greenhouse issues. Its at www.iea.org/ Domestic extempers can find publications and reports from the Department of Energy at www.energy.gov/index.html

4. If You Want To Read More…

Overview

Reliable, Affordable, and Environmentally Sound Energy for America's Future

In his second week in office, President George W. Bush established the National Energy Policy Development Group, directing it to "develop a national energy policy designed to help the private sector, and, as necessary and appropriate, State and local governments, promote dependable, affordable, and environmentally sound production and distribution of energy for the future." This Overview sets forth the National Energy Policy Development (NEPD) Group's findings and key recommendations for a National Energy Policy.

America in the year 2001 faces the most serious energy shortage since the oil embargoes of the 1970s. The effects are already being felt nationwide. Many families face energy bills two to three times higher than they were a year ago. Millions of Americans find themselves dealing with rolling blackouts or brownouts; some employers must lay off workers or curtail production to absorb the rising cost of energy. Drivers across America are paying higher and higher gasoline prices.

Californians have felt these problems most acutely. California actually began the 1990s with a surplus of electricity generating capacity. Yet despite an economic boom, a rapidly growing population, and a corresponding increase in energy needs, California did not add a single new major electric power plant during the 1990s. The result is a demand for electricity that greatly succeeds the amount available.

A fundamental imbalance between supply and demand defines our nation's energy crisis. As the chart illustrates, if energy production increases at the same rate as during the last decade our projected energy needs will far outstrip expected levels of production.

This imbalance, if allowed to continue, will inevitably undermine our economy, our standard of living, and our national security. But it is not beyond our power to correct. America leads the world in scientific achievement, technical skill, and entrepreneurial drive. Within our country are abundant natural resources, unrivaled technology, and unlimited human creativity. With forward-looking leadership and sensible policies, we can meet our fu-

Figure 1

Growth in U.S. Energy Consumption Is Outpacing Production

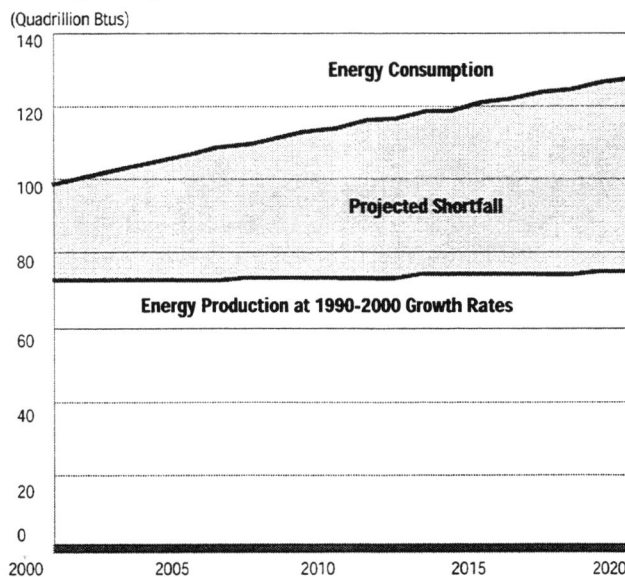

Over the next 20 years, growth in U.S. energy consumption will increasingly outpace U.S. energy production, if production only grows at the rate of the last 10 years.

Sources: Sandia National Laboratories and U.S. Department of Energy, Energy Information Administration.

America's expanding economy, growing population, and rising standard of living will be sustained by our unmatched technological know-how.

ture energy demands and promote energy conservation, and do so in environmentally responsible ways that set a standard for the world.

The Challenge

America's energy challenge begins with our expanding economy, growing population, and rising standard of living. Our prosperity and way of life are sustained by energy use. America has the technological know-how and environmentally sound 21st century technologies needed to meet the principal energy challenges we face: promoting energy conservation, repairing and modernizing our energy infrastructure, and increasing our energy supplies in ways that protect and improve the environment. Meeting each of these challenges is critical to expanding our economy, meeting the needs of a growing population, and raising the American standard of living.

We are already working to meet the first challenge: using energy more wisely. Dramatic technological advances in energy efficiency have enabled us to make great strides in conservation, from the operation of farms and factories to the construction of buildings and automobiles. New technology allows us to go about our lives and work with less cost, less effort, and less burden on the natural environment. While such advances cannot alone solve America's energy problems, they can and will continue to play an important role in our energy future.

The second challenge is to repair and expand our energy infrastructure. Our current, outdated network of electric generators, transmission lines, pipelines, and refineries that convert raw materials into usable fuel has been allowed to deteriorate. Oil pipelines and refining capacity are in need of repair and expansion. Not a single major oil refinery has been built in the United States in nearly a generation, causing the kind of bottlenecks that lead to sudden spikes in the price of gasoline. Natural gas distribution, likewise, is hindered by an aging and inadequate network of pipelines. To match supply and demand will require some 38,000 miles of new gas pipelines, along with 255,000 miles of distribution lines. Similarly, an antiquated and inadequate transmission grid prevents us from routing electricity over long distances and thereby avoiding regional blackouts, such as California's.

"America must have an energy policy that plans for the future, but meets the needs of today. I believe we can develop our natural resources and protect our environment."

— President George W. Bush

Increasing energy supplies while protecting the environment is the third challenge. Even with successful conservation efforts, America will need more energy.

Renewable and alternative fuels offer hope for America's energy future. But they supply only a small fraction of present energy needs. The day they fulfill the bulk of our needs is still years away. Until that day comes, we must continue meeting the nation's energy requirements by the means available to us.

Estimates indicate that over the next 20 years, U.S. oil consumption will increase by 33 percent, natural gas consumption by well over 50 percent, and demand for electricity will rise by 45 percent. If America's energy production grows at the same rate as it did in the 1990s we will face an ever-increasing gap.

Increases on this scale will require preparation and action today. Yet America has not been bringing on line the necessary supplies and infrastructure.

Extraordinary advances in technology have transformed energy exploration and production. Yet we produce 39 percent less oil today than we did in 1970, leaving us ever more reliant on foreign suppliers. On our present course, America 20 years from now will import nearly two of every three barrels of oil – a condition of increased dependency on foreign powers that do not always have America's interests at heart. Our increasing demand for natural gas – one of the cleanest forms of energy – far exceeds the current rate of production. We should reconsider any regulatory restrictions that do not take technological advances into account.

Figure 2

U.S. Oil Consumption Will Continue to Exceed Production

(Millions of Barrels per Day)

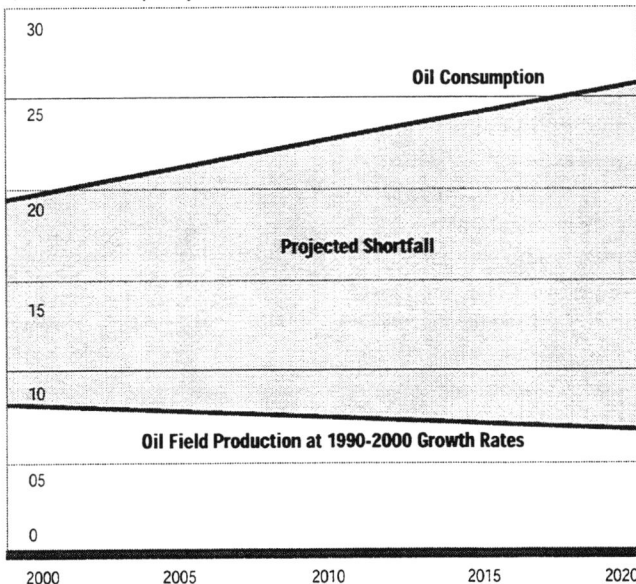

Over the next 20 years, U.S. oil consumption will grow by over 6 million barrels per day. If U.S. oil production follows the same historical pattern of the last 10 years, it will decline by 1.5 million barrels per day. To meet U.S. oil demand, oil and product imports would have to grow by a combined 7.5 million barrels per day. In 2020, U.S. oil production would supply less than 30 percent of U.S. oil needs.

Sources: Sandia National Laboratories and U.S. Department of Energy, Energy Information Administration.

Figure 3

U.S. Natural Gas Consumption Is Outpacing Production

(Trillion Cubic Feet)

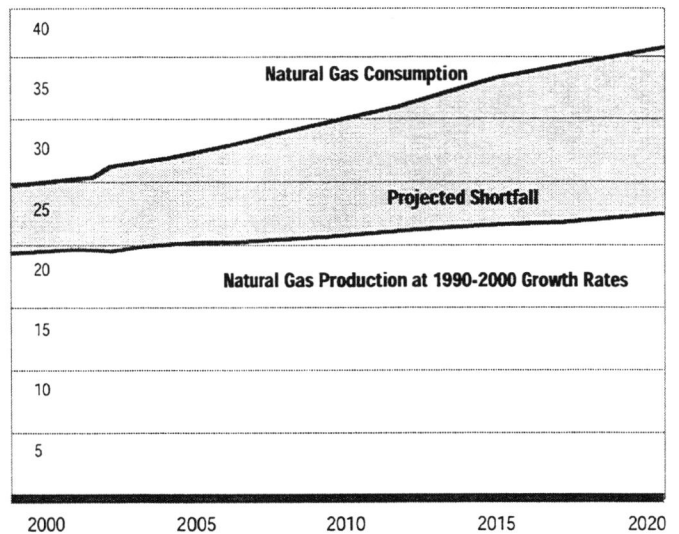

Over the next 20 years, U.S. natural gas consumption will grow by over 50 percent. At the same time, U.S. natural gas production will grow by only 14 percent, if it grows at the rate of the last 10 years.

Sources: Sandia National Laboratories and U.S. Department of Energy, Energy Information Administration.

We have a similar opportunity to increase our supplies of electricity. To meet projected demand over the next two decades, America must have in place between 1,300 and 1,900 new electric plants. Much of this new generation will be fueled by natural gas. However, existing and new technologies offer us the opportunity to expand nuclear generation as well. Nuclear power today accounts for 20 percent of our country's electricity. This power source, which causes no greenhouse gas emissions, can play an expanding part in our energy future.

The recommendations of this report address the energy challenges facing America. Taken together, they offer the thorough and responsible energy plan our nation has long needed.

Components of the National Energy Policy

The National Energy Policy we propose follows three basic principles:

- The Policy is a long-term, comprehensive strategy. Our energy crisis has been years in the making, and will take years to put fully behind us.

- The Policy will advance new, environmentally friendly technologies to increase energy supplies and encourage cleaner, more efficient energy use.

- The Policy seeks to raise the living standards of the American people, recognizing that to do so our country must fully integrate its energy, environmental, and economic policies.

Applying these principles, we urge action to meet five specific national goals. America must modernize conservation, modernize our energy infrastructure, increase energy supplies, accelerate the protection and improvement of the environment, and increase our nation's energy security.

Modernize Conservation

Americans share the goal of energy conservation. The best way of meeting this goal is to increase energy efficiency by applying new technology – raising productivity, reducing waste, and trimming costs. In addition, it holds out great hope for improving the quality of the environment. American families, communities, and businesses all depend upon reliable and affordable energy services for their well being and safety. From transportation to communication, from air conditioning to lighting, energy is critical to nearly everything we do in life and work. Public policy can and should encourage energy conservation.

Over the past three decades, America has made impressive gains in energy efficiency. Today's automobiles, for example, use about 60 percent of the gasoline they

"Here we aim to continue a path of uninterrupted progress in many fields... New technologies are proving that we can save energy without sacrificing our standard of living. And we're going to encourage it in every way possible."

— Vice President
Richard B. Cheney

Figure 4
U.S. Economy is More Energy Efficient (Energy Intensity)
Primary Energy Use

Quadrillion Btus

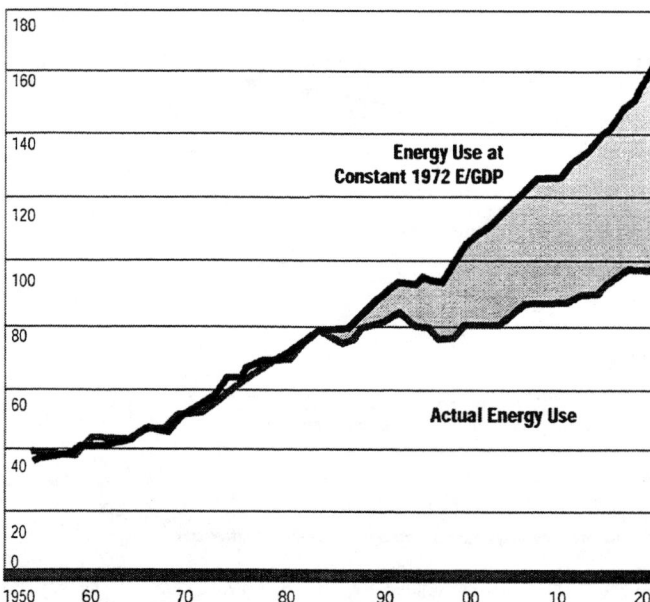

Improvements in energy efficiency since the 1970s have had a major impact in meeting national energy needs relative to new supply. If the intensity of U.S. energy use had remained constant since 1972, consumption would have been about 70 quadrillion Btus (74 percent) higher in 1999 than it actually was.

Source: U.S. Department of Energy, Energy Information Administration.

did in 1972, while new refrigerators require just one-third the electricity they did 30 years ago. As a result, since 1973, the U.S. economy has grown by 126 percent, while energy use has increased by only 30 percent. In the 1990s alone, manufacturing output expanded by 41 percent, while industrial electricity consumption grew by only 11 percent. We must build on this progress and strengthen America's commitment to energy efficiency and conservation.

The National Energy Policy builds on our nation's successful track record and will promote further improvements in the productive and efficient use of energy. This report includes recommendations to:

- Direct federal agencies to take appropriate actions to responsibly conserve energy use at their facilities, especially during periods of peak demand in regions where electricity shortages are possible, and to report to the President on actions taken.
- Increase funding for renewable energy and energy efficiency research and development programs that are performance-based and cost-shared.
- Create an income tax credit for the purchase of hybrid and fuel cell vehicles to promote fuel-efficient vehicles.
- Extend the Department of Energy's "Energy Star" efficiency program to include schools, retail buildings, health care facilities, and homes and extend the "Energy Star" labeling program to additional products and appliances.
- Fund the federal government's Intelligent Transportation Systems program, the fuel cell powered transit bus program, and the Clean Buses program.
- Provide a tax incentive and streamline permitting to accelerate the development of clean Combined Heat and Power technology.
- Direct the Secretary of Transportation to review and provide recommendations on establishing Corporate Average Fuel Economy (CAFE) standards

with due consideration to the National Academy of Sciences study of CAFE standards to be released in July, 2001.

Modernize Our Energy Infrastructure

The energy we use passes through a vast nationwide network of generating facilities, transmission lines, pipelines, and refineries that converts raw resources into usable fuel and power. That system is deteriorating, and is now strained to capacity.

One reason for this is government regulation, often excessive and redundant. Regulation is needed in such a complex field, but it has become overly burdensome. Regulatory hurdles, delays in issuing permits, and economic uncertainty are limiting investment in new facilities, making our energy markets more vulnerable to transmission bottlenecks, price spikes and supply disruptions. America needs more environmentally-sound energy projects to connect supply sources to growing markets and to deliver energy to homes and business.

To reduce the incidence of electricity blackouts, we must greatly enhance our ability to transmit electric power between geographic regions, that is, sending power to where it is needed from where it is produced. Most of America's transmission lines, substations, and transformers were built when utilities were tightly regulated and provided service only within their assigned regions. The system is simply unequipped for large-scale swapping of power in the highly competitive market of the 21st century.

The National Energy Policy will modernize and expand our energy infrastructure in order to ensure that energy supplies can be safely, reliably, and affordably transported to homes and businesses. This report includes recommendations to:

- Direct agencies to improve pipeline safety and expedite pipeline permitting.
- Issue an Executive Order directing federal agencies to expedite permits and coordinate federal, state, and local actions necessary for energy-related project approvals on a national basis

> *"For the electricity we need, we must be ambitious. Transmission grids stand in need of repair, upgrading, and expansion. . . . If we put these connections in place, we'll go a long way toward avoiding future blackouts."*
>
> — Vice President Richard B. Cheney

in an environmentally sound manner, and establish an interagency task force chaired by the Council on Environmental Quality. The task force will ensure that federal agencies set up appropriate mechanisms to coordinate federal, state and local permitting activity in particular regions where increased activity is expected.

- Grant authority to obtain rights-of-way for electricity transmission lines with the goal of creating a reliable national transmission grid. Similar authority already exists for natural gas pipelines and highways.
- Enact comprehensive electricity legislation that promotes competition, encourages new generation, protects consumers, enhances reliability, and promotes renewable energy.
- Implement administrative and regulatory changes to improve the reliability of the interstate transmission system and enact legislation to provide for enforcement of electricity reliability standards.
- Expand the Energy Department's research and development on transmission reliability and superconductivity.

Increase Energy Supplies

A primary goal of the National Energy Policy is to add supply from diverse sources. This means domestic oil, gas, and coal. It also means hydropower and nuclear power. And it means making greater use of non-hydro renewable sources now available.

One aspect of the present crisis is an increased dependence, not only on foreign oil, but on a narrow range of energy options. For example, about 90 percent of all new electricity plants currently under construction will be fueled by natural gas. While natural gas has many advantages, an over-reliance on any one fuel source leaves consumers vulnerable to price spikes and supply disruptions. There are several other fuel sources available that can help meet our needs.

Currently, the U.S. has enough coal to last for another 250 years. Yet very few

coal-powered electric plants are now under construction. Research into clean coal technologies may increase the attractiveness of coal as a source for new generation plants.

Nuclear power plants serve millions of American homes and businesses, have a dependable record for safety and efficiency, and discharge no greenhouse gases into the atmosphere. As noted earlier, these facilities currently generate 20 percent of all electricity in America, and more than 40 percent of electricity generated in 10 states in the Northeast, South, and Midwest. Other nations, such as Japan and France, generate a much higher percentage of their electricity from nuclear power. Yet the number of nuclear plants in America is actually projected to decline in coming years, as old plants close and none are built to replace them.

Enormous advances in technology have made oil and natural gas exploration and production both more efficient and more environmentally sound. Better technology means fewer rigs, more accurate drilling, greater resource recovery and envi-

"As a country, we have demanded more and more energy. But we have not brought on line the supplies needed to meet that demand.... We can explore for energy, we can produce energy and use it, and we can do so with a decent regard for the natural environment."

—Vice President
Richard B. Cheney

Figure 5
Fuel Sources for Electricity Generation in 2000

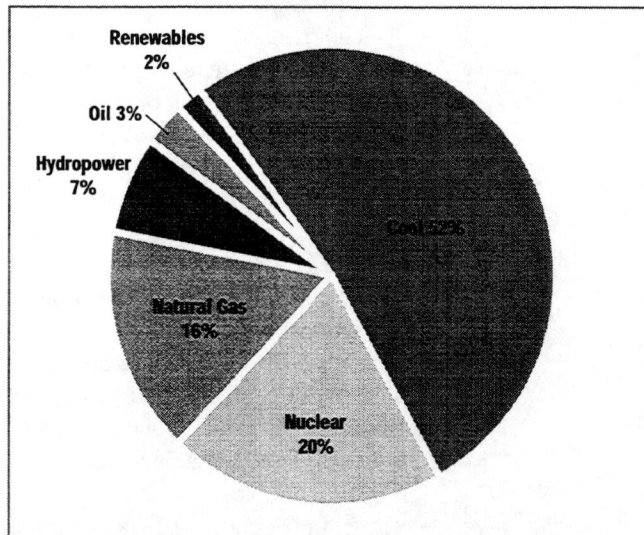

Electricity is a secondary source of energy, generated through the consumption of primary sources. Coal and nuclear energy account for nearly 75 percent of U.S. electricity generation.

Source: U.S. Department of Energy, Energy Information Administration

ronmentally friendly exploration. Drilling pads are 80 percent smaller than a generation ago. High-tech drilling allows us to access supplies five to six miles away from a single compact drilling site, leaving sensitive wetlands and wildlife habitats undisturbed. Yet the current regulatory structure fails to take sufficient account of these extraordinary advances, excessively restricting the environmentally safe production of energy from many known sources.

Our policy will increase and diversify our nation's sources of traditional and alternative fuels in order to furnish families and businesses with reliable and affordable energy, to enhance national security, and to improve the environment. This report includes recommendations to:

- Issue an Executive Order directing all federal agencies to include in any regulatory action that could significantly and adversely affect energy supplies a detailed statement on the energy impact of the proposed action.
- Open a small fraction of the Arctic National Wildlife Refuge to environmentally regulated exploration and production using leading-edge technology. Examine the potential for the regulated increase in oil and natural gas development on other federal lands.
- Earmark $1.2 billion of bid bonuses from the environmentally responsible leasing of ANWR to fund research into alternative and renewable energy resources – including wind, solar, biomass, and geothermal.
- Enact legislation to expand existing alternative fuels tax incentives to include landfills that capture methane gas emissions for electricity generation and to electricity produced from wind and biomass. Extend the number of eligible biomass sources to include forest-related sources, agricultural sources, and certain urban sources.
- Provide $2 billion over 10 years to fund clean coal technology research and a new credit for electricity produced from biomass co-fired with coal.
- Direct federal agencies to streamline the

hydropower relicensing process with proper regard given to environmental factors.
- Provide for the safe expansion of nuclear energy by establishing a national repository for nuclear waste, and by streamlining the licensing of nuclear power plants.

Accelerate Protection and Improvement of the Environment

America's commitment to environmental protection runs deep. We are all aware of past excesses in our use of the natural world and its resources. No one wishes to see them repeated. In the 21st century, the ethic of good stewardship is well established in American life and law.

We do not accept the false choice between environmental protection and energy production. An integrated approach to policy can yield a cleaner environment, a stronger economy, and a sufficient supply of energy for our future. The primary reason for that has been steady advances in the technology of locating, producing, and using energy. Since 1970, emissions of key air emissions are down 31 percent. Cars today emit 85 percent less carbon monoxide than 30 years ago. Lead emissions are down 90 percent. Lead levels in ambient air today are 98 percent lower than they were in 1970. America is using more, and polluting less.

One of the factors harming the environment today is the very lack of a comprehensive, long-term national energy policy. States confronting blackouts must take desperate measures, often at the expense of environmental standards, requesting waivers of environmental rules, and delaying the implementation of anti-pollution efforts. Shortfalls in electricity generating capacity and shortsighted policies have blocked construction of new, cleaner plants, leaving no choice but to rely on older, inefficient plants to meet demand. The increased use of emergency power sources, such as diesel generators, results in greater air pollution.

New anti-pollution technologies hold great promise for the environment. The same can be said of 21st century power generators that must soon replace older models; signifi-

"We will insist on protecting and enhancing the environment, showing consideration for the air and natural lands and watersheds of our country."

— Vice President
Richard B. Cheney

cant new resources for land conservation efforts; and continued research into renewable energy sources. All have a place in the National Energy Policy.

The National Energy Policy will build upon our nation's successful track record and will promote further improvements in the productive and efficient use of energy. This report includes recommendations to:

- Enact "multi-pollutant" legislation to establish a flexible, market-based program to significantly reduce and cap emissions of sulfur dioxide, nitrogen oxides, and mercury from electric power generators.
- Increase exports of environmentally friendly, market-ready U.S. technologies that generate a clean environment and increase energy efficiency.
- Establish a new "Royalties Conservation Fund" and earmark royalties from new, clean oil and gas exploration in ANWR to fund land conservation efforts.
- Implement new guidelines to reduce truck idling emissions at truck stops.

Increase Energy Security.

The National Energy Policy seeks to lessen the impact on Americans of energy price volatility and supply uncertainty. Such uncertainty increases as we reduce America's dependence on foreign sources of energy. At the same time, however, we recognize that a significant percentage of our resources will come from overseas. Energy security must be a priority of U.S. trade and foreign policy.

We must look beyond our borders and restore America's credibility with overseas suppliers. In addition, we must build strong relationships with energy-producing nations in our own hemisphere, improving the outlook for trade, investment, and reliable supplies.

Energy security also requires preparing our nation for supply emergencies, and assisting low-income Americans who are most vulnerable in times of supply disruption, price spikes, and extreme weather.

To ensure energy security for our nation and its families, our report includes these recommendations:

- Dedicate new funds to the Low Income Home Energy Assistance Program by funneling a portion of oil and gas royalty payments to LIHEAP when oil and natural gas prices exceed a certain amount.
- Double funding for the Department of Energy's Weatherization Assistance Program, increasing funding by $1.4 billion over 10 years.
- Direct the Federal Emergency Management Administration to prepare for potential energy-related emergencies.
- Support a North American Energy Framework to expand and accelerate cross-border energy investment, oil and gas pipelines, and electricity grid connections by streamlining and expediting permitting procedures with Mexico and Canada. Direct federal agencies to expedite necessary permits for a gas pipeline route from Alaska to the lower 48 states.

Looking Toward the Future

The President's goal of reliable, affordable, and environmentally sound energy supplies will not be reached overnight. It will call forth innovations in science, research, and engineering. It will require time and the best efforts of leaders in both political parties. It will require also that we deal with the facts as they are, meeting serious problems in a serious way. The complacency of the past decade must now give way to swift but well-considered action.

Present trends are not encouraging, but they are not immutable. They are among today's most urgent challenges, and well within our power to overcome. Our country has met many great tests. Some have imposed extreme hardship and sacrifice. Others have demanded only resolve, ingenuity, and clarity of purpose. Such is the case with energy today.

We submit these recommendations with optimism. We believe that the tasks ahead, while great, are achievable. The energy crisis is a call to put to good use the resources around us, and the talents within us. It summons the best of America, and offers the best of rewards – in new jobs, a healthier environment, a stronger economy, and a brighter future for our people.

"The goals of this strategy are clear: to ensure a steady supply of affordable energy for America's homes and businesses and industries."

— President
George W. Bush

IEA Press (02) 17
Paris, 21 August

ENERGY AND POVERTY :
IEA REVEALS A VICIOUS AND UNSUSTAINABLE CIRCLE

"1.6 billion people today have no access to electricity. 2.4 billion rely on primitive biomass for cooking and heating. What is more shocking, in the absence of radical new policies, 1.4 billion will still have no electricity in 30 years time. This is not a sustainable future," said Robert Priddle, Executive Director of the International Energy Agency (IEA) as he presented today a new document *"Energy & Poverty"*.

The document contains findings from a ground-breaking new study by the IEA on "energy poverty," its magnitude, characteristics and future trends. The objective of this analysis is to provide hard information about global poverty and energy use, seeking, through greater transparency, to contribute to better choices towards solutions.

The study is one chapter in the next edition of the IEA's biennial world energy projections, the *World Energy Outlook 2002*, due for release in Osaka, Japan on 21 September 2002. These findings from the study have been made available now because of their direct relevance to the United Nations World Summit on Sustainable Development, where energy is one of the central themes. The summit will take place from 26 August - 4 September in Johannesburg, South Africa.

The IEA notes that four out of five people without electricity currently live in rural areas of the developing world. They are concentrated in sub-Saharan Africa and South and South East Asia. But the emphasis is changing from rural zones to the booming urban areas. In the next thirty years population growth will be concentrated in the Third World mega-cities. This shift will require dramatic new policies by governments, utility companies and aid agencies, alongside efforts to improve the lot of the rural poor.

Another aspect of energy and poverty is that, throughout the developing world, the poor rely on "biomass" - wood, agricultural residues, and dung. This use gives rise to severe health and environmental impacts. Even in thirty years time, biomass is expected to remain the predominant source of energy for heating and cooking in more than half the homes in the developing world. The number reliant on biomass in this way is expected to increase from 2.4 billion today to 2.6 billion in 2030.

Without adequate supplies of affordable energy, it is virtually impossible to carry out productive economic activity or improve health and education. As a result, poor people remain poor. "There can be no economic development without secure affordable energy," said Robert Priddle.

To access and download Energy & Poverty, click on
http://www.worldenergyoutlook.org/weo/pubs/weo2002/energypoverty.pdf

130

Smart Energy Policies: Saving Money and Reducing Pollutant Emissions through Greater Energy Efficiency

Steven Nadel and Howard Geller

with the Tellus Institute

Report Number E012

©American Council for an Energy-Efficient Economy
1001 Connecticut Avenue, NW, Suite 801, Washington, D.C. 20036
202-429-8873 phone, 202-429-2248 fax, http://aceee.org Web site

EXECUTIVE SUMMARY

Multiple Energy Problems Confront the United States

There are a variety of serious energy challenges confronting the United States. California has experienced power shortages and severe electricity price spikes. Power reliability problems could spread to other regions such as the Pacific Northwest or New York. Even if the lights stay on, electricity prices will continue to climb in many regions of the country—utilities in several states have increased electric rates by 40–50% this year. Natural gas prices have also significantly increased in many parts of the country, causing skyrocketing home energy bills this past winter. Furthermore, our reliance on imported oil has grown—oil imports more than doubled during the past 15 years and oil imports now exceed domestic oil production. Rising demand for oil and tight supplies have also caused gasoline prices to rise; the average price of gas in the United States topped $1.70 per gallon earlier this year and while prices have since abated, price spikes are likely to be a periodic phenomenon in the future.

In addition, emissions of the gases that contribute to global climate change continue to rise. In 2000, U.S. greenhouse gas emissions were up 16% relative to levels in 1990. However, under the Global Framework Convention agreed to in Rio de Janeiro in 1992 by then-President Bush and subsequently ratified by the Senate, the United States voluntarily committed to reducing our emissions to 1990 levels by 2000.

Energy Efficiency—A Critical Foundation for U.S. Energy Policy

Most of these problems—reliability, high prices, and reliance on imports—are all fundamentally due to imbalances between energy demand and energy supply. As demand approaches available supply, prices rise and reliability deteriorates. Rising demand for oil (driven primarily by growing transportation sector energy use) combined with declining domestic production feeds the need for more imported oil. Statements by the current Bush Administration suggest that these problems can largely be solved by increasing energy supplies—more oil wells, coal mines, pipelines, refineries, power plants, and transmission lines. However, a supply-only strategy will be expensive (e.g., energy prices will need to be high to sustain private-sector investments in supply), time-consuming (it takes years to develop new energy sources), and harmful to our environment (e.g, adverse impacts on our land and air). Furthermore, available domestic supplies are not adequate to fully support the domestic economy. The United States accounts for one-quarter of global energy demand but has only 8% of known worldwide oil and natural gas reserves, placing limits on how much expanding energy supply can contribute to our energy needs. Instead of a supply-focused energy strategy, a far more rationale approach would be to first reduce energy demand to the extent that it is cost-effective to do so, and then meet the remaining demand with increased energy supplies (domestic or imported).

i

Energy efficiency improvement has contributed a great deal to our nation's economic growth and increased standard of living over the past 25 years. Total primary energy use per capita in the United States in 2000 was almost identical to that of 1973. Over the same 27-year period, economic output (GDP) per capita increased 74%. In 2000, consumers and businesses spent over $600 billion for total energy use in the United States. Had the nation not dramatically reduced its energy intensity over the previous 27 years, they would have spent at least $430 billion more on energy purchases in 2000.

Even though the United States is much more energy-efficient today than it was 25 years ago, there is still enormous potential for additional cost-effective energy savings. Some newer energy efficiency measures such as hybrid vehicles and sealing home heating ducts have barely begun to be adopted. With proper support, other efficiency measures could be developed and commercialized in coming years. The U.S. Department of Energy (DOE) estimates that increasing energy efficiency throughout the economy could cut national energy use by 10% or more in 2010 and approximately 20% in 2020, with net economic benefits for consumers and businesses. A 1999 ACEEE study estimates that adopting a comprehensive set of policies for advancing energy efficiency could lower national energy use by as much as 18% in 2010 and 33% in 2020, and do so cost-effectively.

Whether the energy savings potential is 20% or 30%, increasing the efficiency of our homes, appliances, vehicles, businesses, and industries should be the cornerstone of national energy policy since it provides a host of benefits. Furthermore, increasing energy efficiency does not present a trade-off between enhancing national security and energy reliability on the one hand and protecting the environment on the other, as do a number of energy supply options. Increasing energy efficiency is a "win-win" strategy from the perspective of economic growth, national security, reliability, and environmental protection.

Energy Efficiency Policy Recommendations

We have identified nine specific policy recommendations that could have a substantial impact on the demand for energy in the United States while also providing positive economic returns to American consumers and businesses. We list these policies in approximate order of energy savings, starting with the policies that yield the largest savings.

1. Increase Corporate Average Fuel Economy

The average fuel economy of new passenger vehicles (cars and light trucks) has declined from about 26 miles per gallon (mpg) in 1988 to 24 mpg in 2000 due to increasing vehicle size and power, the rising market share of light trucks, and the lack of tougher Corporate Average Fuel Economy (CAFE) standards. The original CAFE standards for cars were adopted in 1975 and reached their maximum level in 1985. We recommend increasing the CAFE standards for cars and light trucks by 5% per year for 10 years so that they reach 44 mpg for cars and 33 mpg for light trucks in 2012, with further improvements beyond 2012. Alternatively, the standards

i

for cars and light trucks could be combined into one value for all new passenger vehicles, specifically 38 mpg by 2012. This level of fuel economy improvement is technically feasible, cost-effective for consumers, and can be achieved without compromising vehicle safety.

Higher fuel economy standards should be complemented by (1) implementing tax credits for purchasers of innovative, highly efficient vehicles, (2) expanding taxes on gas-guzzling vehicles, (3) increasing labeling and consumer education efforts, and (4) continuing vigorous research and development (R&D) on fuel-efficient, low-emissions vehicles. This combination of policies would facilitate compliance with the tougher standards.

2. Adopt a National System Benefit Trust Fund

Electric utilities historically have funded programs to encourage more efficient energy use, assist low-income families with home weatherization and energy bill payment, promote the development of renewable energy sources, and undertake R&D. Experience with utility energy efficiency programs in the Northeast, Northwest and Great Lakes region shows that these programs have been highly effective. The value of energy bill savings for households and businesses is about double the costs to produce these savings. Unfortunately, increasing competition and restructuring have led utilities to cut these discretionary "system benefit" expenditures over the past 5 years. Total utility spending on all demand-side management programs (i.e., energy efficiency and peak load reduction) fell by more than 50% from a high of $3.1 billion in 1993 to $1.4 billion in 1999 (1999$).

In order to ensure that energy efficiency programs and other public benefits activities continue following restructuring, 15 states have established system benefits funds through a small charge on all kilowatt-hours flowing through the transmission and distribution grid. We recommend creation of a national systems benefits trust fund that would provide matching funds to states for eligible public benefits expenditures. Specifically, we recommend a non-bypassable wires charge of two-tenths of a cent per kilowatt-hour. This policy would give states and utilities a strong incentive to expand their energy efficiency programs and other public benefits activities.

3. Enact New Equipment Efficiency Standards and Strengthen Existing Standards

Federal appliance and equipment efficiency standards were signed into law by President Reagan in 1987 and expanded under President Bush in 1992. Minimum-efficiency standards were adopted because many market barriers (such as lack of awareness, rush purchases when an existing appliance breaks down, and purchases by builders and landlords) inhibit the purchase of efficient appliances in the unregulated market. Standards remove inefficient products from the market but still leave consumers with a full range of products and features to choose among. Appliance and equipment standards are clearly one of the federal government's most effective energy-saving programs. In 2000, federal appliance and equipment efficiency standards reduced consumer energy bills by approximately $9 billion, with energy bill savings far exceeding any

ii

134

increase in product cost. By 2020, standards already adopted will reduce peak electrical demand by an amount equal to the output of more than 400 power plants of 300 MW each.

In order to provide additional cost-effective savings under this program, we recommend that Congress adopt new efficiency standards for products now or soon to be covered by state efficiency standards. Among the products that should be included are distribution transformers, exit signs, traffic lights, and torchiere lighting fixtures. California is now adopting standards on these products and Massachusetts and Minnesota already have standards on distribution transformers. None of these standards have been controversial and all yield highly cost-effective energy savings. Congress should also adopt standards on commercial refrigeration equipment, commercial unit heaters, and standby power consumption for household appliances and electronic products (such as televisions, VCRs, cable boxes, and audio equipment). In addition, DOE, with adequate funding and encouragement from Congress, should complete equipment standard rulemakings in a timely manner. Finally, the Bush Administration should drop its efforts to roll-back the recently set SEER 13 efficiency standard for residential central air conditioners and heat pumps.

4. Enact Tax Incentives for Highly Energy-Efficient Vehicles, Homes, Commercial Buildings, and Other Products

Many new energy-efficient technologies have been commercialized in recent years or are nearing commercialization. But these technologies may never get manufactured on a large scale or widely used due to barriers such as their initial high cost, market uncertainty, and lack of consumer awareness. Tax incentives would help manufacturers justify mass marketing for innovative energy-efficient technologies. Tax credits also could help buyers (or manufacturers) offset the relatively high first cost premium for the new technologies, thereby helping to build sales and market share. Once the new technologies become widely available and produced on a significant scale, costs should decline and the tax credits could be phased out.

We recommend tax incentives for advanced, high-efficiency appliances, new homes, new commercial buildings, hybrid and fuel cell vehicles, combined heat and power (CHP)systems, and other building equipment such as air conditioners and heat pump water heaters. The total cost to the Treasury would be on the order of $10 billion. These credits would save energy directly due to purchases of equipment eligible for the credits, but even more importantly, if the credits helped to establish these innovative products in the marketplace and reduced the first cost premium so that the products would be viable after the credits were phased out, the indirect impacts would be many times greater than the direct impacts.

5. Expand Federal Energy Efficiency R&D and Deployment Programs

DOE has made many valuable contributions towards increasing the energy efficiency of U.S. buildings, appliances, vehicles, and industries. Consequently, the President's Committee of Advisors on Science and Technology (PCAST) stated in 1997 that "R&D investments in energy efficiency are the most cost-effective way to simultaneously reduce the risks of climate change, oil import interruption, and local air pollution, and to improve the productivity of the economy." A July 2001 National Academy of Sciences review of some of DOE's R&D programs found that a sample of energy efficiency R&D programs resulted in net realized economic benefits of approximately $30 billion (1999$), substantially exceeding the roughly $7 billion (1999$) in total energy efficiency RD&D investment over the 22-year life of the programs. Similarly, the ENERGY STAR deployment programs operated by EPA and DOE have also been very successful.

Based on specific budget recommendations in the PCAST report, we recommend that instead of cutting funding for DOE's R&D programs as proposed this spring by the Bush Administration, funding should instead be increased by about 17% per year for the next 3 years. Funding for EPA's programs should also be expanded at a similar level.

6. Promote Clean, High-Efficiency Combined Heat and Power Systems

CHP systems produce multiple usable energy forms (e.g., electricity and steam) from a single fuel input. These combined systems achieve much greater efficiency than the usual separate systems for producing steam and electricity because the CHP systems recover heat that would otherwise be wasted in separate power production, and use this heat to displace the fuel that otherwise would be used to produce heat in a separate boiler.

Several inequities in government and utility regulations hinder development of CHP resources. These include environmental standards that do not recognize the efficiency gains of CHP systems, utility rules that make it difficult for many CHP systems to connect to the utility grid, and tax depreciation rules that vary the depreciation period for CHP systems from 5–39 years depending on plant ownership. Each of these problems need to be addressed, including: (1) reforming regulations to regulate emissions per unit of energy output rather than per unit of energy input; (2) developing uniform standards for CHP facilities to be interconnected with the local distribution facilities; and (3) standardizing depreciation periods for CHP systems based on the technical and market life of current systems.

7. Voluntary Agreements and Incentives to Reduce Industrial Energy Use

There is substantial potential for cost-effective efficiency improvement in industry. For example, in-depth analyses of specific energy efficiency technologies for the iron and steel, paper and pulp, and cement industries found a total cost-effective energy savings potential of 11–22%. In order to stimulate widespread energy efficiency improvements in the industrial sector, we propose that the U.S. government establish voluntary agreements with individual companies or entire sectors. Companies or sector trade associations would pledge to reduce their overall energy and carbon emissions intensities (energy and carbon per unit of output) by a significant amount, for example, at least 1% per year over 10 years. Companies that make a more substantial commitment (for example, at least 2% per year) could be given ENERGY STAR or similar recognition. The government could encourage participation and support implementation by: (1) providing technical assistance to participating companies that request assistance; (2) offering to postpone consideration of mandatory emissions reductions or tax measures if a large percentage of industries participate and achieve their goals; and (3) expanding federal R&D and demonstration programs for sectors with high participation.

A number of major companies have already made voluntary energy efficiency commitments on their own. For example, Johnson and Johnson set a goal in 1995 of reducing energy costs by10% by 2000 through adoption of "best practices" in its 96 U.S. facilities. As of April 1999, they were 95% of the way towards this goal, with the vast majority of projects providing a payback of 3 years or less. Voluntary agreements between government and industry along the lines proposed here have resulted in substantial energy intensity reductions in some European nations such as Germany, the Netherlands, and Denmark. The United States should build on this experience.

8. Improve the Efficiency and Reduce the Emissions of the Existing Power Plant Fleet

Many old, highly polluting power plants are "grandfathered" under the Clean Air Act. This means that they do not need to meet the same emissions standards for nitrogen oxides (NOx), sulfur dioxide (SO_2), and particulates as plants built after the Clean Air Act of 1970 was enacted. Currently, 850 plants built before 1970 are still operating, with a combined power output of 145,400 MW. In 1999, these plants produced about 21% of our nation's electric generation. These older, dirty power plants emit 3–5 times as much pollution per unit of power generated as newer, coal-fired power plants and 15–50 times as much NOx and particulates as a new combined-cycle natural gas power plant. These older plants also are less efficient than most new plants; the pre-1970 plants have an average heat rate of 11,025 Btus of fuel per kWh generated, compared to modern combined-cycle plants with heat rates of 7,000 or less. When the Clean Air Act was adopted, it was expected that these dirty power plants would eventually be retired. However, many utilities are continuing to operate these plants beyond their "design life" due to their low capital and operating cost.

If old, grandfathered plants were required to meet the same emissions standards as new plants, some plants would be modernized and cleaned up, but many would be shut down and replaced with much more efficient and cleaner generating sources such as combined-cycle natural gas power plants. We recommend that a policy to end "grandfathering" be enacted soon but not take effect until 2010 or thereabouts. This phase-in period would allow owners of these old plants to make plant upgrade vs. replacement decisions and then have sufficient time to implement these decisions without unduly disrupting power markets. Alternatively, the same general objectives would be achieved by adopting new emissions standards as part of a Clean

Air Act "four pollutant" strategy that has been proposed in order to address SOx, NOx, mercury, and carbon dioxide (CO_2) emissions in an integrated fashion. Such a strategy would include tradeable emissions permits, with the number of emissions allowances based on the phase-out of old, dirty, inefficient power plants.

9. Greater Adoption of Current Model Building Energy Codes and Development and Implementation of More Advanced Codes

Building energy codes require all new residential, commercial, and industrial buildings to be built to a minimum level of energy efficiency that is cost-effective and technically feasible. "Good practice" residential and commercial energy codes have been adopted by just over half the states. However, some major states (such as Arizona, Illinois, Michigan, New Jersey, and Texas) have not adopted these "good practice" energy codes. Furthermore, building codes can and should be upgraded. In the case of residential codes, codes can be further improved by including several measures to reduce use of air conditioning in hot climates and by reducing energy losses due to air infiltration and duct leakage. In the case of commercial codes, a new national model standard was published in 1999 that reduces energy use approximately 6% compared to the old "good practice" code. Here too, substantial additional improvements are possible as measures with 10–20% additional savings were included in early drafts but dropped as part of a political process to gain "consensus."

In order to capture the available savings, states should be directed to review their codes and encouraged to revise them. DOE should continue to provide technical assistance for these efforts, with preference given to states that adopt statewide mandatory codes at or above the model codes. The model code organizations (International Energy Conservation Code [IECC] and American Society of Heating, Refrigerating and Air-Conditioning Engineers [ASHRAE]) should also be encouraged to regularly update their codes to incorporate the latest in cost-effective energy-saving measures. IECC has been doing well in this regard, but ASHRAE's 1999 standard revision achieves far less savings than ASHRAE had targeted. Given ASHRAE's conservatism, DOE should broaden its funding activities to include organizations and consortiums of states that are interested in achieving higher levels of energy savings than ASHRAE is able to deliver.

Integrated Analysis

In order to estimate the energy and emissions savings of these nine policies as well as their costs and benefits, we conducted an integrated analysis using the DOE/EIA National Energy Modeling System, known as NEMS. Most of our assumptions for the base case were taken from the NEMS model, specifically as it was applied to produce the *Annual Energy Outlook 2001*. We then modeled each of our policies individually and together to estimate the overall impacts of our policy set and the contribution of each policy towards these combined impacts.

Energy Impacts

Key results of the analysis are summarized in Table ES-1. Overall in the base case, total U.S. primary energy consumption grows 1.3% per year on average. Relative to the base case, the nine policies reduce primary energy consumption by 11% by 2010 and by 26% by 2020. Primary energy use rises slightly during the next decade but falls significantly during 2010-2020 (see Figure ES-1).

Table ES-1. Summary of Overall Results for the Base and Policy Cases

	1990	1999	2010 Base Case	2010 Policy Case	2020 Base Case	2020 Policy Case
End Use Energy (Quads)	63.9	71.6	86.5	79.4	98.3	78.9
Primary Energy (Quads)	84.6	96.1	114.6	102.2	128.1	94.2
Energy Use by Fuel (Quads)						
Coal	19.1	21.4	25.2	18.1	26.2	9.5
Oil	33.5	38	44.9	41.9	51.7	42.1
Natural gas	19.3	22	28.7	26	35.5	27.5
Nuclear	6.2	7.8	7.7	7.8	6.1	6.3
Hydro	3	3.2	3.1	3.1	3.1	3.1
Other renewables	3.5	3.4	4.8	5.1	5.2	5.5
Carbon Emissions (Million Metric Tons)	1,338	1,505	1,817	1,540	2,063	1,338
Other Emissions (Million Metric Tons)						
Sulfur dioxide	19.3	20.5	16.5	14.9	16.9	13.1
Nitrogen oxides	21.9	15.8	12.8	11.6	12.7	6.6
Particulate matter (PM-10)	1.7	1.5	1.5	1.4	1.6	1.4
Cumulative Net Savings ($ billions)			-	152	-	591

In the base case, oil consumption would increase by about one-third by 2020, and oil imports would increase by more than 60% over that period. Thus, the oil import fraction is projected to rise from a little over 50% today to about 70% of total U.S. oil use by 2020. The policies evaluated here would significantly reduce overall oil imports. Relative to the base case, annual oil use would be reduced by about 19% and imports by about 40% by 2020. With implementation of the nine policies, U.S. total energy use in 2020 would be about 2% lower than energy use in 1999. Within this overall trend, use of some fuels would increase and use of other fuels would decrease. For example, use of coal would decline 56% over this period, primarily due to substantial retirements of old coal-fired power plants and replacement with natural gas. Due to increased use of natural gas for electricity generation, natural gas use would grow 25% under the policy case relative to 1999 consumption, indicating that increased natural gas supplies would be needed. This growth in natural gas use in the policy case would be substantially less than the 62% increase in natural gas use in the base case. As for petroleum, even with substantial efficiency improvements, petroleum use in the policy case would be 11% higher than use in

1999. With domestic production at best stagnant, this would mean that oil imports would grow modestly, even with a full array of efficiency policies. (By way of comparison, petroleum use would grow 36% in the base case.) Finally, electricity use in 2020 would be about the same as 1999 use, although growth in CHP systems would decrease the need for centrally generated power relative to 1999. In total, while our nine policies would dramatically reduce the need for new energy supplies, even with these policies, there would be some need for new supplies, particularly natural gas.

Figure ES-1. U.S. Energy Consumption Over Time in the Base and Policy Cases

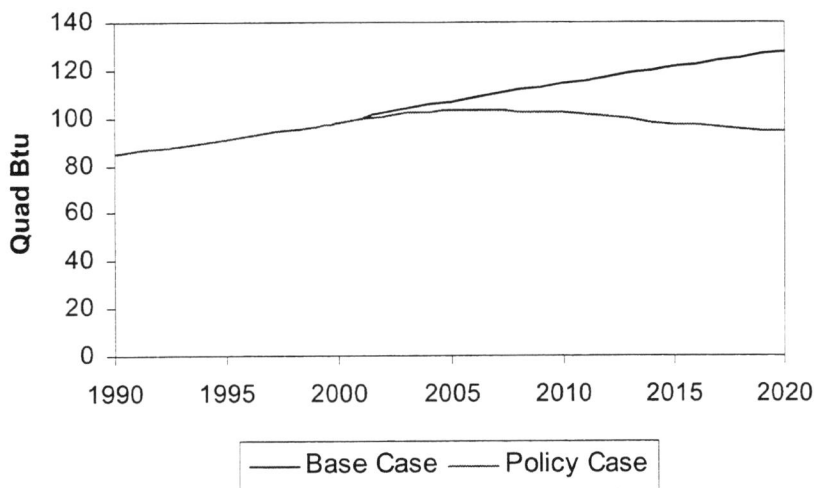

Table ES-2 summarizes savings from the different policies. Each of the policies would have a substantial impact on U.S. energy use, with all saving at least 1.5 quad by 2020 (although tax credits are listed with lower savings since a substantial portion of their savings would be subsumed under the CAFE standards, CHP, appliance standards and building code policies). The largest savings would be achieved by CAFE standards and related policies to improve the fuel economy of light duty vehicles. Public benefit funds and industrial voluntary programs would have the next largest savings. These three policies together would account for about 60% of the savings in our policy case. However, for these policies to achieve such savings, they would need to be stringent along the lines discussed above, with the equivalent of a 38 mpg CAFE standard, a two-tenths of a cent per kilowatt-hour matching public benefit fund, and an industrial targets program backed by significant "carrots and sticks." Scaled-back versions of these policies would result in significantly lower savings.

Intermediate levels of energy savings would be achieved by updated and expanded appliance and equipment efficiency standards, expanded federal R&D and deployment efforts, increased use of CHP systems, and tax credits. Finally, more moderate, albeit still substantial, savings would be achieved by building codes and retirement of old, inefficient power plants. Savings from this latter policy are somewhat limited by our analytical approach, whereby demand-side measures are applied before supply-side measures. With this convention, efficiency programs would lead to substantial power plant retirements, leaving only about half of the old "grandfathered" plants to be affected by the power plant policy. If we had instead considered supply-side policies first, power plant retirements would be included among the policies with intermediate energy savings.

Table ES-2. Energy Use Reductions by Policy

	2010	2020
Total Policy Case Consumption	102.2	94.2
Reduction from industrial policies	4.5	9.5
Reduction from commercial policies	2.7	7.9
Reduction from transport policies	2.1	7.7
Reduction from residential policies	2.5	7.2
Reduction from electric supply policies	0.6	1.5
Total Base Case Consumption	114.6	128.1

Economic Impacts

Figure ES-2 summarizes the direct economic costs and benefits in the policy case. The policies would induce incremental investments in advanced industrial processes; more efficient buildings, lighting, and appliances; more fuel-efficient cars and trucks; cleaner and more efficient power plants; and so on. We estimate a total investment of $127 billion through 2010 and $495 billion through 2020, expressed in 1999 dollars using a 5% real discount rate. To place these figures in context, total U.S. energy expenditures (excluding on-site renewables) equaled a little over $600 billion in 2000. Overall, we estimate that end-users would save over $1,100 billion through 2020 as a result of these policies. The energy bill and operating savings would more than offset the investments costs, with net savings of about $170 billion through 2010 and over $600 billion through 2020. The net savings would grow over time since energy efficiency measures would have more time to pay back their initial cost.

The nine policies would also have a positive impact on the economy by weakening demand for different energy sources, which would result in lower energy prices. In the base case, NEMS projects that domestic electricity and coal prices will decline somewhat in real terms over the 1999–2020 period (e.g., declines of 8% and 25%, respectively), while natural gas prices will increase by 49%. Under the policy case, electricity and coal prices are projected to drop by an additional 7% and 1%, respectively. More dramatically, natural gas prices are projected to decline to below 1999 levels (e.g., to $1.9 per million Btus in 2020), a *37%* decline from the base case.

Figure ES-2. Costs, Savings, and Net Savings for the Policies by 2020

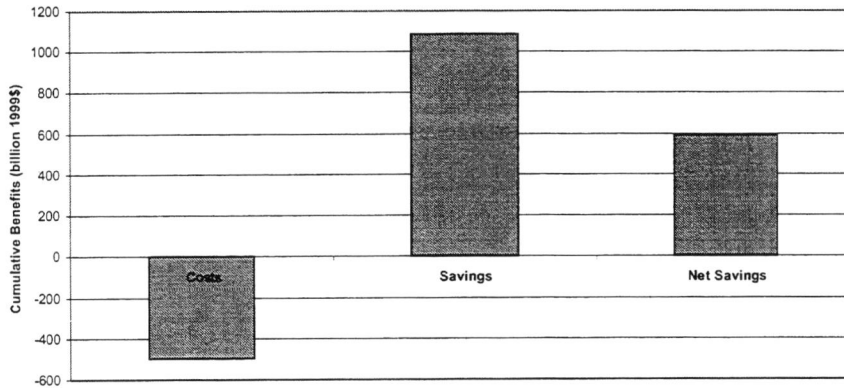

These price declines would have a substantial and positive impact on the U.S. economy and would benefit all consumers and businesses. These indirect benefits are in addition to the direct benefits discussed above. Figure ES-3 summarizes our model results for energy expenditures in the base and policy cases, incorporating both the direct and indirect effects. Viewed on a per household basis, in the base case, energy expenditures per household would gradually climb from $5,355 in 1999 to $6,249 in 2020 (1999$). In the policy case, expenditures per household would be only $4,156, an annual savings of $2,093 per household (a savings of one-third).

Figure ES-3. Energy Expenditures in the Base and Policy Cases

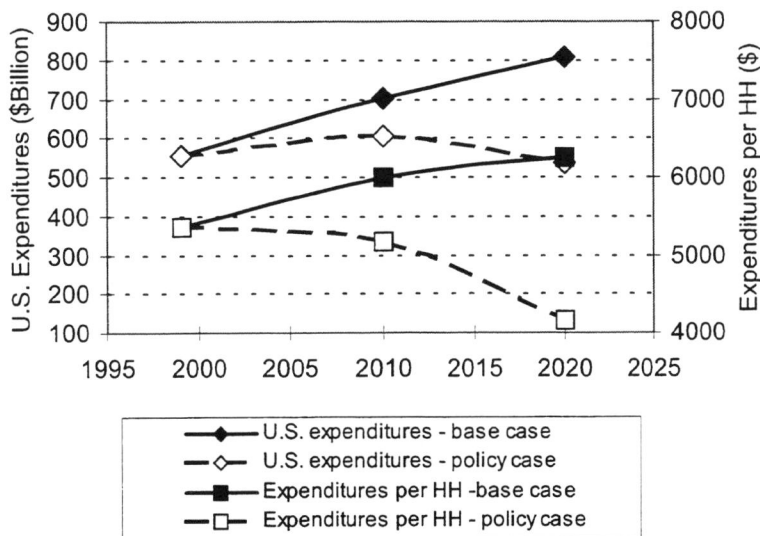

x

Emission Impacts

U.S. carbon emission trends in the base and policy cases are illustrated in Figure ES-4. In the base case, carbon emissions would reach 1,817 million metric tons (MMT) carbon equivalent by 2010 and 2,063 MMT by 2020, a 1.5% annual average growth rate during 2000–2020. Base case emissions would be 36% greater than the 1990 level by 2010 and 54% greater by 2020. In the policy case, carbon emissions would decline by 2010 so that they would be the same as 2000 emissions and about 15% above 1990 emissions. While this would not be enough to reach America's Kyoto Protocol target of 7% below 1990 emissions during 2008–2012, it would be strong steps in that direction. It should be possible to achieve the Kyoto target (i.e., a further 290 MMT annual reduction) through some combination of: (1) further domestic reductions from additional policy initiatives, such as policies to promote use of renewable energy sources and policies to reduce energy use for air and truck transportation and vehicle miles traveled for passenger cars; (2) reductions in emissions of other greenhouse gases; (3) purchase of emissions reductions from other Annex 1 countries; and (4) reductions in developing countries from Clean Development Mechanism projects.

Figure ES-4. U.S. Carbon Emissions Over Time in the Base and Policy Cases

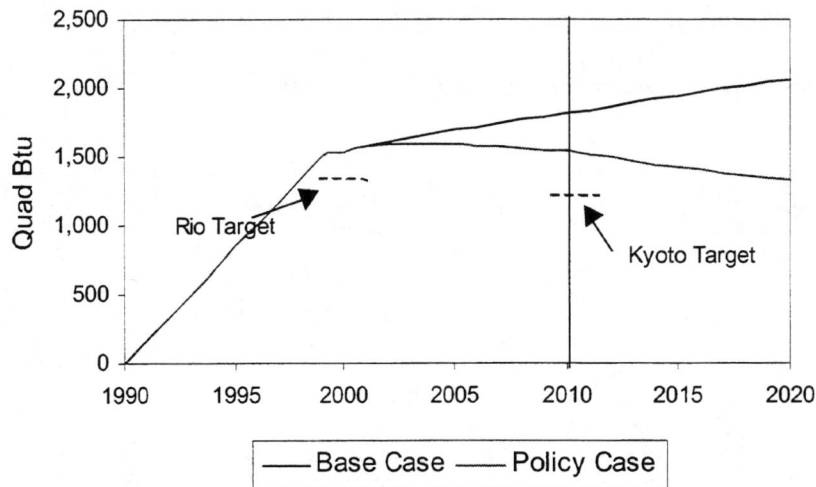

In addition to carbon emission reductions, the set of nine policies would also reduce emissions of criteria air pollutants. Implementing the nine policies would reduce SO_2 emissions the most— 48% by 2020. Emissions of NOx would be cut 19% by 2020 and fine particulate emissions would drop 13% by 2020. Clearly, taking action to reduce energy use as proposed in the policy case would provide significant public health and local/regional environmental benefits.

xi

Discussion and Conclusion

Energy efficiency should be a cornerstone for America's energy policy. Taken together, the nine policies recommended here could reduce U.S. energy use by more than 20% in 2020. These efficiency policies alone would not solve all of our energy problems—energy use would continue to grow for a decade or more while these energy-saving policies would gradually take effect. Furthermore, sustaining current rates of energy use into the long-term future would require new sources of energy supply and distribution. However, these efficiency policies would substantially reduce our energy problems, making it easier to find reasonably priced and environmentally acceptable energy supplies to meet U.S. energy demand. In other words, relative to a supply-focused energy strategy, a balanced energy strategy that complements efforts to expand supplies with a major focus on improving efficiency, would have a greater chance of success in terms of ensuring the reliability of the U.S. energy system, reducing economic costs (since all the efficiency strategies incorporated here save consumers and businesses money at projected future energy costs), and protecting the environment.

The general public voices strong support for increasing energy efficiency and a balanced energy strategy. For example, a recent nationwide poll conducted for the *Los Angeles Times* found that when people were read a list of 11 actions to deal with the energy situation, the top four actions (supported by 85–91% of respondents) were "invest in new sources of energy," "mandate more energy-efficient appliances," "mandate more energy-efficient new buildings," and "mandate more energy-efficient cars." Options for increasing the supply and delivery of traditional energy sources received significantly less support.

Ten years ago the previous Bush Administration issued its National Energy Strategy. It gave considerable priority to greater energy efficiency and called for expansion of energy efficiency R&D and technology deployment programs, new policies to stimulate utility energy efficiency programs, establishing new appliance and equipment energy efficiency standards, and new federal incentives to increase energy efficiency. Many of these proposals were incorporated in the Energy Policy Act of 1992, and the budget for and impacts of DOE's energy efficiency programs rose throughout the previous Bush Administration.

In May 2001 the current Bush Administration released its *National Energy Policy*. This policy calls for "advanc[ing] new, environmentally friendly technologies to increase energy supplies and encourage cleaner, more efficient energy use." Unfortunately the policy details do not bear this rhetoric out. Instead, the plan proposes many specific policies for increasing energy supplies, but the major specific efficiency policy is a call for tax incentives for efficient vehicles and CHP systems (a subset of the tax credits we propose). In addition, the plan calls for "reviewing" CAFE and "tak[ing] steps" to set new appliance efficiency standards. These latter suggestions fall well short of our specific policy prescriptions.

Congress is now beginning to consider energy legislation, and these efforts so far go farther than the Bush Administration proposes, but are still well short of what is needed. As of this writing, legislation passed by the House of Representatives includes many of the tax incentives we call for, some of the appliance standards we call for, and an extremely modest increase in CAFE standards. At the same time, both houses of Congress have passed appropriations bills that reverse the budget cuts proposed by the Bush Administration, but do not provide the growth in funding that is needed. All of our other policies are not included in the House legislation. Congress is so far doing much less than what polls show the American people want. Congress needs to redouble its efforts in order to properly value and support energy efficiency in new energy legislation and in appropriations for energy programs.

This report shows that energy efficiency policies would make a very large contribution towards meeting U.S. needs for new energy sources, while reducing emissions and saving consumers and businesses billions of dollars. However, without aggressive policy intervention, many of these benefits will be lost, costing the United States dearly in terms of economics, public health, dependence on imported energy, and adverse impacts on our environment.

Chapter Eleven
Agriculture

1. The Concepts

The evolution of democratic states has seen a respect, sometimes even a love, for farming. In both England and the United States many early pro-democracy leaders were farmers. Rome's Virgil wrote at the beginning of the Common Era "O farmers excessively fortunate if only they recognized their blessings!" Shakespeare's Hamlet put it well: "Let me be no assistant for a state, but keep a farm". Jefferson's vision of the ideal American was the honest farmer toiling in his fields. When John Adams left the presidency he spent the rest of his long life as a hard-working Massachusetts farmer.

It's easy to see why. Family farms are headed by independent hard-working people used to solving problems. Those who do not have these attributes eventually lose their farm. These same characteristics often describe effective democratic citizens. Good citizenship requires care and involvement. But this outlook has also colored policies and beliefs about agricultural with a tinge on non-empirical interest and bad policies.

Agriculture is crucial to the majority of successful economies. Without food most governments fall and political instability looms. For less developed countries and developing countries no food leaves no option but starvation, their economies lack the **capital formation** necessary to import food needs for very long.

Developed countries sometimes continue to support or subsidize their agricultural sector long after they should. In democracies this can be partially explained by a need to garner votes from the farm community. But in all societies it can be a residue of the societal memory, the memory of fear of shortages and starvation. In the United States it is also a residue of respect, of admiration for the semi-myth of the self-educated yeoman that was the backbone of eighteenth century America. They often ignore **the law of comparative advantage** in their governmental support policies.

But for the United States the last forty years has seen the end of small family farms. Large farmers and corporate agriculture now dominate the agricultural sector. The largest 96,000 farm operators account for 54% of total agricultural sales. The million and a half smallest farms generate less than ten percent of sales. Most American farm subsidies go to the biggest farms, even though they need them the least. In a Kansas survey the 500 most profitable farms (averaging $105,000 in profits each) received on average $41,000 in government subsidies; the 500 least profitable farms (which were losing on average $3,000 each) got only $20,000 apiece in government money.

The future of American farmers is probably brighter than almost any other country on Earth. Great **infrastructure**, good **economies of scale**, better technology and access to high quality **capital goods**, strong worker knowledge, climate and soil advantages all combine to give the United States a decided advantage in this sector for many ranch and farm products. Over the next several years the agricultural sector is expected to improve. Rising world demand for food, continued progress toward freer trade through ongoing **unilateral policy reforms** in foreign countries, and existing **multilateral trade agreements** are expected to lead to steady increases in agricultural exports. **Cash production expenses** are expected to stabilize as fuel prices moderate, but fertilizer and chemical expenses rise, reflecting the **lagged effects** of current higher petroleum prices and modest increases in planted area totals. The biggest unknown is the level of future government subsidies.

Agricultural trade has several important facets. First, beyond the normal trade functions of profit and balance, is its role in forestalling or alleviating famine. National laws, foreign aid, and international famine relief efforts all center on agricultural trade. Conversely, using agricultural exports as a weapon is an important international issue. The War of 1812 was caused partially by failed **embargo** policies. The League of Nations tried to use embargoes to enforce its policies. The United States embargoed food exports to Cuba for decades after Castro proclaimed communism.

But recent years have seen the increased risk of a second agricultural weapon, disease as a terrorist act. Hoof and mouth disease and or a variety of other illnesses might be introduced into an enemy nation's food supply to hurt them. There is speculation that either terrorist groups or **rogue states** might use these or similar **biowarfare agents.** Defenses in most countries against such an act are minimal.

Three controversies surround agricultural trade: subsidies, trade barriers, and **genetically modified** foods. Subsidies violate every major **tenet** of free trade. They violate the law of comparative advantage, and they distort the **law of supply and demand**. They are often **nationalistic** and risk increasing regional or international tensions. They violate both the rule and the spirit of the **W.T.O.** and almost every other trade agreement. Yet they exist in many countries. They are a huge program in the European Union, important to farmers in Japan, and are even a factor in the United States—despite our comparative advantage in many areas of agricultural production. Less developed countries sometimes have subsidies to protect the poor (i.e. keep the price of basic commodities low). Trade barriers often exist for the same reason. In democratic nations they sometimes exist to protect pro-government voting blocks, in poorer countries to protect the income of farmers who would otherwise be driven out of business by cheaper imports.

The agricultural sector of the economy is also being affected by the battle over **genetically modified** foods. GM crops are grown in over 40 countries. 99% of the global transgenic crops are grown in the United States (68%), Argentina (23%), Canada (7%), and China (1%). But some countries have import and or sales bans on genetically modified foods.

Genetic modification is a special set of technologies that alter the genetic makeup of living organisms such as animals, plants, or bacteria. Combining genes from different organisms is known as **recombinant DNA technology**, and the resulting organism is said to be "genetically modified," "genetically engineered," or "**transgenic.**" The principle transgenic crops so far are herbicide and insect resistant soybeans, corn, cotton, and canola. The newest additions are yams resistant to a virus devastating the African harvest, rice with increased iron and vitamins to reduce **malnutrition** in Asia, and a variety of plants able to survive weather extremes.

The debate over benefits of transgenic foods include good arguments on both sides. Advocates point out that:

- ❑ *Crops* have enhanced taste and quality, reduced maturation time, increased nutrients and yields, improved resistance to disease and pests;
- ❑ *Animals* show increased resistance and productivity, they are hardier and feed more efficiently, and their health is better.
- ❑ The *environment* is helped because GM conserves soil, water, and energy as well as producing better waste management.
- ❑ *People* and society benefit because there is increased quantities of healthy food for growing populations.

Opponents have an interesting mix of arguments on their side:

- ❑ *Safety* is unknown. Potential human health **effects** include **allergens**, transfer of antibiotic resistant markers, unknown environmental impacts, unintended transfer of transgenes through cross-pollination (e.g. stronger weeds have already occurred), unknown effects on soil microbes, loss of **flora and fauna biodiversity**.
- ❑ *Society* in LDCs might be hurt because new advances may be skewed to the interests of the rich developed countries, they charge we risk domination of world food production

147

by a few companies, that developing countries will have increased dependence on **post-industrialized states**, and they charge increased risks of **biopiracy**—foreign exploitation of natural resources.

- ❏ *Ethical issues* also play a major role in attacks. Some opponents believe that natural organisms have **intrinsic value**, that we are tampering with mother nature by mixing genes among species, they worry there might be increased stress for animals.
- ❏ *Labeling* is not mandatory in some countries, such as the United States, and mixing genetically modified crops withy non-modified crops confounds labeling attempts

There are three non-trade issues that extemp speakers should get more familiar with. First is the debate over the environmental affects of modern farming. Chemical fertilizer use is very high, the United States saw 22 million tons of nitrogen used last year for example. Farm industrialization and energy use is escalating in many developed countries ranches and farms. Many LDCs use slash and burn land-clearing techniques that clear jungle with very thin topsoil, so the resultant farms can only last a few years before the land is exhausted. And the lost jungle contributes to **species extinction**, loss of animal habitat, reduces **genetic diversity**, and affects global warming because trees are a huge source for absorbing carbon dioxide and replacing it with oxygen. Opponents of some or all of these activities argue for **sustainable agriculture**. This widely used but very vague term has served as a rallying point for other less intrusive methods of farming. Different writers and activists mean different things when they use the phrase "sustainable agriculture". If you advocate it in an extemp speech or debate position be sure to define it. For many people sustainable agriculture means **crop rotation**, reduced fertilizer use, minimal use of growth hormones and genetically altered crops.

Second is the issue of **animal rights** and **factory farms**. Factory farms sometimes pack animals close together for feeding and, in the case of milk cattle, ease of milking. Chickens and pigs are kept in dense groups. **Antibiotic and hormone** use is high because some users see it increasing output. Waste runoff has environmental implications. Opponents have used **boycotts** (e.g. "don't buy veal"), lawsuits, and publicity to fight these business activities. Both sides have active lobbying efforts. The "Humane Farming Association" and a few similar organizations have even opened farm animal refuge ranches.

And finally there is the issue of **organic foods**. Organic food producers claim that pesticides, herbicides, antibiotics, and hormones used in most crop and animal production is harmful to humans. They produce food without using most or all of these tools. But this results in lower production levels and higher costs to consumers. Good quality neutral empirical data is notable missing on the pro-organic side of this debate but that has not deterred a substantial growth curve in developed countries, especially the United States, for organic products. In the Fall of 2002 the Food and Drug Administration finally issued guidelines regulating what is and is not an organic food, thus increasing producer honesty to the consumer.

2. Web Sites

Anti-factory farm material can be found at www.hfa.org/about/index.html. A *huge* collection of articles on genetically modified foods can be accessed at www.connectotel.com/gmfood/. A balanced review of issues plus good links on GM products is offered at www.ornl.gov/hgmis/elsi/gmfood.html. A good broad coverage site with its own internal search engine is www.farms.com/ Agricultural law and policy is very well covered for you at www.nationalaglawcenter.org/agsubject.htm Sustainable agriculture organizations can be reviewed and reach through www.factoryfarm.org/sustainableagricultureorganizations.html

3. Sample Extemp Topics

How can we revitalize the agricultural sector of the American economy?
Organic foods: needed reform or new wave fad?
Who's right in the debate over genetically modified foods?

4. If You Want To Read More…

Global Trade Alone Will
Not End World Hunger

By Jacques Diouf

International Herald Tribune

Rome - Whatever agreement emerges from the next round of multilateral trade negotiations, one thing is clear: Developing countries must be allowed to give priority to their agriculture sectors. Few nations have experienced rapid economic growth and reduction of poverty without first developing domestic agriculture. Economic growth based mainly on exports is not sufficient for broad-based development. Export-led economies frequently benefit only a small segment of the population, bypassing the often-poor majority.

With 790 million people enduring hunger and malnutrition in the developing countries, the UN Food and Agriculture Organization believes that eliminating hunger should be the world's overriding priority. Further liberalization of the global trading regime will not be enough to pull the least developed countries out of poverty.

The huge subsidies and protection that some high-income nations dole out to their farm sectors reduce the chance that farmers in developing countries can "grow" their way out of poverty and hunger. Farm subsidies and protectionism distort world markets and discourage investment in the agriculture sector of developing countries. In the rural areas where most of the world's poor and hungry live, subsidies paid to farmers in richer nations are yet another blow to local farm production.

Just as troubling is the pronounced drop in external assistance to developing countries' agriculture. There is little evidence at this time that private capital will replace public investment in agricultural research and extension, irrigation and infrastructure.

The Uruguay Round agreement on agriculture granted the developing countries "special and differential treatment." That treatment should be made more effective. Developing countries need to negotiate greater access to export markets. Such access is one of the most effective and sustainable kinds of economic assistance.

Globalization can have important benefits for developing countries, stimulating productive enterprises and encouraging investment and technology transfer. But further trade liberalization must be carefully phased in. Import restrictions should not be removed overnight or domestic food security may be harmed. At the same time, produce needs to be improved.

The FAO was mandated by the 1996 World Food Summit to assist developing countries to participate in multilateral agriculture trade negotiations as well-informed and equal partners. Because many developing countries do not have enough technical and legal specialists, the FAO is leading an umbrella program for training, which explains World Trade Organization agreements and prepares specialists to analyze issues

150

likely to come up in future negotiations.

The program shows specialists how to benefit from the process, how to minimize adverse effects, how to evaluate carefully proposals made by other negotiators and how to develop their own negotiating positions. To meet the need for technical assistance in low-income countries, the FAO launched a program for food security, which focuses on sustainable expansion of agricultural production and productivity. It is designed to provide adequate and nutritious food at the national and household levels. It operates in 55 countries, focusing on some of the most vulnerable groups in society, particularly women and the poor.

Trade globalization will not end hunger and poverty, but it has a critical role to play. If developing countries are given an equal opportunity with the wealthier countries to develop agriculture and export farm goods, all will gain. The benefits will be felt both in the North and the South. As the number of hungry people decreases and incomes rise, demand for goods from the wealthier countries can be expected to rise.

It is the moral responsibility of the international community to ensure that globalization does not lead to an ever widening gap between the poor majority and the wealthy few. This would further inflame passions that already bring people into the streets, demonstrating against what many see as manipulation of the world trading system by a cabal of super-conglomerates and the governments that support them.

The writer is director-general of the Food and Agriculture Organization of the United Nations. He contributed this comment to the International Herald Tribune.

More Articles on Inequality

---

777 UN Plaza, Suite 7G, New York, NY 10017 USA
+1 212 557-3161 fax: +1 212 557-3165

globalpolicy@globalpolicy.org

**If you appreciate the information we provide, please support our work.
Make a donation or become a member of Global Policy Forum.**

HUBERT H. HUMPHREY INSTITUTE OF PUBLIC AFFAIRS

SHOULD FOOD BE USED AS A WEAPON? *

G. Edward Schuh**

---

*Presented at WCCO seminar of the same title, North American Farm and Power Show, Minneapolis Convention Center, Minneapolis, November 29, 2001.

** Regents Professor of International Economic Policy and Director, Orville and Jane Freeman Center for International Economic Policy, the University of Minnesota's Humphrey Institute of Public Affairs.

The title of my paper is the subject matter I was asked to address in this session. The explanation that followed in the invitation was "With the war on terrorism underway, exporting of food/agricultural products becomes a consideration. How will those exports impact our security and military policy?"

This is an important and challenging issue. The answer to it has a number of important dimensions, some of which go beyond the explanation provided. I will try to broaden our perspective.

My remarks are divided into four parts. The first section considers the impact of our agricultural exports on our society and military policy. This is followed by a discussion of whether food can be effective as a weapon. The next section addresses the issue of food as a positive weapon. The last section raises the question of whether the United States should support a right to food policy. At the end I will have some concluding comments.

Impact of Agricultural Exports on our Society
and Military Policy

Let me first address the specific question posed in the invitation for me to speak. How will our agricultural exports impact our security and military policy? The short answer to that question is that our agricultural exports earn the foreign exchange needed to undertake the campaign against the terrorists. Thus they are an important resource or asset. We will be making many purchases in other countries to sustain the campaign and to support military and other operations. Obviously, such efforts are not sustainable unless we earn the foreign exchange needed to support them.

The costs of the anti-terrorist campaign will be above and beyond the foreign exchange costs of importing consumer goods and services and the intermediate goods and raw materials

152

needed to support our normal rate of economic growth. Given the degree of integration of our economy into the international economy, these other imports are already rather substantial.

What happens if we do not have adequate exports or foreign exchange earnings to support all of these demands for foreign exchange? One consequence will be a decline in the value of the dollar in foreign exchange markets. That decline will help make us more competitive in international markets and will be good news for export sectors such as agriculture. At the same time, it will make the cost of our imports - and the cost of undertaking the overseas operations - increase over time. In other words, we will have to use a larger share of our domestic resources to do what we need to do. That is equivalent to a decline in our standard of living.

Can Food Be Effectively Used as a Weapon?

Another important dimension to this problem is whether we are able to use our flow of exports as a weapon in the conventional sense of trying to punish those who harbor the terrorists. This is the thought people usually have in mind when they ask whether food should be used as a weapon. The idea is that we could withhold our flow of exports as the means of punishing our enemies.

Many in this audience will recall that that was the strategy Mr. Brezynski used in the embargo on sales to the former Soviet Union back in 1979. We learned a lot from that experience. Among other things, we learned that the market for agricultural commodities is fairly well organized. As a result, we were not able to limit the imports by the Soviet Union, except in a marginal way. The market was simply reshuffled - with the Soviet Union acquiring their supplies from other countries and the U.S. filling the gaps left by those suppliers. In the end, the former Soviet Union acquired all but about 4 million tons of the grain they wanted.

Another important lesson from that experience, and our earlier embargo on soybean exports, was that our reputation as a reliable supplier is important to our interests over the longer term. Instead of developing longer-term relationships that would serve us well over the longer term, potential importers began to diversify their sources so they wouldn't be overly dependent on us. Even if they had to pay a higher price for the commodities, they concluded that the increased security that comes from a diversified source of supplies was worth it.

Finally, there is always the problem that we end up harming the poor and disadvantaged in the country we set out to punish. The regimes we intend to punish by withholding exports are typically insensitive to domestic political pressure - and especially from the poor and disadvantaged. The end result of our using such policies is typically to generate political backlashes that in the longer term work against our own best interests.

Food as a Positive Weapon

There is still a third, positive dimension to using food as a weapon in conflicts with other countries. The current war in Afghanistan provides an excellent example. Although it seems to have disappeared from our television screens, the idea of dropping food to the population in that embattled country was an excellent idea. It should eventually help to alienate the local population against their tyrannical masters.

In a similar way, we can use food aid to promote economic development in the poorer regions of the world. This requires that we take a rather broad and long-term perspective on our posture in the international community. We also have to recognize that much of terrorism is rooted in poverty. By alleviating or eliminating that poverty we can eliminate or reduce the seedbeds of terrorism.

Food aid can in fact be an important means of promoting economic development, although we seldom use it in that way. Moreover, there tends to be strong political support for food aid, in contrast to the support for more general forms of food aid.

Finally, there is the potential for promoting agricultural development in the low-income countries. The argument in this case is essentially the same as above - except that we approach it at a more basic level. In essence, we would collaborate with researchers in the developing countries to help them produce the new production technology needed to promote their own economic development.

There are two issues here. The first is that as we help promote agricultural development in those countries we also help promote their general economic development, and in a low cost way. The increase in per capita incomes associated with that general economic development is the source of future markets for our producers.

Second, by cooperating with the researchers in other countries we learn more about their competitive potential. That can serve as the basis for strengthening our competitive policies. In addition, we gain knowledge that helps us to modernize our own agriculture and thus to be more competitive in international markets.

A Right to Food?

As a final issue, I would like to raise the issue of the right to food - or the access to food as a right. The U.S. position has been strongly against such a posture in international forums, even though we have individual states in this country that have such rights. Should we take such a posture in the international arena? I leave this question with you as you take leave of us.

Concluding Comments

The issue of whether food should be used as a weapon is complicated. Certainly, agricultural exports earn foreign exchange and help to pay for the activities that support the campaign against terrorism, while helping to pay for our other imports. There is a serious question, on the other hand, about whether we can in fact punish other countries by limiting our exports to them. But there are a number of positive ways in which we can use food to strengthen our international posture. These mainly involve activities that would help eliminate or reduce poverty.

Foreword

This report summarizes the main findings of the FAO study, World agriculture:towards 2015/30, which updates and extends the FAO global study, Worldagriculture: toward 2010, issued in 1995. It assesses the prospects, worldwide, for food and agriculture, including fisheries and forestry, over the years to 2015 and 2030. It presents the global long-term prospects for trade and sustainable development and discusses the issues at stake in these areas over the next 30 years.

In assessing the prospects for progress towards improved food security and sustainability, it was necessary to analyse many contributory factors. These range from issues pertaining to the overall economic and international trading conditions, and those affecting rural poverty, to issues concerning the status and future of agricultural resources and technology. Of the many issues reviewed, the report concludes that the development of local food production in the low-income countries with high dependence on agriculture for employment and income is the one factor that dominates all others in determining progress or failure in improving their food security.

The findings of the study aim to describe the future as it is likely to be, not as it ought to be. As such they should not be construed to represent goals of an FAO strategy. But the findings can make a vital contribution to an increased awareness of what needs to be done to cope with the problems likely to persist and to deal with new ones as they emerge. It can help to guide corrective policies at both national and international levels, and to set priorities for the years ahead.

The world as a whole has been making progress towards improved food security and nutrition. This is clear from the substantial increases in per capita food supplies achieved globally and for a large proportion of the population of the developing world. But, as the 1995 study had warned, progress was slow and uneven. Indeed, many countries and population groups failed to make significant progress and some of them even suffered setbacks in their already fragile food security and nutrition situation. As noted in the latest (2001) issue of The State of Food Insecurity in the World, humanity is still faced with the stark reality of chronic undernourishment affecting over 800 million people: 17 percent of the population of the developing countries, as many as 34 percent in sub-Saharan Africa and still more in some individual countries.

The present study predicts that this uneven path of progress is, unfortunately, likely to extend well into this century. It indicates that in spite of some significant enhancements in food security and nutrition by the year 2015, mainly resulting from increased domestic production but also from additional growth in food imports, the World Food Summit target of halving the number of undernourished persons by no later than 2015 is far from being reached, and may not be accomplished even by 2030.

By the year 2015 per capita food supplies will have increased and the incidence of undernourishment will have been further reduced in most developing regions. However, parts of South Asia may still be in a difficult position and much of sub-Saharan Africa will probably not be significantly better and may possibly be even worse off than at present in the absence of

155

concerted action by all concerned. Therefore, the world must brace itself for continuing interventions to cope with the consequences of local food crises and for action to remove permanently their root causes. Nothing short of a significant upgrading of the overall development performance of the lagging countries, with emphasis on hunger and poverty reduction, will free the world of the most pressing food insecurity problems. Making progress towards this goal depends on many factors, not least among which the political will and additional resource mobilization required. Past experience underlines the crucial role of agriculture in the process of overall national development, particularly where a large part of the population depends on the sector for employment and income.

The study also foresees that agricultural trade will play a larger role in securing the food needs of developing countries as well as being a source of foreign exchange. Net cereal imports by developing countries will almost triple over the next 30 years while their net meat imports might even increase by a factor of almost five. For other products such as sugar, coffee, fruits and vegetables the study foresees further export potential. How much of this export potential will materialize depends on many factors, not least on how much progress will be made during the ongoing round of multilateral trade negotiations. Developing countries' trade barriers in all areas, not only in agriculture. In many resource-rich but otherwise poor countries, a more export-oriented agriculture could provide an effective means to fight rural poverty and thus become a catalyst for overall growth. But the study also points at potentially large hardships for resource-poor countries which may face higher prices for large import volumes without much capacity to step-up production.

Numerous studies that assessed the impacts of freer trade conclude that lower trade barriers alone may not be sufficient for developing countries to benefit. In many developing countries, agriculture has suffered not only from trade barriers and subsidies abroad but has also been neglected by domestic policies. Developing countries' from freer trade unless they can operate in an economic environment that enables them to respond to the incentives of higher and more stable international prices. A number of companion policies implemented alongside the measures to lower trade barriers can help. These include a removal of the domestic bias against agriculture; investment to lift product quality to the standards demanded abroad; and efforts to improve productivity and competitiveness in all markets. Investments in transportation and communications facilities, upgraded production infrastructure, improved marketing, storage and processing facilities as well as better food quality and safety schemes could be particularly important, the latter not only for the benefit of better access to export markets, but also for reducing food-borne diseases affecting the local population.

On the issue of sustainability, the study brings together the most recent evaluation of data on the developing they are used now and what may be available for meeting future needs. It does the same for the forestry and the fisheries sectors. The study provides an assessment of the possible extent and intensity of use of resources over the years to 2030 and concludes that pressure on resources, including those that are associated with degradation, will continue to build up albeit at a slower rate than in the past.

The main pressures threatening sustainability are likely to be those emanating from rural poverty, as more and more people attempt to extract a living out of dwindling resources. When these processes occur in an environment of fragile and limited resources and when the circumstances for introducing sustainable technologies and practices are not propitious, the risk grows that a vicious circle of poverty and resource degradation will set in. The poverty-related component of environmental degradation is unlikely to be eased before poverty reduction has advanced to the level where people and countries become significantly less dependent on the exploitation of agricultural resources. There is considerable scope for improvements in this direction and the study explores a range of technological and other policy options. Provided such improvements in sustainability are put in place, the prospects point to an easing of pressures on world agricultural resources in the longer term with minimal further buildup of pressures on the environment

156

caused by agricultural practices.

I conclude by reiterating the importance of developing sustainable local food production and of rural development in the low-income countries. Most of them depend highly on agriculture for employment and income as an important and, often, the critical component of any strategy to improve their levels of food security and alleviate poverty. It is for this reason that sustainable agricultural and rural development is given enhanced priority in The Strategic Framework for FAO: 2000-2015.

Jacques Diouf
Director-General
Food and Agriculture Organization of the United Nations

Policy Analysis

No. 449

Sustainable Development
A Dubious Solution in Search of a Problem

by Jerry Taylor

Executive Summary

From August 26 through September 4, 2002, approximately 100 heads of state and 60,000 delegates will gather in Johannesburg, South Africa, to attend a "World Summit on Sustainable Development." The conference—convened on the 10th anniversary of the Earth Summit in Rio de Janeiro and expected to be the largest U.N. summit in history—will explore domestic and international policy options to promote the hottest environmental buzzwords to enter the public policy debate in decades.

The concept seems innocuous enough. After all, who would favor "unsustainable development"? A careful review of the data, however, finds that resources are becoming more—not less—abundant with time and that the world is in fact on a quite sustainable path at present.

Moreover, the fundamental premise of the idea—that economic growth, if left unconstrained and unmanaged by the state, threatens unnecessary harm to the environment and may prove ephemeral—is dubious. First, if economic growth were to be slowed or stopped—and sustainable development is essentially concerned with putting boundaries around economic growth—it would be impossible to improve environmental conditions around the world. Second, the bias toward central planning on the part of those endorsing the concept of sustainable development will serve only to make environmental protection more expensive; hence, society would be able to "purchase" less of it. Finally, strict pursuit of sustainable development, as many environmentalists mean it, would do violence to the welfare of future generations.

The current Western system of free markets, property rights, and the rule of law is in fact the best hope for environmentally sustainable development.

Jerry Taylor is director of natural resource studies at the Cato Institute.

Both strong and weak definitions of sustainable development pose problems. The narrower the definition, the easier it is to pin down, but the less satisfactory the concept.

What Is Sustainable Development?

The concept of sustainable development is an important milestone in environmental theory because it posits how society itself should be organized, not simply why certain environmental protections should be adopted or how they can be best implemented. This ambitious interpretation is widely shared by business leaders, policy activists, and academics alike.[1] Of course, just how much social and economic change is necessary to achieve sustainability depends upon how "unsustainable" one believes the present to be. Many advocates of the idea clearly believe the present to be quite unsustainable and thus are prepared for radical change.

Unfortunately, sustainable development is rather difficult to define coherently. The UN Commission on Economic Development in its landmark 1987 report titled *Our Common Future* defines sustainable development as that which "meets the needs of the present without compromising the ability of future generations to meet their own needs."[2] But that definition is hopelessly problematic. How can we reasonably be expected to know, for instance, what the needs of people in 2100 might be?

Moreover, one way people typically "meet their own needs" is by spending money on food, shelter, education, and whatever else they deem necessary or important. Is the imperative for sustainable development, then, simply a euphemism for the imperative to create wealth (which, after all, is handed down to our children for their subsequent use)? True, some human needs, such as the desire for peace, freedom, and individual contentment, cannot be met simply by material means, but sustainable development advocates seldom dwell on the importance of those nonmaterial, non-resource-based psychological needs when discussing the concept.[3]

Thus, sophisticated proponents of sustainable development are forced to discard as functionally meaningless the UNCED definition. Otherwise, the UNCED definition can be read as a call for society to maximize human welfare over time. An entire profession has grown up around that proposition. The profession is known as economics, and maximizing human welfare is known not as "sustainable development" but as "optimality." Was Adam Smith's *The Wealth of Nations* really the world's first call for sustainable development?

Since the release of *Our Common Future*, more than 70 competing definitions of sustainable development have been offered by academics and policy analysts.[4] Economists David Pearce and Jeremy Warford, two of the world's more serious thinkers about sustainable development, argue that these competing definitions largely fall into two categories. Many advocates of sustainable development are defining regimes in which the natural resource base is not allowed to deteriorate.[5] This category is generally known as the "strong" definition of sustainability. Other advocates of sustainable development are describing regimes in which the natural resource base would be allowed to deteriorate as long as biological resources are maintained at a minimum critical level and the wealth generated by the exploitation of natural resources is preserved for future generations, who would otherwise be "robbed" of their rightful inheritance. This category is generally known as the "weak" definition of sustainability. Weak sustainability, then, can be thought of as "the amount of consumption that can be sustained indefinitely without degrading capital stocks," defined as the sum of both "natural" capital and "man-made" capital.[6]

Unfortunately, both strong and weak definitions of sustainable development pose problems. As Robert Hahn of the American Enterprise Institute points out, the narrower the definition, the easier it is to pin down, but the less satisfactory the concept.[7]

Strong Sustainability, Flabby Analytics

Numerous analytic problems cripple the utility of strong sustainable development theory.

First, advocates of strong sustainability

are implicitly contending that in most cases natural capital is more desirable than the man-made capital created from its exploitation. Natural capital, it is argued, offers future generations multiple possibilities for its use, whereas man-made capital settles the question for future generations. Future generations, argue advocates of strong sustainability, may have different preferences for the ultimate use of natural capital than the present deciding generation.

Nevertheless, the wealth created by exploiting resources is often more beneficial than the wealth preserved by "banking" those resources for future use. Otherwise, there would be little point in exploiting resources for commercial use in the first place. Moreover, wealth created through resource exploitation is far more versatilely employed than the rock or mineral might be in its unaltered state.

Subscribers to the concept of strong sustainabilty are implicitly suggesting that the world is somehow a poorer place because past generations drew down stocks of oil, iron, and various other minerals and metals to make advanced satellites, modern industry, and—through the wealth thereby created—advanced medicines and dozens of other life-enhancing technologies and practices. Geography professor M. J. Harte of the University of Waikato, New Zealand, underscores the analytic problem:

> We should accept that it is often impractical and perhaps undesirable to hold natural capital intact in its entirety, but it is also counter to the idea of sustainability to bequeath a stock of natural capital to future generations that is incapable of yielding sufficient resource flows (i.e., "income") to fulfill their potential needs and aspirations.[8]

Taken at face value, strong sustainability is wholly inconsistent with a modern economy. Whether a project is sustainable forever or just a very long time has nothing to do with whether it is desirable. If unsustainability were really regarded as a reason for rejecting a project, there would be no mining, no more than subsistence agriculture, and no industry.[9]

A second problem with the concept of strong sustainability is the fact that sustainable resource use can, paradoxically, cause more environmental damage than unsustainable resource use. For instance, economist Richard Rice, ecologist Raymond Gullison, and policy analyst John Reid—a team of scholars who together spent years studying the Amazonian rain forests of Bolivia—concluded recently:

> Current logging practice causes considerably less damage than some forms of sustainable management (which require more intensive harvests of a wider variety of species). Indeed, a more sustainable approach could well double the harm inflicted by logging.... Sustainability is, in fact, a poor guide to the environmental harm caused by timber operations. Logging that is unsustainable—that is, incapable of maintaining production of the desired species indefinitely—need not be highly damaging (although in some forests it is, especially where a wide range of species have commercial value). Likewise, sustainable logging does not necessarily guarantee a low environmental toll.[10]

The third and final problem with strong sustainability is the implicit suggestion that today's natural resource base (and the health thereof) will necessarily be of significant interest to future generations. On the contrary, conserving today's natural resource base does not ensure that tomorrow's natural resource base is secure. Likewise, drawing down today's natural resource base does not necessarily mean that tomorrow's natural resource base will be put in jeopardy.

Resources are simply those assets that can be used profitably for human benefit.

If unsustainability were really regarded as a reason for rejecting a project, there would be no mining, no more than subsistence agriculture, and no industry.

"Natural" resources are a subset of the organic and inorganic material we think of as constituting the biological environment, since not all of that material can be used profitably for human benefit. But what can be used productively by man changes with time, technology, and material demand. Ocean waves, for example, are not harnessed for human benefit today and thus cannot really be thought of as a natural resource. But the technology to harness the movement of waves as a means to generate energy certainly exists, and the day when the cost of doing so is lower than the cost of alternative energy sources is the day when waves become a natural resource. Uranium, to cite another example, would not have been considered a resource a century ago but is most certainly thought of as such today. Petroleum was not an important resource 150 years ago but today is thought of as perhaps the most important resource to modern society. And if cold-fusion technology had panned out, coal would be another example of yesterday's resource but tomorrow's relatively useless rock.

Thus, the natural resource base is itself relative and its components vary greatly with time due to technology and material demand. The composition of the natural resource base of a century ago is substantially different from the natural resource base of today, not because of depletion but owing to advances in the economy, technology, and industrial society. There's little reason to think that tomorrow's resource needs will necessarily match those of today.

The Meaninglessness of Weak Sustainability

What if we embrace the weak definition of sustainable development—allowing natural resources to be depleted as long as they are maintained at a "minimum critical level" and the proceeds of their use are preserved for future generations—rather than the clearly untenable strong definition? Weak sustainability is certainly a more reasonable proposition, but that's largely because it is functionally indistinguishable from the economists'

mission of maximizing human welfare. As economist David Pearce, a strong proponent of weak sustainability, concedes:

> [Sustainable development] implies something about maintaining the level of human well-being so that it might improve but at least never declines (or, not more than temporarily, anyway). Interpreted this way, sustainable development becomes equivalent to some requirement that well-being not decline through time.[11]

The two apparent qualifications of weak sustainability are really no qualifications at all. If, on the one hand, we understand "minimum critical level" as the natural resource base necessary to sustain human life, then one certainly doesn't maximize human welfare by consuming resources beyond that point. As noted by scholars at the Australia-based Tasman Institute:

> Stripped down to its essentials, efficiency means making the best use of resources, including natural resources, capital, labor, knowledge and inherited institutions and cultural values, to ensure that community well-being is maximized. Essential to this are energetic steps to reduce waste and to ensure that valued goods and services are provided with minimum cost. Environmental concerns are a vital part of the notion of economic efficiency and allocations of resources which do not take environmental concerns into account are unlikely to be efficient.[12]

If, on the other hand, we mean that each and every natural resource, regardless of its utility to mankind, should be preserved beyond some minimal critical level—for example, if we construe sustainable development to mean the maintenance of a set of resource "opportunities"[13]—then, without reference to costs and benefits, the concept is simply anti-

Weak sustainability is certainly a more reasonable proposition because it is functionally indistinguishable from the economists' mission of maximizing human welfare.

human and inimical to the interests of future generations.

As a thought experiment, assume that the only way we could have preserved the American bison beyond a minimum critical level was to leave the Great Plains largely untouched by agriculture. Would the sacrifice of what was to become the world's most productive cropland in order to protect the great buffalo herds have been in either the economic or social interest of future generations? A policy paradigm that refuses to consider the costs or benefits of such decisions is incapable of making a moral argument about the interests of future (human) generations. But to include cost and benefit calculations in such decisions brings us right back to the economic concept of "maximizing welfare."

The admonition that the proceeds of such tradeoffs be preserved for our children is superfluous. Since all wealth is eventually inherited by future generations, there would appear to be no rationale for a special state-supervised "account" to be established for their benefit.

The Incoherence of Intergenerational Equity

Perhaps the strongest rationale for both strong and weak variations of sustainable development is, according to its proponents, the case for "intergenerational equity." Indeed, as economist Matthew Cole points out, "despite the countless definitions, a key characteristic of all versions of sustainable development is the principle of equity. Such a notion of equity includes not only providing for the needs of the least advantaged of today's society (intragenerational equity) but also extends to the needs of the next generation (intergenerational equity)."[14] One of the most articulate proponents of this argument is Georgetown University professor of international law Edith Weiss, who argues that future generations have as much right to today's environmental resources as we do, and that we have no right to decide whether or not they should inherit their share of those rights.[15]

Yet the concept of tangible rights to resources for those not even conceived is dubious to say the least.[16] First, it is philosophically inconsistent. Those disincorporated beings not yet even a glimmer in someone's eye are said to have rights to oil, tin, copper, trees, or whatever but not, apparently, to life itself (unless, of course, Western societies decide to outlaw abortion). Moreover, once individuals are conceived, we do not maintain that they have a right to all the resources of the parent. If, for example, a retired couple spends $50,000 on a trip around the world, we do not argue that the couple has violated the resource rights of their children. If intergenerational equity is to be taken seriously, then the claims one generation has on another should not be affected by the distance in time between the two.

The concept of intergenerational equity, moreover, is hopelessly inconsistent. If the choice to draw down resources is held exclusively by future generations, then are we not some previous generation's "future" generation? Why is the present generation bereft of that right? If the answer is that no generation has the right to deplete resources as long as another generation is on the horizon, then the logical implication of the argument is that no generation (save for the very last generation before the extinction of the species) will ever have a right to deplete any resource, no matter how urgent the needs of the present may be. If only *one* generation (out of hundreds or even thousands) has the right to deplete resources, how is that intergentational equity?

Compounding that problem is the fact that future generations will almost certainly be far, far better off economically than present generations. If we were serious about equality between generations, then, we might take economist Steven Landsburg's advice and "allow the unemployed lumberjacks of Oregon to confiscate your rich grandchildren's view of the giant redwoods."[17]

The math is actually quite simple. If U.S. per capita income manages to grow in real terms by 2 percent a year (a conservative assumption), then in 400 years, the average American family of four will enjoy an income

Would the sacrifice of what was to become the world's most productive cropland in order to protect the great buffalo herds have been in either the economic or social interest of future generations?

5

162

of $2 million *a day* in 1997 dollars (roughly, Microsoft CEO Bill Gates's current income). If per capita income grew a bit faster—say, at the rate reported by South Korea over the past couple of decades—it would take only 100 years for an average family of four to earn $2 million daily. "So each time the Sierra Club impedes economic development to preserve some specimen of natural beauty," writes Landsburg, "it is asking people who live like you and me (the relatively poor) to sacrifice for the enjoyment of future generations that will live like Bill Gates."[18]

Furthermore, the notion of resource rights for future generations is premised on the argument that one has a right to forcibly take property from someone else in order to satisfy a personal need. Although that is an argument best left unexplored here, suffice it to say that such a claim is expansive and fraught with moral peril.[19]

Finally, the belief that the interests of future generations are more likely to be protected by political than by market agents is dubious. Indeed, any clear-eyed survey of government versus market decisionmaking finds that market agents are far more likely to invest for the future than governmental agents.[20] As noted by economists Peter Hartley from Rice University and Andrew Chisolm and Michael Porter of the Tasman Institute:

> Future generations do not take part in elections, but they are represented in the capital market. While many voters are concerned about future generations, democratically elected governments have a tendency to reflect the wishes of the marginal voter in the currently marginal electorate, so it is unreasonable to expect governments to be more conservation-minded than such a voter. Markets, on the other hand, can reflect more extreme views on the future value of a resource. Since the value of an asset hinges on expectations of what others may pay for

access in the future, speculators become the representatives of future generations in today's markets.[21]

Since advocates of sustainable development rely upon governmental action to ensure the success of their agenda, it is unlikely—no matter how well-intentioned their efforts or successful their political campaigns—that their goals will be realized through state intervention in the economy.

The Chimera of Resource Scarcity

The call for sustainable development implicitly posits that robust stocks of natural resources are crucial to economic well-being and that current trends in resource consumption are somehow unsustainable.

As to the former claim, it may certainly be the case that resource sustainability is desirable for subjective cultural reasons, but natural resource scarcity is simply not a binding constraint on economic growth as is commonly asserted. Economist Joseph Stiglitz in a classic study found that exogenous technological advances lead to long-run gains in per capita consumption in less-developed countries under conditions of exponential population growth and limited, exhaustible stocks of natural resources.[22] Economist Edward Barbier found that even in a growing economy, technological change is resource augmenting.[23] As Barbier and colleague Thomas Homer-Dixon of the University of Toronto put it, "sufficient allocation of human capital to innovation will ensure that resource exhaustion can be postponed indefinitely, and the possibility exists of a long-run endogenous steady-state growth rate that allows per capita consumption to be sustained, and perhaps even increased, indefinitely."[24]

Regardless, the data clearly show that most natural resources are becoming more—not less—abundant with time. In fact, a proper understanding of resource economics suggests that this trend will actually improve greatly over time and that resource depletion

The belief that the interests of future generations are more likely to be protected by political than by market agents is dubious.

is simply not a significant worry if the correct legal and economic policies are maintained. Accordingly, "sustainable development"—even if we put aside its theoretical difficulties—is a solution in search of a problem.

Agricultural Sustainability

Let's start by examining the data regarding the agricultural sustainability. Figure 1 reveals that, since 1950, food production has greatly outpaced population growth. Figure 2 illustrates the practical effects of figure 1—an overall decline in the price of food throughout the world. Figure 3 reveals that this growing abundance of food has led to a marked increase in daily per capita intake of calories in both rich and poor regions of the world. This massive increase in production came primarily from increased productivity, not from increased cultivation of lands. The amount of land devoted to agricultural purposes expanded by only about 9 percent from 1961 to 1999 while population doubled.[25] Paul Waggoner of the Connecticut Agricultural Experiment Station and Jesse Ausubel of Rockefeller University cal-culate that, given likely trends, cropland will shrink globally by about 200 million hectares, or more than three times the land area of France, by 2050.[26] Ausubel believes that devel-opment will increase global forest cover by about 10 percent.[27]

The UN's Food and Agriculture Organiza-tion reports that, as a consequence, the per-centage of the population subject to famine and starvation declined from 35 percent in 1970 to 18 percent in 1997 and is expected to fall to 12 percent by 2010.[28] Likewise, the per-centage of undernourished children in the developing world has fallen from 40 percent to 30 percent over the past 15 years and is expected to fall to 24 percent by 2020.[29] The continuing existence of large and growing farm subsidies in the developed world is testa-ment to the fact that glut—not scarcity—is the prevailing problem in the agricultural sector.

The positive trend in food availability is unlikely to reverse itself for several reasons. First, there are tremendous unrealized opportunities to exponentially expand global food production simply through the applica-

Given likely trends, cropland will shrink glob-ally by about 200 million hectares, or more than three times the land area of France, by 2050.

Figure 1
World Food Production vs. World Population Growth

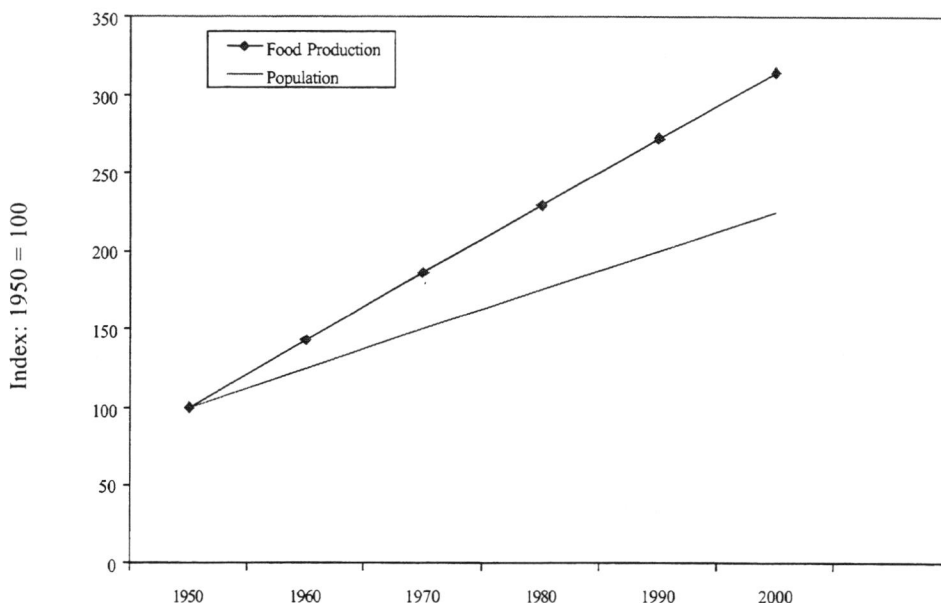

Source: UN Food and Agriculture Organization, data cited in "Loaves and Fishes," *The Economist,* March 21, 1998.

Figure 2
Total Food Commodity Price Index, World

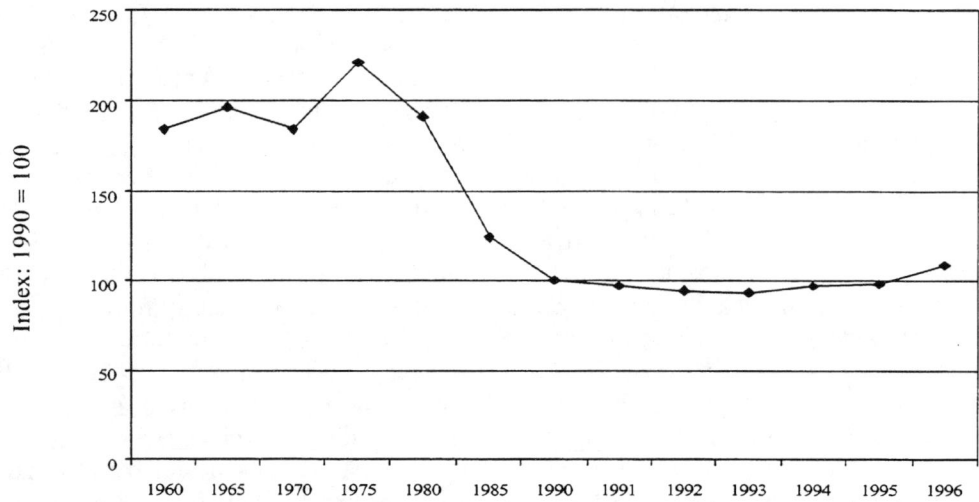

Sources: World Resources Institute, UN Environmental Programme, UN Development Program, and World Bank, *World Resources 1998–1999: A Guide to the Global Environment* (New York: Oxford University Press, 1998), Table 6.3, as cited in Ronald Bailey, ed., *Earth Report 2000* (New York: McGraw-Hill, 2000), p. 265.

Figure 3
Daily per Capita Supply of Calories, 1970 and 1995

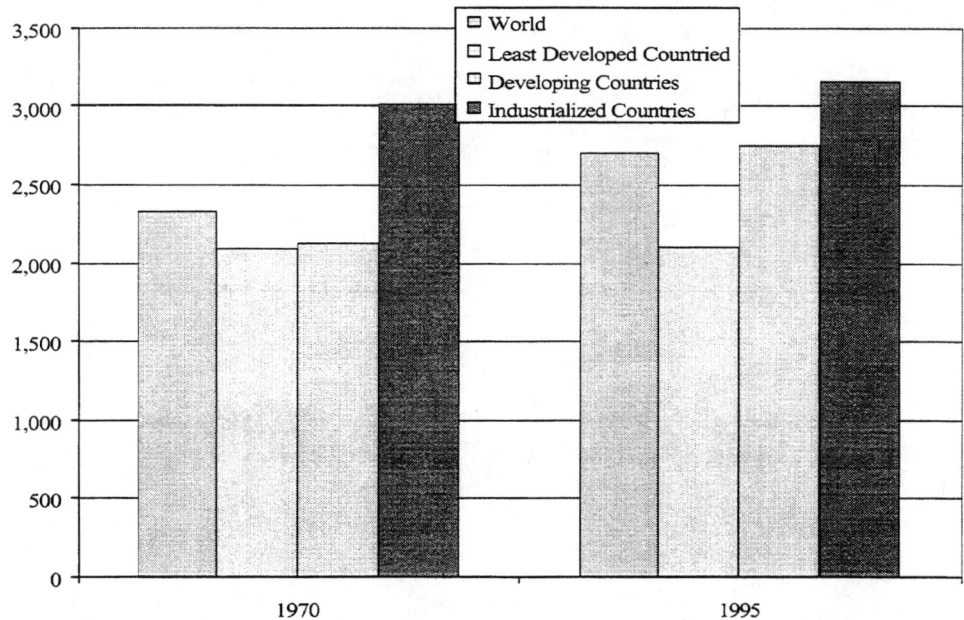

Source: World Resources Institute, UN Environmental Programme, UN Development Programme, and World Bank, *World Resources 1998–1999: A Guide to the Global Environment* (New York: Oxford University Press, 1998), p. 161.

8

165

tion of existing Western technology and agricultural practices in less-developed countries.[30] Second, advances in nonexotic technology and information services are beginning to radically improve yields as they have in many other industries.[31] Third, agricultural science is progressing in record leaps and bounds, promising even greater expansions in agricultural productivity and nutritional improvements.[32] Fourth, economic growth produces greater food availability (largely by making more capital available for advanced agricultural practices), and few economists expect the global economy to stop growing in real terms in the future.[33] Finally, global population is now projected to level off at around 11 billion by the year 2200,[34] a figure well within the agricultural "carrying capacity" of the planet.[35]

Fishery Sustainability

A perennial concern within the subset of issues pertaining to agricultural sustainability is the concern over the depletion of the world's fisheries. As noted above, however, land-based crop and food production is more than capable of meeting future needs. This is particularly the case since fish consumption makes up less than 1 percent of total caloric intake and only 6 percent of protein intake across the global population.[36]

Regardless, there is little evidence for the oft-stated assertion that global fisheries are near collapse. Total catches have increased a bit more than fourfold since 1950 while total catches per capita have doubled over that same period (although they've held steady by that measure since about 1965).[37] While some commercially valuable species are in decline, high prices, consumer tastes, and public awareness campaigns have shifted consumption to less scarce species. So what is commercially valuable today is often not what is commercially valuable tomorrow and visa versa.

Still, there is legitimate concern over the depletion of some species and species subpopulations. Those problems stem from what ecologist Garrett Hardin famously termed "the tragedy of the commons."[38] In short, since

everyone is free to harvest fish but no one owns the schools, individual fisherman maximize their revenue by increasing their harvest regardless of what other fishermen might do. Nobody has any incentive to efficiently manage fish populations. Governments are called in to do the job, but the proliferation of massive subsidies to the fishing industry in virtually all countries and excessively generous allotments for fish harvests demonstrate that well-organized special interests will almost always sacrifice the health of fisheries for the economic interests of the fishing industry.

Here, we confront for the first time in our discussion (but not for the last time) a major cause of "unsustainable" resource use—public ownership and extraction subsidies. The remedy can be found in simple economics—privatization of fishing rights. The most popular method of privatization involves state issuance of individual fishing quotas that could be traded in secondary markets. This approach, which has the support of both conservationists and economists, has proven successful in Iceland and elsewhere at stabilizing fish populations while protecting the economic health of the fishing industry.[39]

Another method is the emerging practice of "fish farming," which not only helps to provide resources at minimal ecological cost but also serves to take the pressure off wild fish stocks.[40] Production from such farms has increased fivefold since 1984—now constituting about 25 percent of total catches[41]—and will continue to grow in the future.[42] The production from such farms could grow even more dramatically with the introduction of fertilizers. Oceanographers etimate that 60 percent of ocean life grows in but 2 percent of the ocean's surface. The limiting factor is primarily the lack of nutrients necessary to sustain phytoplankton. Adding those nutrients—which is conceptually no more difficult than land-based fertilization techniques–could increase fish yields by a factor of hundreds.[43]

Mineral Sustainability

Next, let's consider trends in the availability of commercially important metals, fuels,

> **There is legitimate concern over the depletion of some species and species subpopulations. Those problems stem from what ecologist Garrett Hardin termed "the tragedy of the commons."**

Figure 4

Estimated Annual Trends in Mineral and Metal Prices, 1870–1998 (all commodities indexed to 1990 = 100)

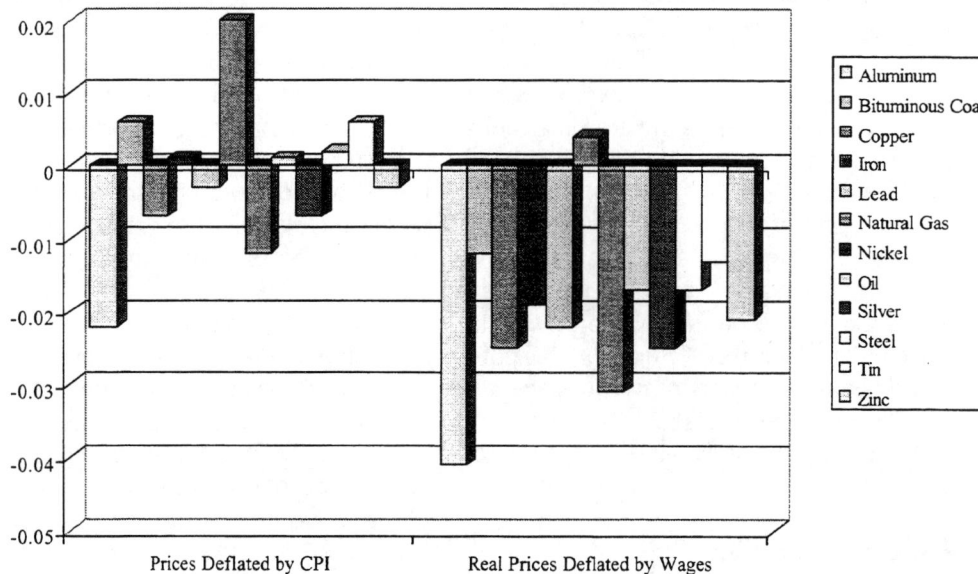

Source: Stephen Brown and Daniel Wolk, "Natural Resource Scarcity and Technological Change," *Economic & Financial Review*, Federal Reserve Bank of Dallas, Q1, 2000, p. 7.

Whether you measure the availability of various mineral resources by inflation-adjusted prices or by the amount of effort necessary to produce a unit of consumption, mineral resources are becoming more abundant.

and minerals. Figure 4 demonstrates that, whether you measure the availability of various mineral resources by inflation-adjusted prices or by the amount of effort necessary to produce a unit of consumption,[44] mineral resources are likewise becoming more abundant—not more scarce—and are on a clearly economically sustainable path.

Perhaps the most provocative suggestion from Figure 4 is that petroleum is becoming more abundant, not more scarce as is popularly believed.[45] This is true even if we examine indicators other than price.[46] The best indicators are development costs and values in-ground. The average cost of finding oil fell from $12 per barrel in 1980 to just $7 per barrel in 1998 despite 40 percent inflation in the interim.[47] While data on petroleum asset values are hard to come by, what is known suggests that those asset values are not trending upwards.[48]

Secondary indicators are less useful but likewise reveal positive trends. Proven reserves of petroleum, for instance, are 15 times larger today than when record keeping began in 1948 and about 40 percent larger than in 1974.[49] Moreover, the amount of those reserves that we use in any given year has remained steady at 2–3 percent since 1950.[50] How much oil can we potentially move from the "unproven" to the "proven" category? One prominent study estimates that 6 trillion barrels of recoverable conventional oil exist today (a reserve of approximately 231 years given present consumption) and another 15 trillion of unconventional oil—such as tar sands, oil shale, and orimulsion) are recoverable (808 years at present levels of consumption) given favorable economics.[51] The argument that we're running out of new fields to discover and that production will accordingly peak in the near future (the so-called Hubbert's Curve hypothesis) ignores the potential for unconventional fossil fuel and grossly underestimates the availability of oil in existing fields given technological advance and adequate pricing signals.[52]

Concerns over the finite nature of mineral resources are ill-considered

10

Chapter Twelve
Immigration

1.   The Concepts

Migration has occurred throughout history, whether it is Europeans stealing America from the Natives or Mexicans illegally entering the United States. Some countries, most notably the classical immigration countries of Australia, Canada, New Zealand and the United States, have usually welcomed the influx. Immigrants often bring valuable ideas, good labor, resources and **cultural diversity**. But over the last four decades immigrants have become increasingly unwelcome in many nations. Any government that proposes to increase immigration is likely to experience a backlash from its citizens. This change occurred for several reasons.

The strong international economic growth that occurred in the decades after the Second World War led to the recruitment of millions off labor immigrants, or "guest workers", by countries in Europe, the Middle East, and elsewhere. Language and cultural differences were a source of some friction. But the 1973 oil embargo signaled an economic downturn that dramatically reduced the demand for immigrant labor. Since then governments have made it much more difficult for people to immigrate.

Because of deteriorating economic conditions, and or ethnic and political persecution, increasingly large numbers of refugees and **asylum** seekers have sought **safe haven** in foreign nations. Because these people tend to come from poorer and less developed countries they often need assistance and are often perceived as burdens. Sometimes conflict between natives and foreigners occur, e.g. the violence that took place in German between natives and asylum seekers during the 1990s. Anti-immigrant movements and parties have risen, such as the Front Alliance in France. Countries on every populated continent have been touched and molded by the movement of people across borders.

There has been a fundamental shift in the level of immigration and the way immigration is viewed by policymakers over the last few decades. Globally the number of immigrants is high, more than 100 million, and rising. In 1976 the United Nations High Commissioner for Refugees (UNHCR) reported 2.8 million refugees. By 1993 the figure had grown to 19 million. Since 1989 the number of refugees and asylum seekers has averaged 15.8 million a year. Moreover, refugee and asylum figures do not include immigrant statistics. The United Nations Population Fund consistently identifies more than 100 million immigrants worldwide. Combining known immigrants, refugees, and **displaced persons** results in 150 million people who have left their homes. This represents approximately 1 of every 38 people on earth, more than 2.5% of the globe's population.

Most immigrants and refugees come from LDCs and developing countries. According to records of the United States Committees for Refugees not a single advanced nation is in the top 40 sources of refugees and asylum seekers. But6 are refugee or immigrant groups mainly in specific regions? Far less than half of the immigrants live in **first world** nations. According to the U.S. Committee for Refugees, Europe and North America have slightly more than 16% of the world's refugees, East Asia and the Pacific have less than 3%. More than 36% of the world's refugees live in Africa, about 33% in the Middle East, and almost 11% in South or Central Asia. Approximately 90%

of the world's refugees are from LDCs or developing countries and move to other LDCs or developing countries. The reality of refugee location is thus a far cry from how the West perceives things.

There is anti-foreigner sentiment in many countries, particularly advanced democracies. Anti-foreigner sentiment has been growing in Europe. Many countries, including France, Austria and Germany, have experienced the growth of right-wing parties that play on anti-immigrant feelings. The greater the cultural differences between natives and immigrants the greater the amount of distrust and fear. A notable extemp example is France, where Jean-Marie Le Pen of the anti-immigration Front National scored second in the 2002 presidential elections. Opinion polls show 50% of Frenchmen are "frightened" by Islam.

Such feelings are not unusual, nor are they limited to Europe. The bhoomiputras in Malaysia regarded the inflow of Chinese and Vietnamese so threatening that the Malaysian government rejected boatloads of Vietnamese refugees even when the vessels were in danger of sinking. In Fiji the native people overthrew a democratically elected government because it was dominated by Indians. Nepal has resisted immigration from northern India, fearing it will erode Nepalese **cultural hegemony**.

Economic issues play a large part in these immigration reactions. Before the 1970s open lands and economic growth encouraged toleration. Then policymakers agreed that the free movement of people added to economic growth. Western Europe's economic recovery after the Second World War, for example, was fueled in part by immigrant labor. But global economic conditions since then have changed dramatically. The 1973 oil embargo, the move from labor intensive to technology intensive industries in advanced nations, and the rising fear of terrorism by non-natives meant that the richest countries have much less need and less desire for immigrants.

When immigrant workers were laid off some used unemployment and other welfare programs they were entitled to. These actions increased fear that immigrants were an economic drain. And as jobs became scarcer native workers increasingly felt that immigrants (who often are willing to work for lower wages) threatened their jobs.

Most Western European countries halted their recruitment of immigrants and tried to **repatriate** their foreign labor. Repatriation has been supported even though it is more expensive, especially in the short run, than it is to provide assistance. The additional cost of repatriation, according to Professor Chapin in the *Journal For the Study of Peace and Conflict*, in a 2000 essay, can be up to 100 times greater than welfare costs. Economic deterioration also increased **xenophobia** (fear of outsiders or foreigners). These economic fears often translated into dubious political voting patterns and increased **nationalism**.

But immigrant labor remains important in other areas of the world. Several million immigrant laborers are employed in the Middle East. Palestinian refugees, for example, are common workers in the oil states around the Persian Gulf.

While voters often think the economic effects of immigration are clear the research is much more murky. The empirical studies that have been conducted often reflect the **ideological predispositions** of their researchers. At one side is Simon, whose 1989 and 1996 studies argue strongly that immigrants increase the wealth and welfare of host countries under all conditions. At the other end are Huddle's 1994 work and the 1985 report by Huddle, Corwin and MacDonald whose data show that immigrants undermine wages and citizen's employment rates.

Sometimes immigration in large numbers has met a **coercive reaction**. For example in 1971 10 million East Pakistan refugees (East Pakistan is now Bangladesh) immigrated to India. India responded by sending troops into Pakistan, partially to stop the flow. Similarly one of the reasons for repeated Israel P.L.O. violence is their intense disagreement over refugee treatment. The Kurdish revolts in Iraq, and Kurdish terrorism in Turkey, are both instances of force reacting to refugee actions and movements. In Bosnia the violence surrounding Moslems resulted in the dislocation of several hundred thousand people, and the death of several thousand. President Clinton's response to Haitian refugees had clearly coercive facets.

How can extempers or debate cases offer to solve such problems? There are at least three possible options: control, accommodation, and or intervention. Greater border control involves more military and police to effectively close borders, stiffer penalties for companies hiring illegal aliens, and quick forced repatriation of illegals. Identity cards can also be used as a control device, though civil liberty issues make them unpopular.

Border control is often used. The United States has long used it, with active strengthening after the September 11, 2001 terrorist attacks. Japan erected clear barriers after World War II to retain its cultural homogeneity. France and Italy have increased their controls, though European Union agreements limit their abilities to do so effectively.

Accommodation means accepting the level of legal immigration and quietly accepting some illegal immigration. The United States from 1944 to 1991 is a good example of accommodation. Canada remains one today. **Neoclassical economic theory** supports this solution by arguing that economic benefits derive from the free movement of **factors of production**.

Your final option is intervention. It is not exclusive, your speech or argument can mix and match solutions. Intervention involves changing the economic, political and or social factors that are causing the immigration. If Mexico's economy is stronger, the theory goes, more Mexicans will stay home to earn there and be with their families. If Turkey is allowed to join the European Union and **joint ventures** plus investment capital strengthens their economy, wages and quality of life will increase; as a result Germany will have fewer Turkish immigrants and repatriation problems will decrease. If east and southern Africa get enough aid and transnational investment to develop an **infrastructure** that restores economic opportunities their conflicts and refugee flow will decrease. Economic assistance, coercive diplomacy, sanctions and military action are all types of intervention.

Almost all economists agree with the carrot part of the "carrot and stick" aspect of intervention. But empirical evidence suggests that, in the short term, emigration increases because the people who were too poor to emigrate acquire the money to do so. A recent book by Myron Weiner, *The Global Migration Crisis*, argues that economic growth is not historically associated with decreases in emigration. In 19th century Germany, for example, hundreds of thousands emigrated even though the nation was experiencing massive economic growth.

2. The Specific Case of the United States*

There are five goals in United States' immigration policy. The economic goal is to increase our productivity and standard of living. But the economic goal must be weighed with or against four other goals:

- ❑ The goal of promoting **human rights**;
- ❑ The security goal—controlling illegal immigration;
- ❑ The social goal—unifying United States citizens with their families;
- ❑ The goal of appreciating and modestly promoting a **multicultural environment**.

About 1.1 million immigrants enter and stay in the United States each year. The vast majority of immigrants are concentrated in only six states. Thus the economic effects of immigration vary depending on the state, the strength of the local economy, and the concentration of immigrants in the area.

Two comparatively recent laws have the most effect on legal United States immigration. The *Immigration Reform and Control Act of 1986* instituted employer sanctions for knowingly hiring illegal aliens, increased border enforcement, and created a legalization program for many then-illegal aliens. The *Immigration Act of 1990* tripled **employment-based immigration** (emphasizing skills needed in our economy), and increased legal immigration ceilings by 40%.

The number of people who speak a language other than English at home is approximately 32 million. Language barriers are expensive, they increase educational costs (e.g. bilingual programs) and lower worker productivity. But over half of those who speak another language at home are native-born.

But your speech can look at education-economy links another way. Immigrants are concentrated at the extremes of the educational spectrum. They are much more likely than native-born Americans to have very high or very low educational achievement. Recent immigrants (24% of them) are more likely than Native Americans to have a college degree. On the other hand, while both immigrants and native-born have made educational gains in the last twenty years, it is Native Americans who are doing so at a faster rate.

The **economic performance** of immigrants can be determined by looking at their employment, occupation, and income. When immigrants enter the labor force they alter economic conditions. As the immigrant population has grown so has its impact on the labor force. 9.5% of the labor force is foreign-born. Unemployment rates for Native-born Americans and immigrants are similar, though some years find a slight edge for immigrants (i.e. they have approximately a .3% lower unemployed rate). At the lowest educational levels native men and women are more likely than immigrants to be without a job, i.e. not in the labor force or unemployed. The average immigrant earns less than the average American citizen.

Labor force projections show that immigrants will continue to add to the diversity of the United States labor force. The foreign-born share of the labor force will rise to 14% in 2010. An additional 6 million new immigrants will join the force in the next decade, accounting for one-third of the labor-force change in the upcoming decade.

The composition of the labor force will continue to change, with white male workers shrinking from 42% to 36% in 2010. White males and females will still constitute a large majority (about 67%)) of labor force entrants, but because they are relatively older than other groups, they will account for over 80% of those who leave the labor force through retirement or death. Racial-ethnic minorities will increase from 26% of the labor force in 2000 to 30% in 2010.

The public costs of immigration, especially their welfare costs, are drawing increasing attention. Tension between the federal government and the states is mounting under the **fiscal pressure** of tight state budgets and stagnant local economies in some of the high immigration areas (such as California). Most state governments argue that since the federal government controls immigration they should not mandate *state* payments for welfare and Medicaid but instead cover it themselves.

One of the reasons state and local governments protest is their belief that immigrants drain money from the tax system. But contrary to perception immigrants generate significantly more in taxes paid than the cost of services they receive. Yet the states do have a valid complaint, because immigrants generate a net surplus in federal taxes but a net loss in state taxes. The biggest complain, about immigrants eating up welfare budgets, is absolutely false. When refugees are excluded immigrants of working age are *considerably* less likely than citizens to receive welfare. In total studies by Prof. Huddle, as well as a 1994 report by Passel and Clark, show a surplus of revenues over social service costs of at least $25 billion.

The evidence indicates that the economic effects of immigration are largely positive. Most immigrants are integrating socially and economically, and they are doing so without broad negative effects on the receiving community.

Legal immigrants give America thee big benefits. The data shows that immigrants pay more in taxes than they receive in public services. The average household incomes of legal and refugee immigrant households rise with time and surpass those of United States citizens after ten years in this country. And, third, immigrants generate more jobs than they take. Native job loss to immigrants is limited to weak **regional labor markets.**

But Illegal immigrants are harder to defend economically. The number of illegals who are poor and live in concentrated poverty areas (geographic regions where 40% or more live in poverty) has grown far faster over the last twenty years than comparable measures for United States citizens and legal immigrants.)

*The information in this section comes primarily from the Urban Institute, and the Immigration and Naturalization Service

3.   Sample Extemp Topics

Should the human rights of refugees outweigh the economic realities of potential host nations?
Who should pay for the economic costs of illegal immigration?
How can the EU better solve its immigration problems?
What should the United States do to resolve the national debate over refugee and immigration policy?

4.   Suggested Web Sites

The "About" series collects links on various topics and groups them for Internet use. They have a good one on immigration at http://immigration.about.com/cs/aboutimmigration/ . The best leads, a *wonderful* set of links for immigration issues (160 different annotated links when I visited it) is at http://dmoz.org/Regional/North_America/United_States/Business_and_Economy/Immigration/.

5.   If You Want To Read More…

U.S. Foreign Policy In Focus

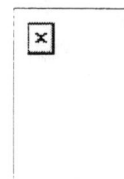

A Project of the Institute for Policy Studies and the Interhemispheric Resource Center

In Focus: The Immigration Debate

Volume 2, Number 31 (Full text)

Editors: Martha Honey (IPS) and Tom Barry (IRC)
Written by David Stoll, author of *Is Latin America Turning Protestant?* and *Between Two Armies in the Ixil Towns of Guatemala.* An anthropologist, he is also interested in the labor implications of immigration.

Key Points

- In the immigration debate, free marketers square off against cultural conservatives on the right side of the political spectrum; while on the left, civil rights and ethnic advocacy groups oppose environmentalists and job protectionists.
- Until 1994 the debate over immigration focused on what the INS calls illegal aliens, particularly those slipping across the Mexican border, even though a larger number of undocumented residents arrived legally and overstayed their visas.
- Immigrants, documented and undocumented, are also the targets of populist backlashes like California's Proposition 187, which bars undocumented immigrants from basic social services.

Immigration into the U.S. is an issue that makes for strange bedfellows. Supporters of current immigration levels include corporate interests that profit from cheap foreign labor, ethnic lobbies seeking to increase their political base, and religious activists, humanitarians, and civil libertarians who focus on human rights and other ethical concerns. Opponents include nativists who view non-European immigrants as a threat to American culture, environmentalists who dread immigration-fueled population growth, and labor advocates who fear that immigration is taking jobs from U.S. citizens and depressing U.S. wages. On the right of the political spectrum, free marketers square off against cultural conservatives. On the left, civil rights and ethnic advocacy groups oppose environmentalists and job protectionists.

Current policy is a reaction to the Immigration Act of 1924, which reduced the number of immigration visas and allocated them on the basis of national origin. Since the quotas for each nationality were based on its proportion of the U.S. population, the system favored northern Europeans and discriminated against Asians. In the 1960s national quotas were finally abolished on equity grounds. Equal opportunity and family reunification became top priorities, opening the door to much larger flows from Latin America, the Caribbean, and Asia.

Refugees became a large immigrant category with mass arrivals from Cuba in the early 1960s and early 1980s, and from Southeast Asia in the 1970s after the collapse of U.S.-supported governments. Refugees fleeing communist-run countries were granted automatic acceptance until steadily rising flows from Vietnam and Cuba forced a halt to this practice.

To reduce economic incentives for illegal immigration, in 1986 Congress passed the Immigration Reform and Control Act (IRCA) to punish employers who hire undocumented immigrants. In addition to authorizing employer sanctions,

IRCA also granted amnesty to undocumented immigrants who had been residing continuously in the U.S. for several years. Immigrant rights groups decried discrimination against undocumented workers, while anti-immigrant groups complained that employer sanctions would be unenforceable and that new arrivals could easily receive amnesty by forging documents.

In 1996 the U.S. Immigration and Naturalization Service (INS) authorized 911,000 legal immigrants, including 595,000 for family reunification, 118,000 for their job skills, and 198,000 for humanitarian reasons and diversity. This represents a rise of almost 30% from the 1995 figure of 716,000. When illegal immigrants receiving amnesty are included, the 1996 total is around one million. In recent years, the largest group of legal immigrants have come from Asia (37%), followed by Mexico/the Caribbean/Central America (32%), and Europe (18%). About 150,000 people apply for political asylum annually, and the backlog of applications for political asylum stands at about 450,000.

Until 1994 the debate over immigration focused on what the INS calls illegal aliens, particularly those slipping across the Mexican border, even though a larger number of undocumented residents arrived legally and overstayed their visas. In response to rising political pressures, the INS launched high-profile campaigns such as Operation Blockade in El Paso and Operation Gatekeeper in San Diego. Blocking the most-frequented entry points, however, shifted immigration flows into isolated deserts and mountains where more border-crossers fall victim to robbers, rapists, and extreme weather conditions.

Immigrants, documented and undocumented, are also the targets of populist backlashes like California's Proposition 187, which bars undocumented immigrants from basic social services. Courts have barred implementation of Proposition 187, but other legislation at the federal and state levels is cutting off both legal and illegal immigrants from public welfare benefits. There are also proposals to end the traditional practice of granting automatic citizenship to anyone born in the U. S., regardless of the legal status of the parents.

Problems With Current U.S. Policy

Key Problems

- Stricter border controls have proved unable to stem illegal immigration flows, leading instead to rising human rights abuses and victimization of border-crossers.
- Immigration clearly contributes to a downward pressure on wage levels and to decreased job availability in certain economic sectors.
- Many refugees fleeing repressive governments and violent political situations find themselves rejected by Washington.

Immigration policy has to address a range of economic, humanitarian, and ethical issues. Central to the raging immigration debate are differing evaluations of the rights of immigrants to be with their families, to find haven from political persecution, to seek a better standard of living, etc. and the rights of native-born citizens (and their government) to determine who lives, works, and benefits from public services in their country.

Among the factors affecting these different assessments are a rising sense of economic and social insecurity in many U.S. communities, dependence of many economic sectors on immigrant labor (from childcare to agribusiness), an increasingly interconnected global economy characterized by the relatively free flow of capital and trade, and rising crime and drug trafficking in border states.

Current immigration policy is failing on numerous accounts. Stricter border controls have proved unable to stem illegal immigration flows, leading instead to rising human rights abuses and victimization of border-crossers. Immigration clearly contributes to a downward pressure on wage levels and to decreased job availability in certain economic sectors. Many refugees fleeing repressive governments and violent political situations find themselves rejected by Washington.

174

Economists tend to agree that immigration is a net benefit to the U.S. economy. Immigrants fill jobs that U.S. citizens often reject, help the U.S. economy maintain competitiveness in the global economy, and stimulate job creation in depressed neighborhoods. But net benefits for the economy can conceal serious losses for vulnerable sectors of the U.S. population. It is no secret that many employers ranging from suburbanites to small contractors to major corporations would rather hire foreigners who often work harder for less pay than U.S. citizens.

As such, immigration has long been a contentious labor issue. The infamous Chinese Exclusion Act of 1882 was, among other things, a reaction to the importation of indentured laborers, who were paid far less than other workers. The immigration debates of the late 19th and early 20th centuries anticipated contemporary alliances between self-interested capitalists and open-door idealists on the one side, and nativists and protectionists on the other. One consequence of the Great Wave from 1880 to 1924 (with immigration averaging more than a half million annually) was that northern manufacturers relied on imported southern and eastern Europeans rather than hiring southern blacks.

Long employed in the agricultural sector, immigrants since the 1970s have become a major presence in other industries that have reorganized to take advantage of cheap labor and undermine union wage scales. A prominent example is the meatpacking industry, which has replaced U.S. workers with Mexicans and Southeast Asians at far lower pay. The chronic oversupply of labor from south of the border has kept farm wages low and obstructed successful labor organizing. The low-wage economy of border towns like El Paso is also partially explained by heavy immigration flows. El Paso, which has grown rapidly in macro terms, is for the most part a low-wage, labor-intensive treadmill with high unemployment, earnings a third lower than the national average, and twice the national poverty rate. Low-skill workers, particularly recent immigrants and blacks, are among the most common casualties of this process. But they are not the only ones. The 1990 expansion slots for high-skill immigrants have contributed to rising levels of unemployment in the U.S. for engineers, computer programmers, and Ph.Ds in technical fields.

Immigration also has implications for U.S. population growth, environmental protection, and the demand for new infrastructure. In the 1970s the U.S. population was approaching stability at less than 250 million around the year 2030. Currently, immigration (including new arrivals and their children) accounts for an increase of about 1.5 million more people a year, which represents more than half of total U.S. population growth. At current levels of immigration, the U.S. population will approach 400 million by the year 2050. If immigration is reduced to half the current level, the U.S. population would still approach 350 million by that year. Given the voracity with which U.S. residents consume a disproportionate share of the world's resources, the accelerated growth of this population is far more troubling than that of third world residents, who consume so much less.

Immigration's fiscal costs and contributions are hotly debated. Rice University economist Donald Huddle argues that, in 1994, legal and illegal immigration drained $51 billion more in social welfare and job displacement costs than immigrants paid in taxes. But according to the Urban Institute, immigrants contribute $25-30 billion more in taxes than they receive in services. Clearly immigrants are stressing the social infrastructure in some states. But cutting them off from hospital care, schooling, and assistance creates conditions of destitution that are even more costly to address apart from the ethical issues such action poses.

Toward a New Foreign Policy

Key Recommendations

- First on the list of reform should be the current definition of family unification a policy that leads to chain immigration and should be restricted to spouses and children followed closely by a drastic reduction in job skills based immigration.
- In humanitarian admissions, national preferences should be eliminated to admit everyone who can demonstrate that they are victims of individual persecution.
- Labor advocates and policymakers should give serious consideration to the national worker identification card.

Backed by rigorous enforcement of labor laws, such cards would deflate the political pressure for militarizing the Mexican border.

The implications of the trends regarding immigrant rights are troubling. The lure of jobs, higher wages, and better living standards is drawing immigrants into situations where U.S. citizens increasingly perceive the protection of immigrant rights as undermining their own. This means that politicians can attract votes by promising to fortify the Mexican border, even if such measures only exact a higher price from border-crossers without significantly altering the flow.

The quandaries of policing borders have generated support for a national worker identity card. Including a photograph and perhaps a fingerprint, the national identity card would be much harder to falsify than current forms of documentation. If issued to legal residents, authorized temporary workers, and U.S. citizens, the card would enable enforcement of sanctions against employers who hire illegal immigrants. It would remove the main incentive for illegal immigration by rendering anyone who didn't have a card unemployable. Opposing the identity card is a broad alliance of liberals and conservatives, ranging from the American Civil Liberties Union to the National Rifle Association, backed by employers who do not wish to see enforceable sanctions.

The jobs/benefits debate has highlighted the fact that the number of legal immigrants is three times the number of undocumented immigrants and that legal immigrants have a correspondingly greater impact hence the proposals in the 1996 Congress to slash legal immigration to as low as 235,000 a year. This figure would approach the level favored by those arguing for replacement level immigration (the same number as those leaving the U.S.). Proposals to reduce quotas were defeated in 1996, but legislation was approved to bolster the strength of the U.S. Border Patrol, expedite deportation proceedings, stiffen the penalties for document fraud, and hold sponsors financially responsible for immigrants who become public charges.

Immigrant labor is, of course, not the main reason for deteriorating wage levels, job opportunities, and labor conditions for U.S. workers. For example, corporations pit workers against each other by threatening to move production to lower-wage locations if their employees make demands. But if current immigration levels are indeed contributing to the transformation of the U.S. into a low-wage economy, then a new immigration policy is in order.

If the labor argument outlined in this policy brief withstands scrutiny, then first on the list of reforms should be the current definition of family unification a policy that leads to chain immigration and should be restricted to spouses and children. Following closely should be a drastic reduction in job skills-based immigration, most of which simply provides an opportunity for businesses to pay foreigners less than what they would have to pay current residents.

With respect to humanitarian admissions, national preferences should be eliminated to admit everyone who can demonstrate that they are victims of individualized persecution. To address illegal immigration, labor advocates and policymakers should give serious consideration to the national worker identification card. Backed by rigorous enforcement of labor laws, such cards would deflate the political pressure for militarizing the Mexican border. Such protections of the U.S. job market should, however, be accompanied by a foreign policy that contributes to broad-based development in low-income countries.

A new immigration policy should do the following:

- Stress ethical and humanitarian objectives by giving priority to refugees fleeing from persecution.
- Streamline and restructure provisional work programs that open the U.S. to temporary workers who take jobs that U.S. residents don't want, while guaranteeing the basic rights of these workers to organize and receive worker benefits such as unemployment compensation.
- Protect the most vulnerable economic sectors from an influx of low-wage competition.
- Lower legal immigration flows to sustainable levels.

- Protect the basic human rights of all U.S. residents, legal or not.

Sources for more information

Organizations

Center for Human Rights and Constitutional Law
256 S Occidental Boulevard
Los Angeles, CA 90057
Voice: (213) 388-8693
Fax: (213) 386-9484

Center for Immigration Studies
1815 H Street NW, Suite 1010
Washington, DC 20006.
(Publishers of *Immigration Review*)

National Immigrant Law Center
1102 South Crenshaw Blvd., Suite 101
Los Angles, CA 90019
Voice: (213) 938-6452
Fax: (213) 964-7940

National Network for Immigrant and Refugee Rights
310 8th Street, Suite 307
Oakland, CA 94607
Voice: (510) 465-1984
Fax: (510) 465-1885
Email: nnirr@igc.apc.org

U.S. Commission on Immigration Reform
2430 E Street South Building
Washington, DC 20037
Voice: (202) 776-8400
Fax: (202) 776-8635

World Wide Web

List of Internet Immigration Organizations
   ft p://heat= her.cs.ucdavis.edu/pub/immigration/index.html
American Civil Liberties Union
   http://www. aclu.org= /issues/immigrant/hmir.html
American Immigation Lawyers Association
   http://aila.org/home.htm
Federation for American Immigration Reform
   http://www.fairus.org/
Urban Institute
   http://www.u rban.org= /hotopics.htm#immigration
U.S. Commission on Immigration Reform
   http://www.utexas.edu/lbj/ uscir/

U.S. Immigration and Naturalization Service

   http://www.us doj.gov/= ins/textonly/index.html

USA Immigration Services - Green Cards, Visas, DV Lottery, Citizenship, INS Visa Status, Immigration Help

Chapter Thirteen
Tax Policy

1.   The Concepts

The government makes many different types of tax policy decisions every year. It is one of their biggest and most controversial tasks.

The dominance of the national government means that the states have to fit the types of taxes they do around tax policies emanating from Washington D.C. If a tax is heavily used by the national government duplicative state taxes can limit its revenue potential. Conversely the national government is reluctant to initiate a national sales tax or use a property tax because these steps would impinge on state and local revenue sources. But many taxes are used by both, the income tax for example. Thus debaters note the start of **fiscal federalism** battles.

The national government gives financial orders and, sometimes, monetary aid to the states. When they are orders the states have to pay to execute they are called **unfunded mandates**, which are resented and cause stress between the states and Washington. When they are funded it is sometimes by **block grants** that are designated by areas (e.g. a welfare grant or an educational grant) that leave the states some flexibility. Other times the federal money is very strictly controlled and can be used only for a specific purposes in a certain way; this approach makes the results more focused but increases **bureaucracy.**

United States **tax revenues** are staggering. But the national government has gotten itself severely restricted in budgetary matters. **Entitlement programs** such as Social Security and Medicare eat up huge amounts of **nondiscretionary funds**. And to make their budgetary impact worse some entitlement programs have automatic **COLAs** or Cost of Living Adjustments, so as inflation increases so does the drain on the tax funds. Payments on the national debt eat at more of the budget. An appreciation for **Keynesian economics** and pressures for a **balanced budget** (i.e. one without a deficit) limit the politicians.

One sure way to raise money is to raise taxes. But some taxes, such as property taxes and sales taxes) are **regressive**, they hurt the poor more than the rich. Most **consumption taxes**, unless they are limited just to luxury goods (yachts, sports cars, etc.) are regressive. Some **progressive** taxes have **loopholes** that let the rich escape. It is possible that some taxes, such as the **capital gains** and **estate taxes**, might discourage investment and economic growth. So tax decisions, reflected in the very complex **United States tax code**, are difficult and challenging policy decisions, the stuff of good extemp topics and debate.

The United States tax code is very complicated and not entirely fair. But taxes are inevitable so the question becomes which taxes are fair, which are best for the nation and our economy. Someone needs to pay for government programs, but who should it be? Should corporations or individuals foot the bill? Should the rich pay more and the poor pay nothing, or should all chip in an equal part of their income? Should "good" behavior be rewarded with tax breaks while "bad" behaviors draw heavy taxation?

A major test for a tax system is whether it is regressive or progressive. A tax is progressive if the rich pay a higher portion of their income to cover the tax. The reason for progressive taxation is that the poor and middle-income groups need a greater percentage of their income for survival (e.g. food, shelter, energy). But if you tax the rich at too high a level they can easily move to another

food, shelter, energy). But if you tax the rich at too high a level they can easily move to another country and or decrease their investments, both of which hurt the poor and middle class because growth declines or stops. A regressive tax forces the poorer people to pay a greater portion of their income in taxes than the rich do. So a flat tax such as a sales tax (e.g. you pay 8% of every purchase) hurts the poor the most; if you have only $100 to spend $8 in taxes is a lot, if you have $1,000 its no big deal.

Federal tax receipts total app. $1.7 trillion dollars. About 50% comes from the personal income tax, 13% from corporate income tax, and the rest from a mix of gift, estate, employment and excise taxes (an excise tax is a tax on the production, sale or consumption of a commodity). Income taxes are progressive, they increase as your income increases. People with incomes over $200,000 account for 31% of total income tax revenue even though they are less than 2% of the total population. At the other end those earning under $28,000 are 55% of individuals but pay only 6% of the total income tax collected.

The income tax has lots of deductions, albeit loopholes to their critics. The biggest are interest on mortgage payments, donations, retirement investments, medical expense, and interest on mortgage payments. There are 5 tax rates or brackets, ranging from 15% of your income to 39.6%. The majority of people are in the lowest bracket. Those earning over $250,000 a year are in the top bracket.

There are always many proposals to change one or another part of the tax system. Many of them are creative and intriguing, and make good speech or block topics. A common cry is for simplification. Most people with anything more than just a single wage income can easily miss or get confused by the record requirements and deduction options on income tax forms. Money that could be used for investment or joy, tens of billions of dollars every year, is diverted top accounting and business records and other expenses that would be unnecessary with a simple tax system.

But there are defenses for the current system. Many of the deductions are incentives that promote something (e.g. alternative energy, home buying, giving to charities) that society has decided should be encouraged. And there are strong arguments to keep this approach going. Environmental tax reform, using the market-based economy to solve the problems it created, is a good example of where there is immense potential for societal good from using existent tax policy strategies.

Another argument against change is that predicting the economic effects of tax changes is difficult. *The Washington Post* wrote as far back as 1998 that "the current system is so embedded that experts say uprooting it could have dramatic and unpredictable effects on all sorts of things, including the value of **assets**, salaries and benefits."

Some of the more common proposals are

- **The Flat Tax.** This is a wonderfully simple but regrettably regressive income tax. It eliminates all loopholes and tax breaks. Everyone pays the same rate. The formula for what you pay is simply income times the percent set by the flat tax.

  The advantages are significant. Money spent on accountants, tax advisers, and diverted into unwanted tax loopholes would now be saved for your own personal use. The stress associated with income tax time would decrease significantly. And advocates say the flat tax could be progressive as long as there was a very large standard deduction so that the poor end up paying nothing, and the middle class a reasonable amount.

  Advocates say a 17% to 19% tax rate would bring in the same level of government revenue that the current income tax brings in.

- **The VAT, the Value Added Tax.** Used extensively in Europe this is a consumption tax that is charged at every production step. The VAT is regressive but that harm is reduced in most plans by exempting basics such as food, medicine, and housing. It generates good revenue but decreases spending because prices appear to be higher. Critics of the present tax system say the current approach increases the incentive to spend when we need to increase savings and investment moneys, defenders say the incentive to spend is good because it promotes economic growth.

- **Repeal the Estate Tax**. Estate and inheritance taxes make some people angry. People pay taxes on what they earn as their life goes along. Every year we pay income tax and sales tax. So what we accumulate has already had taxes paid on it. The estate and inheritance taxes amount to double taxation; when we die our estate and the loved ones we leave our things to get taxed yet again. But the exemption is huge so that only the really rich get hit by the estate tax. And defenders also point out it is a very good way to control the **rich-poor gap** that always threatens **socioeconomic stability.**

    The estate tax brings in $40 billion each year. The Tax Relief Act of 2001 increased the exemption to $1 million. The lifetime gift-tax exemption (the amount you can give away tax-free during your life) also was increased to $1 million. By 2009 the exemption is scheduled to reach $3.5 million! The law expires in 2010 so the tax rate could revert back to a $675,000 exemption then.

Someone inevitably gets hurt more than someone else whatever tax system we use. Its nice to identify who will be helped and quantify how much help will be given by a new tax policy. But the debater or extemper also has to choose whom s/he's wiling to hurt, who you can defend carrying the tax burden in a realistic workable manner.

2.   Web Sites

The Congressional Budget Office has a good variety of less biased publications, links and tax policy cost estimates. Give it a try at www.cbo.gov/. To give yourself a treat go to "Build Your Own Tax Policy" at www.taxpolicy.com/. This is a wonderfully creative and educational site where your skills and knowledge will grow. It represents what education and learning on the web can be at its best! The Tax Policy Center gives good articles and research both for extemp files and debate impacts. Start at its home page on www.taxpolicycenter.org/

For more information on the Flat Tax check out Citizens For A Sound Economy and their advocacy and links at www.cse.org/informed/flatTax.html. A really intriguing mix of articles and links on the Flat Tax is also at www.ncpa.org/pi/taxes/tax71.html

For a glimpse at environmental tax reform visit www.sustainableeconomy.org/

3.   Sample Extemp Topics

How can the states and federal government better balance their tax needs and tax policies?
What should Washington do to regain control of the budget process?
Is there a way to simplify the tax code and still keep it progressive?
Should Europe scratch the VAT?

4.   If You Want To Read More…

LONG-RANGE FISCAL POLICY BRIEF

CBO

A series of issue summaries from the Congressional Budget Office

The Looming Budgetary Impact of Society's Aging

The federal budget-making process is near-term in nature, with rules and procedures that are applicable only five or 10 years into the future. As a result, the looming multidecade rise in government spending associated with society's aging is not in the budget picture on which the Administration and the Congress are required to act annually.

The relatively sanguine budgetary outlook for the next decade does not encompass the demographic shifts--emerging with the retirement of the post-World War II baby-boom generation--that will cause federal spending to begin rising sharply within the next 20 years (*see Figure 1*). At the same time, the near-term outlook offers an opportunity to introduce the necessary policies to mitigate the long-term pressures. Those policy changes affecting federal commitments to the elderly should be implemented far enough in advance to offer future recipients of Social Security and other entitlement benefits time to alter their savings and retirement plans.

For the President and the Congress, the immediacy of having to make year-to-year budgetary policy will always place heavy emphasis on the near term. However, it is critical for policymakers to begin addressing the long-term budgetary pressures associated with the aging of the U.S. population.

Figure 1.

Federal Outlays, Fiscal Years 2002 to 2075

(As a percentage of GDP)

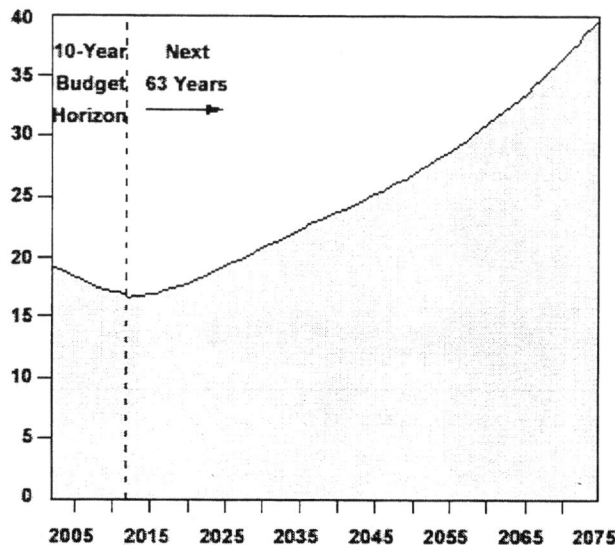

Source: Congressional Budget Office.

Note: For a discussion of these projections, see Congressional Budget Office, *A 125-Year Picture of the Federal*

182

The Looming Budgetary Impact of Society's Aging

Government's Share of the Economy, 1950 to 2075, Long-Range Fiscal Policy Brief (July 3, 2002).

The Near-Term Focus of the Budget-Making Process

Federal budgeting does not have a long time horizon. The Congress enacts annual budget resolutions that look no farther ahead than the next 10 years, and annual budget projections and updates prepared by the Congressional Budget Office (CBO) and the Administration's Office of Management and Budget (OMB) typically are limited to five- and 10-year periods. Appropriations similarly reflect a near-term perspective as they are made from year to year. This emphasis on the near term is set by precedent and long practice.

Although long-range projections are not part of the budget process, they have been made regularly for Social Security and Medicare, as well as for a number of other federal retirement and disability systems.[1] In Social Security's early years, the program's trustees used a projection technique that employed an "infinite" period of valuation, and since 1965, they have used a 75-year period. For Medicare, long-range estimates have been a more recent phenomenon. For the Hospital Insurance portion of the program, 25-year projections were the practice until the mid-1980s. For the Supplementary Medical Insurance part of the program, only annual projections were routinely made.

In recent years, as attention has been drawn to the long-range demographic trends affecting the nation, both the Administration and CBO have been called on to make longer-term estimates. The trustees for both Social Security and Medicare now routinely make 75-year projections, and both OMB and CBO have been issuing long-range budget projections since the mid-1990s.

In a period of stable demographic trends and modest swings in the economy, a short horizon for budgeting may be sufficient as a framework for policymakers to operate in. But it does not provide a long enough perspective to address the very large and continuing rise in government spending that will occur 20 to 30 years from now. The outlook reflected in CBO's baseline projections for fiscal years 2003 to 2012 (the latest of which were issued in March 2002) and in the subsequent decade is relatively favorable, as modest surpluses are expected to arise within the next few years and to continue until the early 2020s (under the assumption that current policies are not altered). However, the first of the baby boomers will become eligible for Social Security in just six years, and the seeds for a long-term rise in federal spending begin to emerge shortly thereafter as more and more members of that generation draw on the government's largest entitlement programs.

Society's Aging and Entitlement Programs

Certainly, long-range projections are subject to unforeseeable economic and political events. In the short term, budget projections can change significantly (even from year to year, as recent experience has shown), and relatively small changes can have very large long-range effects as they are compounded through time. Therefore, skepticism about long-range estimates is justified.

However, a substantial portion of the demographic change underpinning the long-term budgetary outlook is in place. The "baby boom" and subsequent "baby trough" are events that have occurred; the subsequent uptick in birth rates has not been substantial and may now have leveled off; and life expectancy continues to increase (*see Figures 2 and 3*). As a share of gross domestic product (GDP), spending for Social Security, Medicare, and Medicaid--the three entitlement programs most affected by the looming demographics--appears to be relatively stable over the next five years, growing only modestly. However, 10 years out, the outlook starts to change. The population age 65 or older will be growing rapidly. Although that segment constitutes 12 percent of the population today, according to the Social Security and Medicare trustees it is expected to grow to 18 percent in 2025, 21 percent in 2050, and 23 percent in 2075. At the same time, growth in the nation's workforce is expected to slow, resulting in a more slowly growing economy (*see Figure 4*). By 2035, the number of elderly will double, while the number of workers contributing to Social Security and Medicare will rise by only 17 percent. The ratio of the population ages 65 or older to the population in its prime working years (ages 20 to 64) will grow from 21 percent today to 32 percent in 2025 and 42 percent in 2075 (*see Figure 5*).

Figure 2.

Birth Rates

(Births per woman in her lifetime)

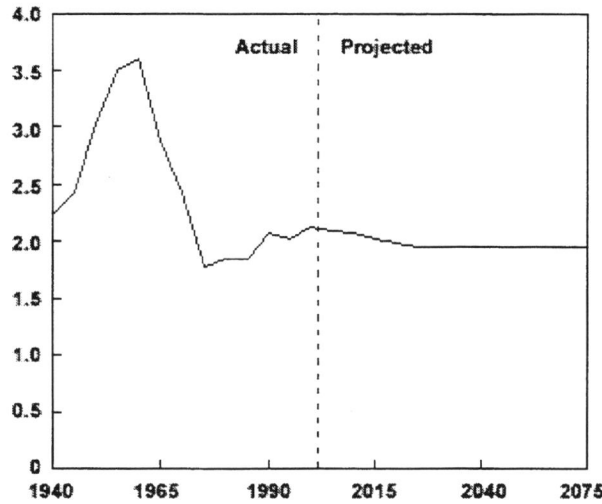

Source: Social Security Administration, *The 2002 Annual Report of the Board of Trustees of the Federal Old-Age and Survivors Insurance and Disability Insurance Trust Funds* (March 26, 2002).

Figure 3.

Years of Life Remaining at Age 65

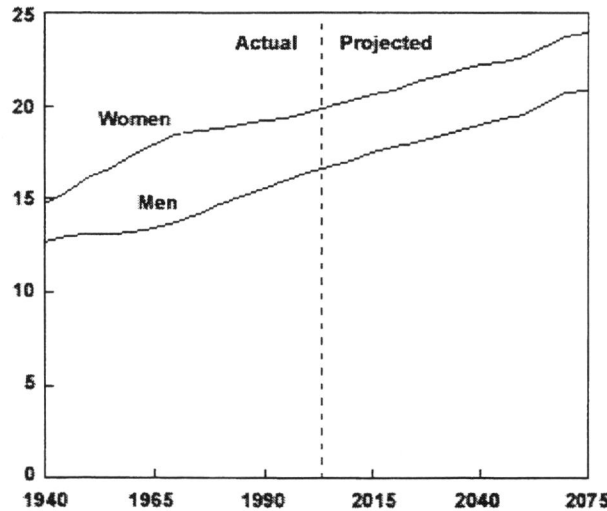

Source: Social Security Administration, *The 2002 Annual Report of the Board of Trustees of the Federal Old-Age and Survivors Insurance and Disability Insurance Trust Funds* (March 26, 2002).

Figure 4.

Growth in Real GDP and the Number of Workers

(Annual percentage)

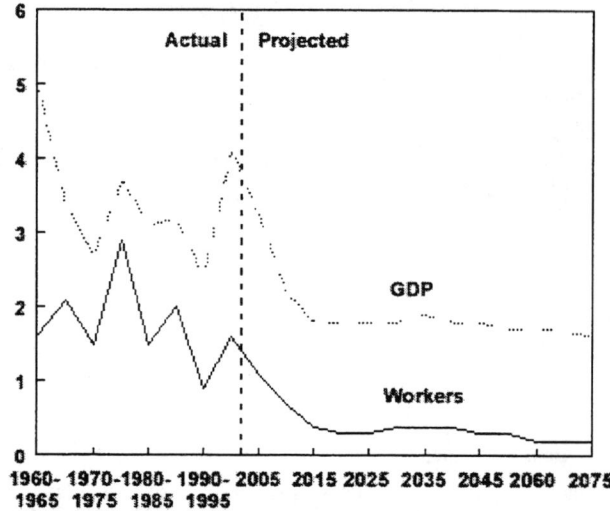

Source: Social Security Administration, *The 2002 Annual Report of the Board of Trustees of the Federal Old-Age and Survivors Insurance and Disability Insurance Trust Funds* (March 26, 2002).

Note: For the period prior to 2001, the figures represent five-year averages.

Figure 5.

The Population Age 65 or Older as a Percentage of the Population 20 to 64

(Percent)

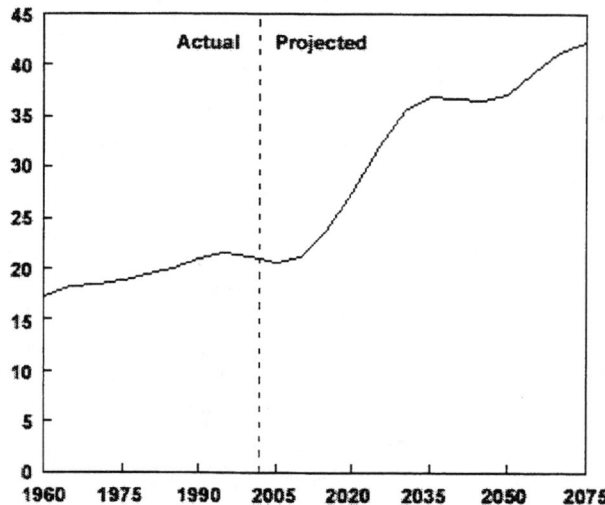

Source: Social Security Administration, *The 2002 Annual Report of the Board of Trustees of the Federal Old-Age and Survivors Insurance and Disability Insurance Trust Funds* (March 26, 2002).

Exacerbating the population trends, Social Security benefits are automatically scheduled to rise in tandem with workers' wages, at a rate that is likely to exceed inflation. And the cost of medical care is expected to continue to climb at an even faster rate because of better technology and the demand for more and better medical services--a rate that for years has consistently outpaced the growth of GDP. As a result, national health expenditures, including those financed by Medicare and Medicaid, will absorb a rising proportion of the nation's production.

The Necessity of Looking Beyond the Near-Term Budgetary Window

185

The Looming Budgetary Impact of Society's Aging

Although these demographic and budgetary trends are not new to fiscal policymakers, the budget process does not provide an effective means to address them. That said, the near-term focus of the process does not preclude a longer view. In the past, major reforms of entitlement programs have taken both near-term and long-range concerns about fiscal policy into account.

However, unlike the circumstances leading to earlier reforms, the situation today poses no imminent threat to anyone's benefits. But the problem with waiting until the rapid escalation in costs falls within the budget window is that doing so may not leave sufficient transition time to deal with it in a gradual fashion.

Reform requires an awareness of the financial pressures that lie ahead and a consensus that legislative changes are necessary. The information presented here and in other long-term budget analyses is intended to help policymakers acquire a fuller perspective about the issue and make prudent decisions.

Supporting Tables

Economic Trends and Projections

(Percent)

Calendar Year	Average Annual Rate of Growth	
	Real GDP	Number of Workers
1960-1965	5.0	1.6
1965-1970	3.4	2.1
1970-1975	2.7	1.5
1975-1980	3.7	2.9
1980-1985	3.1	1.5
1985-1990	3.2	2.0
1990-1995	2.4	0.9
1995-2000	4.1	1.6
2005	3.2	1.1
2010	2.2	0.7
2020	1.8	0.3
2030	1.8	0.4
2040	1.8	0.4
2050	1.7	0.3
2060	1.7	0.2
2070	1.7	0.2
2080	1.6	0.2

Source: Social Security Administration, *The 2002 Annual Report of the Board of Trustees of the Federal Old-Age and Survivors Insurance and Disability Insurance Trust Funds* (March 26, 2002).

Demographic Trends and Projections

Calendar	Life Expectancy at Age 65[a]		Births per	Population Age 65+ as Percent of Population

Year	Women	Men	Woman	20 to 64
1940	79.7	77.7	2.23	11.6
1950	81.2	78.1	3.03	13.8
1960	82.4	78.2	3.61	17.3
1970	83.5	78.8	2.43	18.5
1980	83.8	79.7	1.85	19.5
1990	84.2	80.6	2.07	20.9
2000	84.7	81.4	2.13	21.1
2010	85.3	82.1	2.07	21.2
2020	85.9	82.8	1.99	27.5
2030	86.6	83.4	1.95	35.5
2040	87.2	84.0	1.95	36.8
2050	87.7	84.6	1.95	37.1
2060	88.2	85.2	1.95	39.2
2070	88.8	85.7	1.95	41.3
2075	89.0	85.9	1.95	42.3

Source: Social Security Administration, *The 2002 Annual Report of the Board of Trustees of the Federal Old-Age and Survivors Insurance and Disability Insurance Trust Funds* (March 26, 2002).

a. Projected age at death.

Related CBO Publications: *Social Security: A Primer* (September 2001) and *A 125-Year Picture of the Federal Government's Share of the Economy, 1950 to 2075*, Long-Range Fiscal Policy Brief (July 3, 2002).

Contacts: This policy brief was prepared by Dave Koitz, Melissa D. Bobb, and Ben Page. It and other publications by CBO are available at the agency's Web site.

---

1. The projections made for these programs routinely have been published in separate reports by agencies or trustees as long-range actuarial evaluations of the programs. They have not been published in a single report nor presented in a budget format. However, aspects of them have been consolidated as part of a required analysis of the federal government's financial statements and are now published annually in the Treasury Department's *Financial Report of the United States Government, 2001* (March 29, 2002). The underlying assumptions often are not consistent from program to program.

CBO Home Page

Chapter Fourteen
Poverty

1. The Concepts for the United States

Poverty is a harm in and of itself. But poverty also increases suicides, crime, stress, mental illness, child abuse, spousal abuse, and political instability. One of, perhaps the most important, test of an economic system is how well it can reduce or minimize poverty. The **utilitarianistic** "greatest good for the greatest number" almost always applies to economies and the battle against poverty.

33% of the poor either go hungry or have trouble feeding themselves and their families. They are more likely to get sick and take longer to get well. When they have enough to eat it is more likely to be too high in fats, sugars and carbohydrates and deficient in vitamins and minerals.

The causes of poverty in the United States have been well studied. **Socioeconomic research** has uncovered several clear **causal elements.** An important set combines into a **cycle of poverty**. Children are born into poor homes. Because of the family's poverty nutrition is lacking, the children get sick more often. The children are more likely than children of the non-poor to be exposed to stress, crime, fear and drugs. The parents are often divorced and lack both the time, interest, and or money for home enrichment (such as large numbers of books, trips to museums, vacations to historical cites). Their schools receive less from **property taxes** and are deteriorating so the school does not attract enough good teachers; the children receive an inadequate education. As they grow drugs become increasingly available and promoted, gangs and other criminal activity are more likely to bobby their support and or involvement. They are more likely to participate in unprotected sex. If they graduate they are much less likely to go to college. If they go to college they are much less likely to stay through graduation. If they get jobs they are more likely to be low paying jobs. They have more children than they can afford. Often the parents are not married and or do not live together for very long. The children are born into poor homes and the cycle starts again.

The Bureau of the Census reports that 33.1% of black children live in poverty, 30% of Hispanic children and 13.5% of white children. Prejudice or bigotry appears to be the cause, but empirical data puts **single parent homes** as the top culprit. Statistically the correlations are very high, the number of children in poverty is at the same ratio as single parent homes in each racial or ethnic group. Poverty is highest in single women headed families: 26.4% compared to 4.9% poverty for families with both a male and female adult living at home. Among the least likely to be poor are the elderly (10.2%) and whites (7.8%).

Mental illness also contributes to poverty. The Institute For Policy Research shows that 23% of those who suffer from depression enter the ranks of the poor. Other mental illnesses have high poverty rates. Unemployment is as high as 70% for the mentally ill.

A good extemp speech or disadvantage will avoid spurious links. In other words the reader should be careful not to cite "causes" that are not there. A good example is immigration. Opponents argue that immigrants take job away, drain welfare, and increase poverty. The truth is all in the opposite direction for legal immigration. The National Academy of Sciences research says that legal immigrants add $10 billion a year to the national GDP. Independent studies by the Hoover Institute and Prof. S. Moore document that the communities with heavy immigrant presence have double the level of job creation as compared to other parts of the country and twenty percent lower crime rates, that nationally they increase **per capita** incomes and reduce the poverty rate.

So what are the cures? Some are already in place. Welfare reform has been a huge success. The **TANF** (Temporary Assistance to Needy Families) has contributed to a reduction of 4.2 million in the number of poor since 1996. There are 2.3 million fewer children in poverty, the greatest reduction being among black children where 1.1 million have moved out of poverty according to a Heritage Foundation report.

Economic growth has also helped to reduce the number in poverty. A rising sea lifts all boats. Between 1990 and 2001, for instance economic growth reduced black poverty from 30% to 22.7%, Hispanics from 30% to 21.4%. New policies that increase growth will almost certainly further reduce policy.

Further proposals to reduce poverty include **marriage promotion**, improved school quality, food aid, and perhaps an increased **minimum wage**. The strongest statistical correlation, the easiest to prove causal link, lies in two parent households. Marriage is an obvious way to permanize or lengthen the time a family has two adults in residence. Government policies are now being debated about how to strengthen marriage probabilities among families most prone to poverty. One possible approach is the traditional carrot-and-stick mix: more benefits if both parents are in residence plus tax or aid benefits, but reduced aid and time limited assistance if either parents physically leaves.

Improving ghetto, rural, and economically challenged schools is a longer term but immensely valuable way to break the cycle of poverty. If we can pay teachers more to attract better people (and hold on to the best we have), and get rid of the certification requirements that keep the best content educated people out of education, the result would be to keep more poor kids in school and get them better prepared to successfully enter the job market.

Since the 1950s the United States has given food aid to poorer Americans. Expanding such programs would reduce some of the most obvious harms of poverty. Easier access to **food stamps** would be one step in that direction. Another step would be to expand school free-meal programs. There are modest school breakfast and school lunch programs to give free meals to some of the poor. They could be expanded. The quality of the free meal programs also needs work; many schools that give free meals give nutritionally unsound mixes with too many carbohydrates and too much fat, too little in vitamin and mineral content.

The most controversial and debatable option is too increase the minimum wage. Proponents, mainly Democrats, say that the **working poor** would get a higher income (and thus leave the poverty ranks) if the minimum wage were sufficiently increased. If we do not reward people who try to get off welfare with decent paying jobs, the argument goes, why should we be surprised when welfare and poverty statistics remain too high. Opponents, spearheaded by the Republicans, counter with two arguments. First, the number of low paying jobs would shrink because many those jobs are from businesses that operate on very low profit-margins (examples: agriculture, textiles) and would have to reduce the number of workers or shut down if their wage costs increased significantly. Second, labor cost increases are inflationary.

2. The Concepts and Foreign Issues

International causes and cures are interlocked. **The law of comparative advantage** is ignored in a large number of countries. The result is to produce products that are not competitive. Exports thus suffer and imports are either limited so that inferior products dominate the marketplace, and or imported goods outsells domestic products so that jobs are limited.

What determines if most countries have a high percentage of poor people usually involves many factors:

- ❏ Natural Resources. It is certainly easier to have a high national quality of life if Mother Nature has given us great wealth. Look at the average income in Kuwait or Saudi Arabia. But such wealth can also be easily squandered. Consider the examples of Iran or Russia.

- **Infrastructure**. The more basic elements a nation has (transportation, communication, educational system, capital availability) the more likely incomes will be high and poverty low.
- Political stability. **Capital flight** is endemic to unstable nations. Argentina has been an example several times since the 1940s. But nations with long traditions of successful stable government are much more likely to attract and hold investment. Examples: Switzerland, Singapore.
- Economic system. Despite the idealism of every type of utopian capitalism is far and away the structure most likely to minimize poverty. Socialism, communism, fascism, tyranny, monarchy and theocracy have all been disproven by history. The highest per-capita GDPs are overwhelmingly capitalistic.
- Democracy. Democratic forms give citizens releases and options that promote political stability.
- Integrity and honesty of the legal system. Bribery and corruption can stop an economy from working with any semblance of logic. The **law of supply and demand** gets distorted **Economies of scale** become subservient to under the table payments. The **discipline imposed by competition** is lost to the inefficiencies of government-supported industries.

A good way to analyze international poverty is to show how often it ties to **economic freedom**. An excellent description and study of economic freedom was done by Lawson and Moor in 2002. They considered seven factors: low government spending (to leave private capital available for investment), low government taxes, **property rights**, honest legal system, sound money, liberal trade policies, and minimal government regulations. Using these criteria the top countries dovetailed nicely with the richest countries. The top 20% of free nations had better environmental quality, life expectancy 20 years longer than the bottom nations, and average income of $23,450 and a 2.56% growth rate. At the top, in order, were Hong Kong, Singapore, and the United States.

The bottom 20% of all nations had bad environmental quality, an average income of $2,556 and a *negative* average GDP "growth" of .85%. At or near the bottom were Russia, Romania, and almost every nation in Africa.

It is worth noting, whether you are in extemp or debate, than foreign aid is useless for nations toward the bottom end of the economic freedom scale. The aid is wasted, stolen, diverted to useless projects, or otherwise dissipated.

3.   Web Sites

The **World Bank** and the **IMF** is pushing **PRSP (Poverty Reduction Strategy Plans)**. Each nation that requests or needs help is encouraged to develop and submit the plan and then a follow-up paper(s) noting results. These and good statistics, *organized by country name*, are found at www.imf.org/external/np/prsp/prsp.asp.

The "Hunger, Poverty, and Economic Development" site contains information on the relationship between hunger, poverty, and economic development. Hunger is largely a function, not of the availability of food, but of people's ability to pay for it. The great dilemma is how to create social, economic, and political conditions to ensure that everyone has access to food. http://faculty.plattsburgh.edu/richard.robbins/legacy/hunger_resources.htm

The Institute for Research on Poverty site has research, links, news, and its own search. www.ssc.wisc.edu/irp/ The "Frequently Asked Questions" section is much more useful than most.

4.   Sample Extemp Topics

How can we better reduce poverty?

Why are so many LDCs in perpetual poverty?
Is Africa a continent without economic hope?
Is welfare reform working?
What should the developed world do to help the third world?

5. If you want to read more...

Poverty in the Midst of Plenty
By Douglass C. North
Hoover institution

We live in a world where some countries enjoy a material abundance beyond the wildest dream of our forefathers. Such countries are rich because they are productive. The sources of that productivity—growing markets, technological improvement, and investment in human beings (human capital)—all play an important part in increasing productivity. The new growth economics literature has formalized some of these findings, but economic historians, development economists, and specialists in growth accounting have broadly understood them for some time.

By any standard of measure much of the world's population is still poor, with individuals subsisting on less than two dollars a day. The disparity between the well-being of the average person in the developed world, where per capita annual income may exceed $20,000, and that in low income countries such as Haiti or most of sub-Saharan Africa, where it may be under $500 a year, is striking, especially when one sees up close the living conditions associated with such poverty.

How do we account for the persistence of poverty in the midst of plenty? If we know the sources of plenty, why don't poor countries simply adopt policies that make for plenty? The answer is straightforward. We just don't know how to get there. **We must create incentives for people to invest in more efficient technology, increase their skills, and organize efficient markets.** Such incentives are embodied in institutions. Thus we must understand the nature of institutions and how they evolve.

Institutions are the framework that humans create to structure human interaction. They are made up of formal rules (constitutions, laws, and regulations) and informal restraints (conventions and norms of behavior) and the way both are enforced. Well-specified property right that reward productive and creative activity, a legal system that enforces such laws at low cost, and internal codes of conduct that are complementary to such formal rules are the essential underpinning to productive economies. But well-specified property rights and an effective legal system are the creation of the political structure. Unfortunately, we do not know put such a political structure in place. Informal norms of behavior that make for honesty, integrity, and hard work are the product of long-term human interaction; we do not know how to create them in the short run. The result has been that **efforts to improve the performance of poor countries have been something less than a rousing success.** Sub-Saharan Africa remains a basket case, and our efforts to transform the diverse parts of the Soviet Union into productive economies have so far been a dismal failure. But we are getting a better understanding of the process of political-economic change. The sources of informal constraints such as norms of behavior are a major modern priority in the social sciences and down the road will result in accelerating the reduction.

Douglass C. North is a senior fellow at the Hoover Institution and the Spencer T. Olin Professor in Arts and sciences at Washington University.

Economic Freedom Needed To Alleviate Poverty Around The World

by Robert A. Lawson

Robert A. Lawson is professor of economics and George H. Moor Chair in the School of Management at Capital University in Ohio. He is co-author of Economic Freedom of the World: 2002 Annual Report, produced jointly by the Fraser Institute and the Cato Institute.

Both as an ideology and as a practical system, communism has utterly failed to deliver the goods. Eastern European nations are now rushing to become members of the European Union, and China is undertaking market-oriented reforms. Cuba and North Korea stand as the last remaining communist stalwarts.

One would think that this failure of communist central planning would have unleashed a groundswell of support for its main ideological alternative: economic freedom or market capitalism. But as the anti-globalization protestors in Seattle and at last week's G8 meeting in Canada demonstrate, economic freedom still has a long way to go to win over the hearts and minds of many people.

These protesters believe that free markets lead to widespread poverty, greater gaps between the rich and the poor, and environmental degradation. Only strong government planning through trade tariffs, expansive welfare states, and strict labor and environmental rules can protect the poor of this world from the ravaging forces of the market. These people are dead wrong.

A new study, co-authored by James Gwartney and myself, was recently released by a consortium of think tanks, which includes the Cato Institute in the United States. This publication, Economic Freedom of the World: 2002 Annual Report, presents an economic freedom index for 123 countries. Based on 37 data components drawn from a multitude of sources, this index measures the degree to which nations are pursing policies consistent with economic freedom or market capitalism. To score highly on this index, a nation should have low government spending and taxes, sound property rights and legal system, sound money, liberal trade policies, and few government regulations. Economic freedom means that each individual plays the primary role in his economic life, not the government or central plan.

The most economically free nation in the world remains Hong Kong followed by Singapore and the United States. The rankings of other major economies are the United Kingdom (4th), Canada (8th), Germany (15th), Japan (24th) Taiwan (30th), France (38th), Mexico (66th), and India (73rd). Most of the lowest ranked nations are in Africa and Latin America. Botswana has the best record for an African nation, tied for 38th with six other nations including France and South Korea. Chile, with the best record in Latin America, was tied with three other nations at 15th. Three former communist countries are in the bottom 10: Russia (116th), Ukraine (119th), and Romania (114th) all did worse than communist China (101st). Data for North Korea and Cuba are not available.

The study also shows that economic freedom is strongly linked with both higher levels of income and faster rates of economic growth. The people living in the top one-fifth of the most free countries enjoy an average income of $23,450 and a growth rate in the 1990s of 2.56 percent per year; in contrast, the bottom one-fifth in the rankings had an average income of just $2,556 and a -0.85 percent growth rate in the 1990s.

That economic freedom leads to more and faster wealth creation is no longer a controversial argument. But what of the argument that market capitalism leaves the poor behind? In fact, the poor gain a lot from economic freedom. The share

192

of income going to the poorest 10% of the population is completely unrelated to economic freedom. But poor people are much better off with economic freedom. The poorest 10% of the population have an average income of just $728 in the least free countries compared with over $7000 in the most free countries. Simply put, it is much better to be poor in a free, rich country than an unfree, poor country.

Free people live longer too. The life expectancy of people living in the most free nations is fully 20 years longer than for people in the least free countries. This is quite literally the difference between knowing your grandchildren or not.

Other studies confirm that environmental quality is likely to be enhanced as poor countries become wealthy enough, through economic freedom, to invest in environmental amenities like water treatment plants.

People who are concerned about poverty and environmental issues around the globe must realize that economic freedom and the resulting economic prosperity, not oppressive government taxation and regulation, represent the best hope for the poor and the environment alike.

American Enterprise Institute for Public Policy Research

A≡I Testimony

Statement of Richard Perle
Fellow, American Enterprise Institute
Before the Committee on Foreign Relations
United States Senate

by

Richard Perle

Mr. Chairman,

I appreciate your invitation to participate in the Committee's hearing which poses the question "How do we promote democratization, poverty alleviation and human rights to build a more secure world?" These three ideas, poverty, democracy and human rights are often linked as we try to think our way through the vexing problems of national and international security.

The phrase "a more secure world" is almost certainly prompted by the discovery, on September 11, of how insecure we turned out to be on that day. In any case, hardly any discussion takes place these days that is not somehow related to terrorism and the war against it. For my part, this morning will be no exception.

Let me say, at the outset, that the idea that poverty is a cause of terrorism, although widely believed and frequently argued, remains essentially unproven. That poverty is not merely a cause, but a "root cause," which implies that it is an essential source of terrorist violence, is an almost certainly false, and even a dangerous idea, often invoked to absolve terrorists of responsibility or mitigate their culpability. It is a liberal conceit which, if heeded, may channel the war against terror into the *cul de sac* of grand development schemes in the third world and the elevation of do-good/feel-good NGO's to a role they cannot and should not play.

What we know of the September 11 terrorists suggests they were neither impoverished themselves nor motivated by concerns about the poverty of others. After all, their avowed aim, the destruction of the United States, would, if successful, deal a terrible blow to the growth potential of the world economy. Their devotion to Afghanistan's Taliban regime, which excluded half the Afghan work force from the economy and aimed to keep them illiterate as well as poor, casts conclusive doubt on their interest in alleviating poverty.

Poverty—or poverty and despair--is the most commonly adumbrated explanation for terrorism abroad--and crime at home. Identifying poverty as a source of conduct invariably confuses the matter. We will never know what went through the mind of Mohammed Atta as he plotted the death of thousands of innocent men, women and children, including a number of Moslems. We do know that he lived in relative comfort as did most, perhaps all, of the 19 terrorists—15 of them from affluent Saudi Arabia.

If we accept poverty as an explanation we will stop searching for a true, and useful, explanation. We may not notice the poisonous extremist doctrine propagated, often with Saudi oil money, in mosques and religious institutions around the world.

If we attribute terrorism to poverty, we may fail to demand that President Mubarak of Egypt silence the sermons, from mosques throughout Egypt, preaching hatred of the United States. As you authorize $2 billion a year for Egypt, please remember that these same clerics are employees of the Egyptian government. It is not a stretch to say that U.S. taxpayer dollars are helping to pay for the most inflammatory anti-American ranting.

So when you hear about poverty as the root cause of terrorism, I urge you to examine the manipulation of young Muslim men sent on suicidal missions by wealthy fanatics, like Osama bin Laden, whose motives are religious and ideological in nature and have nothing to do with poverty or privation.

Mr. Chairman, this hearing is about building a more secure future; and I know it will come as no surprise if I argue that doing that in the near term will require an effective military establishment to take the war on terrorism to the terrorists, to fight them *over there* because they are well on the way to achieving their murderous objectives when we are forced to fight them *over here*. For once those who wish to destroy Americans gain entry to the United States and exploit the institutions of our open society, the likelihood that we will stop them is greatly diminished.

This is why President Bush was right to declare on September 11 that "We will make no distinction between the terrorists who committed these acts and those who harbor them." This was not the policy of the last Democratic administration or the Republican one before it. It is not a policy universally applauded by our allies. But it is a right and bold and courageous policy and the only policy that has a reasonable prospect of protecting the American people from further terrorist acts.

Dealing effectively with the states that support or condone terrorism against us (or even remain indifferent to it) is the only way to deprive terrorists of the sanctuary from which they operate, whether that sanctuary is in Afghanistan or North Korea or Iran or Iraq or elsewhere. The regimes in control of these "rogue" states—a term used widely before the last administration substituted the flaccid term "states of concern" — pose an immediate threat to the United States. The first priority of American policy must be to transform or destroy rogue regimes.

And while some states will observe the destruction of the Taliban regime in Afghanistan and decide to end their support for terrorism rather than risk a similar fate, others will not.

It is with respect to those regimes that persist in supporting and harboring terrorists that the question of the role of democratization and human rights is particularly salient. And foremost among these regimes is Saddam Hussein's Iraq.

The transformation of Iraq from a brutal dictatorship, in which human rights are unknown, to a democratic state protecting the rights of individuals would not only make the world more secure, it would bring immediate benefits to all the people of Iraq (except the small number of corrupt officials who surround Saddam Hussein).

I believe that this is well understood in the Congress, which has repeatedly called on the administration to support the Iraqi National Congress, an umbrella group made up of organizations opposed to Saddam's dictatorship. The INC is pledged to institute democratic political institutions, protect human rights and renounce weapons of mass destruction. As we think through the best way to change the regime in Iraq, it is precisely the proponents of democracy who deserve our support, not the disaffected officer who simply wishes to substitute his dictatorship for that of Saddam Hussein.

I hope, Mr. Chairman, that the Congress, which has been well ahead of the executive branch in recognizing this, will succeed in persuading this administration, although it failed to persuade the last one, that our objective in removing Saddam's murderous regime must be its replacement by democratic forces in Iraq and the way to do that is work with the Iraqi National Congress.

Mr. Chairman, it goes without saying that democracies that respect human rights, and especially the right to speak and publish and organize freely, are far less likely to make war or countenance terrorism than dictatorships in which power is concentrated in the hands of a few men whose control of the instruments of war and violence is unopposed. As a general rule, democracies do not initiate wars or undertake campaigns of terror. Indeed, democracies are generally loath to build the instruments of war, to finance large military budgets or keep large numbers of their citizens in military establishments. Nations that embrace fundamental human rights will not be found planning the destruction of innocent civilians. I can't think of a single example of a democracy planning acts of terror like those of September 11.

We could discuss at length why democratic political institutions and a belief in the rights of individuals militate against war and terror and violence. But the more difficult questions have to do with how effectively we oppose those regimes that are not democratic and deny their citizens those fundamental human rights, the exercise of which constitutes a major restraint on the use of force and violence.

Here the issue is frequently one of whether we "engage" them in the hope that our engagement will lead to reform and liberalization, or whether we oppose and isolate them. I know of no general prescription. Each case, it seems to me, must be treated individually because no two cases are alike. Take the three cases of the "axis of evil."

In the case of Iraq, I believe engagement is pointless. Saddam Hussein is a murderous thug and it makes no more sense to think of engaging his regime than it would a mafia family.

In the case of Iran, I doubt that the goals of democratization and human rights would be advanced by engaging the current regime in Teheran. There is sufficient disaffection with the mullahs, impressive in its breadth and depth, to commend continued isolation—and patience. The spontaneous demonstrations of sympathy with the United States are brave and moving. We owe those who have marched in sympathy with us the support that comes from refusing to collaborate with the regime in power. The people of Iran may well throw off the tyrannical and ineffective dictatorship that oppresses them. We should encourage them and give them time.

In the case of North Korea end the policy of bribing them. Such a policy invites blackmail, by them and others who observe their manipulation of us — and it certainly moves them no closer to democracy or respect for human rights. We must watch them closely and remain ready to move against any installation that may place weapons of mass or long-range delivery within their reach.

Mr. Chairman, I have only one recommendation for the Committee and it is this: to support enthusiastically and specifically with substantially larger budgets, the National Endowment for Democracy. On a shoestring it has been a source of innovative, creative programs for the building of democratic institutions, often working in places where democracy and respect for human rights is only a distant dream. It may well be the most cost-effective program in the entire arsenal of weapons in the war against terror and for a more secure world. The Endowment, and even more the organizations that benefit from the Endowment's support, need and deserve all the help we can give them.

Click here for an index of Testimony.

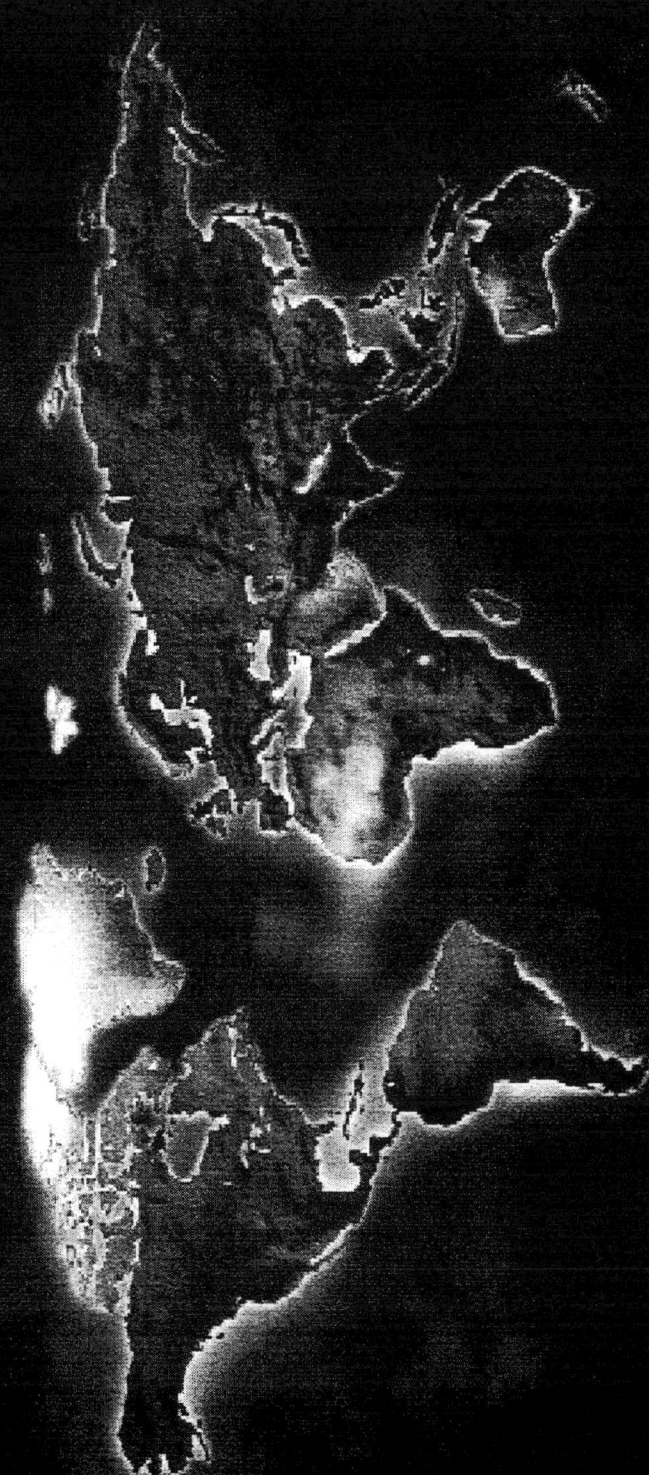

DFID Department for International Development

Making
Globalisation **Work**
for the
World's Poor

An introduction to the UK Government's White Paper on International Development

THE WORLD IS SMALLER THAN IT HAS EVER BEEN … ITS SIX BILLION CITIZENS ARE CLOSER TO EACH OTHER THAN EVER BEFORE IN HISTORY.

Each one of us is increasingly connected to people we will never meet, from places we'll never visit. Many of our clothes or shoes will have been made by people thousands of miles away – perhaps those people are laughing at a dubbed version of one of 'our' sit-coms. The fuel in our cars, the microprocessors in our computers, the coffee in our cup – so many of the products we buy in our high street have journeyed half way around the world. And we're connected in other ways too. For example, jobs in the UK depend on trade

© Chris Stowers/Panos Pictures

CONNECTED WORLD

As the world's population becomes more and more connected the process has been recognised and given a name: globalisation.

And yet, while living standards rise for many as a result of globalisation, more than a billion people on our planet live in extreme poverty, forced to make ends meet on a tiny

© Chris Stowers/Panos Pictures

with, or investment from, faraway countries. People travel more, but so do pollution and diseases.

The International Development Targets

→ A reduction by one half in the proportion of people living in extreme poverty by 2015.

→ Universal primary education in all countries by 2015.

→ Demonstrated progress towards gender equality and the empowerment of women by eliminating gender disparity in primary and secondary education by 2005.

→ A reduction by two-thirds in the mortality rates for infants and children under age 5 and a reduction by three-fourths in maternal mortality – all by 2015.

→ Access through the primary healthcare system to reproductive health services for all individuals of appropriate ages as soon as possible, and no later than the year 2015.

→ The implementation of national strategies for sustainable development in all countries by 2005, so as to ensure that current trends in the loss of environmental resources are effectively reversed at both global and national levels by 2015.

while living standards rise for many more than a billion people on our planet live in extreme poverty

MAKING GLOBALISATION WORK FOR POOR PEOPLE

income and very few basic services. These are the people for whom the shrinking of the planet has delivered no progress.

Eliminating such extreme poverty is the greatest moral challenge the world now faces. In its first White Paper on International Development, published in 1997, the UK Government committed itself firmly to the International Development Targets (see box on page 3) through which the world's governments have agreed to work to halve extreme poverty by 2015.

But reducing poverty is not just a moral issue. The closer we are connected across the continents, the more we become dependent on each other.

And, if we don't take action now to reduce global inequality, there's a real danger that life for all of us – wherever we live –

will become unsustainable.

The UK government believes that globalisation creates unprecedented new opportunities for sustainable development and poverty reduction. It offers an opportunity for faster progress in achieving the International Development Targets.

But – so far – the benefits of globalisation have been unevenly spread – for example while the peoples of East Asia have experienced benefits, millions of people in rural Africa have yet to see any change.

Progress is not inevitable. It depends on political will. And this depends on governments and people across the world.

The challenge is to connect more people from the world's poorest countries with the benefits of the new global

economy. And that means globalisation must be managed properly – to benefit everyone.

In publishing its new White Paper on International Development, in December 2000, the Government is setting out an agenda for managing the process of globalisation in a way that works for the world's poor. This booklet introduces the issues and the Government's key proposals for tackling them.

THE UK GOVERNMENT WILL

◆ Work to manage globalisation in the interests of poor people, creating faster progress towards the International Development Targets.

IT'S NOT ENOUGH FOR PEOPLE IN DEVELOPING COUNTRIES TO SIMPLY SAY, "YES PLEASE, I'D LIKE TO TAKE ADVANTAGE OF THE BENEFITS OF GLOBALISATION." THEY NEED GOVERNMENTS THAT LISTEN AND THAT WORK.

Governments in poorer countries have to create conditions at home that will help the poorest people in their communities find work or a market for their goods that will sustain their families.

While the market fundamentalism of the eighties and early nineties has been discredited, it's now widely accepted that efficient markets are indispensable for effective development.

Developing countries must attract foreign investors. But that's not enough. If the only people who benefit from a new factory or the export of agricultural produce are the rich elite, nothing much has changed.

POLICIES FOR PEOPLE

For globalisation to work for the poorest people, governments must introduce policies that allow companies to conduct their business safely and with a reasonable return. Otherwise they will take their investment elsewhere. So there has to be a stable legal system, where theft is punished, where bribery and corruption are outlawed, where people's human rights are respected and working conditions safeguarded.

Developing countries with effective governments – healthy democracies, with proper management of public finances, effective health and education services, fair law enforcement and a free media – are far more likely to deliver economic growth for their citizens.

States which invest in basic infrastructure such as water and sanitation, transport, electricity and telecommunications can play a major part in giving poor communities access to global markets.

One of the biggest barriers to development is armed conflict. Its threat to investment, stability and security destroys the conditions for growth. The UK government will step up international efforts to regulate the trade in small arms.

Effective and inclusive states – where all people have a stake in the well-being of the country – are much less likely to suffer the tragic human and economic consequences of violent conflict.

STRENGTHENING THE VULNERABLE

The rights of the poor and their influence on government policy must be strengthened – for example by supporting the groups which are helping the poor speak with a stronger voice: religious organisations are particularly close to the poor; co-operatives, women's organisations, human rights groups, development NGOs and trade unions could all help.

But globalisation itself can also work here. New information technologies offer news and information from all over the world which can help the poor to be heard. The increased access to information can also be used to bring to a wider audience the plight of a particular people – thus bringing the weight of international public opinion on those who are abusing or exploiting vulnerable people.

The UK Government believes that creating a sound balance between good social policy and good economic policy will provide the surest way to prosperity for developing countries.

THE UK GOVERNMENT WILL:

- Work to promote effective systems of government and efficient markets in developing countries.
- legislate to give UK courts jurisdiction over UK nationals who engage in bribery overseas.
- Introduce a licensing system to control UK arms brokers and traffickers, and work for tighter controls internationally at the UN conference on small arms.

Good government makes globalisation work for people.

© Fred Hoogervorst/Panos Pictures

THE **GAP** BETWEEN RICH AND POOR ARISES MORE THAN ANYTHING FROM THE KNOWLEDGE AND EDUCATION **AVAILABLE** TO **EACH.**

Speeding the spread of education and skills will make the single greatest difference to the way the world's poorest countries can harness globalisation to eradicate poverty.

When young children learn to read, write and work with numbers they not only build the foundation for further learning, but also learn how to work together, solve problems and assimilate new ideas.

At present, an estimated 113 million children of primary school age have never gone to school. A further 150 million have dropped out before achieving basic literacy and numeracy skills.

EDUCATION – THE WAY OUT

The causes of poverty are many and complex but it's now accepted that education is the quickest route out of it. Research suggests that investing in girls is the single best strategy for development any country can make. Countries which

> Education makes globalisation work.

invest in primary education – especially for girls – develop much more quickly.

International businesses invest more in better educated countries, because there they find an adaptable, more skilled workforce.

© Chris Stowers/Panos Pictures

THE DIGITAL DIVIDE

There is a real risk in poor countries that the existing educational divide will be compounded by a digital divide. Around 80% of the world's population has no access to reliable telecommunications. There are more computers in New York than in the whole of the African continent. More than half the people in Africa have never used a phone.

International business is increasingly built on the rapid movement of information around the world. New communications

© Trygve Bolstad/Panos Pictures

technologies can be harnessed to boost traditional industries – witness the way Indian handicrafts are now marketed through the internet.

Therefore, in tandem with investing in education, we must find imaginative ways of providing telecommunications access to poor communities – at a price they can afford. For example, in Bangladesh poor people in remote villages can get a loan to buy a mobile phone and set up a tiny telecentre for communal use.

THE UK GOVERNMENT WILL

◆ Work to ensure that no government committed to universal primary education is unable to achieve this goal for lack of resources.

◆ Work towards a development perspective within international rules on telecommunications and ICT, and a stronger voice for poorer countries in setting these rules.

8   9

A SIMPLE STATISTICAL COMPARISON CAN SOMETIMES ENCAPSULATE THE DIVIDE BETWEEN THE RICHEST AND POOREST COUNTRIES ON THE PLANET. IN INDIA, FOR EXAMPLE, MORE WOMEN DIE IN PREGNANCY EACH WEEK THAN IN EUROPE EACH YEAR.

Good health care is essential to a country if it's to lift its people out of poverty.

In the developing world, general ill health – not to mention life-threatening diseases – is a constant fear. The knock-on effects of illness can be devastating. For example, if a family member falls sick, someone will have to look after them and medicines will cost extra money.

Good health is a vital component to development. Children, who are at most risk from sickness and disease, need alert minds and healthy bodies if they're to get the most out of learning. Multiply this and you can see how important good health is for the growth of a developing country.

Globalisation, and the shrinking of our world, promise benefits in sharing medical knowledge and positive effects on the health of poor communities. The spread of primary healthcare practices such as the use of clean water, hygienic sanitation and the practice of simple rehydration therapy for diarrhoea has saved hundreds of thousands of lives.

But globalisation also poses risks – increased travel has had a dramatic effect on the spread of killer diseases such as HIV/AIDS and TB. World-wide there are 16,000 new HIV infections every day – 70% in sub-Saharan Africa alone.

This is not only a human tragedy but a developmental catastrophe. For instance, in just 10 months in 1998, Zambia lost 1,300 teachers to AIDS.

At present there is not enough medical research that benefits the poor. Only 10% of international research on health is focused on diseases which affect 90% of the world's population.

Countries which invest in the education and health of their citizens, will inevitably create a more productive workforce which is more attractive to international investment and more likely to harness the opportunities of globalisation.

Good health makes globalisation work.

THE UK GOVERNMENT WILL

- Work with developing countries and international organisations to help strengthen the international effort to tackle HIV/AIDS.
- Seek to increase public and private expenditure on research for development, including by providing new public incentives for private research to benefit poor people.

© Howard Davies/DFID

10

GLOBALISATION CUTS BOTH WAYS

IF OUR INTERCONNECTED WORLD IS TO WORK FOR EVERYONE, THE INTERNATIONAL RULES COUNTRIES PLAY BY MUST BE FAIR.

For a worker producing green beans in Kenya new markets have been a **BOON**.

For an African garment worker prices may have been **UNDERCUT** by competition from elsewhere.

The answer is not to try to **PREVENT** change, but to look for reform that will **IMPROVE** life in the country and provide support for those who are losing out, so that they can adapt and go **FORWARD**.

Globalisation may mean that the fish on our plate has travelled half way round the world to reach our table – but it can also mean that the people in the region where it was fished find stocks so depleted that there's not enough left for their own families, and the long-term sustainability of the resource is threatened. Globalisation can bring consumers in richer countries more choice than ever – but if their own subsidised surpluses are then 'dumped' on poorer countries, hundreds of local businesses in those countries will simply go bust.

Globalisation cuts both ways: for a worker producing green beans in Kenya or Zimbabwe new markets have been a boon.

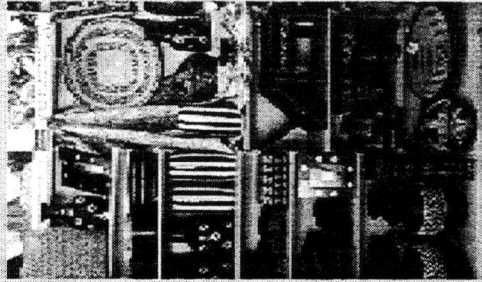

But if you're an African garment worker your prices may have been undercut by competition from elsewhere.

Globalisation must be managed properly so that it does not become merely the survival of the biggest, and the most powerful. The means of management is via global trade rules and if these are fair and transparent for all – not just the most vociferous or historically influential - then globalisation can become a road to prosperity for many.

The fastest-growing developing countries in recent decades have been those promoting exports. In these countries, mainly in east Asia, poverty has fallen most rapidly.

OPEN TRADE IS NOT UNREGULATED TRADE

Effective multilateral trade rules must be applied for open trade

© James Hawkins/Oxfam

12

204

to work for the world's poor. This is what the World Trade Organisation (WTO) does.

But while developing countries are a majority of the WTO's members, its discussions can be dominated by the concerns of older, richer members. Not surprising perhaps, when half the least-developed countries have no representation at its headquarters in Geneva.

Poorer countries can be frustrated by a feeling that their voices are not being heard.

Campaigners demanding the end of the WTO – such as those in Seattle in 1999 and Prague in 2000 – grab headlines. But without a rules-based trading system the powerful countries can bully the rest – not least by striking mutual deals which exclude poorer countries.

The answer to trade rules which are not working is not to scrap the WTO – but to ensure that the trade rules work for all.

The WTO needs reform and as a first step the UK Government will work for more effective participation in the WTO and international trading system by developing countries. We also want to see the WTO commit itself, with the rest of the international community, to achieving the International Development Targets – a powerful signal

of its commitment to poverty reduction and sustainable development, acknowledging that trade is not an end in itself.

© Howard Davies/DFID

The UK will also press for a pro-development European Union (EU) negotiating position in a new Trade Round – including substantial cuts in high tariffs and in trade-distorting subsidies, especially to sectors which are important to developing countries, such as agriculture and fisheries.

We will also press for implementation of a recent European Commission proposal which would allow all exports from least developed countries into the EU duty free, except for arms.

And we recognise that the EU's Common Agricultural Policy (CAP) is an unfair barrier to the access of developing countries to our markets – a barrier that the United Nations has estimated costs developing countries £13.7bn a year. And through

the Common Fisheries Policy (CFP), some of the EU's fishing industry gets the chance to fish in developing countries' waters, making competition harder and sometimes leading to over-fishing. The UK government will lobby for changes to both.

TRADE STANDARDS MUST SERVE DEVELOPMENT

As consumers reasonably press for more information and higher standards to protect labour and the environment, developing country exporters find it hard to keep up with the proliferation of regulators and standards. They fear the 'process standards' – on labour, animal welfare or the environment – may be used to keep their products out of developed country markets. The UK Government is committed to promoting core labour, environmental, social and health standards, but believes that we must provide adequate information and quality to consumers while still enabling developing countries to export and grow their way out of poverty. Standards must not be used to lock developing countries' products out of our markets.

THE UK GOVERNMENT WILL:

◆ Support an open and rules-based international trading system, and work to promote equitable trade rules and an effective voice for developing countries.

◆ Support continuing reductions in barriers to trade, both in developed and developing countries, and work to improve the capacity of developing countries to take advantage of new trade opportunities.

205

ALONGSIDE A **FAIR** AND **ACCESSIBLE** GLOBAL TRADING ENVIRONMENT, DEVELOPING COUNTRIES ALSO REQUIRE THE ABILITY TO **HARNESS** INTERNATIONAL FINANCIAL **INVESTMENT.**

Many poor countries see their own wealth kept in banks outside their country. For example it is estimated that 40% of African private wealth is held overseas, compared with only 4% in Asia. The reforms needed to prevent capital flight also attract inward investment.

In recent years more and more money has been invested in poor countries, increasing private capital levels from £25 billion in 1990 to £137 billion in 1998 – more than four times the level of development aid. But much of this was invested in only a very few countries.

While transnational companies want to invest in new markets – they also want to know that it's a safe proposition. And when the right domestic policies are established, the money follows – look at Mozambique, which has seen a six-fold increase in Foreign Direct Investment since 1994.

Business can also play a greater role in reducing poverty and creating sustainable development. By applying best practice in relation to child labour, corruption, corporate governance, human rights, health and safety, environment and conflict, business can make a real contribution to poverty reduction. Many companies have also realised important commercial benefits, in terms of reputation, managing risk and enhanced productivity.

We will work to improve the monitoring of countries' performances, boosting information to potential investors – and helping avoid sudden shocks and outflows of investors' funds. We will also work to strengthen the international system's capacity to resolve financial crises and improve the stability of global financial markets.

> Mozambique has seen a **SIX–FOLD** increase in Foreign Direct Investment since 1994.

© Howard Davies/DFID

THE UK GOVERNMENT WILL

◆ Work to support developing countries to put in place conditions that will allow them to attract private financial flows and deal with the problem of capital flight.

◆ Work to strengthen the global financial system to manage the risks associated with the scale, speed and volatility of global financial flows, and promote international co-operation on tax, competition and investment issues.

◆ Work to encourage corporate social responsibility by national and transnational companies, and more investment by them in poor countries.

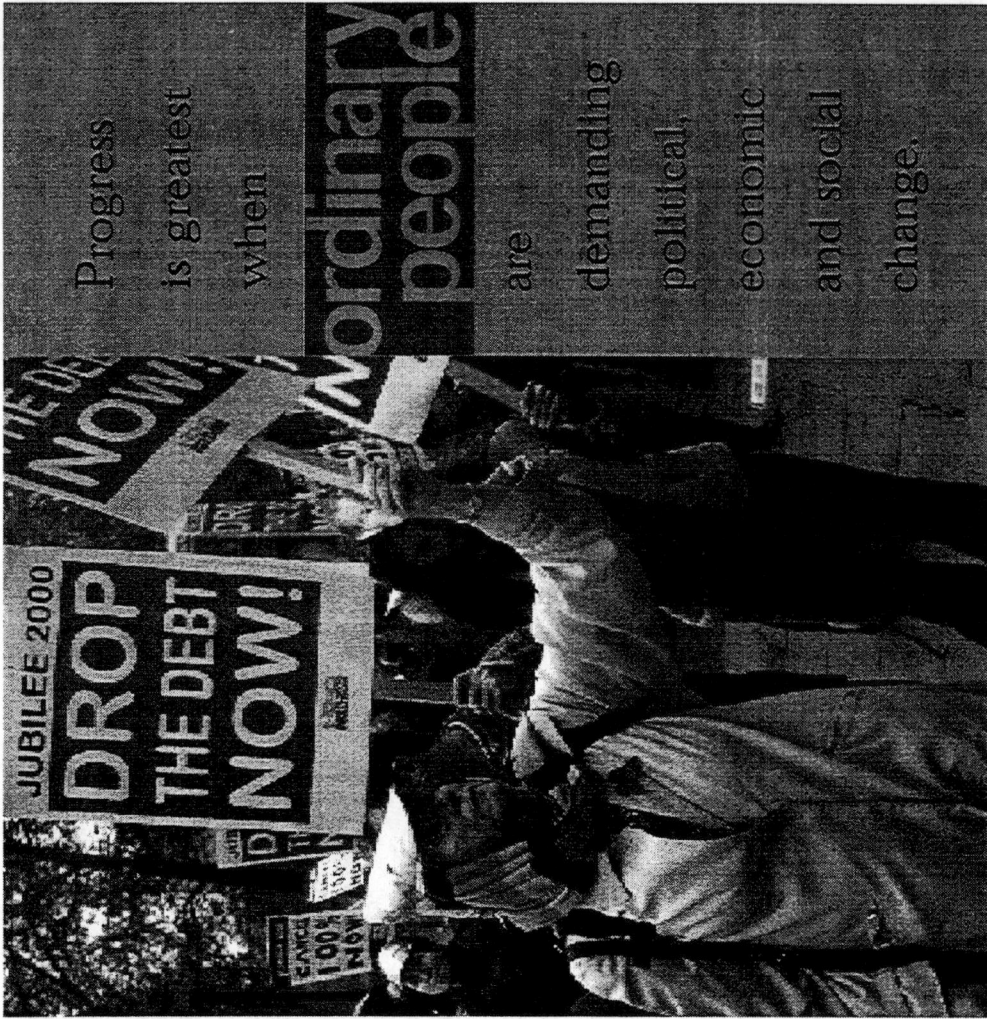

Progress is greatest when **ordinary people** are demanding political, economic and social change.

JUBILEE 2000 DROP THE DEBT NOW!

© Howard Davies/DFID

IF WE ARE TO ENHANCE THE WAY THAT KEY INTERNATIONAL INSTITUTIONS CONTRIBUTE TO THE REDUCTION IN POVERTY, WE MUST GIVE POOR PEOPLE AND COUNTRIES A MORE EFFECTIVE VOICE WITHIN THESE INSTITUTIONS.

We also need national and global civil society to demand policies which will deliver on the International Development Targets. Progress is greatest when ordinary people are demanding political, economic and social change.

AGENTS OF CHANGE

Governments in developing countries are more likely to prioritise the needs of the poor if there is an active civil society insisting that they do. Governments will act when they feel the heat from their people, from religious groups, trade unions, human rights organisations, women's groups, the professions and academia.

The voice of civil society in developed countries is also vital; and in the UK, for example, the revised national curriculum in England incorporates a commitment to sustainable development and the global dimension.

THE UK GOVERNMENT WILL

◆ Work with others to build an effective, open and accountable international system, in which poor people and countries have a more effective voice.

18

EXISTING PATTERNS OF PRODUCTION AND CONSUMPTION ARE PLACING ENORMOUS STRAINS ON THE ECO-SYSTEMS OF THE PLANET.

Pollution in one part of the world has knock-on effects in another.

The release of greenhouse gases into the atmosphere from our burning of fossil fuels and the destruction of forests threaten to change the weather patterns across the world and put at risk coastal areas.

Poor countries contribute least to these environmental problems, but they are most likely to be the victims of environmental disasters. The Red Cross estimates that in 1998, for the first time, the number of refugees displaced by 'natural' disasters, caused by floods, storms and droughts, outnumbered those who had the leave their homes because of war.

People in developed countries consume more per head than those in developing countries and often actively contribute to the environmental challenges we must solve. For example, our demands for timber, minerals, cheap food and tourism can result in deforestation, water pollution, erosion, loss of traditional land use patterns and the destruction of fragile habitats. Developed countries should

do more to reduce their contribution to climate change, pollution and the depletion of natural resources. They should lead by example and work closely with developing countries to enable them to manage environmental assets sustainably.

Developing countries will need help to make their emerging industries conform to global environmental agreements

and objectives (such as on emissions of greenhouse gases) as well as their own national priorities for sustainable development.

Protecting the fragile resources of the planet, and the people who depend on them, makes globalisation work.

Poor countries contribute least to environmental problems but are most likely to be the victims of ENVIRONMENTAL DISASTER

THE UK GOVERNMENT WILL

◆ Meet our global environmental responsibilities, including our goal of reducing our CO_2 emissions by 20% by 2010.

◆ Work with developing countries to integrate environmental sustainability into their poverty reduction strategies and increase assistance for them to benefit from multilateral environmental agreements.

© Panos Pictures

208

GLOBALISATION MUST BECOME A FORCE FOR **GOOD** FOR POOR COUNTRIES. BUT IT'S AN **ENORMOUS** CHALLENGE FOR DEVELOPING COUNTRIES TO TURN THIS INTO A **REALITY**.

Richer countries cannot expect them to do this alone.

Over the years, immense sums of money have been handed or lent to developing countries in the name of aid, but it's not always been wisely given or wisely used. We have to make sure that aid does what it's supposed to do – reduce poverty by strengthening the arm of the poor, but also create conditions to attract inward investment and boost economic growth.

In the past too much aid has been:

→ used as a sweetener to win lucrative contracts.

→ tied to the purchase of goods from the donor country.

→ given as part of a donor-led project which is not necessarily in the best interests of the country.

Research indicates that the best results come when aid is focused on the poorest people in countries where the government has good policies of pro-poor reform.

Aid from developed nations needs to dovetail with realistic strategies to reduce poverty,

designed and led by developing countries themselves. This is also true in the case of debt relief – on which the UK has led international efforts for faster and more substantial progress.

World Bank research suggests that aid given in this way would be as valuable as increasing the aid budget by 50%.

The right kind of aid makes globalisation work.

THE UK GOVERNMENT WILL

◆ Provide more money in development aid – rising to 0.33% of GNP by 2003/4 and continuing our progress to 0.7% thereafter.

◆ Allocate more of our aid to low income countries.

◆ Stop tying UK aid only to UK suppliers and work to get all other donors to act similarly.

◆ Work to ensure that EC aid is more effective and is focused on low income countries.

GLOBALISATION CAN WORK FOR THE WORLD'S POOREST PEOPLE

WHILE AID, EFFECTIVELY TARGETED, CAN MAKE A **SIGNIFICANT** DIFFERENCE TO THE LIVES AND PROSPECTS OF POOR PEOPLE, IT'S **NOT** A SOLUTION BY **ITSELF.**

If globalisation is to work for poor people then all the issues we've mentioned in this publication will need to be tackled.

This involves all the players, right across the board – governments at home and abroad, business, international institutions (such as the World Bank and the World Trade Organisation) and NGOs. It also demands reform and fresh thinking across a broad swathe of policy areas, including trade, economics and foreign policy. This is not something the UK

unified, global approach.

We must combine our efforts with a wider international commitment to improve the lot of the poor. It's also in all of our interests to do so. Therefore, we believe we have an unrivalled opportunity at the beginning of the 21st century to harness the benefits of globalisation to give people living in some of the poorest countries the chance to build a viable future for themselves and their families.

Government can do on its own. We can make sure we pull our own weight by getting our own policies right, but poverty is such an enormous, global challenge that it demands a

→ Want to know more about globalisation?

→ Want to find out about what this government is doing to encourage development around the world?

→ Want a copy of the full text of the White Paper?

→ Want to have your say?

WRITE TO

DFID public enquiry point
Abercrombie House
Eaglesham Road
East Kilbride
Glasgow G75 8EA UK

CALL 0845 300 4100

VISIT www.dfid.gov.uk

22

Chapter Fifteen
Researching Economic Topics

Many debates are won by research. Extemp championships may rest on fluency, but knowledge is the crucial second variable. In every chapter the author has included recommendations for Internet sites. What follows is an annotated alphabetical list of the "best of the rest", locations you should know and use if you are going to be dominant in your knowledge and research.

www.aei.brookings.org/ is the home page for the AEI-Brookings Joint Center. A moderate political position with good coverage on in-the-news issues. Has publications, internal search feature, stories, good "Hot Topics".

Almanac of Policy Issues economic focus is at www.policyalmanac.org/economic/index.shtml .Has good internal search, good selection of pre-done focus areas (Antitrust Law through Rent Control), Directories, Congressional links, news, data links, more. Its home page reminds us how important economics is to every other area: "Economic policy often drives other forms of policy. A nation's economic strength often dictates how much it can afford to spend on public needs like health care, transportation, science or education. It can also affect a nation's ability to afford new regulatory policies targeting things like the environment or safety in the workplace.

More fundamentally, economic policy often drives elections, and elections affect issues across the policy spectrum. As a wag once noted when prioritizing the most important issues in a presidential campaign, 'it's the economy stupid.'

Economic policy has many components, including **fiscal policy** (government spending and taxes), **monetary policy** (determining the size of the money supply), and **regulatory policy** in all its forms, including regulation of business, labor relations, consumer protection, and rules of international trade. In fact, most matters of public policy, even those that are not primarily economic in nature, have some impact on the economy."

Also check out their business issues section at www.policyalmanac.org/economic/business.shtml

Ask Henry at www.askhenry.com/ lists economics as one of its strengths.

CDE at www.cdedebate.com has four sections the reader will want to check out. The texts and handbooks for extemp and debate are plentiful and useful. The summer camp offerings are the best available. Debaters will want to take advantage of the free blocks. And every reader should tap into the CDE FREE LINKS section, it is *very* useful.

Maybe somebody has already built arguments and or blocks on the very issue you are prepping. Or there's an already ongoing web debate on it. Check and see at *The Debate Club*, www.geocities.com/freetradeforever/debateclub.htm It's a fun idea and there's no registration or password requirement.

The Freedom Network offers us *the Directory of General Economic Theory Online Resources Directories*. It gives you 4 sections: global, United States, Latin America, and Europe. Links noted by source, country and abstract. www.free-market.net/directorybycategory/homepages/T25/

EconDebates Online "keeps you informed on today's most crucial economics policy debates. Each EconDebate, created by John Kane (SUNY-Oswego), provides a primer on the issues and links to background information and current, in-depth commentaries from experts around the world." Review the brief introductions and, for EconDebates that interest you, click to see publications and links for the full debate. www.swcollege.com/bef/policy_debates/econ_debates_scarcity_choice.html

This is a wonderful resource. The end of this chapter shows you the home page and a sample of what you find when you select a topic. See it and then use it.

Teachers will be very pleased with the Economic Education site hosted by the Federal Reserve Bank of New York. "This page provides information about programs and services available to students and teachers to promote economic and financial literacy and a greater understanding of the role of the Federal Reserve System." Includes an economics bowl, the history of money, publications, financial indicators, 5 strategies on teaching economics, more. www.ny.frb.org./pihome/educator/?expand=4

Economy.com They describe themselves as "a leading independent provider of economic, financial, and industry research. Our economic research and data are used by clients in 65 countries across the globe." Some free content, some costs you. www.economy.com/default.asp

For college and graduate students (or the truly well read high school senior) there is the Economic Modeling web site. It has hundreds of white papers on useful and **esoteric** topics. www.itpapers.com/

The Economic Policy Institute is useful. They update by topic weekly. They have an excellent "Issue Guide" to help you focus. The home page also includes a "Paycheck Economics" section with good subdivisions. At the top of the home page is a good third feature, big headings (e.g. trade and globalization, education, ...more) that you are likely to use. Extempers will like one more feature, its even titled like an extemp speech, "How To Stimulate The U.S. Economy." www.epinet.org/epihome.html

Economics Working Paper Archive, like ItPapers, is for college level. "This award winning service (provided by the Economics Department of Washington University) is devoted to the free distribution of working papers in eco0nomics. There are 22 subject areas...and an area for data." http://econwpa.wustl.edu/

The Energy and Environmental Research Center (EERC) focuses on two important areas with heavy economic subcomponents. Has a good internal search feature, news, and literature. www.eerc.und.nodak.edu/

Essays on International Trade, Economics and Politics by Jock O'Connell has great links to specific news stories from a multitude of newspapers. Excellent for your extemp files. www.members.tripod.com/jockoconnell/articles.html

Federal Reserve Bank off New York staff reports are good college level publications. These are "technical papers intended for publication in leading economic and finance journals". www.ny.frb.org./rmaghome/staff_rp/

The Foundation For Economic Education has a <u>fine</u> "ECONOMICS" site. It also has CX debate, LD debate and extemp sections plus an internal search engine. The Economic sections include lesson plans, transportation, taxes, development, ethics, environment, poverty, law and economics, globalization and trade. www.freespeaker.org/economics/index.html

The Fraser Institute has an "Economic Freedom" location. It includes access to its annual *Economic Freedom of the World Report*. Also has nice "Recent News" section. On its home page check out the left side for links to editorials, publications, education, environment, health, and many other useful options. www.fraserinstitute.ca/economicfreedom/index.asp?snav=ef

Foreign extempers and debaters looking for impact stories need to get very comfortable with Global Issues That Affect Everyone at www.globalissues.org/ The home page gives you easy, well organized options with logical useful plentiful subdivisions: Trade Related Issues (Third World Debt, Free Trade and Globalization, Sustainable Development, etc.), Human Rights, Geopolitics (with Arms Control, Int'l Criminal Court, NATO, Foreign Policy, more), Environmental Issues (Biodiversity, Genetic Engineering, Global Warming, more). Has internal search engine.

The Organization for Economic Cooperation and Development is an objective respected keeper of statistics and economic advice. Be sure to use two features on its home page: "What's New" for economic indicators and noteworthy actions, and "Themes" on the left side of the page where everything from Ageing Society to Trade and Transport get their coverage. www.oecd.org/

Victory Briefs has extemp "How To" books and briefs.
www.victorybriefs.net/web-extemp/ext-products.asp

EconDebate Online
Economic policy
debates on today's
pressing issues

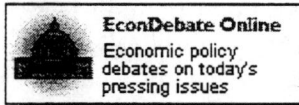

Economics Policy Debates

EconDebate Online keeps you informed on today's most crucial economics policy debates. Each EconDebate, created by John Kane (SUNY-Oswego), provides a primer on the issues and links to background information and current, in-depth commentaries from experts around the world.

Hot Debates

- Does U.S. immigration policy harm domestic workers?
- Does the anti-sweatshop movement help or harm workers in low-wage economies?
- Does an increase in the minimum wage result in a higher unemployment rate?
- Should the antitrust exemption for baseball be eliminated?
- Do OSHA regulations benefit or harm workers?
- Does international trade harm the environment?
- Do slave redemption programs reduce the problem of slavery?
- Does a gender wage gap still exist?
- Has Deregulation Caused the Energy Shortage in California?
- Is a college education a good investment?
- Should Medicare Provide Prescription Drug Coverage?
- Should the Strategic Petroleum Reserve be used to Reduce Fluctuations in Oil Prices?
- Should Napster and similar MP3 distribution mechanisms be banned?
- Should there be a market for human organs?
- Does Public Investment in Municipal Sports Stadiums Pay Off?
- Is There A New Economy?
- Can Open-Source Software Survive?
- Is Workfare Working?
- Does the U.S. economy benefit from the WTO?

TOPIC INDEX

Select the topic of interest to you to review an index of policy debates.

Economic Fundamentals I Microeconomics I Macroeconomics I World Economy

Economic Fundamentals

- Scarcity, Choice, and Opportunity Cost
- Supply and Demand

Microeconomics

- Economics and the Environment
- Government and the Economy
- Income Distribution and Poverty
- Labor Markets

- Market Failure, Regulation, and Public Choice
- Monopolistic Competition
- Monopoly
- Oligopoly
- Utility and Consumer Choice

Macroeconomics

- Employment, Unemployment, and Inflation
- Fiscal Policy
- Monetary Policy

- Money and the Financial System
- Productivity and Growth
- Taxes, Spending, and Deficits

World Economy

- Comparative Economics Systems
- Developing and Transitional Economies

- International Finance
- International Trade

213

South-Western EconDebate Online

- Should the Death Tax Be Abolished?
- Do School Vouchers Improve the Quality of Education?
- Is the death penalty an efficient crime deterrent?
- Does dollarization benefit developing countries?
- Do technological advances result in higher unemployment?
- Should the Fed pursue a fixed policy rule?
- Should marijuana be decriminalized?
- How should the U.S. budget surplus be used?
- Is Microsoft a Monopoly?
- Does globalization require a change in antitrust policy?
- Is there a need for health-care reform?
- Will Social Security survive into the 21st century?
- How should we reform the current tax system?
- Will the European Monetary Union succeed?
- Does the U.S. economy benefit from foreign trade?
- Should the Federal Reserve aim at a zero inflation policy?
- Should U.S. financial markets be deregulated?
- What accounts for recent increases in income inequality?
- Does foreign direct investment hinder or help economic development?
- What are the pros and cons of IMF involvement with global economies?
- Have Learnfare programs resulted in improved school attendance?

©2002 South-Western. All Rights Reserved   webmaster | DISCLAIMER

Economics

EconDebates Online

EconDebates Online keeps you informed on today's most crucial economics policy debates. Each EconDebate, created by John Kane (SUNY-Oswego), provides a primer on the issues and links to background information and current, in-depth commentaries from experts around the world. Review the brief introductions and, for EconDebates of interest, select the full debate.

Scarcity, Choice, and Opportunity Cost	
Title	*Introduction*
Does the anti-sweatshop movement help or harm workers in low-wage economies? **Full Debate**	The anti-sweatshop movement in the U.S. and other industrialized economies has, in recent years, attempted to use consumer boycotts to eliminate sweatshop working conditions and child labor in less developed economies. Unions and college student groups have been leading the drive for sweatshop boycotts.
Should Medicare Provide Prescription Drug Coverage? **Full Debate**	Recent advances in medical care have resulted in the development of many new pharmaceutical therapies for a variety of health conditions. Many of these newly introduced drug therapies, though, are relatively expensive due to the high costs associated with developing and testing these drugs. Medicare, however, does not currently provide prescription drug coverage. Instead, retired individuals either have no prescription drug coverage, or purchase relatively expensive "Medigap" insurance coverage to cover the medical expenses not covered by Medicare.
Should there be a market for human organs? **Full Debate**	Advances in medical treatments have resulted in a dramatic increase in the number of organ transplants performed each year. A limited supply of organs, however, prevents many individuals from receiving organ replacements that could either save a life or substantially improve the recipient's quality of life.
Does Public Investment in Municipal Sports Stadiums Pay Off? **Full Debate**	There has been an extensive amount of public investment in the construction of municipal sports stadiums in recent years. Cities wishing to either attract or keep a professional sports team are often forced to provide new stadiums as a result of competition with other cities.
Should marijuana be decriminalized? **Full Debate**	Marijuana is a product derived from the cannabis sativa plant. This plant, also known as "hemp," was a major agricultural product in the United States from the colonial period until the early part of the 20th century. Hemp was used to produce rope, cloth, lacquer, and bird seed. There is evidence suggesting that hemp was grown on the plantations of George Washington and Thomas Jefferson.

Will Social Security survive into the 21st century? **Full Debate**	The online resources listed below provide a wide range of opinions concerning the magnitude of the problems facing the social security system. Part of the reason for this is that forecasts of future social security revenue depend on factors such as future rates of economic growth, the level of future unemployment and labor force participation rates, and similar factors. Small differences in rates of economic growth can have dramatic effects on the level of output (and tax revenue) over the course of a 20-30 year period. Different assumptions about such future outcomes result in very different conclusions about the future solvency of the social security system.
Should anti-pollution standards be strengthened? **Full Debate**	Nearly everyone agrees that pollution is undesirable (the only likely exceptions are those individuals whose income depends on the provision of pollution abatement services). It is socially optimal, however, that some level of pollution be tolerated. The reason, of course, is that there is an opportunity cost associated with pollution abatement. A cleaner environment requires higher production costs and a lower level of output.
Is there a need for health-care reform? **Full Debate**	Health-care reform was one of the major issues in the 1992 U.S. Presidential campaign. While no major reform bill was passed during Bill Clinton's first term in office, health-care reform has remained a major topic of congressional debate.
Is the death penalty an efficient crime deterrent? **Full Debate**	The economic argument in favor of the death penalty is rather simple. Economists assume that individuals weigh the expected costs and benefits when deciding to undertake any activity. Thus, rational individuals considering criminal activities would weigh the expected benefits against the expected cost of the criminal endeavor. The expected cost of any given crime is affected by the probability of being detected, the probability of being convicted given detection, and the expected penalty that results from a conviction. Since the death penalty provides a higher cost than alternative punishments, it is expected to generate a larger deterrent effect, ceteris paribus.
Do School Vouchers Improve the Quality of Education? **Full Debate**	Several experimental voucher programs have been introduced in the past decade. One of the oldest and largest is a pilot program begun in 1990 in Milwaukee, Wisconsin. Initial analyses of this data have suggested little or no improvement in the quality of education as the result of a voucher system. These results, however, are quite controversial and are the subject of a good deal of debate. More recent pilot programs in New York City and Cleveland are also beginning to provide additional evidence for this debate. Preliminary, and equally controversial, results from the New York Choice Scholarship Program suggest that a voucher system has resulted in modest improvements in test scores for low-income students that transfer to private schools as a result of a scholarship program.

Return to <u>EconDebates Topic Index</u>   Return to <u>Economics Resource Center</u>

©1998-2001 South-Western. All Rights Reserved <u>webmaster</u>

Economics

EconDebates Online

EconDebates Online keeps you informed on today's most crucial economics policy debates. Each EconDebate, created by John Kane (SUNY-Oswego), provides a primer on the issues and links to background information and current, in-depth commentaries from experts around the world. Review the brief introductions and, for EconDebates of interest, select the full debate.

Supply and Demand	
Title	*Introduction*
Does U.S. immigration policy harm domestic workers? **Full Debate**	Most U.S. residents today are the descendants of immigrants who arrived in the U.S. during the past 150 years. Concern over the effect of immigration on domestic workers, however, have resulted in the passage of several laws designed to restrict immigration. Unions, in particular, have argued for more restrictive immigration policy on the grounds that immigration lowers the wage and employment levels for domestic residents.
Does the anti-sweatshop movement help or harm workers in low-wage economies? **Full Debate**	The anti-sweatshop movement in the U.S. and other industrialized economies has, in recent years, attempted to use consumer boycotts to eliminate sweatshop working conditions and child labor in less developed economies. Unions and college student groups have been leading the drive for sweatshop boycotts.
Does an Increase in the Minimum Wage Result in a Higher Unemployment Rate? **Full Debate**	Minimum wage laws in the U.S. were first introduced during the 1930s in response to the Great Depression. This period was characterized by falling output, falling prices, and falling employment. The National Industrial Recovery Act (NIRA) of 1933 attempted to stop this downward spiral by encouraging the formation of trade association agreements that established price floors and minimum wages. This was the first national attempt to introduce minimum wages in major industries. Those firms that participated in the trade association agreements were able to display a "blue eagle" logo in their establishments. In 1935, the U.S. Supreme Court ruled that the NIRA was unconstitutional, and these initial minimum wage agreements were terminated.
Do slave redemption programs reduce the problem of slavery? **Full Debate**	In the U.S. and other industrialized countries, slavery is generally viewed as a part of the distant past. Slavery, however, still exists in some parts of the world. In recent years, substantial attention has been focused on the existence of slavery in Sudan. As world attention focused on the problem of slavery in Sudan, several religious and human rights groups attempted to deal with this issue by buying the freedom of these slaves. Several concerns have been raised, however, about the unintended consequences associated with these slave redemption programs. A simple demand and supply model of the market for slaves can effectively illustrate these concerns.
Does a gender	The average wage rate for female workers has been below that for male workers for as long as statistics have been recorded. In recent years, female wages have been

wage gap still exist? **Full Debate**	approximately equal to 3/4 of the level of male wages. At first glance, statistics such as this may suggest that females are the subject of substantial discrimination in the labor market. There is, however, a fair amount of disagreement among economists concerning the cause of this wage differential.
Has Deregulation Caused the Energy Shortage in California? **Full Debate**	California began experiencing a serious energy shortage in the summer of 2000. Power blackouts became relatively frequent in many areas of the state. These problems appeared to have begun with the deregulation of the electrical power industry in California. Are these problems the result of deregulation? Or are they the result of regulations that result in inefficient outcomes? This question is of particular importance since many other states are in the process of following California's path to deregulation.
Is a college education a good investment? **Full Debate**	One of the questions asked every year by many college students and their parents is: "Is a college education a good investment?" A large body of statistical evidence indicates that, on average, college graduates have higher lifetime earning streams than high school graduates. The rate of return to a college degree, however, is affected by a variety of factors, including: choice of college major, choice of occupation, labor market conditions, college quality, and individual ability. There are, however, several problems that make it difficult to measure the return to education for an individual.
Should there be a market for human organs? **Full Debate**	Advances in medical treatments have resulted in a dramatic increase in the number of organ transplants performed each year. A limited supply of organs, however, prevents many individuals from receiving organ replacements that could either save a life or substantially improve the recipient's quality of life.
Do School Vouchers Improve the Quality of Education? **Full Debate**	Several experimental voucher programs have been introduced in the past decade. One of the oldest and largest is a pilot program begun in 1990 in Milwaukee, Wisconsin. Initial analyses of this data have suggested little or no improvement in the quality of education as the result of a voucher system. These results, however, are quite controversial and are the subject of a good deal of debate. More recent pilot programs in New York City and Cleveland are also beginning to provide additional evidence for this debate. Preliminary, and equally controversial, results from the New York Choice Scholarship Program suggest that a voucher system has resulted in modest improvements in test scores for low-income students that transfer to private schools as a result of a scholarship program.
Is there a need for health-care reform? **Full Debate**	Health-care reform was one of the major issues in the 1992 U.S. Presidential campaign. While no major reform bill was passed during Bill Clinton's first term in office, health-care reform has remained a major topic of congressional debate.
Should marijuana be decriminalized? **Full Debate**	Marijuana is a product derived from the cannabis sativa plant. This plant, also known as "hemp," was a major agricultural product in the United States from the colonial period until the early part of the 20th century. Hemp was used to produce rope, cloth, lacquer, and bird seed. There is evidence suggesting that hemp was grown on the plantations of George Washington and Thomas Jefferson.

Return to EconDebates Topic Index

Return to Economics Resource Center

©1998-2002 South-Western. All Rights Reserved webmaster

Economics

Issues and Background

The average wage gap is not proof of widespread discrimination, but of women making choices about their educational and professional careers in a society where the law has granted them equality of opportunity to do so. Comparable worth promotes a dependence for women, and a reliance on government for protection. Given women's achievements, such dependence is unnecessary. American women enjoy historically unparalleled success and freedom, and the progress they have made in the past half century will continue.
~Diana Furchtgott-Roth

Equal pay has been the law since 1963. But today, 37 years later, women are still paid less than men—even when we have similar education, skills and experience.

In 1999, women were paid 72 cents for every dollar men received. That's $28 less to spend on groceries, housing, child care and other expenses for every $100 worth of work we do. Nationwide, working families lose $200 billion of income annually to the wage gap.

It's not like we get charged less for rent or food or utilities. In fact, we pay more for things like haircuts and dry cleaning.
~AFL-CIO

The average wage rate for female workers has been below that for male workers for as long as statistics have been recorded. In recent years, female wages have been approximately equal to 3/4 of the level of male wages. At first glance, statistics such as this may suggest that females are the subject of substantial discrimination in the labor market. There is, however, a fair amount of disagreement among economists concerning the cause of this wage differential.

No one seriously disputes the existence of a gender wage differential. The disagreement primarily focuses on the cause of the wage differential. Is it the result of gender discrimination? Or is it the result of differences in other characteristics that are correlated with gender? A study by Jacob Mincer and Solomon Polachek indicates that much of the gender wage difference is the result of differences in educational attainment and work experience. Erica Groshen and others have found that most of the remaining gender wage differential can be explained by differences in occupational choice.

Thus, the empirical evidence indicates that most (or all) of the male-female wage differential is due to gender-related differences in occupational choice, educational attainment, and prior work experience. Those who argue that the male-female wage differential is not a symptom of discrimination suggest that this difference is the result of voluntary

219

decisions on the part of individuals in selecting their careers, educational attainment, and the level and timing of labor force participation. Those who believe that the gender wage differential is due to discrimination argue that discrimination affects women's choice of careers, educational attainment, and labor supply decisions.

One of the main reasons for the male-female wage differential is that those occupations that are disproportionately filled by women tend to be relatively low-paying occupations while male-dominated occupations tend to offer high wages. Most secretaries, nurses, and elementary school teachers are women while most engineers, surgeons, computer programmers, and chemists are men. The "crowding" hypothesis suggests that the low wages received by women in these occupations is due to a relatively large supply of labor in these female-dominated occupations. If women voluntarily select these low-paid occupations then the lower wage is the result of voluntary choice, not discrimination. This part of the wage differential is the result of discrimination, though, if women are crowded into these occupations as a result of barriers to their entry into higher-paying male-dominated professions. It is expected, however, that as the proportion of women in male-dominated occupations continues to increase, the wage differential is likely to narrow.

While there are substantially more women than males in college today, this is a relatively recent historical phenomena. Until the past 20 years, the proportion of women attending college was substantially less than the proportion of males attending college. While the educational attainment of young male and female workers is quite similar today, older women in the labor force have lower levels of educational attainment than older males. Part of the wage differential is due to the lower average level of educational attainment for women. It is expected that this portion of the wage differential will narrow over time as more highly educated women enter the labor market and older women retire.

Until the 1980s, most women withdrew from the labor force for a few years after the commencement of childbearing. Today, most women with young children remain in the labor force. A typical woman in the labor force, though, still has fewer years of prior work experience than a typical male. Since earnings are strongly related to prior work experience, differences in work experience explain part of the gender wage gap. It is expected that this part of the wage differential will decline over time due to declining fertility rates over the past few decades and the more continuous labor force attachment of younger female workers.

Those who argue that the wage differential is the result of discrimination argue that women are more likely to withdraw from the labor force because they have less to lose by leaving. Lower wages and reduced chances of promotion lower the incentives of women to remain in the labor force. This argument suggests that the causality between work experience and wages is bidirectional. While lower female wages may be partly due to lower levels of work experience, these lower levels of work experience are also partly caused by lower female wages.

Those who believe that the male-female wage differential is the result of labor market discrimination sometimes suggest that a "comparable worth" pay structure be introduced to eliminate the gender wage gap. Under a comparable worth pay system, jobs are rated according using a number of criteria such as: educational requirements, manual dexterity requirements, job stress, risk of injuries, etc. Jobs that have similar ratings are assigned the same pay. Advocates of such a system suggest that this system results in equal pay for equivalent work. Some studies, for example, have suggested that secretaries and truck drivers are "comparable" jobs. Both involve long periods of sitting, similar amounts of training, and repetitive tasks. Therefore, it is argued, the pay of secretaries (a female-dominated occupation) should be equal to the pay of truck drivers (a male-dominated occupation).

Opponents of comparable worth pay structures argue that the lower wage rate for secretaries is the result of "crowding" in this labor market. Higher pay rates would encourage more people to enter an occupation in which wages were initially low because there were already too many workers in this labor market. A reduction in the pay rate for truck drivers would cause fewer people to enter an occupation in which pay is initially high because there are relatively few people willing to work in this occupation. Those who oppose comparable worth pay structures argue that they would result in economic inefficiency by causing surpluses in labor markets in which pay is raised and shortages in those labor markets in which pay is lowered.

While there are several reasons to believe that the gender wage gap will be reduced in the future, this wage gap remains relatively large. As long as this gap remains, this issue is likely to provide a major source of debate among economists, policymakers, and the general public.

Primary Resources and Data

- ### Equal Pay Act of 1963
  http://www.eeoc.gov/laws/epa.html
  The Equal Pay Act of 1963 was designed to eliminate gender discrimination in wages. This Act prohibits sex discrimination in wages for male and female workers in a given firm. It allows pay differentials based upon length of job tenure, merit, and productivity differentials.

- ### Title VII of the Civil Rights Act of 1964
  http://www.eeoc.gov/laws/vii.html
  Title VII of the Civil Rights Act of 1964 explicitly banned gender discrimination in hiring or in establishing wage rates.

- ### U.S. Council of Economic Advisers, "Explaining Trends in the Gender Wage Gap"
  http://clinton4.nara.gov/WH/EOP/CEA/html/gendergap.html
  This June 1998 report examines the reasons for the existence of the gender wage gap. It is noted that a substantial portion of the wage gap may be explained by differences in education, work experience, hours of work, and occupational choice. The difficulties in separating the effects of discrimination from the effects of preferences and choice are also discussed.

- ### U.S. Equal Employment Opportunity Commission (EEOC)
  http://www.eeoc.gov/
  The U.S. Equal Employment Opportunity Commission (EEOC) web site contains information on employment law related to gender discrimination. Methods of remedying discrimination are also discussed.

- ### U.S. Equal Employment Opportunity Commission, "Job Patterns For Minorities And Women In Private Industry, 1999"
  http://www.eeoc.gov/stats/jobpat/jobpat.html
  This web site, provided by the U.S. Equal Employment Opportunity Commission, shows the proportion of women employed in an extensive set of occupations. Data is sorted by 3-digit SIC code and by job category within the industry.

- ### National Organization for Women
  http://www.now.org/
  The web site of the National Organization for Women contains arguments suggesting that gender discrimination is a significant factor in explaining the male-female wage differential. The Economic Equity and Affirmative Action pages on this site are of particular relevance.

- ### National Committee on Pay Equity
  http://www.feminist.com/fairpay/
  The National Committee on Pay Equity argues for the elimination of the gender wage gap. They provide statistics on the magnitude of the male-female wage gap over time, and a table listing earnings by education (this does not take into account, however, the effect of occupation and work experience). This group argues for legislation that attempts to eliminate the gender wage gap.

- *U.S. Department of Labor Women's Bureau*
  http://www.dol.gov/dol/wb/
  The Women's Bureau of the U.S. Department of Labor posts an extensive collection of information related to female labor force activity.

- *U.S. Department of Labor Women's Bureau, "Earnings Differences Between Men and Women"*
  http://www.dol.gov/dol/wb/public/wb_pubs/wagegap2000.htm
  This online document, provided by the U.S. Department of Labor Women's Bureau, contains a good discussion of the history and causes of the gender wage gap.

- *U.S. Bureau of the Census, "Money Income in the United States, 2000"*
  http://www.census.gov/prod/2001pubs/p60-213.pdf
  This Census Bureau document contains detailed statistics on the distribution of income and earnings in the United States. It documents the magnitude of the male-female earnings differential. Income statistics are available by gender, educational attainment, and ethnicity. The Adobe acrobat viewer plugin is required to view this document. You may download this viewer by clicking here.

- *Bureau of Labor Statistics, "Highlights of Women's Earnings in 2000"*
  http://www.bls.gov/cps/cpswom2000.pdf
  This report summarizes data on the male-female wage gap in 2000. It finds that average weekly earnings of full-time women workers was 77% of the level of full-time male workers. This study also notes that the wage gap is larger for older workers than for younger workers. Evidence of a decline in the wage gap over time is also discussed in this report. The Adobe acrobat viewer plugin is required to view this document. You may download this viewer by clicking here.

- *U.S. Department of Labor Women's Bureau, "Median Annual Earnings in Current and 1999 Dollars for Year-Round Full-Time Workers by Sex, 1951-99"*
  http://www.dol.gov/dol/wb/public/wb_pubs/achart.htm
  This web page contains statistics on nominal and real median earnings for full-time male and female workers during the years 1951 through 1999. A small narrowing of the gender wage gap during this period is apparent.

- *U.S. Department of Labor Women's Bureau, "Women's Earnings as Percent of Men's, 1979-2000"*
  http://www.dol.gov/dol/wb/public/wb_pubs/2000.htm
  The table appearing on this page lists hourly, weekly, and annual earnings for women as a percent of men's income for the years 1979-2000. The effect of lower average weekly and yearly hours of work for women is apparent in the smaller earnings gap that occurs when this is measured in terms of hourly earnings.

- *Philip L. Rones, Randy E. Ilg, and Jennifer E. Gardner, "Trends in Hours of Work since the mid-1970s"*
  http://stats.bls.gov/opub/mlr/1997/04/art1full.pdf
  Philip L. Rones, Randy E. Ilg, and Jennifer E. Gardner find that women are exhibiting more continuous labor force participation in this April 1997 *Monthly Labor Review* article. The Adobe acrobat viewer plugin is required to view this document. You may download this viewer by clicking here.

- *U.S. Department of Labor, "Nontraditional Occupations for Women in 2000"*
  http://www.dol.gov/dol/wb/public/wb_pubs/nontra2000.htm
  The U.S. Department of Labor provides this list of occupations in which relatively few women are employed. Statistics are provided on the number of women employed in each occupation, the average weekly wage, the gender wage gap, and the proportion of women in each occupation.

- *U.S. Department of Labor, "20 Leading Occupations of Employed Women, 2000 annual averages"*

http://www.dol.gov/dol/wb/public/wb_pubs/20lead2000.htm
This page, provided by the U.S. Department of Labor, contains information on the 20 occupations that employ the largest number of women. Statistics are provided on the number of women employed in each occupation and the proportion of women in each occupation.

- *U.S. Department of Labor, "Women's Jobs 1964-1999: More than 30 Years of Progress"*
  http://www.dol.gov/dol/wb/public/jobs6497.htm
  This online document contains a series of charts and graphs that illustrate the expanding role of women in the labor market during the years 1964 to 1999.

- *U.S. Department of Labor, "Occupational Outlook Handbook"*
  http://www.bls.gov/oco/
  The *Occupational Outlook Handbook* contains detailed descriptions of job duties and employment prospects in a wide variety of occupations.

- *Christopher Snowbeck, "Study Uncovers Gender Gap in Physician Pay"*
  http://shns.scripps.com/shns/story.cfm?pk=WOMENDOCTORS-07-18-00&cat=AH
  This July 18, 2000 news article discusses a University of Pittsburgh study that finds that female physicians earn significantly less than male physicians. In particular, this study finds that the hourly wage of female physicians is 14% below the wage of male physicians.

- *Cornell University, "Cornell Couples and Careers Study"*
  http://www.lifecourse.cornell.edu/cci/current.html
  This web site contains information about the Couples and Careers Study conducted by Cornell University. This study collected information on dual-earner households using "focus groups, in-depth interviews, surveys, and organizational records." This study finds that workers feel constrained by career considerations to work more than their desired number of hours. Evidence is also presented that indicates that men still spend more time in paid market labor than their working wives.

Different Perspectives in the Debate

- *Anita U. Hattiangadi, "'Where's My 26 Cents?': Choices Explain Gender Wage Gap"*
  http://www.epf.org/ff/ff4-6.htm
  Anita U. Hattiangadi, in this Employment Policy Foundation article, discusses the magnitude and causes of the gender wage gap. She notes that most of the observed differences in male and female wages can be explained by differences in average hours, work experience, educational attainment, and career choice.

- *Diana Furchtgott-Roth, "The Statistically Misleading 74 Cent Wage Gap"*
  http://www.aei.org/ct/ctdfr.htm
  Diana Furchtgott-Roth argues that the observed gender wage gap is due to educational, career, and family choices on the part of women in this April 12, 1999 testimony before the Equal Employment Opportunity Commission. She suggests that a comparison of the average wages of male and female full-time workers is meaningless since it does not control for gender differences in average hours, educational attainment, occupation, and other factors that affect wages. She argues that existing laws are sufficient to deal with actual cases of gender discrimination and warns that comparable worth plans result in inefficient outcomes.

- *Women Employed Institute and the Office for Social Policy Research at Northern Illinois University, "Two Sides of the Coin: A Study of the Wage Gap Between Men and Women in the Chicago Metropolitan Area"*

http://www.ssri.niu.edu/wei.html
This October 1994 study found that the gender wage gap in Chicago was larger than that measured at the national level. They found that differences in educational attainment could not account for the observed wage gap. A mix of corporate and government policies were recommended to reduce this gap.

- *Howard J. Wall, "The Gender Wage Gap and Wage Discrimination: Illusion or Reality?"*
  http://www.stls.frb.org/publications/re/2000/d/pages/economic-backgnd.html
  Howard J. Wall discusses the gender wage gap in this October 2000 article appearing in *The Regional Economist*, a publication of the St. Louis Federal Reserve District Bank. He argues that the evidence indicates that at most 25% of the gap is due to discrimination; the remaining 75% or more of the wage gap is due to differences in hours worked, educational attainment, work experience, and occupation. Wall cites a study by Blau and Kahn that indicates that 6.2 cents of the gender wage gap is due to unexplained factors. This unexplained component may be the result of discrimination, or unobservable differences in human capital investment. Wall notes that it is difficult to determine whether occupational segregation is the result of voluntary choice or of labor market discrimination that limits employment choice for women.

- *Deborah Walker, "Value and Opportunity: The Issue of Comparable Pay for Comparable Worth"*
  http://www.cato.org/pubs/pas/pa038es.html
  Deborah Walker examines the economic arguments concerning comparable worth legislation in this May 31, 1984 *Policy Analysis* article. She argues that wage differentials across occupations reflect differences in society's evaluation of the services provided by workers in these occupations. Market determined wages encourages the flow of labor to those markets in which the labor services are most highly valued. Walker argues that a comparable worth pay system disrupts this process and encourages labor to shift from high-valued to low-valued uses.

- *AFL-CIO, "Working Women"*
  http://www.aflcio.org/women/index.htm
  This web site contains links to a variety of pages discussing the AFL-CIO's position on the gender wage gap. Numerous statistics are presented supporting the existence of a gender wage gap.

- *AFL-CIO, "How Much Will the Pay Gap Cost You?"*
  http://www.aflcio.org/women/calculat.htm
  This page, provided by the AFL-CIO provides an online calculator that measures the impact of the wage gap on women's lifetime earnings. (The assumptions and underlying model used to compute these results do not appear to be specified on this page.)

- *Borgna Brunner, "The Wage Gap: A History of Pay Inequity and the Equal Pay Act"*
  http://www.infoplease.com/spot/equalpayact1.phtml
  Borgna Brunner provides a brief history of the gender wage gap and the Equal Pay Act in this article. She notes that, until the early 1960s, jobs were listed separately for men and women with different pay rates, even for identical jobs. Brunner observes that a substantial gender wage gap still exists nearly 30 years after the passage of the Equal Pay Act.

- *Patricia Hausman, "I Am Woman, Hear Me Whine"*
  http://www.dadi.org/wom_whin.htm
  Patricia Hausman argues, in this April 3, 2001 online article, that the gender wage gap is very small. She suggests that many activists ignore studies that indicate that most of the male-female wage differential is the result of differences in hours worked, previous work experience, educational choice, and occupational choice.

- *Naomi Lopez, "Free Markets, Free Choices II: Smashing the Wage Gap and Glass Ceiling Myths"*

http://www.pacificresearch.org/pub/sab/health/ceiling/0499ceiling.html
Naomi Lopez argues, in this online article, that the wage gap does not exist when fields of study, educational attainment, and work experience are held constant. She suggests that unequal outcomes are the primarily the result of individual preferences and decisions, not discrimination.

- *Tony Dobbins, "Gender Wage Gap Examined"*
http://www.eiro.eurofound.ie/2000/11/features/ie0011160f.html
In this November 2000 article appearing on Eironline, Tony Dobbins discusses trends in the gender wage gap in Ireland. He notes that the gender wage gap had fallen from 20% in 1987 to slightly over 15% in 1997. Dobbins cites studies that suggest that approximately three-fourths of the wage gap can be explained in terms of differences in labor force participation and other factors. The remaining one-fourth of the wage gap may be the result of discrimination. He argues that "high-quality, affordable childcare, particularly for low-income families and single mothers, is crucial" if the gender wage gap is to be reduced.

- *U.S. Department of Education, "The Condition of Education 1995: Educational Progress of Women"*
http://www.ed.gov/pubs/CondOfEd_95/ovw3.html
This 1995 report describes the increase in female educational attainment that has been occurring for the past several decades. It notes that women tend to start school earlier and are less likely to repeat a grade. It is observed that females tend to receive higher verbal scores on standardized tests, but lower science and math scores. This report also notes that women are much more likely to major in education, English, foreign languages, communications, psychology and health-care fields. Women are less likely to declare college majors in math, engineering, computer science, or the physical sciences.

- *National Center for Educational Statistics, "Women in Mathematics and Science"*
http://nces.ed.gov/pubs97/97982.html
This July 1997 report examines trends in women's education in mathematics and science. It is observed that males and females have similar performance levels in math and science until age 13. While there gender difference in math scores appears to be declining, the gender difference in science scores has remained relatively large. While similar proportions of males and females complete advanced math and science classes in high school, their performance tends to be lower. This report indicates that women are much less likely to select math or science related majors in college. It is also observed that female science majors tend to receive lower salaries than their male counterparts in their first job after college.

- *Alicia C. Dowd, "Collegiate Grading Practices and the Gender Pay Gap"*
http://epaa.asu.edu/epaa/v8n10.html
Alicia C. Dowd examines the effect of grading policies by academic departments on the gender pay gap in this January 27, 2000 article appearing in *Education Policy Analysis Archives*. She observes that math related majors (such as mathematics, economics, chemistry, engineering, and physics) assign lower average grades to students than do departments in which verbal skills are more important (such as English, history, and education). Dowd cites studies that indicate that women are more likely than males to avoid majors in which they experience relatively low grades. This, combined with the fact that college-age females tend to have higher verbal and lower math skills, encourages females to major in those disciplines in which verbal skills are highly valued. Males are more likely to major in disciplines that rely on high levels of mathematical skills. Because math-oriented majors are more highly valued in the labor market, males receive higher wages. Dowd suggests that grading policies should be standardized across academic departments to allow grades to be a better signal of relative performance.

- *Brown University, "Achieving Gender Equity in Science Classrooms: A Guide for Faculty"*
http://www.brown.edu/Administration/Dean_of_the_College/homepginfo/equity/Equity_handbook.html
This online document examined methods of retaining more women in math and science related majors. Several studies are cited that examine why women are less likely to major in such disciplines. It is argued that the gender gap in science related fields could be reduced if teaching styles are modified to accommodate a wider variety of

learning styles.

- *Minnesota Department of Employee Relations, "Pay Equity / Comparable Worth"*
http://www.doer.state.mn.us/lr-peqty/lr-peqty.htm
The Minnesota Department of Employee Relations web site contains detailed information about the implementation of their comparable worth pay system. This site even includes downloadable pay equity analysis software that may be used to assist in the implementation of a comparable worth pay system.

- *Steven E. Rhoads, "Would Decentralized Comparable Worth Work? The Case of the United Kingdom"*
http://www.cato.org/pubs/regulation/reg16n3e.html
In this in this *Cato Regulation* article, Steven Rhoads examines the "equal value" pay system used in England. This system is essentially a decentralized form of a comparable worth pay structure in which firms can use any nondiscriminatory pay system. Disputes are resolved in industry tribunals consisting of three people, one of whom is a lawyer. Independent experts render opinions on the merits of these cases. Rhoads notes that the lack of uniform standards result in the use of a wide variety of standards by these experts in evaluating discrimination cases. He finds that the U.K. system provides arbitrary results. Rhoads believes that concerns over this arbitrary process will eventually result in the adoption of centralized standards. He suggests that such a centralized system will still result in arbitrary and inefficient outcomes.

- *Ann Crittenden, "Mothers Pay Price for Nurturing Human Capital"*
http://www.womensenews.org/article.cfm?aid=456
In this February 21, 2001 article, Ann Crittenden argues that society generally undervalues the role that women play in creating human capital. She notes that women play the largest share in creating human capital through childbearing and childrearing. Yet, these activities tend to be unrecognized because no salary is attached to these tasks. GDP undercounts the value of women's contribution because it does not measure the value of unpaid activities. Crittenden argues that divorce laws in many states also do not fully take into account the value of the household services provided by women. She suggests that this results in a dependency that is harmful to women.

- *Infoplease.com, "The Wage Gap in Pro Sports"*
http://ln.infoplease.com/spot/sptwagegap1.phtml
This online article describes gender differences in wages in professional sports as well as gender differences in access to sports scholarship funds.

©2002 South-Western. All Rights Reserved webmaster@swcollege.com | DISCLAIMER

Chapter Sixteen
Eat The Rich

By P. J. O'Rourke*

WE'RE SO CLOSE to being rich. Everybody in the world could be rich as hell. The benighted masses of India could quit pedaling bicycle rickshaws and start dragging Lear jets through the streets of Calcutta. Indians in the Brazilian rain forest could be *singing* in the rain. The endangered fauna would wear thong bikinis: "Save the Girl from Ipanema." Eskimos could give up clubbing baby seals and devote their arctic vastness to building an Olympic-quality ice dancing team.

When we're all wealthy, Sally Struthers will be featured in magazine ads headlined, YOU CAN SEND THIS CHILD TO SUMMER WEIGHT-LOSS CAMP OR YOU CAN TURN THE PAGE. CARE packages will contain oyster forks and truffles. And altruistic musicians will hold benefit concerts to raise enough money to pay the Rolling Stones to retire.

Money won't solve all our problems. But money will give us options—let us choose the problems we want to have. Leisure conglomerates may open franchises in Bosnia and Herzegovina where Muslims and Serbs can blast each other in paintball wars. Self-destructive individuals will still exist, but instead of dying from drug overdoses in pay-toilet stalls, they will be able to expire in luxury at the Chateau Marmont like John Belushi. The Taliban fundamentalists might continue to keep women in seclusion but they could do so by opening a Bergdorf Goodman's in Kabul. They'll never see those wives again.

All this is possible because the modern industrial economy works. Obviously it works better in some places than in others. But it works, even in the poorest areas. Côte d'Ivoire now produces as much per-capita wealth as the United States did when the Monroe Doctrine was declared, and Egypt produces more. America did not consider itself a poor country during the 1820s, and, in fact, at that time it was one of the world's most prosperous nations.

Extensive research has been done on the history of the industrial economy, much of it by the Organization for Economic Cooperation and Development. The OECD was founded by the Marshall Plan countries in the wake of World War II, and its purpose is what its name says. The OECD wants to make everyone rich as hell, although it never quite confesses to this in its literature.

In 1995 the OECD published a book by economist Angus Maddison titled *Monitoring the World Economy 1820-1992*. Maddison has been studying economic growth since the 1950s, and has examined and weighed the subject's statistics and statistical estimates. On the strength of these, Maddison calculates that until the industrial revolution, economic growth was paltry. Measured in 1990 U.S. dollars, the world gross domestic product—the value of everything produced on earth—went from $565 per person in 1500 per person in 1820. That was an increase in wealth of about 27 cents a year.

But after the industrial Revolution, something wonderful happened. The total world GDP grew from $695 billion in 1820 to almost $28 trillion n 1992. This planet has the same amount of arable land in 1992 as they as it had in 1820, and, arguably, fewer natural resources. Plus, population had grown from a little more than 1 billion to nearly 5.5 billion. But even so, world GDP per capita swelled from $6541 to $5,145. Prosperity increased by $26 a year. Wealth has been growing a hundred times faster than it did before the Industrial Age.

The modern economy works, and we know how to make it work better. Free markets are extremely successful. The evidence is there for anyone who wants to look. Hong Kong, with 6.5

million people in 402 square miles, has an annual GDP of $163.6 billion. Tanzania, with 29.5 million people in 342,1000 square miles, has a GDP of $18.9 billion.

And the free market trumps education and culture. North Korea has a 99 percent literacy rate, a disciplined, hard-working society, and a $900 per-capita GDP. Morocco has 43.7 percent literacy rate, a society that spends all day drinking coffee and pestering tourists to buy rugs, and a $3,260 per-capita GDP.

We know what to do, and we know how to do it. So what's wrong with the world? To a certain extent, it's the same thing that's wrong with me. Because the prosaic, depressing, and somewhat shameful fact that the secret to getting ahead is just what my parents told me it was.

The whole miracle of the modern industrial economy is based upon the things that our folks were trying to drum into our heads before we went off to college to grow sideburns and leg hair—or, as the modern case is, get pierced eyebrows and neck tattoos. It's the advice we received at the dinner table while the Jell-O dessert puddle and our friends were waiting for us at the mall. It's the clumsy set-piece speech our parents made in the heart-to-hearts they'd spring on us when we were really high. It's what we heard in capital letters when we brought home grades that looked like a collection of *Baywatch* bra cup sizes or wrecked the car.

- Hard Work
- Education
- Responsibility
- Property rights
- Rule of Law
- Democratic government

Actually, most parents didn't get all those items into the lecture. In fact, I've never heard of a parent saying, "Listen here, if I catch you running around without property rights again, I'll take away your cell phone." But when our parents said, "Be honest," they were assuming that property rights were real. And when our parents said, "Obey the law," they were making a logical inference that the law existed and that I merited obeying. And many of our parents had served in the military, defending democracy, and would remind us of this at length.

Of course, by "hard work" our parents didn't mean that we should be doing the hard things that constitute as work for the poor people in the world. Few parents hope that their children will get jobs carrying forty-pound buckets of water on their heads. Our parents wanted us to do hard work that was intelligent, fulfilling, and promised advancement in life. (Although they also wanted us to mow the lawn.) The hard work was linked to education.

However, billions of people don't have a chance to get an education, and some of them, like religious fundamentalists and deconstructionist college professors, don't believe the education when they get one. This is one reason that dinner0table parental advice is difficult to apply to the earth's impoverished masses. There are also billions of people who don't have property rights, not to mention property. Or the property rights are arbitrary, and the property can be taken away by anybody with a gun or a government title. These billions of people have trouble being responsible because being responsible means thinking of the future. They haven't got one.

Rule of law is crucial. And it has to be good law, not Albania's Law of Lek. So if what our parents tell us is going to be globally effective, Mom and Dad will need to bring world leaders into the dining room. All the presidents, prime ministers, dictators, generals, chairmen of idiot political parties, lunatic guerrilla chieftains, and fanatical heads of crazed religious sects will need to squeeze around the imitation Queen Anne mahogany veneer (with extra leaves in) and get a real talking-to.

Then there is democracy to be considered. Democracy is a bulwark against tyranny—unless the *demos* get tyrannical. People can vote themselves poor, as the Swedes seem to be trying to do.

Now all the people are coming over to the house. And when they get there, what they're going to do is . . . exactly what we did. They're not going to listen.

There is a worldwide pigheadedness about money. There is a willful and even belligerent ignorance concerning ways and the means. There is a heartfelt and near-universal refusal to understand the basic economic principles behind the creation of wealth.

Not all of this ignorance is irrational. Some people profit from economic privation. Economists, for instance. John Maynard Keynes couldn't have become a big shot, guiding government intervention in business and finance, if it hadn't been for the Great Depression. And Alan Greenspan is successful because we all lost our wallets when inflation scared our pants off.

We fear the power that others have over us, and wealth is power. We're afraid that Kathie Lee Gifford is going to make us sew jogging suits for thirty cents and hour. But are the rich really any scarier than the poor? Take a midnight stroll through a fancy neighborhood, then take a midnight stroll a few blocks from the U.S. Capitol. Sure, we can get in trouble in Monte Carlo. We can lose at roulette. We can get suckered into a shady business deal with Princess Stephanie's ex-husband. But we're more likely to be mugged in the District of Columbia.

Not that we should begrudge the crimes of those poor people. They're just practicing politics on a small scale. If they'd listen to their own political leaders, they'd put down the gun and pick up the ballot box, and steal from everyone else instead of just us.

Political systems must love poverty—they produce so much of it. Poor people make easier targets for a demagogue. No Mao or even Jiang Zemin is likely to arise on the New York Stock Exchange floor. And politicians in democracies benefit from destitution, too. The United States has had a broad range of poverty for thirty years. Those programs have failed. Millions of people are still poor. And those people vote for politicians who favor keeping the poverty programs in place. There's a Matt Drudge conspiracy theory in that somewhere.

Many religions claim to admire poverty. And some religions even advocate the practice of being poor. (Although all those religions seem willing to accept large cash donations.)

You'd think that businessmen, in the search for new customers, would always be opposed to impecuniousness. But Kathie Lee Gifford is not alone in depending on destitute workers to take pay-nothing jobs.)

Then there is a certain kind of environmentalist who thinks that human deprivation means plant and animal wealth. Tanzania's experience of rhino-subsidizing rich tourists versus rhino-killing impoverished poachers argue against this. (And an Asia where every man could afford Viagra would be the best things that could happen to the rhinoceros.) But many "greens" still believe that increasing human prosperity is wrong. For example, the famous population-control advocate Paul Ehrlich has said, "Giving society cheap, abundant energy . . . would be the equivalent f giving an idiot child a machine gun."

Finally, general poverty benefits specific wealth. If most people are broke, that's great for the wealthy few. They get cheap household help, low ancestral-manor real-estate prices, and no crowds on Martha's Vineyard. This explains the small, nasty plutocracies in impoverished countries. Maybe it also accounts for the rich socialist prominent on the political landscape for the last two centuries.

I began this book by asking why some parts of the world are rich and others are poor, and I naturally had prejudices about what the answers would be. I favored the free market, not because I knew anything about markets, but because I live in a free (or nearly free) country and I'm a free man (as long as I call home frequently), and it works for me. I was skeptical about the ability of politics to deliver economic benefits because I did know something about that. I'd been writing about politics, at home and abroad, for years. I had a low opinion of the trade and its practitioners. And I considered culture, as an economic factor, to be a joke. How is ballet going to make the Tanzanians wealthy?

I was stupidly surprised to find out how important law is. Law, of course, derives from politics. And a political system is ultimately a product of a society's attitudes, ideas, and beliefs—that damned conundrum, its culture.

Which brings me back to the free market. I started out looking at the free market in terms of its effectiveness, its "efficiency," as an economist would say. I ended up looking at the free market as a moral device. My initial prejudice was right in one respect. The most-important part of the free market is the part that's free. Economic liberty cannot be untangled from liberty of other kinds. You may have freedom of religion, if the rabbi can get off night shifts on Fridays. You may have freedom of assembly, but where are you all going to go if it rains?

The U.S. Constitution is (at least I hope it is) a statement of American Cultural value. The First Amendment implies a free market. Six of the remaining nine articles in the bill of rights defend private property specifically. And two of the others concern rights reserved to the people, some of which are certainly economic rights. We are a free-market nation, though the electors and the elected sometimes forget it.

A belief in the free market means a belief that people have an innate right to the fruits of their endeavors, and the right to dispose of the fruit the way they see fit, as long as other people don't get pasted in the face with a rotten peach or something.

There are people who don't believe this. Some of these people are just bad. They steal. Some of these people are "nationalistic" and think it's okay to take things from other people if they live more than a peach toss away or speak another language or have a different religion or look funny. And the kinds, emperors, and so forth who ruled mankind during most of history were under the impression that everything belonged to kings, emperors, and so forth.

Now that the kings and emperors have been shot or reduced to pathetic ceremonial posts, the most common reason given for not believing in economic liberty is that the free market is unfair. Socialists, Social Democrats, American Liberals, and all other kinds of economic levelers think that unconstrained industry, agriculture, and commerce lead to the exploitation of people who aren't very good that these things. A bit or immoral wealth and a great deal of unconscious poverty is supposedly created.

It was Adam Smith in *The Wealth of Nations* (published with happy coincidence in 1776) who originally argued that a free market is good for everybody. Smith seems to have been the first person to realize that all voluntary exchanges increase prosperity. Wealth is created by any swap. It may seem like an even trade, but each trader gives up something he values less in order to receive something he values more. Hence the wealth of both traders grows. When Neolithic spear makers did business with Neolithic basket weavers, the spear makers were able to carry things around in a manner more convenient that skewering them on spear points, and the basket weavers were able to kill mastodons by a method more efficient than swatting them with baskets.

The free-market outcome benefits all. It's moral. And the beautiful thing about this morality is that we don't have to be good to achieve it. In the most, perhaps only, famous passage from an economics book, Adam Smith states, "It is not from the benevolence of the butcher, the brewer, or the baker, that we expect our dinner, but from their regard to their own interest." Smith saw that a man's selfish concern with his own well-being is a desirable, indeed a splendid thing for society. "[He] intends only his own gain," wrote Smith, "and he is in this . . . led by an invisible hand to promote an end which was no part of his intentions." That end is the end this book is about: economic progress.

The general morality of the free market, however, does not answer the specific objection of unfairness. Economic liberty leads to differences in wealth. And the differences are enormous. The "wealth gap" is the subject of a critical debate about economics. The perception of unfairness is the reason enormous numbers of the world's decent and well-meaning people, in fact the majority of them, do not rush to embrace the free market in its totality. Complete economic liberty would mean a system like Hong Kong's under John Cowperthwaite with no barriers to trade or capital flow, and no barriers to labor flow, either: no check on immigration, no minimum wage, no cost controls, and no attempt to create a fair society. This is a daunting prospect, and it's not just the Swedes and Fidel Castro who are daunted by it.

Socialists and capitalists naturally take opposing sides on the question of how economically fair life should be. But so do various political parties which claim to be pro-market. So do theologians and ·philosophers. And so do ordinary people when they're voting for school-bond issues or deciding how much to cheat on their taxes.

Fairness is a potent emotional issue, but how is fairness to be delivered? It's hard to build a political structure that provides economic fairness. The map is full of failed attempts, and so is this book. When a government controls both the economic power of individuals and the coercive power of the state, we get, at best, Shanghai. A businessman finds that one of his stockholders has tanks, artillery, and jet fighter planes. This violates the fundamental rule of happy living: Never let the people with all the money and people with all the guns be the same people.

There is another difficulty with political control of the economy which keeps even the best-behaved governments from using resources as well. This problem was explained by the economists Milton and Rose Friedman in their book, *Free to Choose*. The Friedmans' argued that there are only four ways to spend money:

1. Spend money on yourself.
2. Spend money on other people.
3. Spend other people's money on yourself.
4. Spend other people's money on other people.

If you spend your money on yourself, you look for the best value at the best price—knockoff Pings on sale at Golf-*fore*-Less. If you spend your money on other people, you still worry about price, but you may not know—or care—what the other people want. So your brother-in-law gets a Deepak Chopra book for Christmas. If you spend other people's money on yourself, it's hard to resist coming home with real Pings, a new leather bag, orange pants with little niblicks on them, and a pair of Foot-Joy spikes. And if you spend other people's money on other people, any damn thing will do and the hell with what it costs. Almost all governments spending falls into category four. This how the ungrateful residents of Ukraine got Chernobyl.

Also, if fairness is important, that is really fair? We may say something like, "People have a right to food, a right to housing, and a right to a good job for decent pay." But from an economist's perspective, all those rights involve making finite goods meet infinite wants. Unless the fair society generates tremendous economic growth—which societies that put fairness first have trouble doing—the goods will come from redistribution. Try rephrasing the rights statement thus: "People have a right to my food, a right to my housing and a right to my good job for my decent pay."

Accepting the free market allows us to avoid the political abuse and financial mismanagement inherent in trying to design an economy that's fair. It also allows us to see that economies can't be designed. Economics is the measurement of how human nature affects the material world. The market is "heartless." So are clocks and yardsticks. Saying that economic problems are the result of the free market's failure is like gaining twenty pounds and calling the bathroom scale a bum.

Adam Smith recognized that markets are self-organizing. Man has a "general disposition to truck, barter, and exchange," wrote Smith. If people are protected from coercion by other people, and from coercion by that agglomeration of other people known as the state, human brains and greed create economic growth. "The strength of the mastiff is not in the least supported either by the swiftness of the greyhound, or the by the sagacity of the spaniel," wrote Smith. "Among men, on the contrary, the most dissimilar geniuses are of use to one another."

I had thought that economic problems were the result of ignorance about economics. I was wrong again. I asked a friend, who's knowledgeable in the field: "Why is the concept of the 'invisible hand' so difficult to comprehend?" He said, "It's invisible." The hardest thing to understand about economics is that it doesn't need to be understood. My beatnik friends and I, when were in college, were perfectly justified in expending our intellectual energy on love and death instead of money.

But there was one thing that we did need to learn. And still do. And it's a piece of knowledge that seems to contradict psychology, life experience, and the dictates of conscience: Economics is not zero sum. There is so fixed amount of wealth. That is, if you have too many slices of pizza, I don't have to eat the box. Your money does not cause my poverty. Refusal to believe this is at the bottom of most bad economic thinking.

True, at any given moment, there is only so much wealth to go around. But wealth is based on productivity. Without productivity, there wouldn't be any economics, or any economic thinking, good or bad, or any pizza, or anything else. We would sit around and stare at rocks, and maybe later have some dinner.

Wealth is based on productivity, and productivity is expandable. In fact, productivity is fabulously expandable, as Angus Maddison has shown in *Monitoring the World Economy*. Yet a person who is worried about fairness can recite the old saw: "The rich get richer and poor . . ."

"Get entertained by *People* magazine stories about divorces among the rich." That is not how the worrier was going to finish his sentence. "Get lower mortgage rates because banks have more money to lend." No, that's not it, either. "Get better jobs because there's more capital to be invested in businesses." No, the cliché is, "The rich get richer, and the poor get poorer."

Except there is no evidence of this in recent history. Per-capita GDP is a tricky figure and it doesn't tell us much about the well being of individual people. But there are other statistics that don't present the same problems of averaging. Life expectancy and infant-mortality rates *do* tell us how things are going for ordinary folks. No matter how rich a nation's elite, its members aren't going to live to be 250 and wildly skew the numbers. And a country can't fake a low infant-mortality rate by getting a few rich babies to live while letting all the poor babies die.

The United Nations study *World Population Prospects: 1996 Revision* contains historical statistics on life expectancy and infant mortality. Figures are given for Most Developed Regions, Less Developed Regions, and Least Developed Nations. The last being places that are truly poor, such as Tanzania. In the early 1950s the richest countries has an average infant-mortality rate of 58 deaths per 1,000 live births. By the early 1990s the average was down to 11. During the same period the infant mortality rate in the poorest countries dropped from an average of 194 deaths per 1,000 to 109 per 1,000. infant-mortality rates declined in both rich and poor countries, and so did the gap between those rates. A difference of 136 deaths per 1,000 had diminished to a difference of 109 deaths forty years later. This is still too many dead babes (and it's hard to imagine a number of dead babies that wouldn't be too many, unless the fair-minded worrier is also a zealous pro-choice advocate). But infant-morality rates give us some hopeful information about world economic growth. Yes, the rich are getting richer, but the poor aren't becoming worse off. They're becoming parents.

Life expectancy tells the same story. In the early 1950s, people in rich countries lived, on average, 66.5 years. By the early 1990s they were living 74.2 years. In the poorest countries, average life-spans increased from 35.5 to 49.7 years (which, somewhat unnervingly, was my exact age when I wrote that sentence, and I was glad I didn't live in Tanzania and had to die that night). Anyway, the difference in life expectancy between the world's rich and poor has decreased by 6.5 years. The rich are getting richer. The poor are getting richer. And we're all getting older.

So if wealth is not a worldwide round robin of purse snatching, and if the thing that makes you rich doesn't make me poor, why should we care about fairness at all? We shouldn't.

Fairness is a good thing in a marriage and at the day-care center. It's a nice little domestic virtue. But a liking for fairness is not that noble a sentiment. Fairness doesn't rank with charity, love, duty, or self-sacrifice. And there's always a tinge of self-seeking in making sure that things are fair. Don't you go trying to get one up on me.

As a foundation for a political system, fairness may be no virtue at all. The Old Testament is clear on this point. The Bible might seem like an odd place to be doing economic research, especially by someone who goes to church about once a year, and only then because that's when my wife says the Easter Bunny comes. However, I have been thinking—in socioeconomic terms—about the tenth Commandment.

The first nine Commandments concern theological principles and social law: Thou shalt not make graven images, steal, kill, etc. Fair enough. But then there's the Tenth Commandment: "Thou shalt not covet thy neighbor's house, thou shalt not covet thy neighbor's wife, nor his manservant, nor his maidservant, nor his ox, nor his ass, nor anything that is thy neighbor's."

Here are God's basic rules about how we should live, a very brief list of sacred obligations and solemn moral precepts, and right at the end of it is, "Don't envy your buddy's cow."

What is that doing in there? Why would God, with just ten things to tell Moses, choose, as one of them, jealously about the livestock next door? And yet, think about how important to the well-being of a community this Commandment is. If you want a donkey, if you want a pot roast, if you want a cleaning lady, don't bitch about what the people across the street have. *Go get your own.*

The tenth commandment sends a message to socialists, to egalitarians, to people obsessed with fairness, to American presidential candidates in the year 2000—to everyone who believes that wealth should be redistributed. And the message is clear and concise: go to hell.

If we want the whole world to be rich, we need to start loving wealth. In the difference between poverty and plenty, the problem is poverty, not the difference. Wealth is good.

You know this about your own wealth. If you got rich, it would be a great thing. You'd improve your life. You'd improve your family's life. You'd purchase education, travel, knowledge about the world. You'd invest in worthwhile things. You'd give money noble causes. You'd help your friends and neighbors. Your life would be better if you got rich. The lives of the people around you would be better. Your wealth is good. So why isn't everybody else's wealth good?

Wealth is good when a lot of people have it. It's good when a few people have it. This is because money is a tool, nothing more. You can't eat or drink money, or wear it very comfortably as underwear. And wealth—an accumulation of money—is a bunch of tools.

Tools can be used to do harm. You can break into a house by driving a forklift through a window. You can hit somebody over the head with an hydroelectric turbine. Tools are still good. When a carpenter has a lot of tools, we don't say to him, "You have too many. You should give some of your hammers, saws, screws, and nails to the guy who's cooking omelets."

Making money thought hard work and wise investment is a fine thing to do. Other ways of making money aren't so bad either, as long as everybody who's in on the deal is there voluntarily. Better sleazy productivity than none. As terrible as Albania's pyramid schemes were, Albania's riots were worse.

233

And the Hong Kong of John Cowperthwaite shows that even the most resolutely free-market system makes use of private means for the public weal. If the United States radically reduced the size of its government, eliminated all subsides, price controls, and corporate welfare, and abolished all its entitlement programs, we'd still pay taxes. And those tax revenues would be spent—ideally on such reasonable things as schools, roads, and national defense, in case the British invade again and try to hand over Wall Street to the Red Chinese.

Or take the real-world example of two kids who graduate from college with honors. One is an admirable idealist. The other is on the make. The idealist joins Friends of the Earth and chains himself to a sequoia. The sharpie foes to work for an investment bank selling fishy derivatives and makes $500,000 a year. Even assuming that the selfish young banker cheats the IRS—and he will—he'll end up paying $100,000 a year in taxes: income tax, property tax, sales tax, etc.

While the admirable idealist has saved one tree (if the logging company doesn't own bolt cutters), the pirate in a necktie has contributed to society $100,000 worth of schools, roads, and U.S. Marines, not to mention Interior Department funding sufficient to save any number of trees and the young idealist chained thereto.

And if the soulless yuppie cheats the IRS so well that he ends up keeping the whole half million? That cash isn't going to sit in his cuff link box. Whether spent or saved, the money winds up invested somewhere, and maybe that investment leads to the creation of the twenty-first century's equivalent of the moldboard plow, the microchip, or the mocha latte. Society wins. Wealth brings great benefits to the world. Rich people are heroes. They don't usually mean to be but that's their problem, not ours.

Almost everyone in the world now admits that the free market tells us the economic truth. Economic liberty makes wealth. Economic repression makes poverty.

Poverty is hard, wretched, and humiliating. Poverty is school-girl prostitutes trying to feed their parents in Cuba. Poverty is John driving around in the Tanzanian night looking for the doctor while his daughter dies. It's grandmother begging on the streets of Moscow. But what poverty is not sad. Poverty is infuriating. These things don't have to happen. These conditions don't need to exist. We can't solve all the problems of life, but we can solve the problem of gross, worldwide material deprivation. The solution doesn't work perfectly. The solution doesn't work uniformly. Nonetheless, the solution works. If we can't fix everything, let's fix the easy stuff. We know how to get rid of poverty. We know how to create wealth. But because of laziness, fear, complacency, love of power, or foolish idealism, we refuse to do it.

We think we can dabble in freedom—allow a few of its liberties and leave our favorite constraints in place. We think we can screw around with the free market—skip its costs and get all of its benefits anyway.

There is a joke that I think President Reagan used to tell to illustrate the attitude that some people have towards the blessings they get from freedom and private property. If Reagan didn't tell the joke, he should have. He won't mind the attribution. Doubtless he's forgotten all about economics now. And I'm with the president on that. I intend to start forgetting all about economics as soon as I can—keeping in mind, however, a few rudimentary conceits, such as the one about the traveling salesman who is staying overnight with a farm family. When the family sits down to eat, there's a pig in a chair at the table. The pig has three medals hanging around its neck and a wooden leg. The salesman says, "Um, I see a pig having dinner with you."

"Yep," says the farmer. "That's because he's a very special pig. You see those medals around his neck? Well, the first medal is from when our baby son fell in the pond and was drowning, and that pig dove in, swan out, and saved his life. The second medal, that's from when our little daughter was trapped in a burning barn, and that pig ran inside, carried her out, and saved her life. And the third medal, that's from when our oldest boy was cornered in the stockyard by a mean bull, and that pig ran under the fence, bit the bull's tail, and saved the boy's life."

"Yes," says the salesman, "I can see why you let that pig sit right at the table and have dinner with you. And I can see why you awarded him the medals. But how did he get the wooden leg?"

"Well," says the farmer, "a pig like that—you don't eat him all at once."

*© Copyright by P.J. O'Rourke, Reprinted by permission of Grove/Atlantic, Inc.

P.J. O'Rourke is the Mencken Research Fellow of the CATO Institute. He is the best-selling author of eight previous books, including *Holidays in Hell, Parliament of Whores,* and *All the Trouble in the World.* He has written for such publications as *Automobile, The Weekly Standard, Esquire, Forbes FYI, the New Republic, The New York Times Book Review, The Wall Street Journal* and *Rolling Stone,* where he is currently foreign affairs desk chief.

Visit P.J.'s Web Site at www.pjrourke.com

Tool Number One:
Economic Humor and Jokes

An economics solution should be like a woman's skirt: short enough to be provocative; long enough to have something substantial underneath.

A real story:

One day, the professor who taught Money and Banking in Buenos Aires told us: "I do not know if you will find jobs as economists, but I am sure you will know why you are going to be poor."

Why God Never Received Tenure at the University

1. Because he had only one major publication.
2. And it was in Hebrew.
3. And it had no cited references.
4. And it wasn't published in a reference journal or even submitted for peer review.
5. And some even doubt he wrote it Himself.
6. It may be true that He created the world, but what has He done since?
7. His cooperative efforts have been quite limited.
8. The scientific community has had a very rough time trying to replicate His results.
9. He never applied to the Ethics Board for permission to use human subjects.
10. When one experiment went awry, He tried to cover it up by drowning the subjects.
11. When subjects didn't behave as predicted, He often punished them, or just deleted them from the sample.
12. He rarely came to class, just told students to read the book.
13. He had His son teach the class.
14. He expelled His first two students for learning.
15. Although there were only ten requirements, most students failed His tests.
16. His office hours were infrequent and usually held on a mountaintop.

Kenneth Boulding said, "Mathematics brought rigor to Economics. Unfortunately, it also brought mortis."

Definition: Policy Analyst is someone unethical enough to be a lawyer, impractical enough to be a theologian, and pedantic enough to be an economist.

Robert Kuttner, the Poverty of Economics, The Atlantic Monthly, Feb 1985, p. 79, which says: "George Stigler Nobel laureate and a leader of Chicago School was asked why there were no Nobel Prizes awarded in the other social sciences, sociology, psychology, history, etc. 'Don't worry,' Stigler said, 'they already have a Nobel Prize in . . . Literature.'"

A mathematician, a theoretical economist, and an econometrician are asked to find a black cat (who doesn't really exist) in a closed room with the light off:

The mathematician gets crazy trying to find a black cat that doesn't exist inside the darkened room and ends up in a psychiatric hospital.

The theoretical economist is unable to catch the black cat that doesn't exist inside the darkened room, but exits the room proudly proclaiming that he can construct a model to describe all his movements with extreme accuracy.

The econometrician walks securely into the blacked room, spends one hour looking for the black cat that doesn't exist and shouts from inside the room that he has it by the neck.

Two strangers, a man and a woman, meet in a café. The man asks,
"My dear, would you go to bed with me for a million dollars?
"Well, yes, I guess I would."
"How about $100?"
"What kind of person do you think I am?"
"My dear, we have already established that. We are merely haggling over the price!"

According to Ross Emmet, the story was told by George Bernard Shaw. The man and the woman are Winston Churchill and Lady Astor and the incident allegedly did occur.

True story:

I attended an ASSA/AEA convention in Dallas. During the third day of the convention, one of the bellhops at the convention asked me who the people attending the convention were and what we did for a living.
"We're economists," I replied. "Why do you ask?"
"I don't know . . . no women, no drugs, just booze, booze, booze."

John Palmer.

One night a policeman saw a macroeconomist looking for something by a light pole. He asked him if he had lost something there. The economist said, "I lost my keys over in the alley." The policeman asked him why he was looking by the light pole. The economist responded, "It's a lot easier to look over here."

An economist is someone who gets rich explaining to others why they are poor.

Heard at the Wharton School.

Man walking along a road in the countryside comes across a shepherd and a huge flock of sheep. Tells the shepherd, "I will bet you $100 against one of your sheep that I can tell you the exact number in this flock." The shepherd thinks it over; it's a big flock so he takes the bet. "973," says the man. The shepherd is astonished, because that is exactly right. Says "OK, I'm a man of my word, take an animal." Man picks one up and begins to walk away.

"Wait," cries the shepherd, "Let me have a chance to get even. Double or nothing that I can guess your exact occupation." Man says sure. "You are an economist for a government think tank," says the shepherd. "Amazing!" responds the man, "You are exactly right! But tell me, how did you deduce that?"

"Well," says the shepherd, "put down my dog and I will tell you."

A mathematician, an accountant and an economist apply for the same job. The interviewer calls in the mathematician and asks "What do two plus two equal?" The mathematician replies "Four." The interviewer asks "Four, exactly?" The mathematician looks at the interviewer incredulously and says "Yes, four, exactly." Then the interviewer calls in the accountant and asks the same question "What do two plus two equal?" The accountant says "On average, four - give or take ten percent, but on average, four."

Then the interviewer calls in the economist and poses the same question "What do two plus two equal?" The economist gets up, locks the door, closes the shade, sits down next to the interviewer and says, "What do you want it to equal?"

TOP 10 REASONS TO STUDY ECONOMICS

1. Economists are armed and dangerous: "Watch out for our invisible hands."
2. Economists can supply it on demand.
3. You can talk about money without every having to make any.
4. You get to say, "trickle down" with a straight face.
5. Mick Jagger and Arnold Schwarzenegger both studied economics and look how they turned out.
6. When you are in the unemployment line, at least you will know why you are there.
7. If you rearrange the letters in "ECONOMICS", you get "COMIC NOSE".
8. Although ethics teaches that virtue is its own reward, in economics we get taught that reward is its own virtue.
9. When you get drunk, you can tell everyone that you are just researching the law of diminishing marginal utility.
10. When you call 1-900-LUV-ECON and get Kandi Keynes, you will have something to talk about.

ECONOMISTS do it at bliss point
ECONOMISTS do it cyclically
ECONOMISTS do it in an Edgeworth Box
ECONOMISTS do it on demand
ECONOMISTS do it risk-free (in reference to the risk-free interest rate)
ECONOMISTS do it with a dual
ECONOMISTS do it with an atomistic competitor
ECONOMISTS do it with crystal balls
ECONOMISTS do it with interest

"Economists do it with models"

Econometricians do it if they can identify it.
Applied econometricians do it even if they can't.

"Econometricians do it with dummies"?

An economist is a trained professional paid to guess wrong about the economy. An econometrician is a trained professional paid to use computers to guess wrong about the economy.

Talk is cheap. Supply exceeds Demand.

Bentley's second Law of Economics: The only thing more dangerous than an economist is an amateur economist!

An economic forecaster was known to have a horseshoe prominently displayed above the doorframe of his office. Asked what it was for, he replied that it was a good luck charm that helped his forecasts. But do you believe in that superstition? He was asked, and he said, "Of course not!" But then why do you keep it? "Well," he said, "it works whether you believe in it or not."

An economist was standing at the shore of a large lake, surf-casting. It was the middle of winter, and the lake was completely frozen over, but this didn't seem to bother the economist, who stood there patiently casting his lure out across the ice, slowly reeling it in again, then repeating the process.

A mathematical economist came sailing by on an ice boat, and pulled to the shore beside the surf-fishing economist to scoff. "You'll never catch any fish that way," said the mathematical economist. "Jump on my ice-boat and we'll go trawling."

Three econometricians went out hunting, and came across a large deer. The first econometrician fired, but missed, by a meter to the left. The second econometrician fired, but also missed, by a meter to the right. The third econometrician didn't fire, but shouted in triumph, "We got it! We got it!"

True story. I'm riding up the elevator at the Boston ASSA meetings a few years back. In the car with me is a woman who works in the hotel. I ask her if economists are really as dull a bunch as they're made out to be. She responds that she used to be stationed at the NYC branch of the chain when the meetings were held there and that even the hookers had taken the week off.

Carlos Bonilla

Practice economy at any cost.

From "The Hitchhiker's Guide to the Galaxy" by Douglas Adams, Chapter 16.

Arthur awoke to the sound of argument and went to the bridge. Ford was waving his arms about. "You're crazy Zaphod," he was saying, "Magrathea is a myth a fairy story, it's what parents tell their kids about at night if they want them to grow up to be economists, it's..."

From the preface to Paul Krugman's book, "Peddling Prosperity: Economic Sense and Nonsense in the Age of Diminished Expectations" (1994, page xi): An Indian-born economist once explained his personal theory of reincarnation to his graduate economics class. "If you are a good economist, a virtuous economist," he said, "you are reborn as a physicist. But if you are an evil, wicked economist, you are reborn as a sociologist."

When two economists are out for a stroll together, how do you identify the U of C economist? He's the one walking randomly.

Economist poem

If you do some acrobatics
, with a little mathematics
it will take you far along.
If your idea's not defensible
don't make it comprehensible
or folks will find you out,
and your work will draw attention
if you only fail to mention
what the whole thing is about.

Your must talk of GNP
and of elasticity
of rates of substitution
and indeterminate solution
and oligonopopsony.

  Kenneth E. BOULDING

Q. What do economists and computers have in common??
A. You need to punch information into both of them.

Why does Treasury only have 10 minutes for morning tea??
A. If they had any longer, they would need to re-train all the economists.

Two economists were walking down the street when they noticed two women yelling across the street at each other from their apartment windows.

Of course they will never come to agreement, stated the first economist.

And why is that, inquired his companion,

Why, of course, because they are arguing from different premises.

A civil engineer, a chemist and an economist are traveling in the countryside. Weary, they stop at a small country inn. "I only have two rooms, so one of you will have to sleep in the barn," the innkeeper says. The civil engineer volunteers to sleep in the barn, goes outside, and the others go to bed. In a short time they're awakened by a knock. It's the engineer, who says, "There's a cow in that barn. I'm a Hindu, and it would offend my beliefs to sleep next to a sacred animal." The chemist says that, OK, he'll sleep in the barn. The others go back to bed, but soon are awakened by another knock. It's the chemist who says, "There's a pig in that barn. I'm Jewish, and cannot sleep next to an unclean animal." So the economist is sent to the barn. It's getting late, the others are very tired and soon fall asleep. But they're awakened by an even louder knocking. They open the door and are surprised by what they see: It's the cow and the pig!

Three economists and three mathematicians were going for a trip by train. Before the journey, the mathematicians bought 3 tickets but economists only bought one. The mathematicians were glad their stupid colleagues were going to pay a fine. However, when the conductor was approaching their compartment, all three economists went to the nearest toilet. The conductor, noticing that somebody was in the toilet, knocked on the door. In reply he saw a hand with one ticket. He checked it and the economists saved 2/3 of the ticket price.
The next day, the mathematicians decided to use the same strategy- they bought only one ticket, but economists did not buy tickets at all! When the mathematicians saw the conductor, they hid in the toilet, and when they heard knocking they handed in the ticket. They did not get it back. Why? The economists took it and went to the other toilet.

A party of economists was climbing in the Alps. After several hours they became hopelessly lost. One of them studied the map for some time, turning it up and down, sighting on distant landmarks, consulting his compass, and finally the sun.
Finally he said, ' OK see that big mountain over there?'
'Yes', answered the others eagerly.
'Well, according to the map, we're standing on top of it.'

Did you hear of the economist who dove into his swimming pool and broke his neck?

He forgot to seasonally adjust his pool.

If all the economists were laid end to end they would be an orgy, of mathematics.

A wealthy labor economist had an urge to have grandchildren. He had two daughters and two sons and none of them had gratified his desire for a grandchild. At the annual family gathering on Thanksgiving Day, he chided them gently to bless his old age with their progeny. "But I haven't given up hope," he said, "Yesterday I went to the bank and set up a one hundred thousand dollar trust fund to be given to the first grandchild that I have. Now we will all bow our heads while I say a prayer of thanks." When he looked up, he and his wife were the only ones at the table.

NATURAL RATE OF UNEMPLOYMENT
Newlan's Truism: An "acceptable" level of unemployment means that the government economist to whom it is acceptable still has a job.

Q Why did the market economist cross the road?
A To reach the consensus forecast.

These were created by Pat Marren 2/14/96

Subject: TOP TEN ECONOMIST VALENTINES

10. YOU RAISE MY INTEREST RATE THIRTY BASIS POINTS WITHOUT A CORRESPONDING DROPOFF IN CONSUMER ENTHUSIASM
9. DESPITE A DECADE OF INFLATION, I STILL DIG YOUR SUPPLY CURVE
8. WHAT DO YOU SAY WE REMEASURE OUR CROSS-ELASTICITY?
7. YOU BRING THE BUTTER, I'LL BRING THE GUN.
6. LET'S RAISE HOUSING STARTS TOGETHER

5. FURTHER STIMULUS COULD RESULT IN UNCONTROLLED EXPANSION
4. TELL ME WHETHER MY EXPECTATIONS ARE RATIONAL
3. LET'S ASSUME A RITZY HOTEL ROOM AND A BOTTLE OF DOM
2. YOU STOKE THE ANIMAL SPIRITS OF MY MARKET
1. A LOAF OF BREAD, A JUG OF WINE, AND THOU BESIDE ME WATCHING RUKEYSER

When Albert Einstein died, he met three New Zealanders in the queue outside the Pearly Gates. To pass the time, he asked what were their IQs. The first replied 190. "Wonderful," exclaimed Einstein. "We can discuss the contribution made by Ernest Rutherford to atomic physics and my theory of general relativity". The second answered 150. "Good," said Einstein. "I look forward to discussing the role of New Zealand's nuclear-free legislation in the quest for world peace". The third New Zealander mumbled 50. Einstein paused, and then asked, "So what is your forecast for the budget deficit next year?" (Adapted from Economist June 13th 1992, p. 71).

Two men are flying in a captive balloon. The wind is ugly and they come away from their course and they have no idea where they are. So they go down to 20 m above ground and ask a passing wanderer. "Could you tell us where we are?"

"You are in a balloon."

So the one pilot to the other:

"The answer is perfectly right and absolutely useless. The man must be an economist"

"Then you must be businessmen", answers the man.

"That's right! How did you know?"

"You have such a good view from where you are and yet you don't know where you are!"

Q: How many Chicago School economists does it take to change a light bulb?

 A: None. If the light bulb needed changing the market would have already done it.

Q: How many mainstream economists does it take to change a light bulb?

A1: Two. One to assume the existence of ladder and one to change the bulb.
A2: Two. One to assume the existence of latter and one to change the bulb.

Q: How many neo-classical economists does it take to change a light bulb?
A: It depends on the wage rate.

Q: How many conservative economists does it take to change a light bulb?

A1: None. The darkness will cause the light bulb to change by itself.

A2: None. If it really needed changing, market forces would have caused it to happen.

A3: None. If the government would just leave it alone, it would screw itself in.

A4. None. "There is no need to change the light bulb. All the conditions for illumination are in place.

A5. None; they're all waiting for the unseen hand of the market to correct the lighting disequilibrium.

The above light bulb jokes originated from an article in The Wharton Journal, by Selena Maranjian, who undoubtedly pilfered the humor from someone else.

Q: How many Trotskyites does it take to change a light bulb?
A: None. Smash it!

Q: How many central bank economists does it take to screw in a light bulb?
A: Just one -- he holds the light bulb and the whole earth revolves around him.

Q: How many Marxists does it take to screw in a light bulb?
A: None - the bulb contains within it the seeds of its own revolution.

How many environmental economists does it take to change a light bulb? Eight - one to turn the light bulb and seven to do the environmental impact study. ---

---

It's not easy being an economist. How would you like to go through life pretending you knew what M1 was all about?

An elderly economics professor is standing at the shallow end of the campus pool. A Coed is standing at the deep end taking pictures. She suddenly drops the camera into the pool. Then she motions for the professor to come to her. He goes and she asks him to retrieve the camera. He agrees and dives in and retrieve its.

Upon returning he says to her, "Why did you ask me to retrieve the camera when there were many younger and more athletic males closer to her?" She replied, "Professor you seem to forget that I'm in your Econ I class, and I don't know anyone who can go down deeper, stay down longer and come up drier than you."

Economics is the painful elaboration of the obvious.

True story: The scene is a conference of professors of marketing. The keynote speaker is an eminent economist. The chairman, who sees himself as a bit of a wag, says,

"I would like to introduce my eminent colleague and friend. He's an economist, one of those people who turn random numbers into mathematical laws."
The economist, not to be outdone, replies,
"My friend, here, is a marketer. They reverse the process."

Q. What's the difference between an economist and a befuddled old man with Alzheimer's?

A. The economist is the one with the calculator.

One day a woman went for a walk in her neighborhood and came across a boy with some puppies. "Would you like a puppy? They aren't ready for new homes quite yet, but they will be in a few weeks!"

"Oh, they're adorable," the lady said. "What kind of dogs are they?"
"These are economists."
"OK. I'll tell my husband."

So she went home and told her husband. He was very interested to see the puppies. About a week later he came across the lad; the puppies were very active.

"Hey, Mister. Want a puppy?"
"I think my wife spoke with you last week. What kind of dogs are these?"
"Oh. These are decision analysts."
"I thought you said last week that they were economists."
"Yeah, but they've opened their eyes since then."

An economist is someone who doesn't know what he's talking about - and make you feel it's your fault.

The definition of "waste": a busload of economists plunging over a precipice with three of the seats unoccupied.

Bill and Boris are taking a break from a long summit, Boris says to Bill, -Bill, you know, I have a big problem I don't know what to do about. I have a hundred bodyguards and one of them is a traitor. I don't know which one. -Not a big deal Boris, I'm stuck with a hundred economists I have to listen to all the time before any policy decision, and only one tells the truth but it's never the same one.

Two government economists were returning home from a field meeting. As with all government travelers, they were assigned the cheapest seats on the plane so they each were occupying the center seat on opposite sides of the aisle. They continued their discussion of the knotty problem that had been the subject of their meeting through takeoff and meal service until finally one of the passengers in an aisle seat offered to trade places so they could talk and he could sleep. After switching seats, one economist remarked to the other that it was the first time an economic discussion ever kept anyone awake.

Robert J. BARRO in his 1989 paper in the Journal of Economic Perspectives:
"A colleague of mine argues that a 'normative' model should be defined as a model that fits the data badly."

Found in a paper of Anatol RAPOPORT (Scientific American, July 1967) who tells the following joke which he found in 'The Complete Strategist' by J. D. Williams:
"Two policemen are considering the problem of catching the bandit. One of them starts to calculate the optimal mixed strategy for the chase. The other policeman protests.
'While we're doodling,' he points out, 'he is making his getaway.'
'Relax,' says the game-theorist policeman. 'He's got to figure it out too, don't he?'"

During the waning days of communism in the Soviet Union, an inspector was charged with visiting local poultry farmers and inquiring about the amount of feed they were giving their chickens. Central planning was still in effect and each farmer was allocated 15 Rubles to spend on chicken feed.

One farmer very honestly answered that he spent five of the allocated 15 Rubles on chicken feed. The inspector took this to mean that the thieving farmer pocketed the other ten and promptly had him imprisoned.

Hearing of this through the rumor mill, the next farmer down the road insisted that he spent all 15 Rubles on food for the chickens. The inspector saw this as a case of budget-padding and the farmer as a wasteful opportunist. He too was imprisoned.

The third farmer heard of both episodes and was more prepared for the inspector's arrival.

"How many of the 15 Rubles do you actually spend on chicken feed," asked the inspector.

Like a true nascent capitalist, the farmer threw his hands in the air and answered, "hey! I give 15 Rubles to the chickens. They can eat whatever they want!"

Experienced economist and not so experienced economist are walking down the road. They get across shit lying on the asphalt.

Experienced economist: "If you eat it I'll give you $20,000!"
Not so experienced economist runs his optimization problem and figures out he's better off eating it so he does and collects money.
Continuing along the same road they almost step into yet another shit.
Not so experienced economist: "Now, if YOU eat this shit I'll give YOU $20,000."
After evaluating the proposal experienced economist eats shit getting the money.
They go on. Not so experienced economist starts thinking: "Listen, we both have the same amount of money we had before, but we both ate shit. I don't see us being better off."
Experienced economist: "Well, that's true, but you overlooked the fact that we've been just involved in $40,000 of trade."

An economist is someone who knows the price of everything and the value of nothing.

Economists are people who are too smart for their own good and not smart enough for anyone else's.

A woman hears from her doctor that she has only half a year to live. The doctor advises her to marry an economist and to live in South Dakota. The woman asks: will this cure my illness? Answer of the doctor: No, but the half year will seem pretty long.

A boy was crossing a road one day when a frog called out to him and said, "If you kiss me, I'll turn into a beautiful princess." He bent over, picked up the frog and put it in his pocket. The frog spoke up again and said, "If you kiss me and turn me back into a beautiful princess, I will stay with you for one week." The boy took the frog out of his pocket, smiled at it, and returned it to his pocket. The frog then cried out, "If you kiss me and turn me back into a princess, I'll stay with you and do ANYTHING you want." Again the boy took the frog out, smiled at it and put it back into his pocket. Finally, the frog asked, "What is the matter? I've told you I'm a beautiful princess, that I'll stay with you for a week and do anything you want. Why won't you kiss me?" The boy said, "Look, I'm an economist. I don't have time for a girlfriend, but a talking frog is cool."

Q: Why did God create economists?

A: In order to make weather forecasters look good.

Q: Why did the economist cross the road?

A: It was the chicken's day off.

Q. What does an economist do?

A. A lot in the short run, which amounts to nothing in the long run.

To an economist, real life is a special case.

I asked an economist for her phone number.... and she gave me an estimate.

One more light bulb joke:

Q: How many economists does it take to change a light bulb?
A: Eight. One to screw it in and seven to hold everything else constant.

Economists have forecasted 9 out of the last 5 recessions.

An econometrician and an astrologer are arguing about their subjects. The astrologer says, "Astrology is more scientific. My predictions come out right half the time. Yours can't even reach that proportion". The econometrician replies, "That's because of external shocks. Stars don't have those".

SOCIALISM: You have two cows. The state takes one and gives it to someone else.
COMMUNISM: You have two cows. State takes both of them and gives you milk.
FASCISM: You have two cows. State takes both of them and sell you milk.
NAZISM: You have two cows. State takes both of them and shoot you.
BUREAUCRACY: You have two cows. State takes both of them, kill one and spill the milk in system of sewage.
CAPITALISM: You have two cows. You sell one and buy a bull.

Alternative: A COWSMIC VIEW OF WORLD ORGANIZATION

FEUDALISM: You have two cows. Your lord takes some of the milk.

PURE SOCIALISM: You have two cows. The government takes them and puts them in a barn with everyone else's cows. You have to take care of all the cows. The government gives you as much milk as you need.

BUREAUCRATIC SOCIALISM: You have two cows. The government takes them and puts them in a barn with everyone else's cows. They are cared for by ex-chicken farmers. You have to take care of the chickens the government took from the chicken farmers. The government gives you as much milk and as many eggs as the regulations say you should need.

FASCISM: You have two cows. The government takes both, hires you to take care of them, and sells you the milk.

PURE COMMUNISM: You have two cows. Your neighbors help you take care of them, and you all share the milk.

RUSSIAN COMMUNISM: You have two cows. You have to take care of them, but the government takes all the milk.

DICTATORSHIP: You have two cows. The government takes both and shoots you.

SINGAPORE DEMOCRACY: You have two cows. The government fines you for keeping two unlicensed animals in an apartment.

MILITARIANISM: You have two cows. The government takes both and drafts you.

PURE DEMOCRACY: You have two cows. Your neighbors decide who gets the milk.

REPRESENTATIVE DEMOCRACY: You have two cows. Your neighbors pick someone to tell you who gets the milk.

AMERICAN DEMOCRACY: The government promises to give you two cows if you vote for it. After the election, the president is impeached for speculating in cow futures. The press dubs the affair "Cowgate".

BRITISH DEMOCRACY: You have two cows. You feed them sheep's brains and they go mad. The government doesn't do anything.

BUREAUCRACY: You have two cows. At first the government regulates what you can feed them and when you can milk them. Then it pays you not to milk them. After that it takes both, shoots one, milks the other and pours the milk down the drain. Then it requires you to fill out forms accounting for the missing cows.

ANARCHY: You have two cows. Either you sell the milk at a fair price or your neighbors kill you and take the cows.

CAPITALISM: You have two cows. You sell one and buy a bull.

HONG KONG CAPITALISM: You have two cows. You sell three of them to your publicly listed company, using letters of credit opened by your brother-in-law at the bank, then execute a debt/equity swap with associated general offer so that you get all four cows back, with a tax deduction for keeping five cows. The milk rights of six cows are transferred via a Panamanian intermediary to a Cayman Islands company secretly owned by the majority shareholder, who sells the rights to all seven cows' milk back to the listed company. The annual report says that the company owns eight cows, with an option on one more. Meanwhile, you kill the two cows because the Feng Shui is bad.

ENVIRONMENTALISM: You have two cows. The government bans you from milking or killing them.

FEMINISM: You have two cows. They get married and adopt a veal calf.

TOTALITARIANISM: You have two cows. The government takes them and denies they ever existed. Milk is banned.

POLITICAL CORRECTNESS: You are associated with (the concept of "ownership" is a symbol of the phallo-centric, war-mongering, intolerant past) two differently-aged (but no less valuable to society) bovines of non-specified gender.

COUNTER CULTURE: Wow, dude, there's like... these two cows, man. You got to have some of this milk. Far out! Awesome!

SURREALISM: You have two giraffes. The government requires you to take harmonica lessons.

JAPANESE DEMOCRACY: You have two cows. You give the milk to gangsters so they don't ask any awkward questions about who you're giving the milk to.

EUROPEAN FEDERALISM: You have two cows which cost too much money to care for because everybody is buying milk imported from some cheap east-European country and would never pay the fortune you'd have to ask for your cows' milk. So you apply for financial aid from the European Union to subsidize your cows and are granted enough subsidies. You then sell your milk at the former elevated price to some government-owned distributor which then dumps your milk onto the market at east-European prices to make Europe competitive. You spend the money you got as a subsidy on two new cows and then go on a demonstration to Brussels complaining that the European farm-policy is going to drive you out of your job.

EASTERN EUROPEAN DEMOCRACY: You have two cows. You sell the milk (diluted with some water) at a high price to the neighbors or to anyone at the open-air market. If somebody asks for receipt, you charge for a two times higher price, so nobody will request an invoice. For concerned families with small babies you claim that the milk is "bio", though you collect the grass for feeding at the side of the highway and you keep the milk in plastic barrels used previously as containers of dangerous chemicals. Later, your neighbor or anybody from town will steal the cows and will buy their meat for a high price, and if you ask for a receipt, you will be charged for a two times higher price.

David Gunn (Scotland): "Eighty percent of rules of thumb only apply 20 percent of the time"

This one I attribute to Richard Thaler, now at the Univ of Chicago.

When an economist says the evidence is "mixed," he or she means that theory says one thing and data says the opposite.

This tale is said to be told by John Kenneth Galbraith on himself. As a boy he lived on a farm in Canada. On the adjoining farm, lived a girl he was fond of. One day as they sat together on the top rail of the cattle pen they watched a bull servicing a cow. Galbraith turned to the girl, with what he hoped was a suggestive look, saying, "That looks like it would be fun." She replied, "Well.... she's your cow."

"I'd rather be vaguely right than precisely wrong."

- J.M.Keynes; Found in Forbes magazine 01/25/1999 issue. In the Numbers Game column by Bernard Cohen

---

"I'm thinking of leaving my husband," complained the economist's wife.
"All he ever does is stand at the end of the bed and tell me how good things are going to be."

Q: Why do social workers refuse to sleep with economists?
A: They have learned it's a sunk cost.

Q: Why do Economists provide estimates of inflation to the nearest tenth of a percent?
A: To prove they have a sense of humour.

"Economic statistics are like a bikini, what they reveal is important, what they conceal is vital"
- Attributed to Professor Sir Frank Holmes, Victoria University, Wellington, New Zealand, 1967.

"An economist is a person who confronted with a eight foot high wall, immediately assumes he is ten feet tall."
- Attributed to John Zanetti, Senior Lecturer, Victoria University, Wellington, New Zealand 1971.

Seven habits that help produce the anything-but-efficient markets that rule the world by Paul Krugman in Fortune.

1. Think short term.
2. Be greedy.
3. Believe in the greater fool
4. Run with the herd.
5. Overgeneralize
6. Be trendy
7. Play with other people's money

Phelson's Law (or so I was told)
Copying an idea from an author is plagiarism. Copying many ideas from many authors is... research!!

When doctors make mistakes, at least they kill their patients. When economists make mistakes, they merely ruin them.

An economist is someone who has had a human being described to him, but has never actually seen one.

There are three sorts of economist. Those who can count, and those who can't.

Grow your own dope -- plant an economist.

Economic forecasters assume everything, except responsibility.

Economics is to be found in the library -- beyond fiction.

You know the difference between a dead economist and a dead cat. There are usually skid marks in front of the dead cat.

Economics-everything we know in a language we don't understand.

A voice from history.

"Not all Germans believe in God but they believe in the Bundesbank"

Jacques Delors former president of European Commission
in FT December 15,1998

An economics limerick

Folks came from afar just to see
Two Economists who'd agreed to agree.
While the event did take place,
It proved a disgrace;
They agreed one plus one adds to three.

Robley E. George

A joke on the streets of Moscow these days, according to World Bank staffer John Nellis, goes this way: "Everything the Communists told us about communism was a complete and utter lie. Unfortunately, everything the Communists told us about capitalism turned out to be true."

A Scorpion begged a Frog to carry him across the river because he could not swim. The Frog hesitated for fearing being stung by the Scorpion. The Scorpion said: "Don't worry, you know I won't sting you since we will both get drowned if I do that". So the Frog carried Scorpion across the river. But in the middle of the river, it happened--the Frog got a sting. Before he died, the Frog asked Scorpion in disbelief: "I don't understand why you did this!?" "Because I am not a game theorist and you are", replied the Scorpion.

A real story

250

Last year at the SEA meetings in Baltimore, I was in the elevator and witnessed the following: the elevator gets to the lobby, and there is a woman (economist) waiting to get in and a man (economist) waiting to get out. The woman pauses to allow the man to exit first, the man pauses to allow the woman to enter the elevator first. After a couple of seconds of just standing there, they both make a move for the door - but as each sees the other moving, they pause again to allow the other to go first. More standing still occurs until finally the door starts to close. The man in the elevator jabs his arm out at the last instant to prevent the doors from closing, and the two stumble past each other as they simultaneous switch places. The door finally closes, and as the elevator starts to move the economist is heard to say, under her breath, "Manners are never optimal."

- Edward Bierhanzl

INTEREST GROUP ECONOMIST VIRUS - Divides your hard disk into hundreds of little units, each of which does practically nothing, but all of which claim to be the most important part of the computer.
ECONOMETRICIAN VIRUS - Sixty percent of the PCs infected will lose 38 percent of their data 14 percent of the time (plus or minus a 3.5 percent margin of error)
POLITICAL THINK TANK ECONOMIST VIRUS - Doesn't do anything, but you can't get rid of it until next election.
GOVERNMENT ECONOMIST VIRUS - nothing works on your system, but all your diagnostic software says everything is just fine.
MARXIAN ECONOMIST VIRUS - Helps your computer shut down whenever it wants to.
SOVIET ECONOMIST VIRUS - Crashes your computer, but denies it ever happened.
MAINSTREAM ECONOMIST VIRUS - It claims it feels threatened by the other files on your PC and erases then in "self-defense."
CENTRAL BANK ECONOMIST VIRUS - Makes sure that it's bigger than any other file.
MULTINATIONAL CORPORATION ECONOMIST VIRUS - Deletes all monetary files, but keeps smiling and sending messages about how the economy is going to get better.
SUPPLY SIDE ECONOMIST VIRUS - Puts your computer to sleep for four years. When your computer wakes up, you're trillion more dollars in debt.
NEW ECONOMY VIRUS - Also known as the "Tricky Dick Virus." You can wipe it out, but it always makes a comeback.
ENVIRONMENTAL ECONOMIST VIRUS - Before allowing you to delete any file, it first asks you if you've considered the alternatives.

A friend of mine was taking a class by Milton Friedman at the U of Chicago, and after a late night studying fell asleep in class. This sent Friedman into a little tizzy and he came over and pounded on the table, demanding an answer to a question he had just posed to the class, my friend, shaken but now awake said " I'm sorry Professor, I missed the question but the answer is increase the money supply."

What does it take to be a good economist? An unshakeable grasp of the obvious!

" I have come to appreciate how Monetarists view the holiness of this principle ['Friedman's x% rule'] by watching Friedman advising on the appropriate monetary policy in diverse complex situations and each time coming up, unfailingly, with the same practical answer: 3 percent."
-Franco Modigliani
Contemporary Policy Issues (1988) 6 October

Achieving free trade is like getting to heaven. Everyone one wants to get there, but not too soon.

Value of human capital

Engineers and scientists will never make as much money as business executives. Now a rigorous mathematical proof that explains why this is true:

Postulate 1: Knowledge is Power.
Postulate 2: Time is Money.

As every engineer knows,

$$\frac{Work}{Time} = Power$$

Since Knowledge = Power, and Time = Money, we have

$$\frac{Work}{Money} = Knowledge$$

Solving for Money, we get:

$$\frac{Work}{Knowledge} = Money$$

Thus, as Knowledge approaches zero, Money approaches infinity regardless of the Work done. Conclusion: The Less you Know, the more money you Make.

A traveler wandering on an island inhabited entirely by cannibals comes upon a butcher shop. This shop specialized in human brains differentiated according to source. The sign in the shop read:

Artists' Brains $9/lb
Philosophers' Brains $12/lb
Scientists' Brains $15/lb
Economists' Brains $19/lb

Upon reading the sign, the traveler noted, "My those economists' brains must be popular!" To which the butcher replied, "Are you kidding! Do you have any idea how many economists you have to kill to get a pound of brains?!"

In Canada there is a small radical group that refuses to speak English and no one can understand them. They are called separatists. In this country (USA) we have the same kind of group. They are called economists.

On the first day God created the sun - so the Devil countered and created sunburn. On the second day God created sex. In response the Devil created marriage. On the third day God created an economist. This was a tough one for the Devil, but in the end and after a lot of thought he created a second economist!
CHEER February 1993

Three leading economists took a small plane to the wilderness in northern Canada to hunt moose over the weekend. The last thing the pilot said was, "Remember, this is a very small plane and you will only be able to bring ONE moose back."

But of course, they killed one each and come Sunday, they talked the pilot into letting them bring all three dead moose onboard. So just after takeoff, the plane stalled and crashed. In the wreckage, one of the economists woke up, looked around and said, "Where the hell are we. Oh, just about a hundred yards east of the place there we crashed last year."

"Economic man" never gets a hangover, if he doesn't decide that the advantages of acquiring it exceed the drawbacks.

An Economist is someone who didn't have enough personality to become an accountant.

An economist is someone who knows 100 ways to make love, but doesn't know any women/men.

Q: What is a recent economics graduate's usual question in his first job?

A: What would you like to have with your French fries sir?

An economist returns to visit his old school. He's interested in the current exam questions and asks his old professor to show some. To his surprise they are exactly the same ones to which he had answered 10 years ago! When he asks about this the professor answers: "the questions are always the same - only the answers change!"

Economics is extremely useful as a form of employment for economists.

A central banker walks into a pizzeria to order a pizza.

When the pizza is done, he goes up to the counter get it. There a clerk asks him: "Should I cut it into six pieces or eight pieces?"

The central banker replies: "I'm feeling rather hungry right now. You'd better cut it into eight pieces."

Reproduced below is an Economist Joke that illustrates the separate facilities solution to an externality problem.

Three guys decide to play a round of golf: a priest, a psychologist, and an economist.

They get behind a *very* slow two-some, who, despite a caddy, are taking all day to line up their shots and four-putting every green, and so on. By the 8th hole, the three men are complaining loudly about the slow play ahead and swearing a blue streak, and so on. The priest says, "Holy Mary, I pray that they should take some lessons before they play again." The psychologist says, "I swear there are people that like to play golf slowly." The economist says, "I really didn't expect to spend this much time playing a round of golf."

By the 9th hole, they have had it with slow play, so the psychologist goes to the caddy and demands that they be allowed to play through. The caddy says O.K., but then explains that the two golfers are blind, that both are retired firemen who lost their eyesight saving people in a fire, and that explains their slow play, and would they please not swear and complain so loud.

The priest is mortified; he says, "Here I am a man of the cloth and I've been swearing at the slow play of two blind men." The psychologist is also mortified; he says, "Here I am a man trained to help others with their problems and I've been complaining about the slow play of two blind men."

The economist ponders the situation-finally he goes back to the caddy and says, "Listen, the next time could they play at night."

A physicist, a chemist and an economist are stranded on an island, with nothing to eat. A can of soup washes ashore. The physicist says, "Lets smash the can open with a rock." The chemist says, "Lets build a fire and heat the can first." The economist says, "Lets assume that we have a can-opener..."

An economist, a philosopher, a biologist, and an architect were were arguing about what was God's real profession. The philosopher said, "Well, first and foremost, God is a philosopher because he created the principles by which man is to live." "Ridiculous!" said the biologist "Before that, God created man and woman and all living things so clearly he was a biologist." "Wrong," said the architect. "Before that, he created the heavens and the earth. Before the earth, there was only complete confusion and chaos!" "Well," said the economist, "where do you think the chaos came from?"

The First Law of Economists: For every economist, there exists an equal and opposite economist.

The Second Law of Economists: They're both wrong.

If all the economists were laid end to end

a) it would be a good thing

b) they would be more comfortable

c) they would never reach conclusion

d) all of the above

e) none of the above

f) they would point in different directions

Two economists are walking down the street. One sees a dollar lying on the sidewalk, and says so.

"Obviously not," says the other. "If there were, someone would have picked it up!"

We have 2 classes of forecasters: Those who don't know . . . and those who don't know they don't know.

- John Kenneth Galbraith

The experience of being proved completely wrong is salutary. No economist should be denied it, and none are.
- J K Galbraith

"Murphy's law of economic policy": Economists have the least influence on policy where they know the most and are most agreed; they have the most influence on policy where they know the least and disagree most vehemently.

- Alan S. Blinder

An economist is an expert who will know tomorrow why the things he predicted yesterday didn't happen today.

- Laurence J. Peter

A study of economics usually reveals that the best time to buy anything is last year.

- Marty Allen

Having a little inflation is like being a little pregnant--inflation feeds on itself and quickly passes the "little" mark.

- Dian Cohen

If you put two economists in a room, you get two opinions, unless one of them is Lord Keynes, in which case you get three opinions.

- Winston Churchill

Shall I tell you the opinion of a famous economist on jealousy? Jealousy is just the fact of being deprived. Nothing more.

- Henry Becque

There is also a joke about the last Mayday parade in the Soviet Union. After the tanks and the troops and the planes and the missiles rolled by there came ten men dressed in black.

"Are they Spies?" Asked Gorby?

"They are economists," replies the KGB director, "imagine the havoc they will wreak when we set them loose on the Americans"

"Having a house economist became for many business people something like having a resident astrologer for the royal court: I don't quite understand what this fellow is saying but there must be something to it." Linden. (Jan. 11, 1993). Dreary Days in the Dismal Science. Forbes. Pp. 68-70.

If an economist and an IRS agent were both drowning and you could only save one of them, would you go to lunch or read the paper?

The National Institute of Health (NIH) announced that they were going to start using economists instead of rats in their experiments. Naturally, the American Agricultural Economics Association was outraged and filed suit, but NIH presented some compelling reasons for the switch:

1) NIH lab assistants become very attached to their rats. This emotional involvement was interfering with the research being conducted. No such attachment could form for an economist.
2) Economists breed faster.
3) Economists are much cheaper to care for and PETA won't object regardless of the experiment.
4) There are some things even rats won't do.
However, it is difficult to extrapolate test results to human beings.

How many economists does it take to screw in a light bulb?

1. Just one, but it really gets screwed.
2. One to prepare the proposal, an econometrician to run the model, one each MS and PhD students to write the theses and dissertations, two more to prepare the journal article (senior authorship not assigned), four to review it, and at least as many to refine the model and replicate the results.

A guy walks into a DC curio shop. While browsing he comes across an exquisite brass rat. "What a great gag gift" he thinks to himself. After dickering with the shopkeeper over the price, the man purchases the rat and leaves. As he's walking down the street, he hears scurrying noises behind him. Stopping and looking around, he sees hundreds, then thousands of rats pouring out of the alleys and stairwells into the street behind him. In a panic he runs down the street with the rats not far behind. The street ends at a pier; he runs to the end of the pier and heaves the brass rat into the Potomac. All of the rats scurry past him into the river where they drown. After breathing a sigh of relief and wiping his brow, the man heads back to the curio shop, finds the shopkeeper and asks, "Do you have any brass economists?"

TEN THINGS TO DO WITH A GRADUATE ECONOMICS TEXTBOOK

1. Press pretty flowers.
2. Press pretty insects.
3. Use it as paperweight on your already overcluttered desk.
4. Leave out in obvious places to impress uninformed undergraduates.
5. Mail to the White House as an intimidation tactic.
6. Give it a walk-on part in a boring European existentialist play.
7. Just throw the damn thing away.
8. Leave out for the rain and other forces of nature to reckon with.
9. Read it (ha ha ha), and weep.
10. Get a refund from bookstore so you can buy weekend's beer supply.

How can you tell when an economist is lying?
His lips are moving.

Why won't sharks attack economists?
Professional courtesy.

Q: What do you get when you cross the Godfather with an economist?

A: An offer you can't understand.

Q: How many economists does it take to change a light bulb?

A: Hell, you need a whole department of them just to prepare the research grant.

They say that Christopher Columbus was the first economist. When he left to discover America, he didn't know where he was going. When he got there he didn't know where he was. And it was all done on a government grant.

A grade school teacher was asking students what their parents did for a living. "Tim, you be first. What does your mother do all day?"

Tim stood up and proudly said, "She's a doctor."
"That's wonderful. How about you, Amy?"
Amy shyly stood up, scuffed her feet and said, "My father is a mailman."
"Thank you, Amy" said the teacher. "What does your parent do, Billy?"
Billy proudly stood up and announced,
1. "Nothing. He's an economist."
2. "My daddy plays piano in a whorehouse." The teacher was aghast and went to Billy's house and rang the bell. Billy's father answered the door. The teacher explained what his son had said and demanded an explanation. Billy's dad said, "I'm actually an economist. How can I explain a thing like that to a seven-year-old?"

A Berkeley economist died and went to heaven (No, that's not the joke). There were thousands of people ahead of him in line to see St. Peter. To his surprise, St. Peter left his desk at the gate and came down the long line to where the economist was, and greeted him warmly. St. Peter took the economist up to the front of the line, and into a comfortable chair by his desk. The economist said, "I like all this attention, but what makes ME so special?" St. Peter replied, "Well, I've added up all the hours for which you billed your consultation clients, and by my calculation you're 193 years old!"

A Chicago economist died in poverty and many local futures traders donated to a fund for his funeral. The president of (the Merc, the Board of Trade, etc.) was asked to donate a dollar. "Only a buck?" said the president, "only a dollar to bury an economist? Here's a check; go bury 1000 of them."

An economist and a physician had a dispute over precedence. They referred it to Diogenes, who gave it in favor of the economist as follows: "Let the thief go first, and the executioner follow."

What's the difference between mathematics and economics?

Mathematics is incomprehensible; economics just doesn't make any sense.

A judge was hearing a drunk-driving case and the defendant, who had both a record and a reputation for driving under the influence, demanded a jury trial. It was nearly 4 p.m. and getting a jury would take time, so the judge called a recess and went out in the hall looking to empanel anyone available. He found a dozen economists and told them that they were a jury. The economists thought this would be a novel experience (none had ever been at a trial before, except as a defendant or an expert witness) and followed the judge into the courtroom. The trial was over in about 10 minutes and it was very clear that the defendant was guilty. The jury went into the jury-room, the judge started getting ready to go home, and everyone waited. After three hours, the judge sent the bailiff into the jury- room to see what was holding up the verdict. When the bailiff returned, the judge said, "Well, have they arrived at a verdict yet?" The bailiff shook his head and said, "Verdict? Hell, Judge, they're still doing nominating speeches for the foreman's position!"

For three years, the young assistant professor took his vacations at a country inn. He had an affair with the innkeeper's daughter. Looking forward to an exciting few days, he dragged his suitcase up the stairs of the inn, then stopped short. There sat his lover with an infant on her lap! "Why didn't you write when you learned you were pregnant?" he cried. "I would have rushed up here, we could have gotten married, and the child would have my name!" "Well," she said, "when my folks found out about my condition, we sat up all night talkin' and talkin' and we finally decided it would be better to have a bastard in the family than an economist."

Santa Claus, the tooth fairy, a practical economist, and an old drunk are walking down the street together when they simultaneously spot a hundred dollar bill. Who gets it? The old drunk, of course, the other three are mythological creatures.

A Harvard economist had a summerhouse in the Maine woods. Each summer he'd invite a different friend (no, that's not the punch line) to spend a week or two. On one occasion, he invited a Czechoslovakian to stay with him. They had a splendid time in the country - rising early and living in the great outdoors. Early one morning they went out to pick berries for their morning breakfast. As they went around the berry patch along came two huge bears. The economist dashed for cover. His friend wasn't so lucky and the male bear reached him and swallowed him whole. The economist ran back to his car, drove to town as fast has he could, and got the sheriff. The sheriff grabbed his rifle and dashed back to the berry patch with the economist. Sure enough, both bears were still there. "He's in THAT one!" cried the economist, pointing to the male. The sheriff looked at the bears, and without batting an eye, leveled his gun, took careful aim, and SHOT THE FEMALE. "Whatd'ya do that for?!" exclaimed the economist, "I said he was in the other!" "Yep," said the sheriff, "and would YOU believe a economist who told you that the Czech was in the Male?"

WASHINGTON DC GOVERNMENT ECONOMIST HUNTING REGULATIONS AND BAG LIMITS

GENERAL

1. Any person with a valid Washington DC hunting license or a Federal Income Tax Return may harvest government economists.
2. Taking of economists with traps or deadfalls is permitted. The use of currency as bait is prohibited.
3. Killing of economists with a vehicle is prohibited. If one is accidentally struck, remove the dead economist to side of the road and proceed to the nearest car wash.
4. It is unlawful to chase, herd, or harvest economists from limousines, Mercedes Benz's, the Metro, or Porsches.
5. It shall be unlawful to shout "research contract" or "I need a policy consultant" for the purpose of trapping economists.
6. It shall be unlawful to hunt economists within 100 feet of government buildings.

7. It shall be unlawful to use decision memos, draft legislation, conference reports, or RFP's to attract economists.

8. It shall be unlawful to hunt economists within 200 feet of Senate or House hearing rooms, libraries, whorehouses, massage parlors, special interest group offices, bars, or strip joints.

9. If an economist is elected to government office, it shall be a felony to hunt, trap, or possess it. It will also be a shame.

10. Stuffed or mounted economists must have a DC Health Department inspection certificate for rabies and vermin.

11. It shall be illegal for a hunter to disguise as a reporter, drug dealer, pimp, female congressional aid, sheep, legislator, policy maker, bookie, lobbyist, or tax accountant for the purpose of hunting economists.

Given 1000 economists, there will be 10 theoretical economists with different theories on how to change the light bulb and 990 empirical economists laboring to determine which theory is the *correct* one, and everyone will still be in the dark.

Tool Number Two:
Quotes About Economics and Economists

The assertion of the law of economy as the law of history is the only contribution the socialists have made to my library of ideas.
> Henry Adams in a letter to Brooks Adams

Men in great places are thrice servants: servants of the sovereign, servants of fame, and servants of business.
> Francis Bacon, **Of Great Place**, 11

A servant's too often a negligent elf;
  --If it's business of consequence, do it yourself!
> Rev. R. H. Barham (1788-1845), **The Ingoldsby Penance**

There is nothing more requisite in business than dispatch.
> Joseph Addison, **Ancient Medals**, 5

The Crown is . . . the 'fountain of honor'; but the Treasury is the spring of business.
> Walter Bagehot, 1867

Society cares about the individual only in so far as he is profitable.
> Simone De Beauvoir, **The Coming of Age**, 1970

Business is more exciting than any game.
> Lord Beaverbrook

The nature of business is swindling.
> August Bebel, German Socialist leader, speech in Zurich, Dec. 1892

The happiest time in any man's life is when he is in red-hot pursuit of a dollar with a reasonable prospect of overtaking it.
> Josh Billings, nineteenth century humorist/writer

I must create a system or be enslaved by another man's;
I will not reason and compare; my business is to create.
> William Blake (1757-1827), **Jerusalem**

You cannot strengthen the weak by weakening the strong. You cannot help the wage earner by pulling down the wage payer. You cannot help the poor by destroying the rich. You cannot help men permanently by doing for them what they could and should do for themselves.
> John Henry Boetcker

Business makes a man as well as tries him.
> H. G. Bohn, **A Handbook of Proverbs**, 1855, p. 334

Mere parsimony is not economy. . . expense, and great expense, may be an essential part of true economy.
> Edmund Burke

Business is a good game – lots of competition and a minimum of rules. You keep score with money.
> Nolan Bushnell, founder of Atari

The maxim of the British people is 'Business as usual'.
> Winston Churchill, speech at Guildhal, Nov. 9, 1914

The inherent vice of capitalism is the unequal sharing of blessings; the inherent vice of socialism is the equal sharing of miseries.
> Attributed to Winston Churchill

Corporations cannot commit treason. . . for they have no souls.
> Edward Coke

The business of America is business.
> Calvin Coolidge, speech before the Society of American Newspaper Editors, Jan. 17, 1925

Civilization and profits go hand in hand.
> Calvin Coolidge, speech in New York, Nov. 27, 1920

Commerce is greedy. Ideology is bloodthirsty.
> Mason Cooley

Capitalism in the United States has undergone profound modification, not just under the New Deal but through a consensus that continued to grow after the New Deal. Government in the U.S. today is a senior partner in every business in the country.
> Norman Cousins

'Do other men, for they would do you.' That's the true business precept.
> Charles Dickens, **Martin Chuzzlewit**, chapter 11

There are an enormous number of managers who have retired on the job.
> Peter F. Drucker

Whenever you see a successful business, someone once made a courageous decision.
> Peter Drucker

It is not the employer who pays wages – he only handles the money. It is the product that pays wages.
> Henry Ford

There is only one social responsibility of business – to use its resources and engage in activities designed to increase its profits without deception or fraud.

Milton Friedman, second American to win the Nobel Prize for Economics

What kind of society isn't structured on greed? The problem of social organization is how to set up an arrangement under which greed will do the least harm; capitalism is that kind of system.
    Milton Friedman

Business is the salt of life.
    Thomas Fuller, **Gnomologia**, 1732

In economics, the majority is always wrong.
    John Kenneth Galbraith, Prof. of Economics

No one can possibly achieve any real and lasting success or 'get rich' in business by being a conformist.
    Interview with J. Paul Getty (multimillionaire businessman) in **Herald Tribune**, Jan. 10, 1961

Power over a man's subsistence amounts to a power over his will
    Alexander Hamilton, first Sec. Of the Treasury and founder of the Federalist Party

He's happy who, far away from business, like the race of men of old, tills his ancestral fields with his own oxen, unbound by any interest to pay.
    Horace (65-8 B.C.), **Epodes**

Competition means decentralized planning by many separate persons.
    Friedrich Hayek

Mathematics has given economics rigor, but alas, also mortis.
    Robert Heilbroner, economist

Practical men, who believe themselves to be quite exempt from any intellectual influences, are usually the slave of some defunct economist.
    J.M. Keynes (1883-1946), **The General Theory of Employment, Interest and Money**, chapt. 24

The best way to destroy the capitalist system is to debauch the currency. By a continuing process of inflation, government is can confiscate, secretly and unobserved, an important part of the wealth of their citizens.
    John Maynard Keynes

…they use economic data the way a drunkard uses a lamppost: for support rather than illumination. Or as Disraeli put it, there are three kinds o0f lies: lies, damn lies, and statistics.
    Paul Krugman

Big business is basic to the very life of this country; and yet many – perhaps most – Americans have a deep-seated fear and an emotional repugnance to it. Here is a monumental contradiction.
    David Lilienthal

America's great achievement has been business.
    Henry Robinson Luce (1898-1967), co-founder of **Time**

The business of business is to take part in the creation of the Great Society.
    Henry Robinson Luce

Capital is past savings accumulated for future production.
    Jackson Martindell

Even when a society has got on the right track . . . to lay bare the economic law of motion of modern society—it can neither clear by bold leaps, nor remove by legal enactments, the obstacles offered by7 the successive phases of its normal development. But it can shorten and lessen the birth pangs.
    Karl Marx, **Das Kapital**, Preface to the first German edition, 1867

Business is a combination of war and sport.
    Andre Maurois

When you've got them by   their wallets, their hearts and minds will follow.
    Fern Naito

The forces in a capitalist society, if left unchecked, tend to make the rich richer and the poor poorer.
    Jawaharlal Nehru, former Prime Minister of India

No praying, it spoils business.
    Thomas Otway, **Venice Preserved**, Act 2, scene 1, 1681.

Expenditure rises to meet income.
    C. Northcote Parkinson

In a hierarchy every employee tends to rise to his level of incompetence.
    Laurence J. Peter

Crime is a logical extension of the sort of behavior that is often considered perfectly respectable in legitimate business.
    Robert Rice

No business which depends for existence by paying less than living wages to its workers has any right to continue in this country.
    Franklin D. Roosevelt (1882-1945), speech of June 16, 1933

Good management consists of showing average people how to do the work of superior people.
    John D. Rockefeller

The growth of a large business is merely a survival of the fittest.
    John D. Rockefeller Sr., quoted in **Social Darwinism in American Thought**, 1944

An economist's guess is liable to be as good as anybody else's.
    Will Rogers, humorist/columnist/actor, 1879-1935

WE demand that business give the people a square deal...
    Teddy Roosevelt, **Autobiography**, p. 615, 1913

I believe in property rights; I believe that normally the rights of property and humanity coincide; but sometimes they conflict, and when this i9s so, I put human rights above property rights.
     Teddy Roosevelt, article in **Outlook**, Nov. 15, 1913

Man exploits man. Under communism it's just the opposite.
     Contemporary Russian proverb

The big print giveth and the fine print taketh away.
     J. Fulton Sheen.

The national debt is a very good thing and it would be dangerous to pay it off for fear of political economy.
     W. C. Sellar, **1066, And All That**, chapter 38, 1930

To business that we love we rise betime, and go to it with delight.
     William Shakespeare, **Antony and Cleopatra**, Act. 4, scene 4

The white man knows how to make everything, but he does not know how to distribute it.
     Sitting Bull

By pursuing his own interest (the individual) frequently promotes that of the society more effectually than when he really intends to promote it. I have never known much good done by those who affected to trade for the public good.
     Adam Smith

Business first, pleasure afterwards.
     William Thackeray, **The Rose and The Ring**, chap. 1, 1855

But the rich man . . . is always sold to the institution that made him rich. Absolutely speaking, the more money, the4 less virtue; for money comes between a man and his objects, and obtains them for him.
     Henry David Thoreau (1817-1862), **On The Duty of Civil Disobedience**, 1849

The big unions served a noble purpose once, and bless them for it. Now they're part of the problem and must give way if America is to move and participate in management and achieve reasonable productivity.
     Robert Townsend

Economists are people who work with numbers but who don't have the personality to be accountants.
     Unknown

My rule always was to do the business of the day in the day.
     Duke of Wellington, Nov. 2, 1835

One man's wage rise is another man's price increase.
     Harold Wilson, former Prime Minister of Great Britain

Go to your business, I say pleasure, whilst I go to my pleasure, business.
     William Wycherley, **The Country Wife,** Act 2, 1672.

INDEX

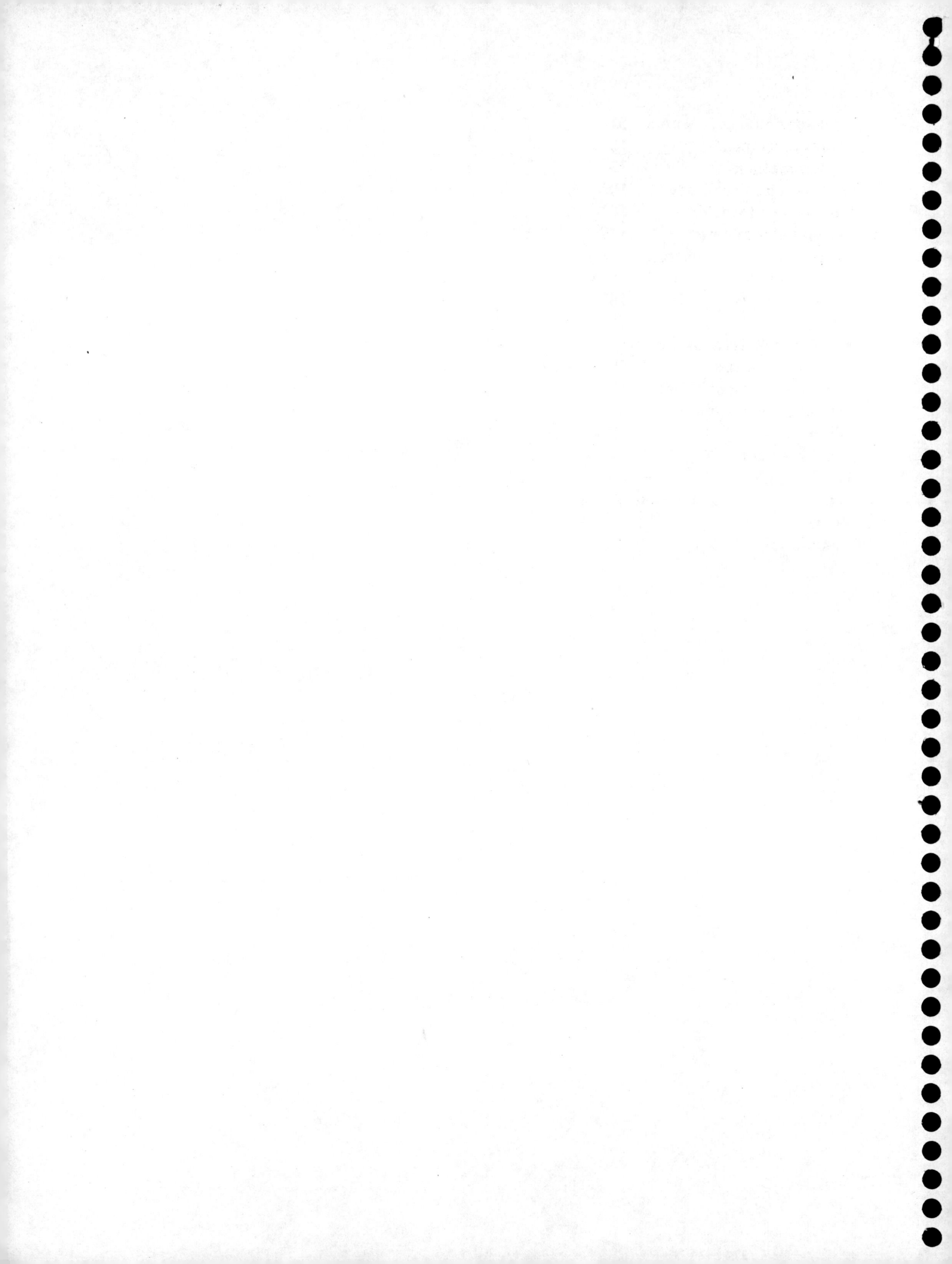